D1306003

To
Jennifer from Elsa

EX LIBRIS

1-24-01

Daily Guideposts, 2001

GUIDEPOSTS®
Carmel, New York 10512
www.guideposts.org

Copyright © 2000 by Guideposts, Carmel, New York 10512. All rights reserved.

No part of this publication may be reproduced, stored in a retrieval system or transmitted, in any form or by any means, electronic, mechanical, photocopying, recording or otherwise without the written permission of the publisher. Inquiries should be addressed to the Rights & Permissions Department, Guideposts, 16 E. 34th St., New York, NY 10016.

Every attempt has been made to credit the sources of copyrighted material used in this book. If any such acknowledgment has been inadvertently omitted or miscredited, receipt of such information would be appreciated.

ACKNOWLEDGMENTS

All Scripture, unless otherwise noted, are taken from *The King James Version of the Bible*.

Scripture marked (NIV) are taken from *The Holy Bible, New International Version*. Copyright © 1973, 1978, 1984 International Bible Society. Used by permission of Zondervan Bible Publishers.

Scripture marked (RSV) are taken from the *Revised Standard Version of the Bible*. Copyright © 1946, 1952, 1971 by Division of Christian Education of the National Council of Churches of Christ in the U.S.A. Used by permission.

Scripture marked (NAS) are taken from the *New American Standard Bible,* © The Lockman Foundation, 1960, 1962, 1963, 1968, 1971, 1972, 1973, 1975, 1977. Used by permission.

Scripture marked (TLB) are taken from *The Living Bible.* Copyright © 1971 by Tyndale House Publishers, Wheaton, IL 60187. All rights reserved.

Scripture marked (NKJV) are taken from *The Holy Bible, New King James Version*. Copyright © 1997, 1990, 1985, 1983 by Thomas Nelson, Inc.

Scripture marked (GNB) are taken from *Good News Bible, Today's English Version*. Copyright © 1966, 1971, 1976, 1978 by American Bible Society.

Scripture marked (NEB) are taken from *The New English Bible.* Copyright © The Delegates of the Oxford University Press and The Syndics of the Cambridge University Press, 1961, 1970, 1972, 1976.

"When God Reaches Out . . . Through Other People" was written by Elizabeth Sherrill.
"A Whole and Holy Love" was written by Marilyn Morgan King and Robert King.
"Into Africa" was written by Eric Fellman.
"Simple Lives, Single Hearts" was written by Isabel Wolseley.
"To Walk in Jerusalem" was written by Kenneth Chafin.
"The Leaning Log" was written by Roberta Messner.
"Rehab for the Heart" was written by John Sherrill.
"A Weekend Away" was written by Van Varner.
"A Birdsong at Sunset" was written by Mary Brown.
"Image in the Mirror" was written by Carol Knapp.

www.guideposts.org
Designed by Holly Johnson
Artwork by Jeremy Jarvis/www.jeremyjarvis.com
Indexed by Patricia Woodruff
Cover photo copyright © The Stock Market Photo Agency/Craig Tuttle, 1992
Typeset by Allentown Digital Services Division of R.R. Donnelley & Sons
Printed in the United States of America

TABLE OF CONTENTS

INTRODUCTION

The year 2001 is special indeed. Even the purists will admit that we're well launched into the new millennium, and that emphatic number *1* is like a final farewell to all the Y2K commotion. But 2001 is also a particularly important year for us here at Guideposts: You are holding in your hands the twenty-fifth edition of *Daily Guideposts,* our annual devotional.

Way back in 1977, Fred Bauer wrote down 365 inspirational thoughts and stories and put them together as *Daily Guideposts, 1977.* Fred is still sharing his wisdom—and his poems—with you, although now he has plenty of company. In 1979, Arthur Gordon, Drue Duke, Marilyn Morgan Helleberg, Penney Schwab, Marion Bond West and Van Varner joined the *Daily Guideposts* family; in 1980, Oscar Greene and Shari Smyth came on board. You'll find them all here in *Daily Guideposts, 2001,* along with forty-one more of the dear friends we've come to love over the years, all with new stories of God working in the ordinary and extraordinary events of their lives. And you'll also hear a new voice or two, ready to give you a boost in the morning or a quiet reflection at night. All of them, friends old and new, are waiting to reach out and touch your life, just as God has used parents, teachers, pastors, neighbors, co-workers, children, even people whose names they'll never know, to reach out and touch theirs.

So our theme for this, our Silver Anniversary edition of *Daily Guideposts,* is "Reaching Out." Our fifty-three writers will take us with them on a voyage of discovery as they come to recognize a fundamental law of life: In reaching out to those around us, we encounter the loving God Who is always reaching out to us.

Joining our family this year are three exciting new voices: Brian Doyle, an editor and father of three from Portland, Oregon, who shows you how to take an inventory of your life as you fold your laundry; Richard Hagerman, a retired dentist from Wendell, Idaho, who shares a life-changing experience in an old English church during World War II; and Robert King, husband of Marilyn Morgan (Helleberg) King, of Green Mountain, Colorado, who gives you his perspective on their life together.

No anniversary would be complete without presents, and we've got some great ones for you: nine very special series to illustrate our theme. At the beginning of each month, in "When God Reaches Out . . .

Through Other People," Elizabeth Sherrill will tell you about some of the people who, without knowing it, have brought a word from God into her life. Then, in the middle of the month, Marilyn Morgan Helleberg, now Marilyn Morgan King, and her husband Robert King will share their story of "A Whole and Holy Love." Come to their wedding in January and then find out how it happened—and how they learned that God must be the center of every love.

In February, Isabel Wolseley will take you far off the usual traveler's path to Papua New Guinea, where she finds the key to emotional wholeness in its wonderfully open and giving people. Eric Fellman spent three weeks in Africa in 1999, and six times during this year, he'll share some of the ways Africa changed his mind and touched his heart. During Holy Week and Easter, Kenneth Chafin invites you "To Walk in Jerusalem" and experience the events of that week of weeks as if they were happening for the very first time. In May, we'll go with Roberta Messner as she begins the difficult process of rebuilding her life and restoring the dilapidated cabin she calls "The Leaning Log." In July, John Sherrill, on the grueling but joyous road to recovery from a hidden heart attack, will take you to "Rehab for the Heart." In August, spend "A Weekend Away" with Van Varner. Then in October, join a reluctant Mary Brown as God helps her to give a dying neighbor "A Birdsong at Sunset." Finally, in Advent, Carol Knapp will show you the "Image in the Mirror": the events of Christmas as only a mother can see them.

And in addition to all of this, you'll find another special gift: twelve prayers from our new two-volume collection *Prayers for Every Need*, one for every month of the year. If you'd like to find out more about this unique, original prayer resource, write to Guideposts, EK# 201419191, 39 Seminary Hill Road, Carmel, NY 10512, or call 1-800-938-3322.

Over the last quarter of a century, *Daily Guideposts* has helped more than 14 million readers to see the signs of God's presence in their lives and to live richer, faith-filled lives. Along the way, we've become a family, writers and readers united by shared stories and memories and, above all, by prayer. We pray that through *Daily Guideposts, 2001,* we will be able to reach out even further with the message of the love that reaches us, whoever we are and wherever we are, day after day, and that opens our hearts to reach out to others.

—THE EDITORS

January

Declare his glory among the heathen, his wonders among all people.

—PSALM 96:3

S	M	T	W	T	F	S
	1	2	3	4	5	6
7	8	9	10	11	12	13
14	15	16	17	18	19	20
21	22	23	24	25	26	27
28	29	30	31			

1/MON *"See, I am sending an angel ahead of you to guard you along the way and to bring you to the place I have prepared."* —EXODUS 23:20 (NIV)

I sometimes think New Year's Day comes at the wrong time of year. I'm usually facing a bunch of tasks left over from the old year, like taking down the Christmas tree and putting away all the decorations, writing thank-you notes and dealing with decisions about what to do with the stack of Christmas cards. Throw them away? Save the ones with pictures? Check the addresses? Then there's the thought of trying to catch up with all the work I put off during the holidays. I'm behind before the New Year even starts.

"Who can think about new beginnings or inspirational goals in the midst of old concerns?" I asked my lawyer-husband Lynn as he came in the door after a quick trip to the office to complete a couple of year-end responsibilities.

"Let me show you a gift I just received," he said, pulling an attractively wrapped package out of his briefcase. On it was a card: "To Lynn. May this gift encourage you in the coming year." It was signed by a friend in his Bible study group.

Lynn tore off the paper and lifted out a beautifully framed message, penned by a professional calligrapher. The message read:

> *Lynn,*
> *Trust Me. I have everything under control.*
> *Jesus*

He set the frame down amidst the clutter on the kitchen counter so I could see that simple message as I went about my tasks.

Slowly those words began to change my frame of mind. If I needed something to help me carry my old concerns into the New Year, I'd just found it . . . the determination to face each day's concerns, trusting in the words of this promise from the Source of all comfort and strength.

Father, each day in this new year, please help me remember that You are in control of everything. —CAROL KUYKENDALL

WHEN GOD REACHES OUT . . . THROUGH OTHER PEOPLE

How does God reach out to us? Some say it's through a sunset or a symphony, a Bible verse or the song of a bird. For Elizabeth (Tib) Sherrill, God communicates most often through encounters with other people. Sometimes it's a friend, sometimes a stranger. Whoever it is, he or she is probably unaware of relaying a message from God! At the start of each month, Tib recalls one of these "two-level" meetings, when behind human words and acts we perceive the outstretched hand of God. —THE EDITORS

2/*TUE*   *Cleanse thou me from secret faults.* —PSALM 19:12

It was our friend Brother Andrew who started me on the adventure of seeing God in the people around me. "He can reach out to us," Andrew said, "through even the briefest contact." Then he told this story.

Andrew is a Dutchman who for decades ministered secretly to Christians behind the Iron Curtain. Yet this selfless man carried a burden of guilt he could not lay down. Years earlier, Andrew had been among the Dutch soldiers sent to Indonesia to put down the independence movement.

When the Cold War ended, Andrew decided to return to now-independent Indonesia to serve the people he once fought. Nothing he did for them, however, served to ease his conscience. The place he most dreaded revisiting was the town of Ungaran, where his army unit had been headquartered.

"At last," he said, "I forced myself to go back there." He made himself walk up the single main road, past the mosque, to the big U-shaped school building the Dutch had used as a barracks. The building had been turned back into a school; on the former drill ground inside the U, some children in ragged clothing were playing.

As Andrew stood watching, a little girl, maybe eight years old, suddenly broke away from her playmates and ran toward him. The other children stopped their game and stared after her, clearly puzzled. The child ran straight up to Andrew, put her small hand in his, looked up into his eyes and smiled. Then she ran back to join her companions.

Andrew stood where he was, tears running down his face. "I knew Who it was Who'd come to me. It was Jesus. Jesus telling me, 'I forgive you, Andrew. Now forgive yourself and serve these beautiful people with joy.'"

Speak to me this year, Lord, in the people You will send me.

—ELIZABETH SHERRILL

EDITOR'S NOTE: How is God reaching out to you as you begin this exciting new year? We hope you'll take time out to record some of the gifts and graces God is giving in the diary pages "Daily Gifts" at the end of each month.

$3/$ WED *Remember, O Lord, thy tender mercies and thy lovingkindnesses; for they have been ever of old.*
—PSALM 25:6

Right after Christmas last year my wife Joy's dad went into the hospital with flu that turned into pneumonia. For years he has had a condition called chronic pulmonary disease, so the situation was serious. Joy is a nurse, and she flew out to California to make sure he was getting the best care at the hospital and to help her family prepare for the long-term medical problems he might have.

After a few days the situation became worse, and each time I talked to Joy, I heard her professionalism taking over as she described working with her dad's doctors and nurses to take every step possible and monitor every response. Then one night she called crying, and told me, "Today, when I went into the room, it wasn't a patient who was lying there dying, it was my daddy."

I felt helpless. I was three thousand miles away and unable to hold her or even think of the right things to say over the phone. We prayed, asking God for His help and entrusting Joy's father to His wisdom. When we finished, Joy said to me, "That old word in the Bible, *lov-*

ingkindness, is what I feel right now. He will hold my father and my family in His hands, and whatever comes will be all right."

God has brought back Joy's dad, for now. But eventually he will leave us, as we will leave our children, to pass from life into lovingkindness. His life and ours are in God's hands, and we are safe there.

Lord, thank You for planning a life beyond this one, and for carrying us over when we come to the doorway between the two.

—ERIC FELLMAN

4/*THU* *For God is not the author of confusion, but of peace. . . .* —I CORINTHIANS 14:33

Some folks eat chocolate when they're under stress. Some people bite their nails. My reaction to stress is more unusual: I lose things.

My TV remote control somehow finds its way into my laundry. My economics books migrate under my bed. My keys, purse, trombone oil, student ID and floppy disks all disappear, though you wouldn't think I could lose much in a ten-by-ten dorm room. To make matters worse, in a frantic search for my homework, I'll ransack the room, burying my hole-punch, my journal and a disgruntled cat.

My keys are the best at hiding. I've tried everything to keep from losing them. The "key receptacle" by my door worked until the cats discovered the keys made good prey and could be reliably hunted near the dish. I tried a key chain attached to my wallet, which attached to my purse, which attached to my backpack, and was always getting tangled. I've considered building a homing device for my key chain, but I haven't yet invested the time. Anyway, if I did, I'd lose the homing end just after I lost my keys.

Though I would like to be more organized, my current system does have its advantages. My busy student's schedule doesn't have enough time in it to get everything done, and often one of the first things I pass over is prayer. Soon enough, though, I lose something critical, and when I can't find it anywhere, I have no alternative to sitting down to pray. Usually, with God's helping hand and some careful excavation, I find what I'm looking for, be it my stapler, that book of stamps or even some time to pray.

Jesus, no matter how much I have to get done, help me pencil in some time for prayer today.

—KJERSTIN EASTON

5/<small>FRI</small>   *Repent, then, and turn to God, so that your sins may be wiped out. . . .*   —ACTS 3:19 (NIV)

My son John was dawdling again, and I was getting impatient. We needed to be at the subway soon if we wanted to be on time for church. But the dead leaves and dry sticks at the corner of the street were too fascinating to pass by quickly.

"John, let's go," I said, reaching down to take his hand.

"No, I want to play!" John answered, avoiding my grasp.

"Now, John." I started to pull him toward me.

"No! No! No!" John shouted. He broke away from me and ran toward his mother and his sisters, halfway down the block. Julia turned to see what was going on; one-year-old Mary, snug in the backpack, peered over her mother's shoulder and smiled at the commotion. "Come on, John!" five-year-old Elizabeth shouted encouragingly.

When I caught up with him, he was crying. He knew he had done something wrong and was trying to figure out a way to make it better. "Daddy, I have to go back to the corner," he said between sobs. Then he turned and started running back to where things had started to go wrong.

For the last few weeks, this has been a pattern for John: When he misbehaves or makes a mistake, he wants to retrace his steps to the place where the trouble started and begin again from there.

I understand what John is trying to do. When I was a boy, I hoped someone would invent a time machine that would take me back to the point just before I'd talked back to my mother or ignored my homework or been rude to Aunt Bess. But life doesn't work like that; when I do wrong, I can't run the film backward and play the scene again. I've got to face up to what I've done, say I'm sorry and go forward from there. It's a hard lesson for a three-year-old to learn, and even now, when I'm all grown up, it's a hard lesson for me, too.

Lord, help me to make a new beginning by acknowledging, not evading, the mistakes I've made.   —ANDREW ATTAWAY

6/<small>SAT</small>   *In the world ye shall have tribulation: but be of good cheer; I have overcome the world.*   —JOHN 16:33

Each year in early January we invite all our godchildren and extended church family over for a potluck meal and one last singing of

Christmas carols. Last year we included our ninety-four-year-old adopted grandma, whom we fondly call "Baba Draga." She bubbled with joy to "be with all you young people." (We middle-agers were pleased to be considered young.)

At one point my husband Alex was at the piano taking requests for everyone's favorite carols. Baba Draga astonished us all by requesting "Home on the Range"! As we searched for the music, Draga explained it was her very favorite song because of the line, "Where seldom is heard a discouraging word, and the skies are not cloudy all day!" She said, "I taught this to my boys, and when they would get into scraps or start complaining, we would sing this song!" Chuckling, we sang "Home on the Range," while Baba Draga beamed and waved her arms conducting us.

A few months later Baba Draga asked me to take her to the eye doctor. Her eyesight had been diminishing, and she was anxious to get some test results. To our disappointment, the doctor confirmed the diagnosis of macular degeneration. It was getting worse, and nothing could be done to stop her loss of vision.

Baba Draga insisted on taking me out to lunch afterward and surprised me by her good humor. When I commented on her happy mood despite the doctor's grim prognosis, she peered across the booth at me. "You know," she said, "everyone at my age has some loss or pain to bear. But I memorized something years ago that I tell myself every day: 'When cheerfulness is kept up against all odds, it is the finest form of courage.'"

Dear God, thank You for Baba Draga and her example of courage. Today, and all year long, please help me refrain from discouraging words or thoughts. —MARY BROWN

7 / SUN *In the beginning was the Word, and the Word was with God, and the Word was God.* —JOHN 1:1

How well I remember my childhood church. It stood stiff and tall on Orange and Concord streets in Lancaster, Pennsylvania. A pair of broad steps led to the impossibly heavy wooden doors. Inside, twelve more steps, which I counted each week, took me to the sanctuary, cool and dark, smelling of dust and old wood.

We children sat in the front pew with instructions not to kick under the seat or bang the hymnals. The minister loomed high in the pulpit above us. As the sermon zinged over my head, I craned my neck and my eyes traveled to an ornate iron plaque bolted to the wall. It said, THE WORD OF OUR GOD SHALL STAND FOREVER. ISAIAH 40:8. Over and over I read it, week by week, year by year. And week by week and year by year, that Scripture grew with me and in me.

Today, whenever I feel myself sinking in the quagmire of a broken promise or whirled about by a sudden, jarring change, those words come back to me as truth that can't be bent, broken or shaken. *The Word of our God shall stand forever.*

Lord, in all the changes and chances of my life, You and Your Word are solid rock.   —SHARI SMYTH

8/ MON   *The God of hope fill you with all joy and peace in believing. . . .*   —ROMANS 15:13

The road ahead was dark and deserted. My car's wipers whined as they pushed a mixture of snow and ice back and forth across the windshield. I grasped the steering wheel with white knuckles and prayed silently. My daughter Keri and I were driving toward Birmingham, Alabama, where she was to participate in a scholarship competition the next morning. Winter storms are an oddity in the South, and I was terrified. I didn't want Keri to know.

She sat silently beside me, eyes straight ahead.

"If you want, you can turn on the radio," I said. Static followed, then a jumble of voices and music, and finally Elton John filled the car with a love song.

My heart melted, thinking of the child beside me. Then, in the midst of my anguished prayers for all the dark unknowns, the presence of God filled my heart with a confident knowing. "Keri," I said, "someday we'll remember this moment and everything I'm about to say will already be true. You are going to get a good scholarship. You are going to excel in college. Someone very wonderful is going to fall in love with you, and all the scattered, confusing pieces of your life will fit perfectly together. I know this because God has put it in my heart to say this to you.

"Someday we'll be dancing at your wedding, and we'll remember this night, and we'll laugh with happiness. Who knows? I might even get Elton John to sing this very song as you walk out onto the floor for the first dance!"

Five years later, I pick up the phone. Keri gives me a glowing report of her first class in graduate school. She speaks of the teenage girls she will be counseling and offers an update on her boyfriend, who attends another graduate school nearby. "Mama, have you written to Elton John yet?" she says with a chuckle. And with those words she tells me everything a mother needs to know.

Dear God, in my scariest moments, You point me to the place where, in Your time, You fit the pieces of my life together into a perfect whole. Thank You.
—PAM KIDD

9 / TUE
"Let the children come to me . . . because the Kingdom of heaven belongs to such as these."
—MATTHEW 19:14 (GNB)

All New England was prepared for the "Blizzard of the Century." Technically, so was I. I'd bought groceries, waxed the shovel, gassed the car, posted mail and taken out the garbage. I was safely ensconced like everyone else in the region, fortified against the onslaught.

My emotions were a different story. There are no pre-blizzard grocery runs to stock up on faith and cheer. The snow this season had started before Thanksgiving and continued through Christmas. It seemed appropriate during the holidays. With Christmas two weeks past, this storm was different. Starting on Sunday, the snow continued falling through the night and into the next day. When it finally ended Monday night, snow filled the streets, sidewalks and yards, transforming even the darkness with an eerie glow. And it filled me as well, numbing my mind and quenching my spirit.

Sleepless, I wandered to my window. It faced a parking lot, uncharacteristically empty for the past forty-eight hours except for maintenance trucks. At 4:00 A.M., they'd been plowing now for nearly two full days. Two trucks plowed endless rows in a seemingly impossible task. The monotony was hypnotizing, further deadening already paralyzed senses as I continued watching.

Suddenly, both vehicles swung dramatically around to face each other. Simultaneously, their bright lights beamed on. In one concerted movement, they began to whirl around like dervishes in tight, wild circles in the snow. I felt an incredulous spark that grew into delight, until I heard myself laughing aloud at their antics. The two weary, dispirited drivers had become children on a joyous ride. For ten minutes they kept it up, until I was dizzy with laughter.

I finally fell asleep, knowing that God had been there all the time, smiling, and just waiting for me to notice Him and smile back.

Lord, help me to gaze on Your world with childlike delight.
—MARCI ALBORGHETTI

10/ *In that day shalt thou not be ashamed for all thy doings. . . .*   —ZEPHANIAH 3:11

10/ WED

It was a bone-chilling January evening, and I was attending a Cultural Council meeting at our local TV station. We were sending letters telling grant applicants that their requests for funding for their community art projects had been approved.

I enjoyed the group and felt comfortable expressing myself. I looked across the table at Mary Ellen and said, "What should be the most exciting days of my life are the most troubling." Mary Ellen looked puzzled, so I continued. "They're Ruby's February birthday, Mother's Day and our anniversary in September. I don't know what to give her anymore. I've given her a radio, a bread maker, a four-quart cooker, a food processor and more. And they're still in their cartons, unopened!"

Mary Ellen's pen dropped and her eyes flashed, "Don't you know any better?" she asked. "On *her* days, you don't give appliances. You don't give her anything that plugs in! Give something personal that shows you care. How many times have you told her you loved her? When was the last time you escorted her to a movie?"

Mary Ellen's words jolted me. The last time I'd taken Ruby to the movies was to *Fiddler on the Roof* on January 5, 1973! Mary Ellen was saying that the greatest gifts I could give Ruby were my time and myself. It hurt to admit I was always busy, constantly reading or lost in thought. I would have to change.

I'll begin by asking Ruby what she'd like for her birthday. Then I'll put her first in my day instead of giving her my leftover time. And maybe tonight we could go to a movie!

Father, pleasing a loved one is so simple. Help me follow Your example by being available always.
—OSCAR GREENE

11/_{THU} *Therefore I take pleasure . . . in distresses for Christ's sake: for when I am weak, then am I strong.*
—II CORINTHIANS 12:10

It had promised to be a long day from the start, but traveling on New York City's mass transit system with three small children in a cold January rain made it stretch on forever. There were simply not enough hands for kids and umbrellas and a stroller, too. My tote bag was crammed to its soggy brim, and the buses were crowded.

When we finally headed home on the subway, "No-Nap John" was asleep in the stroller, Mary drowsed in my arms, and Elizabeth was reading a book. The woman next to me was absorbed in a gourmet food magazine. As I glanced over her shoulder, a postcard insert slipped from the magazine to the train floor. Awhile later another card fell, and then another. The woman did nothing. When she got up to leave the train, I tapped her on the shoulder and said, "Excuse me, but you dropped something."

She shrugged and walked off.

I was furious. *A full-grown adult who leaves trash in public spaces? Why, even my kids pick up the cereal they drop on the floor!* My thoughts were interrupted by the need to get off the train.

As I stood on the platform with two sleeping children and a tired five-year-old, it suddenly occurred to me that there was no way I was going to get everyone up the stairs to the street.

Just then a gentle voice from behind me said, "May I help?" I turned around. There was a petite woman, motioning that she would carry John up the stairs. I said no; he probably weighed half as much as she did. The woman nodded a determined yes, picked up the stroller and carried John up the two flights of stairs to the street. I felt like kissing her, but instead settled for thanking her profusely.

Walking slowly home under gray but dry skies, I asked myself, *So what are you going to remember about today? The woman with the magazine or the woman on the stairs?*

Lord Jesus, You cover my sins with Your perfect righteousness. Take my irritations and turn them into praise. —JULIA ATTAWAY

12/ FRI

Do ye look on things after the outward appearance?
If any man trust to himself that he is Christ's . . .
that, as he is Christ's, even so are we Christ's.

—II CORINTHIANS 10:7

A couple of years ago I was given the job of editor-in-chief of *Guideposts* after working at the magazine for a dozen years. I was a little apprehensive, not so much about the work as about being the public face of such a beloved publication.

I decided to introduce myself to the readers in an editor's column, a more-or-less standard practice for which I needed a current photograph. After sifting through my recent snapshots, our photo editor decided we needed to have professional photographs taken. "All right, you know best," I agreed, though secretly I wanted to use a shot of me hiking the Appalachian Trail with my dogs, wind-blown hair, two-day stubble and all.

I got my hair trimmed and wore my best suit. The photographer shot what must have been several thousand rolls of film. A few days later, I picked out what I thought was the best shot.

Responses to my column were warm, for the most part. A few worried folks wrote in that I looked a little young to be in charge of such a big magazine, and one suggested I find someone with some experience to help me.

Then I got the most surprising letter of all. "I was a neighbor of your sister's," the correspondent wrote, "when she and Ken and the boys lived in Columbus. I've seen many pictures of you. I remember when you graduated from college. I saw pictures from your wedding and your mom's eightieth birthday party. Don't take this the wrong way. Your picture in the magazine is nice—very official looking—but I have to say I prefer you in all those family shots I've seen through the years, where you looked natural and relaxed. That's the Ed Grinnan I know. Just remember, be yourself. Good luck!"

It was too late to do anything about the picture, but there was plenty of time to get used to my new job by just being myself. But next time, maybe I'll use the shot with the dogs after all.

You make me who I am, Lord. Help me to be true to You by being true to myself.
—EDWARD GRINNAN

A WHOLE AND HOLY LOVE

In Daily Guideposts, 1993, *she shared the heartache of her broken marriage with us in a memorable Holy Week series. Now Marilyn Morgan Helleberg has a vibrant new marriage and a new name— Marilyn Morgan King. Today, you're invited to her wedding. Then in the middle of every month, Marilyn and her husband Robert King will show you the milestones on Marilyn's journey from divorce to the whole and holy relationship that now fills her life with joy, and share with you some of the ways their relationship has helped them grow together in the Spirit.* —THE EDITORS

13/SAT   *This is my beloved, and this is my friend. . . .*
              —SONG OF SOLOMON 5:16

"I, Marilyn, take you, Robert, to be my cherished husband. I promise to love you, aspire to treat you always with respect and dignity, to be true and faithful to you, and to hold our relationship sacred for as long as we both shall live."

Suddenly, this candlelit room, in the Rocky Mountain home where we are now becoming husband and wife, takes on a gentle, holy glow.

For a moment, I flash back to 1989, a time when the wounds of divorce were cutting their scars into my life. God seemed eternities away, and I felt sure of only one thing—another marriage was totally out of the question for me. How could I have known then that if I could learn to respond freely to God's love, I would be led to the spiritual companion I had longed for all my life?

And yet here we stand, Robert and I, on New Year's Day 1999, looking into each other's eyes and speaking these holy words: "With this ring, I thee wed. . . ." Just minutes after the New Year begins, we are pronounced husband and wife, and seal our commitment with a kiss. The music swells, and Robert and I walk arm-in-arm into the New Year . . . and into our new life together.

I glance at Saralisa, my five-year-old granddaughter who earlier danced her way down the makeshift aisle, showering everyone with rose petals. In her cherry-red velvet dress, with matching flowers in her hair and a tear of joy on her cheek, she is fresh and beautiful. I send out a little prayer that she will someday know the joy of a love as deep and true as this. I pray the same for you.

Spirit of Love, I ask to wake each day of this year with fresh eyes, that I may see Your light shining through all my loved ones.

—MARILYN MORGAN KING

14 / SUN

All the congregation are holy, every one of them, and the Lord is among them. . . . —NUMBERS 16:3

This was not one of our better Sunday mornings. Maria, just four, was fidgety. She tried coloring but kept dropping her crayons on the floor. She repeatedly wandered to the end of our row of empty chairs, and I pulled her back as if she were a wayward dog on a too-long leash.

"She should be in Sunday school," the woman behind me scolded. My face burned with embarrassment, then anger. Maria had been in Sunday school the previous hour; I had taken her into the service to see her daddy sing. *Is that so bad?* I hastily gathered up our things and moved to the back row. *What nerve!* I thought. Then I glanced at the picture Maria had been coloring. It showed Jesus talking with several children. The caption read, "The disciples thought Jesus wouldn't want to be bothered by children. They soon learned Jesus loves children."

See there! I thought. Jesus invited everyone to follow him, even fidgety four-year-olds. I felt more than a little smug until I remembered the previous week. I'd been critical of the teenager sitting in front of us in her short dress and spaghetti straps. Wouldn't Jesus have welcomed her, too? And I was annoyed by the man a few rows back who sang so loudly and off-key. I'm sure Jesus would have loved his enthusiasm.

I've been guilty of trying to impose my standards on other people's worship, whether it's a dress code or a judgment about their worship style. But my way of praising God certainly isn't the only way that pleases Him. Whether it's fidgety little ones, the dressed-down or the shaky singers—all of us unique souls who fill God's house every week—He sees past the packaging to what's inside. Now I try to do the same.

Each Sunday, Lord, help me to join with—and not judge—those around me praising You. —GINA BRIDGEMAN

15/ MON *"In a dream, in a vision in the night, When deep sleep falls upon men . . . Then he opens the ears of men. . . ."* —JOB 33:15-16 (NKJV)

It's almost as if he knew he didn't have much time. Young Martin Luther King, Jr. was always in a hurry. Skipping grades of school, he entered college at age fifteen and became an ordained minister at age nineteen. He was only thirty when he saw the signing of the Civil Rights Act, and at thirty-five he was the youngest person ever to receive the Nobel Peace Prize. Just four years later his life was over.

How could one man do so much in such a short time? Maybe the answer is in a line from his speech at Selma, Alabama, in 1965. When asked how long it would take to win the reforms he was fighting for, he said, "How long? Not long, for mine eyes have seen the glory of the Lord."

I wonder how many good works I have neglected because I thought they would take too much time and effort. I can usually think of dozens of reasons why something can't be done:

"I'm too old to start."

"I'm not exactly rich, you know?"

"I'm a low-energy person."

"I'm too shy, I'm not the leader type."

All of these may be true, but I think the real reason I don't accomplish more is that I don't have a clear vision of what I want to do, and I fail to include the Lord on my list of resources.

It stirs me to think of the possibilities for good if everyone learned to see with the eyes of a dreamer. Today, on the birthday of Dr. King, would be a good time to look up at the stars and ask God for a clearer vision of what needs to be done.

Thank You, Father, for men and women who show us what we can do when we dare to dream. —DANIEL SCHANTZ

PRAYER FOR JANUARY

Today is a new day, Lord, and I'm glad.
Yesterday was not so good.
I said some things I shouldn't have said.
I ate more than I needed to eat.
I didn't love my children well enough,
or accomplish enough.

But in Your Word, You promise that
the old has passed away
and the new has come;
And when we confess our shortcomings to You,
You forgive us.
So here I am, Lord,
at the beginning of this new day,
asking Your forgiveness.

I surrender myself to You, right now,
recognizing my total dependence on You.
So as I go forward from this moment of prayer
and walk through this day,
help me carry the reality of Your presence,
Your forgiveness and Your love
into all that I say . . . all that I do . . . and all that I think.
Starting right now.

—CAROL KUYKENDALL

16/ *TUE*   *In returning and rest shall ye be saved; in quietness and in confidence shall be your strength. . . .*
—ISAIAH 30:15

I had been away from the office for some weeks due to illness, and when I returned to work I was full of the anxieties typical of editors. Did those proofs get sent out in time? Was this freelance doing a good job on the art for that project? Is editor X on top of project Y? In and out of different offices I trotted, asking questions, worrying about the answers, feeling that I would never catch up with all that I had missed, feeling sure we were headed for some kind of corporate train wreck.

Finally, on my third day back, I flopped down exhausted in the office of my colleague Elizabeth and asked, "What am I missing? I'll never get this all straight. What do I need to make sure all this gets done on schedule? How can I get that report for the board done by Friday?"

She was silent for a moment, looking as though she were reluctant to answer my barrage of questions. Finally, she said slowly, "Well, there are two things that would help."

"Great," I said. "What are they? I'll get right on it." I stood up, almost ready to run out of her office before I had the magic recipe.

"Patience and trust," said Elizabeth quietly. "I think they are what you need right now."

I gulped and sat down again. As her words sank in, I realized that all the staff had been working hard and conscientiously in my absence. My questions were just taking up their valuable time, making them feel second-guessed. And I realized, too, that impatience, my old enemy, had crept up on me as I lay unable to work and now was busy upsetting everybody, including me.

"Thanks," I said, and I went to sit in my own office repeating to myself silently, *Patience and trust. Patience and trust.*

Lord, teach me to trust others and to approach every situation with patience.
—BRIGITTE WEEKS

17/ WED

> "Simply let your 'Yes' be 'Yes,' and your 'No,' 'No'. . . ." —MATTHEW 5:37 (NIV)

"Where are you going?" I asked my three-year-old son Julian as he climbed out of his bed not two seconds after I'd tucked him in.

"To get my other dinosaur," he replied.

"Get back in bed. You already have three dinosaurs right here." Julian got back in bed. Then he started to get back out. "Now where are you going?"

"I want to say good night to Mommy."

"You already did. Now get back in bed." He got back in bed. He started to get out again. "Where in the world are you going now, Julian?"

"I want to kiss the baby good night."

"No, she's already asleep and you'll wake her up. Now look, I want you to get back in bed, and I do not want you to get back out, okay? Under no circumstances do I want you to get out of this bed. It's late!"

Julian promptly got back under the covers and started thrashing about from side to side. At this I got up and grabbed my guitar. Perhaps the lullaby I wrote for him would calm him down.

As I sang the final note, I looked at Julian, who gently looked at me and gave a deep sigh—then started to climb back out of his bed.

"Julian!"

"What, Daddy?"

"I told you not to get out of bed. What possible reason could you have to get up?"

"I want to tell Mommy what an amazing songwriter you are."

I looked him in the eyes. "Okay, go ahead... but hurry!"

Lord, if I have convictions, help me to stand by them, no matter what. —DAVE FRANCO

18/*THU*   *Hold thou me up, and I shall be safe. . . .*
—PSALM 119:117

It was a scary night! The Santa Ana winds whistled through our California canyon, snapping branches off the oaks and bouncing them across our bedroom roof. "One huge mess to clean up in the morning," my husband John grumbled as he tried to snatch a bit of sleep in between the thumps and bumps.

The next morning I stood shivering in my dressing gown on the patio, braced against the still howling wind, and looked at the tangled, twisted rubble that filled our pool and covered our lawn. The phone rang. It was Jan, the young musician who rents the little cottage that was once my mother's, just a few blocks from where we live in the hills of Sierra Madre.

"Come quick! The big pine tree across the fence is leaning over and maybe one or two more gusts of wind will crash it down on top of my roof."

"We'll be right over," I said. "Get out of the house—now—and wait for us in your car! That tree could fall and crush the cottage."

Protect him, Lord, I prayed. *And please protect our cottage.*

It took us exactly four minutes to get to the cottage. Jan, John and

I huddled together, feeling helpless as we watched the huge tree tipping over, perilously close to falling. "My drums are still in there," said Jan.

"Leave them. It's just too dangerous," my husband warned.

After an hour or so of waiting, Jan decided to go back in. A short time later, the huge tree fell. Jan rushed out of the cottage, and we all stopped and looked in awe. The spreading arms of the massive avocado tree that shelters the little cottage from the hot summer sun caught the falling pine and held it up, steady and firm. One side of our cottage roof was slightly cracked and dented, but Jan, his drums and the cottage were safe, held in the arms of answered prayer.

Most blessed Lord, in the stormy seasons of my life and the lives of those I love, put the strength of Your arms under and around us and keep us safe.
—FAY ANGUS

19/ *FRI*   *And I will give them one heart, and I will put a new spirit within you. . . .* —EZEKIEL 11:19

I felt empty, self-centered, all wrapped up in me, me, me. God seemed remote. *I need You to do something, Lord. I don't even know what.* Silence.

One lonely Friday morning I finally curled up with a book a friend had sent for no apparent reason. *Some Wild Flower In My Heart* by Jamie Langston Turner captivated me. I read all day—slowly, like a second-grader. Nearing the end of the book on Saturday afternoon, I savored each word as I would an expensive chocolate. When I finished, I couldn't bear to put it down, so I sat holding it close to me, fully aware that God had worked His way into my heart—even the stubborn part—through this remarkable book. I'd rediscovered the key to Christian joy—genuinely loving others, even the unlovely, from the reservoir of God's unconditional love.

That very afternoon I visited an unbelieving neighbor, a classic grouch. I took flowers to a sick friend I somehow hadn't been able to make time for before. Back at my desk, I wrote out a generous check for a missionary and sent letters of encouragement to each of my six grandchildren. Finally, I looked my astonished husband right in the eye and told him a few of the reasons I loved him so completely.

I decided I had to call the author of this life-changing book to say thank-you. Then my common sense took over, and I attempted to talk myself out of the idea. How would I locate her? Exactly what would I say? Where would I begin?

Five phone calls later, Jamie Turner and I were talking excitedly like old friends. We spoke from the heart for nearly an hour that Saturday afternoon. I could hardly believe it when she insisted that my call had made her day. I know that her book—and her graciousness—had made mine.

Father God, fill my heart with Your love so that I may pass it on to friends and strangers. Amen. —MARION BOND WEST

20/SAT   *I press toward the mark. . . .* —PHILIPPIANS 3:14

My wife set the goal: "You should exercise to this videotape a couple of times a week." I groaned.

"All right, class," the woman on the tape said. "Ready...begin...lift. Again. One, two, three, four. Hold it, hold it. Again. One, two, three, four. . . . Keep it up. Good!" I could only be glad she couldn't see me huff and puff.

"Ouch, ugh. Ouch, ugh," were the sounds I made to the woman's relentlessly cheery voice. "Out, in. Up, down." *I wish we didn't have to meet like this,* I told myself day after day. She and I might have had a nice chat. Instead she was always asking me to do exhausting things.

As the weeks passed, the exercise lady and I got to know each other quite well. I could tell in a heartbeat exactly what she was going to say and when. I would even get ready for the next exercise before she announced it. We weren't exactly friends, but gradually I did a little less huffing and puffing.

And then one day I wore her out. I put in the video and pressed Play. Nothing happened. "I beat her!" I announced to my wife. "I wore the exercise lady out!" I said jubilantly, holding up the broken tape.

"We'll get a new tape," my wife announced. "You can set yourself a new goal."

"Well, for today, I want to celebrate." I had the perfect things in mind: a big piece of chocolate cake, and a little prayer:

Dear Lord, thanks for the discipline that helps me meet my goals. Give me more! —RICK HAMLIN

21 / SUN

And he called his ten servants, and delivered them ten pounds, and said unto them, Occupy till I come.
—LUKE 19:13

There are days when I come home from work and just want to lie down. No, make that pass out. After a long day on the job, the bed, the blankets and the pillows look awfully tempting.

Then I think about Bishop Howard Oby. I remember the first time I saw him more than twelve years ago, preaching in a country church in North Carolina. His skin the color of coffee without cream, he stood about six feet tall, with short-cropped salt and pepper hair. Bishop Oby's hands often dangled loosely at his sides, as if they were unconnected to his body. Except, that is, when he was using a hammer or playing the piano to accompany the choir, a soloist or the congregation. In his church, he was preacher, repairman and musician. On the quiet back roads, people whispered that Bishop Oby could lay those hands on sick people and make them well. They said he could stare at you and know you'd done wrong before you could tell him.

In addition to preaching and playing, Bishop Oby often chauffeured his flock in his van, to and from church on Sunday and from their rural homes to town, to market, to the Laundromat throughout the week. Each Sunday he bathed, clothed, fed and preached to one homebound member of his flock. And with all this, he listened patiently each time one of us called. He never said a word about money and received no salary.

Bishop Oby still doesn't say a word about money. Now, having spent forty-six of his seventy years in ministry, he just keeps moving, keeps serving, keeps praying—keeps doing what he can with what he has, he says, until the Lord comes.

Lord, help me to be a good investor of my time and to be faithful in Your service.   —SHARON FOSTER

22 / MON

"You are the God who sees me. . . ."
—GENESIS 16:13 (NIV)

Our college-age son Jeff received a new gadget for Christmas, a mini-cam to attach to his computer so he could broadcast live shots of his dorm room on his Web site. One January evening my husband

Gordon beckoned me to the computer to see this new technological—a live look at Jeff's room nearly three hundred miles away! The first shot showed Jeff's head in the foreground. In the background, a pair of legs extended from the top bunk and rested on a chest of drawers nearby. In the second shot, the legs were standing on the chest of drawers.

Gordon immediately telephoned Jeff. His roommate Paul answered. "This is the World Wide Web furniture police," Gordon teased. "We've seen you standing on the furniture."

There was a long, startled silence, followed by a meek, "Yes, sir?"

"Just kidding," Gordon replied. "This is Jeff's dad."

Apparently Paul didn't remember the new WebCam. "Oh. Are you here looking in our window?"

The next time we visited Jeff's dorm room, I noticed a piece of tape on the carpet that said, "Now entering WebCam zone. Be careful!"

It's easy to forget that, wherever I am, Someone is watching me. No matter how careful I am to keep up appearances, God always sees deep down inside my heart. And even in my darkest, loneliest moments, God is there, watching me with loving eyes. Sometimes it takes a newfangled gadget to remind me of an age-old truth.

Dear God, help me always to remember that You see me better than I can see myself.   —KAREN BARBER

$23/_{TUE}$ *They that had any sick . . . brought them unto him; and he laid his hands on every one of them, and healed them.*   —LUKE 4:40

Shirley and I belong to the contingent that believes, like the old evangelist, "It's better to stand on the promises than sit on the premises." Since coming to Florida, we've found two volunteer efforts beyond church service that are particularly rewarding: Meals on Wheels, and a pet therapy program for nursing homes and assisted-living centers. The philosophy behind pet therapy is that animals are wonderful expressers of love, capable of bringing smiles to the faces of people whose circumstances are often less than joyful.

Not long ago Shirley and I took a long-legged, sweet-spirited dog named Lady, a greyhound-Labrador mix, to a nursing home. We led her from one room to the next, and dozens of people enjoyed petting her shiny black coat, feeding her treats and getting hand licks in return. Then in the hallway we came upon a wheelchair-bound woman in her eighties.

"Would you like to pet Lady, Mabel?" I asked, reading the woman's name off a tag. She tried to talk, but her words came out in gibberish. Taking her gnarled hand, which was arthritically knotted in a ball, I put it on top of Lady's head. The woman seemed to be unable to pet the dog, so I moved her hand for her. An amazing thing happened: With great willpower, Mabel slowly opened her closed fist until her palm lay on Lady's head, and in the slowest of motions she gently moved her hand from side to side. The smile that broke from the woman's face rivaled the most beautiful sunsets I've ever seen.

There is great healing in touch. Sometimes it is as dramatic as it was for the ailing woman who touched the hem of Jesus' garment. Other times, as with Mabel, touch is a transitory heart healer. But I'm convinced God needs more agents willing to be conduits of His caring who with simple gestures—a spontaneous hug or kiss on the cheek—can help soul-mend the ill, worried, lonely, aging and depressed. If a dog can be God's instrument of love, so can we.

> *Remind me, God*
> *When I stammer and words fail,*
> *To study a dog and its wagging tail.*

—FRED BAUER

24 / WED   *Thou, O Lord, remainest . . . from generation to generation.*   —LAMENTATIONS 5:19

When I went to college, I didn't have much money. Every semester I wondered where my next tuition dollars would come from. But I was rich in one thing: my mother's prayers. When she found out that I often studied past midnight and got up before dawn to study again, she had a practical solution. "I'll just pray that you get two hours of rest for every one hour of sleep." Knowing that made those short nights more bearable, somehow. And I always managed to get through my days—and my tests.

Now my daughter Amy Jo is in her first year of law school. Her days are filled with legal research, detailed lectures, hours spent writing briefs. And her nights are often very short. When she confided this to me on the phone the other day, I instantly knew what to say. "I'll pray that you get two hours of rest for every one hour of sleep."

So that's what I'm doing. And I know—firsthand—that God will answer this prayer.

Thank You, God, for a mother who prayed for me. And for a daughter who needs my prayers. —MARY LOU CARNEY

25/*THU* *For the Lord thy God blesseth thee, as he promised thee. . . .* —DEUTERONOMY 15:6

When my husband Bob was first diagnosed with Parkinson's disease and I began to learn of the many ill effects it might have on him, I became very frightened. How would I be able to cope with the drastic life change awaiting both of us? I outlined my fears to God in prayer. And almost immediately I began to see those prayers answered.

One of my fears was that as Bob's condition worsened, we would be stranded at home. I had given up driving the car years ago, following serious eye surgery, and there is no public transportation in our area. Now a dear friend comes every Friday night after she leaves her job and takes me to buy groceries. Another calls midweek when she is going shopping to see if she can buy anything for me. Trips to the doctor's office or short sprints to the mall are readily taken care of by other friends and neighbors.

And the blessings do not stop there! Church members remember us with cards, phone calls, visits and hot food each time a supper is held in the fellowship hall.

A major problem with Bob's illness is that it causes the muscles to deteriorate, which results in his falling unexpectedly. A man across the street from our house responds immediately to my telephone calls—day or night—and helps me to lift Bob from the floor into his chair or bed.

And, of course, our daughter and granddaughter come almost every weekend and perform countless tasks about our house and yard.

Bob and I were gadabouts when we were healthy—traveling, dancing, participating in senior-citizen doings and church activities. Now all of that has ceased. But I am not restless or resentful. Instead, God has given me a sense of quiet peace and satisfaction, which, at this time in my life, I feel might be the greatest blessing of all.

Thank You, Father, for the blessings You send me daily. Please shower Your love on those who reach out to help us. Amen.

—DRUE DUKE

26/FRI

The Lord is gracious and . . . full of compassion.
—PSALM 116:5 (NIV)

Exhausted and overwhelmed, I drop into the chair. I am midway through a battery of medical tests, and I'm wilting under the barrage of needles and high-tech machines. Just two weeks ago I was diagnosed with malignant melanoma, and in a few days I will be scheduled for major surgery.

While waiting for our next appointment, my husband Harry and I wander into The Park, a sunny atrium on the third floor of this giant cancer center. Wicker chairs with chintz cushions are arranged in comfortable clusters with small tables and reading lamps. Suspended from the high glass ceiling are brightly colored, child-shaped cutouts, and the space is filled with what seems like acres of lush green plants. But in spite of the surrounding beauty, my heart is full of fear.

White-coated staff members walk briskly through to the adjoining hospital, and an older man in a hospital gown and slippers, accompanied by his wife, shuffles along pushing his IV tree. A young girl, entirely bald, rolls by in her wheelchair with her parents walking alongside.

I lean my head back against the chair, too discouraged even to read my book. Then, unexpectedly, from the grand piano across the room comes a familiar melody: "Amazing Grace." Suddenly, I'm wiping the tears from my cheeks as I consider all the things I have to be grateful for.

My doctor, who probably saved my life by recognizing the need to do a biopsy.

The last-minute phone call from friends that helped us make arrangements to come here.

The laptop computer that keeps us in close touch with friends all over the world who are praying for us.

The competent, caring staff who keeps this from being a cold, impersonal place.

This semi-retired time in our lives that frees us to focus on this unexpected need.

And this young woman (a patient or a staff person on lunch break?), whose simple gift has shifted my focus from feeling sorry for myself to being grateful for all that has brought us to this place of healing.

Loving Father, thank You for being able to change tears of self-pity into tears of gratitude. —MARY JANE CLARK

27 / SAT   *Hereafter ye shall see heaven. . . .*   —JOHN 1:51

"In heaven," says my four-year-old son, with the confidence of a man talking about his native country, "everyone is one hundred inches tall." He goes on at some length about the geography and nature of heaven, what sort of boots people wear there (red ones), what the angels do all day long (play basketball), what's for breakfast (cookies).

These pronouncements draw guffaws and scorn from his brother and sister, but he holds forth with undiminished verve. "Yeah, I remember that heaven," he says, with affection. "God was there all the time. He really big guy. He laughing all the time. He funny guy. He have really big hands. He bigger than Daddy. I was not scared because He was laughing."

More scorn from his siblings and a grin from his mother, but his father is moved to ruminate on the topography of heaven, and not for the first time, either. Did not this boy come to me from God? Didn't his long-legged sister and his exuberant brother? And the lovely woman sipping coffee and smiling across the table? And the air we all breathe and the vast country outside and the crow on the fence cocking a curious eye at the heavenly boy in the house? None would be but for the Maker. And who is to say that this boy does not remember a place he was a mere four years ago?

So I listen with care, and hear of a country filled with joy and peace and light and laughter. Many days I think that I am in heaven right now, right here, in the sea of love that is my family. But listening to the little prophet at the head of the table, I dream for a moment of the world to come, the world we work for, in the end an ocean of love in which there are no islands of lovelessness.

Lord, give me ears to hear Your voice and Your music, to savor the heaven around me every moment. And give me the grace never to shush a child telling tales.   —BRIAN DOYLE

28/ *SUN*   *"Then you will present your petitions over my signature! . . ."*   —JOHN 16:26 (TLB)

When our daughter Gae began her second semester in Bible college, some five hundred miles from home, she needed to pay for her courses in advance. But she wouldn't know the courses she'd be taking until she arrived on campus, so she couldn't tell us the exact amount of her tuition. Too young to have her own credit card, she asked her father how she should go about paying.

As only a loving father would do, Leo sat down at the kitchen table and wrote his signature on the bottom of a blank check. "Here, Gae. Once you've enrolled, fill in the exact amount of your tuition."

"But what if you don't have enough money to cover it?" Gae asked.

"There's more than enough. Just trust me," replied Leo.

"Oh, boy!" Gae teased. "Maybe I'll spend it on a new car or something!"

"Just remember," said Leo, shaking his finger at her in mock warning, "I can put a stop payment on it."

"Oh, so you've got me all figured out!" Gae said with a laugh. After giving her dad a big hug, she started off to her bedroom to finish packing. "And don't worry, Dad. I'll find a good safe place for that check. Thanks again!"

That little scene replayed itself in my mind this morning during prayer time. Do I ask for too much? And yet the Bible says, "My God shall supply all your needs according to His riches in glory in Christ Jesus" (Philippians 4:19, NAS).

Is what I want within His will? And yet Psalm 84:11 (NAS) says, "No good thing does He withhold from those who walk uprightly."

If God has given me a blank check, why am I so unwilling to fill it out?

Heavenly Father, help me to believe that You are both willing and able to grant those petitions that will bring me closer to You.

—ALMA BARKMAN

29 / MON   *[Jesus] gave them power . . . to heal all manner of sickness and all manner of disease.*

—MATTHEW 10:1

The feeble line etched by the fetal monitor told the grim story: The baby wasn't doing well. As first-time childbirth coach for my daughter Tess, in labor with her first child, I sensed a growing uneasiness in the hospital room.

Normally chipper Nurse Leah wasn't smiling. "We'd like to see more baby activity," she explained. Every few minutes she would check the monitor, then slip out to the nurses' station to phone the doctor. Even a sonogram and extra oxygen didn't convince her that the baby could rally.

"I've called the doctor. He'll be here right away."

We had met Dr. Culwell, the obstetrician on call, only once. Trim, white-haired, slow-talking, he had seemed pleasant enough during our brief office visit. But could he handle what was fast becoming an emergency?

The doctor strode into Tess's room, chatted calmly, checked the fetal monitor and quickly made his decision. "We need to do a Caesarean section so we don't compromise this baby. She might have trouble with ten or twelve more hours of labor."

Major surgery and we don't even know this guy!

As the nurses began to prepare Tess for the operating room, Dr. Culwell confided to me on his way out the door, "I started praying about this at home."

"You're the man for us !" I said. My tension melted away.

A few minutes later, wearing scrubs, blue paper booties and hair net, I held Tess's hand in the operating room. Suddenly, our praying doctor whisked a tiny baby the color of cement through the air to the warming table. As the pediatrician deftly suctioned her, she began to turn pink as a sunrise. Her throaty wail assured us all was well.

The next day as Tess snuggled her tiny Hannah, I met Dr. Culwell in the hall. "I don't know how to thank you," I said haltingly.

"Oh, it wasn't just me," he drawled, looking heavenward with a grin. "I had a lot of help."

Merciful Father, thank You for skilled professionals who humbly put their trust in You. —GAIL THORELL SCHILLING

30/*TUE*   *In everything give thanks. . . .*
                                —I THESSALONIANS 5:18

Sometimes it's hard to remember to thank friends or neighbors for recent favors. It's even harder to reach back across two centuries. But that's just what happened to me the other day.

My wife Pam and I were visiting one of the Zuni Communities in New Mexico where work was being done on a very old chapel. A small sign invited visitors to make a contribution that would help with the restoration. Pam, who was born in England, said to me, "Your family goes back a long way in this country. Are there any family stories about Indians?" So I told her about my great-great-grandmother Eleanor Lytle and a Seneca chief named Cornplanter.

During the Revolution, little Eleanor, age nine, was captured along with her mother and small brother by a raiding party of Senecas, who sided with the British in those days. Eleanor's brother and mother were quickly ransomed, but the Seneca chief took such a fancy to the nine-year-old girl that he adopted her as his sister and refused to let her go. For four years she remained with the Senecas, who treated her with great kindness. Finally, Cornplanter agreed to let her have a meeting with her parents, but he made her promise never to leave him without his consent.

The meeting took place near Fort Niagara soon after the war ended. Eleanor, now thirteen, could not contain herself. She jumped from the canoe and flung herself into her mother's arms. Watching this, Cornplanter said, "The mother must have her child again. I will go back alone." And he did. Some years later, in 1798, Eleanor married a frontiersman named John Kinzie, my great-great-grandfather.

"So you see," I said to Pam, "if it weren't for that act of unselfishness, I might not be here at all."

"Let's help the Zunis with their restoration plans," Pam said. "I think Cornplanter would be pleased."

So we did, and we hope he was.

Father, help us to remember that it is never too late to be grateful for a kindness.
—ARTHUR GORDON

31 / WED

Casting all your care upon him; for he careth for you.
—I PETER 5:7

I was leaving my parents' apartment after a daylong visit with them before heading on to my sister's house. "We'll walk you to the bus stop," my mother said.

"Oh, that's not necessary," I began. "I'm sure I can find—"

They were already putting on their coats. We walked the few blocks, the snow crunching under our feet. But louder than the snow came the list of instructions. "Now, be extra careful that you get on the right bus. Both the N-20 and the N-21 stop here, and you don't want to get on the wrong one."

I'm sure I can figure that out, I thought. Then my mother held up her MetroCard—it was a new development since I'd last been in New York City, when I'd used a token. "Here," she said, "take my Metro-Card. Just slide it in the money changer on the bus. Make sure you put it in with the arrow facing down."

"Thanks, Ma," I muttered, thinking, *Next, they'll tell me to look both ways before I cross the street!*

Sure enough, "And this is a busy intersection," my stepfather Joe instructed me. "Make sure to look both ways."

As soon as I was settled into a place in the line, I gave a sheepish smile to the lady in front of me, a stranger, who was cuddling a baby swathed in a yellow crocheted blanket. "Everybody was somebody's baby once," she said, looking lovingly at her own child.

Suddenly, I felt the love and caring that my parents' instructions conveyed. All they wanted was for me to be safe. I turned to look for them. I didn't have to look far—they were waiting to see that I got on the bus safely.

"Thanks!" I mouthed. "Thanks for caring about me."

God, today let me be grateful for, not grumpy about, the concern of those who love me. They are extensions of Your love.
—LINDA NEUKRUG

DAILY GIFTS

1 _____

2 _____

3 _____

4 _____

5 _____

6 _____

7 _____

8 _____

9 _____

10 _____

11 _____

12 _____

13 _____

14 _____

15 _____

16 _____

17 _____

18 _____

19 _____

20 _____

21 _____

22 _____

23 _____

What a wonderful day this was
24 *Elsa treated me to lunch & gave this book*

25 _____

26 _____

27 _____

28 _____

29 _____

30 _____

31 _____

February

I delivered the poor that cried, and the fatherless, and him that had none to help him . . . . I was eyes to the blind, and feet was I to the lame.

—JOB 29:12, 15

S	M	T	W	T	F	S
				1	2	3
4	5	6	7	8	9	10
11	12	13	14	15	16	17
18	19	20	21	22	23	24
25	26	27	28			

WHEN GOD REACHES OUT . . . THROUGH OTHER PEOPLE

1/_THU_   *Stand still, and see the salvation of the Lord. . . .*
—EXODUS 14:13

Kathy Halpern could not have known about my dilemma. She lives in California, where I was visiting, far from the situation waiting for me back home in New York. Two of my closest friends had separated after forty years of marriage; now each wanted me to hear their side of the story. How could I befriend either one without being disloyal to the other?

It was a relief to escape for a few days to the West Coast, where Kathy's church had recently witnessed the near-miraculous recovery of one of its members. The young man had been pronounced brain-dead after a car accident. The church mounted a round-the-clock prayer vigil, and now, four months later, he was sitting up, talking, recognizing members of his family.

"Do you know what the hardest thing was for me?" Kathy said. "Not rushing to the hospital with everybody else, the night of the accident." That had been her first instinct—to jump in her car and get there as fast as she could. "I was on my way out the door when God simply stopped me." She thought she heard Him say that there would be a string of daunting medical negatives at the hospital. The role God had for Kathy was to focus on His power. *Keep your eyes on Me,* He said, *not on the problem.*

And so she had, contacting the young man's family the next day with a message of faith instead of fear.

As I say, Kathy couldn't have known about the situation back in New York. But of course, God did. Through her words shone God's wisdom for me as well: *You don't need to know the details of your friends' breakup. Right now, right here in California, you can lift them both to Me.*

When problems come this month, Lord, keep my eyes on the One Who has the answers.
—ELIZABETH SHERRILL

2/ *FRI*   *A light to lighten the Gentiles, and the glory of thy people Israel.*   —LUKE 2:32

I'll admit it. I've never looked forward to or enjoyed Groundhog Day. No matter what that groundhog sees when he comes out of his hole, we Wisconsin realists already know that we're going to have at least six more weeks of winter. Probably more like twelve weeks of cold, dreary weather, if the truth be known.

Personally, I like the other holiday that falls on February 2 much better: Candlemas Day. Candlemas commemorates the presentation of the infant Jesus in the Temple by Mary and Joseph. As Luke tells the story in his gospel, the old man Simeon, who has been waiting to see the deliverance of Israel, takes the baby in his arms and declares that He is the light of the nations and Israel's glory. Since the eleventh century, candles have been blessed on Candlemas Day in many churches to recall Simeon's words.

In northern Europe, where Candlemas Day is celebrated with gusto, tradition says that dark, snowy skies on February 2 offer hope of a quick end to winter, much like the Groundhog Day tradition in the United States. An old Scottish couplet proclaims:

> If Candlemas is fair and clear,
> There'll be two winters in the year.

But if that happens, at least we'll have the warm, bright light from those candles to give us hope for an early spring and warmer weather.

Today, in my home in Oak Creek, I'm going to light candles on the table at supper time. I'm going to think about how the light of Christ shines bright in our lives no matter what the weather. I'll also dream about springtime and warmer weather and perhaps even plan a few warm-weather vacations. I'll leave Groundhog Day to those folks around the country who truly do have a chance for less than six more weeks of winter.

Heavenly Father, today as I light these candles, help me to spread the light of Your Son Jesus Christ into a few dark corners.

—PATRICIA LORENZ

3/*SAT*   *Your word is a lamp to my feet and a light for my path.*   —PSALM 119:105 (NIV)

There's a wonderful outdoor flea market held one weekend a month in a town near my home. The gates open at 4:00 A.M., and for a small early buyer's fee, you can shop by flashlight while the dealers are setting up.

My sister Rebekkah and I could hardly wait to check it out, and we didn't sleep a wink the night before. We parked on a patch of grass near a lady selling vintage linens. But in all the excitement, we left our flashlight in the trunk, and we didn't even attempt to retrace our steps back to the car in the dark.

A man on a bicycle with a lantern welded to a wire basket the size of a washtub seemed to be grabbing everything in sight. We followed his light for a while. When he stopped to inspect some old tools, I trailed behind a lady with a flashlight clipped to a baby stroller-turned-shopping cart. I thought Rebekkah was right behind me, but she was nowhere to be found.

Over the next couple of hours, I purchased a chair I planned to stencil, a blue graniteware stove and a primitive ladder perfect for displaying an old quilt I'd snapped up. Three hours and a backache later, I still hadn't located my sister or the car.

When I finally spotted Rebekkah, lying down with a lemonade in a wicker chaise by the entrance gate, I collapsed beside her and we scrutinized our finds. The vintage Santa she'd bought had a big rip that was seeping sawdust, and my prized quilt had a terminal stain. "If I'd seen this stuff in broad daylight, I would've kept on walking," I said. "Me, too," she agreed, pointing to yet another major ding on my graniteware stove.

In the dark, our "treasures" had been irresistible, and following the lights in the crowd had seemed so exciting. But ever since, when I set out for unfamiliar, dark territory, I make certain the light for my path is close beside me.

Dear Lord, please light my path, lest I lose my way.

—ROBERTA MESSNER

4 / *SUN*

Beloved, I pray that all may go well with you and that you may be in health; I know that it is well with your soul. —III JOHN 2 (RSV)

When I was a child in a small Missouri village during World War II, I caught a bad case of the mumps. The only doctor in the area was off on a trip and the nearest hospital was over sixty miles away, beyond the reach of our gas-ration stamps. I developed a fever of 105 degrees and a long-lasting headache that threatened to split open my skull. At last I slipped into a lethargy so profound that I could not move, speak or open my eyes, but I could still hear my mother rocking in a chair near my bed. Her soft murmuring reassured me and eased the pain.

When I finally began to recover after days of illness, I asked my mother, "Who were you talking to while I was sick?"

"God," she replied.

Today we have antibiotics to help combat severe illness, and I believe in accepting the help that doctors can offer. But I know through experience that prayer, too, is a "miracle medicine" that reaches through pain, sickness and despair to strengthen us with God's healing touch.

What a blessing to have the Great Physician always ready to make a house call! (It helps to have Him around on the good days, too!)

Father, today I will reach out to someone who needs the comfort of Your healing presence. —MADGE HARRAH

SIMPLE LIVES, SINGLE HEARTS

Two years ago, Isabel Wolseley lost her beloved husband Roland. Isabel tried her best to hide her grief, but she was still hurting months later, when her son John asked her to go with him to Papua

New Guinea, where he had been a missionary years before. For the next seven days, join Isabel as she discovers healing for her heartache in a new and very different land. —THE EDITORS

5/MON

DAY ONE: HALF A WORLD AWAY
"God be gracious to you, my son."

—GENESIS 43:29 (NIV)

"I'm making a business trip back to Papua New Guinea," my son John said. "Marie and the girls will be staying home. Would you like to go with me?"

His phone call came only a few months after the death of my husband—John's stepfather—and doubtless John sensed I was tired of putting on a brave front, keeping outward emotions under control when inwardly I felt far from fine.

This is my chance to get away . . . anywhere where I don't have to pretend!

"Yes," I answered, "I'd love to go." During the eighteen years John and his family had lived in Papua New Guinea as missionaries, I'd always wanted to visit them, but circumstances had never allowed it.

It was a six-hour flight from Syracuse, New York, to Los Angeles, fourteen hours from L.A. to Sydney, Australia, then another three from Sydney to the bird-shaped island nudging the southern edge of the equator above Australia. Landing in Papua New Guinea's coastal capital, Port Moresby, was like entering another world. Everyone wore sandals or went barefoot. Everyone carried *bilums,* colorful string bags, to and from the outdoor markets. The bilums held fruit, vegetables, eggs, beadwork. And babies. John said their youngest child, born in Papua New Guinea, napped best in a bilum.

Our destination was in the island's remote highlands, so we headed to another part of the airport where the missionary aircraft were based. When I saw the plane we were to take—a mosquito compared to the mammoth 747 from which we had so recently debarked—I felt a few jitters in my stomach.

Evenly distributed cargo was stowed all over the plane. Then we four slithered into seats so cramped our knees nearly hooked over our ears. Our mosquito's two props reluctantly hiccuped a bit, then buzzed furiously as we raced down the runway for liftoff.

A line of sharp, sky-reaching mountains loomed ahead. Even

though I was confident with my son at the cockpit controls, I found myself remembering the words from an old hymn and making them my prayer:

Jesus, Savior, pilot me. . . .
Chart and compass come from Thee. . . .
May I hear thee say to me,
"Fear not, I will pilot thee."
(EDWARD HOPPER, 1816–1888)

—ISABEL WOLSELEY

6/TUE
DAY TWO: KUAMI'S TEARS
I have seen thy tears: behold, I will heal thee. . . .
—II KINGS 20:5

Cumulus clouds alongside our tiny missionary aircraft seemed so huge, billowy—and close—that I wanted to reach out and touch them to see if they really were as wispy as they appeared. With their flat undersides, they looked like meringue mounded on transparent glass, their tops browned by the setting sun.

Piloting and shouting above the Cessna's noisy engines, my son John pointed out "Shaggy Ridge," the last area of fighting in Papua New Guinea during World War II. Even yet, he often saw planes "rusting in peace" in rainforest so dense their dying descent into the fronds of the tall palms undoubtedly caused only a momentary ripple. Behind us was the Coral Sea, once the scene of a titanic naval battle, now pink and serene.

After cresting the mountains, we dropped into a valley—still nearly six thousand feet up—and touched down on Aiyura Airport's narrow dirt runway.

John had not been back in Papua New Guinea for five years, and when people learned of his upcoming visit, many waited hours for his arrival. As he unfolded his six-foot three-inch frame to exit the Cessna, men whose heads reached only to John's chest took turns hugging him, their wives and children shyly standing nearby.

One elderly man, Kuami, tears of joy zigzagging down his cracked-ebony face, kept clinging to John, murmuring "John, John." My son laid his own head on top of the old man's and the two, arms entwined, melded into one—like a marbleized block of black and white.

The scene made me uncomfortable. *People—men especially—aren't supposed to show their emotions.* Since my husband's death several months earlier, I'd made certain no one saw my tears.

Then, surprisingly, my eyes suddenly filled with tears, too, and I wondered: Could the Lord be using this trip to crack my pretense that all was well?

Precious Lord, You are the Great Physician. You can heal whatever hurt we have if we turn it over to You. —ISABEL WOLSELEY

7 / WED

DAY THREE: A DIFFERENT SKY
When I consider your heavens, the work of your fingers, the moon and the stars, which you have set in place, what is man that you are mindful of him, the son of man that you care for him?
—PSALM 8:3–4 (NIV)

It was my first night in the missionary compound, where one of the houses had been made available for my son and me. Its green, rattan-braided walls provided privacy but also allowed the wind to seep through. *Neat,* I thought. *Natural air-conditioning!*

The nicest time of day always seemed to be around 4:00 or 5:00 P.M., when there was a slight breeze. But as the sun went down, so did the wind. Even the trees seemed to lose heart; their leaves hung listlessly, and by bedtime a steamy shroud clung to everything. It took heat and high humidity to create a rainforest so lushly green and fluorescent it almost hurt to view it.

From dusk into the dark, night creatures awoke to form an orchestra of their own: insects chirping; birds calling; frogs and geckos rasping their own noises. I regretted not having brought a tape recorder to capture their sounds.

I lay there in the friendly darkness. A fingernail-clipping of a moon seemed to hang on nothingness as I looked for the Southern Cross amid a multitude of stars. At six thousand feet with no smog or city lights, the stars looked like back-lit crystals pricked into an arching, velvety-black, celestial dome with the Milky Way like powdered sugar sifted among them.

I marveled at the heavens God had made. But mostly I marveled, *Amidst all this, God made and cares for me!* I rolled over and was soon lulled to sleep by the music of His night creatures.

How wonderful it is to know, heavenly Father, that You—Who never sleeps—watch over and cradle me while I do. —ISABEL WOLSELEY

*8/*THU
DAY FOUR: GIFTS OF LOVE
There is no speech nor language, where their voice is not heard. —PSALM 19:3

There are about eight hundred language groups in Papua New Guinea, but Tok Pisin is the common trade language, and it was what my son used to introduce me to his friends.

"This is Mama," John said to those gathered nearby to greet him after a five-year absence. "I'm her number one."

Kuami, the elderly man who had greeted John at the airport, was called Papa because of his advanced age and was the acknowledged spokesman for the group. He offered me his hand, gave a bow—as courtly as if I'd been the island's queen—and an "Ah, Mama." He stretched *Mama* into a reverent *Mah-ma.* He then added something else; I turned to John for its interpretation. "He's given you the highest form of address—parents are honored in Papua New Guinea."

Suddenly, a young woman darted up and thrust a string bilum into my hands. "*Mah-ma,*" she said, then just as suddenly was swallowed back in the fringe of women and children.

At first glance, the bag was not all that pretty. Its strings were scratchy and bore a design in washed-out red. Its handle was too long to hand-carry but too short to slip over my shoulder. But I smiled warmly and hugged the bilum—the only way I knew to say "thank you."

Later my son told me how the bag had been made. First, the woman had pounded palm and banana leaves to a pulp, then rolled the fibers between her hands to make pale brown strings as fine as pencil leads. The coloring for the pale burgundy painted bird on one side was made by pressing seeds from red, milkweedlike pods. It was knitted with fingers—not needles. The purse had taken her two months to make.

I didn't need to understand Tok Pisin to sense the love for John that went into this gift to his mama. And in spite of my determination to conceal my own vulnerability, in the warmth of that love my reserve was beginning to melt.

Dear Lord, help me always to remember that love can be expressed in any language.
                                                              —ISABEL WOLSELEY

9/ FRI

DAY FIVE: A FEAST OF FRIENDSHIP
They ate and drank with great joy in the presence of the Lord that day.   —I CHRONICLES 29:22 (NIV)

My son—this time in the copilot's seat of a two-propeller missionary plane—the pilot, and four of us passengers, left the six-thousand-foot valley in Papua New Guinea's highlands. Our destination was Madang, a small town on the island's northern edge where a white obelisk-shaped monument honors the coastwatchers of World War II.

In Madang John picked up a missionary-owned all-terrain vehicle, and we began the ascent to a village where he had lived during his eighteen years on the island. The final mile took us up a thousand feet on a one-lane sand-and-rock road, which zigzagged up the mountainside. Our quarters for the next several days was a house with the usual rattan-braided walls, sitting atop a knoll. Below us stretched flowering trees, vines, almost impenetrable undergrowth and, in the distance, the Bismarck Sea. Sudden night showers often pelted our corrugated tin roof.

One day John said, "Tolop and his family will be joining us for supper. Would you cook chicken and noodles? I know they like that."

"How many are coming?"

"I'm not sure. It's not polite to ask."

Tolop, his wife, three children, son-in-law and baby showed up; there were nine of us around the table. Tolop carried in their contribution to the meal: a large cast-iron kettle filled with green beans, sweet potatoes, taro and other vegetables cooked in coconut milk. We women smiled a lot but listened in silence while the men did the talking—in Tok Pisin, of course, which I could not understand—as we all ate together.

After the meal, I was anxious to get things cleaned up and go to bed. The baby, up past its bedtime, cried, but the family lingered and the men continued chatting (about spiritual matters, John later told me) for what apparently was the traditional length of time.

Finally I relaxed, accepting something that was new to me . . . a slower pace of life.

Calm my frantic pace, Lord, and show me how to still my heart so that I can better appreciate Your presence. —ISABEL WOLSELEY

10/SAT

DAY SIX: KUAMI'S FAREWELL
Rejoice with them that do rejoice, and weep with them that weep. —ROMANS 12:15

Several days before my son and I were due to leave Papua New Guinea, he told me he and Tolop needed to bring up some supplies from Madang. Then he added, "I want to stop and say good-bye to Papa Kuami at his home village on the way."

John turned the missionary van off the road, skillfully navigating across a cracked-earth opening that could easily have torn off or swallowed its wheels. In an acre-sized opening hacked out of the rain-forest was a typical Papua New Guinea village: six or eight frond-thatched dwellings on stilts, the domestic animals beneath them.

Papa was waiting; doubtless he'd heard the approaching vehicle's growl. Again, Papa clung to John, shaking his head, so emotionally spent he was unable even to utter my son's name. I sensed that he knew this was their final meeting on earth.

Finally, Papa released his hold. Then, balancing himself with a crooked-stick cane in one bony hand and two bags of rice (a parting gift from John) in the other, he turned weeping back to his dirt-floored hut.

I raised my camera to record the event. Then I lowered it. A *National Geographic* crew might have made that scene part of an award-winning documentary. But for me, this final good-bye was too tender, too intimate to show to anyone else. I wanted to protect Papa in this moment of intense feeling.

Back down in Madang, while my son scurried through stores looking for last-minute gifts for those who'd remained at home in the

States, I noticed that Tolop was dogging my every step. It took a few minutes before I understood why: Tolop was protecting John's widowed *Mah-ma* while her son was out of sight.

Lord, help me learn when to cry, when to laugh and when to watch over my fellow human being.
—ISABEL WOLSELEY

11 / SUN

DAY SEVEN: ALMOST HOME
Heal me, O Lord, and I shall be healed . . . for thou art my praise.
—JEREMIAH 17:14

In spite of Papua New Guinea's heat and humidity and the threat of malaria, I was reluctant to leave the island and its people, both so easy to love. With my son behind the wheel of the missionary van, we navigated the wildly zigzagging lane back down the mountainside to Madang's airport.

Tolop was already there. While we waited to board—seated below signs announcing "This is a no-smoking, no-betel nut-chewing flight"—John gestured to Tolop, who kept repeating, "No savvy."

John, obviously puzzled himself, turned to me. "How do you explain the international dateline in Tok Pisin?"

I had a hard time "savvying" it myself. You see, we left Papua New Guinea on the longest day of the year in the Southern Hemisphere, but when we crossed the equator and the international dateline, it was the shortest day in the northern half of the world. I experienced both the longest and the shortest day, all within one twenty-hour flight to California via Sydney, Australia!

I stayed in the Los Angeles area with a cousin, whose exquisite home is like a museum. And when her thirty-plus guests arrived for a catered dinner and she introduced me, each woman gave me a perfunctory hug and a midair kiss, which landed somewhere near my left ear. Later that evening we attended a musical program at church, where spotlights painted the elegantly robed professional choir, the organ pipes and the ornate walls with a kaleidoscope of colors. I couldn't help but contrast my present surroundings with those I'd just left. *Why was I so touched during my visit to Papua New Guinea?* I asked myself.

It was as if the Lord Himself answered: *The people didn't put on a brave front or try to keep their emotions from showing—as you've been doing recently. It's refreshing, isn't it?*

Heavenly Father, let me never be ashamed to display and share what's truly important—my feelings. —ISABEL WOLSELEY

12/MON

But I say unto you, Love your enemies, bless them that curse you, do good to them that hate you, and pray for them which despitefully use you, and persecute you; That ye may be the children of your Father which is in heaven. . . . —MATTHEW 5:44-45

The American Civil War was the greatest tragedy that the American people ever endured. It was a brutal struggle of brother against brother. In four years of combat, more than 620,000 soldiers lost their lives. The number of civilian casualties is unknown. More Americans lost their lives in the Civil War than in all of our nation's other wars combined.

Toward the end of the Civil War, when hatred between North and South had reached a demonic peak, Abraham Lincoln was asked to speak to a group of staunch Unionists, mothers and fathers who had lost their sons and husbands in battle. In his remarks Lincoln spoke compassionately of Southerners. He pitied their plight and their suffering, and plainly said so.

After his speech an elderly lady rebuked the President for speaking kindly of his enemies. Rather, she admonished, he should be concerned with wiping the Confederates off the face of the earth and bringing the war to an immediate conclusion. Lincoln gently replied to her, "Why, madam, do I not destroy my enemies when I make them my friends?"

It was this tender spirit of Lincoln that kept the fabric of America from being totally destroyed. And though Lincoln himself died a violent death at the hands of an assassin, his example lived long after him, helping Americans to bind up their wounds and seek reconciliation.

Our world today still desperately needs men and women with the heart of Lincoln who will transform enemies into friends.

Lord, make me an instrument of Your peace. Where there is hatred, let me sow love; where there is injury pardon. Amen. (ATTRIBUTED TO ST. FRANCIS OF ASSISI) —SCOTT WALKER

13/ TUE

Teach me good judgment and knowledge, for I have believed thy commandments. —PSALM 119:66

Tuesday morning is garbage pickup at our country home. One Monday evening I hauled several heavy bags to the edge of the road. Wanting to make the lifting easier for the pickup man, I overturned a wheelbarrow and placed one heavy bag on top of it. Early the next morning the wheelbarrow was gone.

"Somebody stole our wheelbarrow," I fumed.

"Nobody *stole* your wheelbarrow," my brother said with a laugh. "Whoever took it thought you were throwing it out with the garbage."

"Well, then, I'll make a sign and ask for it back," I said.

"Mom, if you do that, I'm not coming home," my teenage son warned.

"Forget it," my brother said.

But I made a sign anyway. It read, PLEASE RETURN OUR WHEELBARROW. WE NEED IT. THANK YOU.

A couple of mornings later my daughter bounced into the kitchen. "Look, Mom," she said, pointing toward the living room window. There beside the road in the early dawn stood our wheelbarrow.

I never did find out who took our wheelbarrow or who brought it back. No matter. That wheelbarrow incident has taught me a good lesson: Sometimes what seems like mischief is just an honest mistake.

Lord Jesus, help me see others clearly, as You see them, and to believe the best about them.
                                        —HELEN GRACE LESCHEID

14/ WED

Love covers a multitude of sins. —I PETER 4:8 (RSV)

Sometimes I feel overwhelmed by the challenges of parenting. I especially struggle to control my temper. But on my refrigerator is a paper heart, pasted on red construction paper, to remind me of a lesson I learned one February.

That day I just lost it with my then-six-year-old daughter—about valentines, of all things! I insisted Elizabeth sign her name to the last three cards for her kindergarten class. "Elizabeth, there will be no time in the morning to finish before school, so please finish now."

Tears and refusals from Elizabeth. Loud demands from me. She had written her name seventeen times and simply couldn't sign three more. Yes, she could—and must. No, she couldn't—and wouldn't. Angrily, I sent her upstairs to get ready for bed. I tossed the valentines into the box and slammed cupboard doors while cleaning up the kitchen.

Then, clearing papers off the counter, I picked up a worksheet from Sunday school, a page of six hearts with jagged lines through them. Inside each heart was a Bible verse about love. The children could cut out the heart pieces, then match up the Scripture verses to paste them back together.

As I stared at the paper, the verse in the first heart pierced my own: "Love one another; as I have loved you" (John 13:34). How I'd failed to love Elizabeth as God loves me, so patient with my weaknesses, holding back His anger, understanding and giving constant help! I tiptoed upstairs to tuck her in. "Elizabeth, please forgive me for shouting at you," I said.

To my surprise, she murmured, "Oh, Mom, I'm sorry I didn't want to do what you wanted me to do." With a forgiving hug, our relationship was glued back together.

Dear God, when I've done something to break a relationship, help me to admit my mistakes and ask for forgiveness. —MARY BROWN

PRAYER FOR FEBRUARY ❧

I'm never quite sure
whether it's You talking to me,
dear Lord,
or me talking to me.
Keep me from hearing my own voice
when all I want is to listen
to You and only You.
Your plan, Your purpose,
Your will, not mine,
in everything I do.

—FAY ANGUS

A WHOLE AND HOLY LOVE

15 / *THU* *"I am with you always."* —MATTHEW 28:20 (RSV)

The year was 1990, and I'd just arrived home from a delightful evening of reminiscing, laughter and comradeship. A couple who'd moved away had come back for a visit, so Helen and Bob had invited the old gang over for the evening. It was nice of them to include me, but there was no way to avoid the glaring truth that I was now single—one-half of a couple.

As I walked into my dark and empty house, I felt more alone than ever before, and the chill of the February night went all the way into my bones. At that moment, I looked up to the framed needlepoint cross hanging by my prayer chair. Sewn by a *Daily Guideposts* reader who had sent it to comfort me at this difficult time in my life, it bore the words of Jesus:

I
AM
WITHYOU
A
L
W
A
Y
S

Oh, how desperately I wanted to believe it! But could I honestly claim such a wild, unprovable truth? As the wind howled outside my window, I sank into my prayer chair, closed my eyes and fell into the waiting silence. Then I began to breathe those words into my heart, repeating them silently, letting them fill my empty heart: *I am with you always . . . I am with you always . . . I am . . . .*

I continued the practice daily, and as the weeks and months unfolded, I found the words taking up residence in my heart. From this sturdy rock my life began to flow like a trusting river. Without trying to *make* anything happen, I felt led to reach out to form new friendships, to find spiritual companionship in group prayer and Bible study, and to get to know myself better through keeping a daily journal. There were down days, too, when I was ambushed by loneliness or when a friend's death brought awareness of my own diminishing years. At such moments, those five aligning words would come up unbidden from my heart to remind me I could trust God to bring me through the rockiest of riverbeds.

Knowing You are with me always, Lord, I can trust You to carry me to wholeness. —MARILYN MORGAN KING

16/ *FRI* *And as the bridegroom rejoiceth over the bride, so shall thy God rejoice over thee.* —ISAIAH 62:5

"Mom, we're engaged!" Kendall's words tumbled out of the telephone late one afternoon. Little did she know that I'd been waiting all day for her call, because I knew she was getting engaged that day. One week earlier, her then-boyfriend David Parkhurst flew to Colorado and took Lynn and me to dinner to ask our blessing on his intention to propose to Kendall. His gesture, and the sacrifices he made to carry it out, not only endeared him to us but gave us the privilege of anticipating this phone call.

David actually surprised us. He didn't tell us the reason for the dinner, instead saying something about his parents were flying through Denver and had arranged for a layover so the four of us could meet for the first time. The plan was to get together at a restaurant at 6:30 on a Friday evening. When we showed up, the maitre d' greeted us warmly. "Your table is ready," he said, "and a young man is here waiting for you." Lynn and I looked at each other with the first inkling of what might be unfolding. Sure enough, when we got to our table, there was David—*only* David.

"Your parents aren't coming, are they?" I asked as I gave him a hug.

"No," he grinned, "it's just me."

For the next couple of hours, the three of us talked and prayed and ate and laughed and, of course, I cried as he told us why he loved Kendall and wanted to marry her. We joyfully gave him our blessing, and he shared with us his plan for proposing to Kendall the next weekend. That's why I expected her phone call on this day.

As Kendall overflowed with excitement on the telephone, I overflowed with gratitude for a future son-in-law who cared enough to carry out that ageless tradition of asking for our daughter's hand, which included us in their circle of love on this day.

Thank You, Lord, for the way an engagement enlarges and enriches a whole family.
—CAROL KUYKENDALL

17/ SAT *And let ours also learn to maintain good works for necessary uses, that they be not unfruitful.*
—TITUS 3:14

If I had had the courage, I would have stood up like David before Goliath. My Philistines were the powers-that-be of the American Museum of Natural History here in New York City.

Life was good until three years or so ago when it was revealed that the Hayden Planetarium would be torn down, and more than that, Theodore Roosevelt Park was in danger. I live across the street from the museum, and the low-lying planetarium building and the green space in front of it meant sunshine for my second-story apartment, a rare commodity in New York. Though I hadn't been to the planetarium often (well, once), it was there for me just the same. And what would happen to the dog run on the eastern end of the park?

I watched sadly while they did their worst to the noble planetarium. Then they dug a hole, an enormous one—for a garage, I figured, which was okay by me, since parking in the neighborhood was terrible. I waited for the end of the dog run, and waited, and waited, but after two and a half years, it was still there.

I was unprepared for the next phase, it happened so rapidly. Huge curtains hid something momentous from view; the dog run was moved south, but retained; a fence went up around the park; and men scooped dirt and masons got to work. By New Year's Eve there was a sudden scurrying, the fence went down, and behold, The Rose Center for

Earth and Space had arrived! I was agog. A giant sphere enclosed in a glass box and lighted in a soft blue, it was the new planetarium, and it was sitting, almost flying, in my own front yard. I loved it.

I was embarrassed, humbled. Suppose I *had* played David, and somehow had stopped this beautiful addition to the city?

You know, Father, I am too quick to take sides. Help me with this.

—VAN VARNER

18/*SUN*   *"And if you greet only your brothers, what are you doing more than others? Do not even pagans do that?"*
—MATTHEW 5:47 (NIV)

Going to church together on Sunday morning is very important for our family. One particular Sunday when our son Reggie was home from college, I was scheduled to preach at a church in a nearby town. We had never been to this church before, and as we walked in, no one spoke to us or reached out to shake our hands and make us welcome. In the midst of this cold environment, we felt out of place and unwanted.

As I went to the vestry to get ready for the service, I encouraged Reggie and my wife Rosie to take the initiative in breaking the ice. We could judge this congregation of strangers and stereotype them as self-absorbed folks who didn't want to like us, or we could trust God, treat them like brothers and sisters, and see what happened.

Reggie and Rosie sat down in a pew and turned to greet the people sitting around them. To their surprise, they discovered that here was a group of Christians who loved Christ and had nothing against us, but just didn't know how to reach out to us. If we had been unwilling to take the first step, we would have been confirmed in our uncharitable opinion—and we would have missed the chance to get to know some wonderful people.

Lord, thank You for revealing to my heart that nothing should stop me from reaching out to people from all backgrounds and cultures.

—DOLPHUS WEARY

19/ MON

For we wrestle not against flesh and blood, but against principalities, against powers, against the rulers of the darkness of this world, against spiritual wickedness in high places.   —EPHESIANS 6:12

My husband Bill and I stood by the elegantly curtained ten-foot window, looking out through the white columns of the portico at the lights of cars passing on Pennsylvania Avenue. The air around us was charged with power. I shivered with excitement.

We had entered the White House on the lower level, passed the China Room and slowly climbed the marble stairs to the main floor. We wandered wide-eyed from the East Room through the Green, Blue and Red rooms to the State Dining Room. White-gloved servers handed us beverages. From candlelit tables spread along the walls, I sampled my first caviar and smoked salmon. The Air Force Strolling Strings played softly from room to room, complementing the Marine Band performing in the center hall.

Soon the President would come downstairs and, because he knew and loved my in-laws, we would have personal messages to take from him back to them in Ohio. For now, we had paused in a quiet place just to collect our thoughts on being where we were. I wondered if anyone ever got used to being in this supercharged atmosphere.

"Your first time?"

We turned to find a famous columnist grinning at us. We nodded.

"Well, this is my thirty-fourth one of these. And I *still* get goose bumps."

Ever since that first electrifying evening at 1600 Pennsylvania Avenue more than twenty-five years ago, I have prayed regularly for each of our presidents, regardless of party. I have sensed firsthand how great is the power that surrounds them, and how deeply they need our prayers.

How good it is on this Presidents Day to pray for those in authority. If only we remember every day!

Lord, may You always be the Power behind the throne for this nation. Please grant both knowledge and wisdom to our leaders, from the top down.   —ROBERTA ROGERS

20/_{TUE} *Surely goodness and mercy shall follow me all the days of my life: and I will dwell in the house of the Lord for ever.* —PSALM 23:6

Sitting front and center at old Uncle Hubert's funeral was my Aunt Ruth, a tiny woman flanked by her two elderly sons. All three sported a cloud of fluffy white hair.

The minister began the service. "The Lord is my shepherd, I shall not want—"

Aunt Ruth jumped in. "He maketh me to lie down in green pastures." Embarrassed, she lifted both hands to her mouth. Uncle Rodney, on her right, tucked a comforting arm about her slight shoulders to let her know the outburst didn't matter.

The preacher continued. "He leadeth me beside the still waters. He restoreth my soul."

"He leadeth me in the paths of righteousness—" Aunt Ruth blushed this time and bowed to hide her face. To her left, Uncle Bill reached for one of her hands. Affectionately, he patted her gnarled old fingers.

"—for his name's sake," continued the preacher. "Yea, though I walk—"

Aunt Ruth couldn't help herself. Every time the preacher started in, she interrupted. The words of the Twenty-third Psalm were so alive in her soul she couldn't keep still, no matter her embarrassment and my amused smile.

Suddenly, the minister looked up from his Bible with his own smile for Aunt Ruth, and he held out his hand in invitation. "Thou preparest a table before me in the presence of mine enemies: thou anointest my head with oil. . . ."

Aunt Ruth sat tall—though still very tiny—between her two sons. "My cup runneth over," she joyfully joined in. "Surely goodness and mercy shall follow me all the days of my life: and I will dwell in the house of the Lord for ever. And ever and ever and ever and ever and ever!" She clasped her hands and then opened them like the wings of a butterfly. "Forever!"

Thank You, Lord, for this invitation to dwell with You forever, and for Aunt Ruth's faith. May I, too, know this comfort when in need.
—BRENDA WILBEE

21 / WED *Watch thou in all things. . . .* —II TIMOTHY 4:5

When I was little, *watch* was one of my favorite words.

"Watch, Dad! See how far I can throw the ball!"

"Watch, Mom! I can run fast!"

"Watch, Keri! I can dive like a champ!"

I'll have to admit, though, that sometimes my desire to be watched took a less-than-happy turn. One winter I took a walk along a creek with my grandmother. The creek was frozen, a temptation that renders most twelve-year-old boys helpless. "Hey, Babe, watch me slide on the ice!" She didn't have enough time to stop me. *Crunch.* I was up to my knees in frigid water. Fortunately, we weren't far from home and she quickly got me under a hot shower.

Then there was the time I attempted to jump the garbage can with my bike. I came sailing down the driveway as my dad walked out the front door. "Watch me, Dad! I'm just like Evel Kneivel!" The homemade ramp I had constructed gave out, and my bike did at least two flips in the air. When I landed, I wasn't seriously injured, but I got the breath knocked out of me, was a bit skinned up and, worst of all, I was grounded.

As the years passed, I became aware that people were watching me without my having to ask them. As a financial consultant, I help clients pick stocks to invest in. Knowing they're going to watch their stocks closely makes me work extra hard to do a good job. My mentors in my company are also watching my performance, and it fires me up to know that they're keeping close tabs on me. At church, a lot of the younger kids watch my behavior with the elderly folks, and that helps me be extra considerate.

And then there's another Watcher, the most important of all, Who helps me keep my life in focus. God our Father has told us over and over that He's watching over us, and that's a great reason to try to become a better person every day.

Heavenly God, I know You're watching. Thank You. —BROCK KIDD

22 / THU *Remember the days of old, consider the years of many generations. . . .* —DEUTERONOMY 32:7

This year my wife Julia decided that it was time Elizabeth and John started learning something about American history. So she headed to the children's room at the library and came home with an arm-load of books about colonial America and the Revolution.

The book that got five-year-old Elizabeth's attention was *Phoebe and the General,* about the daughter of Samuel Fraunces, the African American owner of the Queen's Head Tavern, where General Washington and his officers met for food and conversation during the early days of the Revolution. In the story, thirteen-year-old Phoebe saves Washington from an assassination plot.

Elizabeth couldn't get enough of *Phoebe and the General.* The plot was exciting, the setting was our own New York, and the protagonist was a girl! So as a special treat, we decided one Saturday to take her to the Fraunces Tavern Museum to see where it had all taken place.

We looked at the recreated Long Room, where Washington said farewell to his officers after the war; we looked at a gallery with por-traits of Washington and Samuel Fraunces; we listened to a concert by a fife-and-drum corps in Revolutionary War uniforms—three-year-old John was enthralled—but we saw nothing in the museum about Phoebe Fraunces and the plot to kill Washington.

We were browsing through the small museum shop before going home when Julia came across a copy of *Phoebe and the General.* She took it over to the man behind the counter and asked him what he thought of the story.

"We get lots of questions about that," he said. "It's a fine book, and children love it, but it's more fiction than fact."

Oh, dear, I thought, *how will we explain that to Elizabeth?*

As it turned out, explaining it to Elizabeth wasn't hard at all. She understood the difference between things that really happened and things that were made up, and that some books have both kinds of things in them. And now she'd learned enough about Washington to know that the things that really happened to him were more fasci-nating than even the most skillfully crafted story.

Lord, thank You for George Washington, a man my children can look up to, even without the varnish. —ANDREW ATTAWAY

23/*FRI* *Behold, I will extend peace to her like a river. . . .*
—ISAIAH 66:12

"Mama, Ben asked me to marry him," my daughter Keri said. She stood before me, holding out her hand; a diamond sparkled from her third finger. Her words seemed to be coming to me from the end of a long tunnel.

"Oh, no," I said.

I've always had a fantasy of being the perfect mother. *"How lovely, Keri,"* that perfect mother would say. *"I'm so happy for you."* But this was real life, and I'm far from perfect, so I answered back, "When? Surely you're smart enough to wait a few years? You're still in graduate school. We have no money saved for a wedding. You're waiting until Ben finishes dental school, aren't you?"

The answer, of course, was "No."

Ben seemed shaken by my reaction, but Keri knows me, so she didn't miss a beat. "Actually, we were thinking this May. Since I was born on your birthday, we thought it would be cool to get married on your and Daddy's anniversary."

David's and my marriage had begun with too many debts and too little money. I wanted something different for my daughter. "Keri, you have no idea how much it hurts not to be able to buy the groceries you need, to stand in line at the store trembling at the total."

"Mama," she answered, "you and Daddy are happy. If being poor is part of what got you here, then I want to experience the same thing. I want a marriage like yours."

What could I say back? The truth? The truth is, I wouldn't sell a second of my life with David for any sum of money. I stood in the living room and looked at the young woman whom I call daughter. She seemed very wise, and I was awed by the mystery of being her mother.

Father, trusting those I love to You, I find incredible peace. Thank You.
— PAM KIDD

24 / SAT

God is not a man, that he should lie. . . .
— NUMBERS 23:19

One time my husband Keith and I were driving to Yosemite National Park in the late winter. We had reached the town of Fresno, California, when we encountered signs on the sides of the road that chains would be required before we could proceed. We didn't have chains, having driven up from Los Angeles, where snow is nonexistent. So we pulled into the parking lot of an old auto parts warehouse and went in to ask for chains for our VW Bug.

The man behind the counter wore a red plaid flannel shirt, overalls with frayed suspenders and a huge mustache that hadn't been trimmed recently. When he smiled, he was missing a front tooth. His hands were big and greasy, and he looked like he would be more at home tinkering with a tractor than greeting us.

We told him what we needed, and he turned to the computer terminal on the counter. "Let's see what this thing says," he said. He input his request and then stared at the monitor screen for a long time.

Then he looked up at us. "We just put this in a couple of weeks ago. It says we don't have any of those chains, but you know, I just don't believe it. You folks wait here."

He vanished into the cavernous depths of the warehouse and emerged in a minute with our chains in his hands. "I don't never fall for false prophets," he said with satisfaction.

In this age of high technology, dear God, keep me grateful for the human touch.
—RHODA BLECKER

25/SUN *The Lord is my shepherd. . . .* —PSALM 23:1

Years ago, when our daughters were very young, we'd drop them off at our church's children's chapel on Sundays before the eleven o'clock service. One Sunday, just as I was about to open the door to the small chapel, the minister came rushing up in full vestments. He said he had an emergency and asked if I'd speak to the children at their story time. He said the subject was the Twenty-third Psalm.

But just as I was about to get up from the back row and talk about the good shepherd, the minister burst into the room and signaled to me that he would be able to do the story time after all. He told the children about sheep, that they weren't very smart and needed lots of guidance, and that a shepherd's job was to stay close to the sheep, protect them from wild animals and keep them from wandering off and doing dumb things that would get them hurt or killed. He pointed to the little children in the room and said that they were the sheep and needed lots of guidance.

Then the minister put his hands out to the side, palms up in a dramatic gesture, and with raised eyebrows said to the children, "If you are the sheep, then who is your shepherd?" He was pretty obviously indicating himself.

A silence of a few seconds followed. Then a young visitor said, "Jesus. Jesus is the shepherd."

The young minister, obviously caught by surprise, said to the boy, "Well, then, who am I?"

The little boy frowned thoughtfully and then said with a shrug, "I guess you must be a sheep dog."

I remember the look on that young minister's face every time I get to thinking that I'm the shepherd in charge of some of God's sheep. There's only one Shepherd of the flock—and I'm not He.

Lord, help me always to follow You as You guide Your flock to green pastures. Amen. —KEITH MILLER

26/MON *I myself am satisfied about you, my brethren, that you yourselves are full of goodness, filled with all knowledge, and able to instruct one another.*
—ROMANS 15:14 (RSV)

Tom Harken is a self-made millionaire. But at age twenty, he couldn't read. As a child, Tom had spent a year in an iron lung with polio, followed by a year in quarantine with tuberculosis. He fell behind in school and never caught up; he dropped out in the seventh grade.

Miss Melba, Tom's wife, knew she could teach him to read. It was a struggle because Tom would get very angry, but she was not a person to give up. Because of Tom's shame, they kept his illiteracy a secret until he shared his story at a gala Washington, D.C., ceremony in 1992, where Tom was honored with the Horatio Alger Award.

Together, Tom and Melba have had a wonderful life and do a tremendous amount of good in helping people. The Harkens are especially interested in children and have had great success in promoting literacy and educational achievement. They're living proof of the truth of the phrase, "It can be done, and you can do it."

Many of us are satisfied with just living our lives for our own gratification. But life is filled with joy and excitement when we start doing kindnesses for others. Brilliant minds often emerge as young people are motivated to really achieve. And the radiant smile that comes to the face of a lonely person when a neighbor or friend comes to call is one of life's great blessings. Let's resolve this year to make time every day to do that extra thing that makes a difference in someone's life.

Lord, open my eyes to see the need I can minister to today.

—RUTH STAFFORD PEALE

27 / *TUE* *Jesus himself drew near, and went with them.*

—LUKE 24:15

Sister Janice handed me a white business card that read MINISTRY OF PRESENCE, followed by a telephone number. "Our desire is to be present with God's people in need," she said. "Please call if Sister Rosarita or I can help you or your clients."

"I will," I said automatically. Secretly I doubted that two nuns would be of much help. The community was full of people with real needs—for food, decent housing, legal aid and affordable medical care. Our church-sponsored service agency had trained staff to help meet those needs. Along with the Salvation Army, Emmaus House and Family Crisis Center, we took care of just about everything.

Or did we? Sister Janice discovered that several families were without shelter on sub-zero nights. She found temporary housing, then organized a Winter Cold Shelter program. Sister Rosarita conducted a comprehensive survey of the poor that led to better access to daycare. Did a family need transportation? Both sisters would drive, and also listen and pray.

During His earthly ministry, Jesus preached to the multitudes and fed thousands—the same work as our helping agencies. But He was also fully present for people with special needs, just like Sisters Janice and Rosarita. He wasn't too busy to heal a bleeding woman who touched the hem of his robe (Luke 8:43–48). He took time to bless little children (Luke 18:16). He noticed a poor widow putting two mites into the temple treasury and praised her generosity (Luke 21:1–4).

The ministry of presence, I realized, doesn't need to be done by an agency or trained staff. Jesus gives the privilege of presence to anyone with a caring heart, the willingness to listen and a genuine desire to help.

Lord, who needs my ministry of presence today? —PENNEY SCHWAB

28/ WED *They that dwell in the land of the shadow of death, upon them hath the light shined.* —ISAIAH 9:2

As I walked down the corridor of the second floor of the nursing home where my dad has lived for the past three years, I noticed the silence. Usually there were residents in wheelchairs along the way, and by this time I knew many of them by name. Then I realized that those who could get around were probably downstairs at an Ash Wednesday worship service conducted by several churches in our area. My dad always used to attend, but this year he wasn't well enough to spend much time out of bed. Poor guy—although he was in the advanced stages of Alzheimer's and sometimes didn't even know who I was, he did remember every word of the Lord's Prayer. Would he realize what day this was and wonder why he wasn't a part of it? What would he think when he saw the ashes on my forehead? I wasn't looking forward to the visit.

A man and a woman came out of his room. I didn't recognize them, but they stopped and smiled. "Are you Ray's daughter?" the woman asked. When I nodded, she told me they were ministers from one of the local churches, and while the regular service was going on downstairs, they were visiting residents who were confined to bed.

"Thank you!" I said. "This means a lot to both of us."

When I walked into Dad's room, he was sitting up in bed and smiling. He pointed to my forehead and said, "Hey, just like you!" And there on his own forehead was a smudgy cross. He was part of the worship service, after all, and he knew it.

In that moment I understood that God never excludes any of us from His love and concern. Even if we can't get to Him, He comes to us—wherever we are.

Dear Lord, when times of darkness lie ahead of us, let us remember that the light of Christ's love shines through them. Amen.

—PHYLLIS HOBE

DAILY GIFTS

1 _____

2 _____

3 _____

4 _____

5 _____

6 _____

7 _____

8 _____

9 _____

10 _____

11 _____

12 _____

13 _____

14 _____

15 _____

16 _____

17 _____

18 _____

19 _____

20 _____

21 _____

22 _____

23 _____

24 _____

25 _____

26 _____

27 _____

28 _____

March

I will seek that
which was lost, and
bring again that
which was driven
away, and will bind
up that which was
broken, and will
strengthen that
which was sick . . . .

—EZEKIEL 34:16

S	M	T	W	T	F	S
				1	2	3
4	5	6	7	8	9	10
11	12	13	14	15	16	17
18	19	20	21	22	23	24
25	26	27	28	29	30	31

WHEN GOD REACHES OUT . . . THROUGH OTHER PEOPLE

1/*THU*   *Jesus wept.*   —JOHN 11:35

God can reach out without a word.

I'd been in Switzerland, teaching a writing seminar for Christians from the former Communist bloc. It had been an exhilarating two weeks—so many moving stories waiting to be told now that these countries had relaxed their censorship.

To end our time together, the seminar's host Rudi Lack put on a traditional Swiss fondue party. We sat around a big table spearing chunks of bread with long-handled forks and thrusting them into a great communal pot of bubbling cheese. We'd grown close through the days of sharing. Now we were laughing, joking, very much in a festive mood.

Then I noticed that one fork lay on the crisp white cloth untouched. Across the table from me, young Gazmond Shtylla from Albania was staring down at his plate. This was Gazmond's first trip outside his country, the poorest in Europe. During the seminar he'd told us vivid tales of the food shortage there, how a little black bread moistened with water was often all a family had to eat.

Suddenly, I saw our merry party as a hungry person might—forks plunging again and again into the brimming pot, laughing mouths open to gobble dripping cheese. I glanced across the table again, just as a tear splashed onto Gazmond's empty plate. He swiped quickly at his cheek, tugged his lips into a smile and picked up his fork.

But I had seen.

Not Gazmond's tears, but the tears of Jesus. Jesus, Who loved parties, too. Jesus, Who surely rejoiced that Christians in Albania could now share the Good News with their countrymen.

But I'd also seen the Jesus Who cares today as He did two thousand years ago, for the needy, the homeless, the hungry. "This new freedom is good," that tear said to me. "But don't forget My poor."

When my own plate is heaped high, Lord, help me remember those whose plates are empty. —ELIZABETH SHERRILL

2/ *FRI* *If a man love me, he will keep my words: and my Father will love him. . . .* —JOHN 14:23

Words. I am surrounded by them. As an editor, I poke and scratch and rework them. As a writer, I try to make them sing. As an avid magazine and newspaper reader, I use them to gather information. But sometimes I think there are too many words in the world—or at least, in my world.

So for Lent this year, I'm reading only certain words in my Bible. The words of Jesus. They are conveniently printed in red—bright patches of scarlet among all the lines of black. When I leaf through the Gospels, I see that Jesus is, indeed, a man of few words. "Let your light so shine" (Matthew 5:16). "Love your enemies" (Matthew 5:44). "Come and follow me" (Matthew 19:21). "Make disciples of all nations" (Matthew 28:19, NIV). "I am the resurrection, and the life" (John 11:25).

I find comfort in His words. But I find challenge, too. There is an energy in their sparseness. It makes much of my world seem unduly wordy. It makes much of what I say seem unduly wordy. I begin to understand: More is not always better.

So during this holy season, I will immerse myself in the red words. They are my salvation.

Dear Jesus, let me find quiet time to meditate on the most important words ever spoken: Yours. —MARY LOU CARNEY

3/ *SAT* *The woman said to him, "Sir, give me this water, that I may not thirst. . . ."* —JOHN 4:15 (RSV)

I have a bad case of the "wants." I know the Psalmist says, "The Lord is my shepherd; I shall not want" (Psalm 23:1), but somehow that hasn't had the desired effect on me.

I want a house. I want a car. I want an amp for my piano. I want a bed frame. I want an entertainment center. The list goes on. And on.

Recently a friend from my church invited me to her apartment to help her write a song for our Sunday-night service. She lives on the nineteenth floor of a building that overlooks New York's Central Park. When I walked into her apartment, I was immediately confronted by one of the most spectacular views in New York City—in all the world, for that matter—beautiful Central Park West to the left, breathtaking Fifth Avenue to the right, and the grandest, most photographed, painted and written about park that ever was, smack-dab in between. It was dusk, and the early lights shimmered like fairy dust.

I just stood there for a while, taking it all in—*wanting* it. Our modest apartment way uptown, across the street from a dusty little park-and-playground, couldn't compare with this. "This is unbelievable!" I said. "You must stand here and look out this window for hours."

"Truth is," she said, "I rarely even notice it's there anymore."

Truth is, that's how it would be with me, too. If I had all the things I think would really bring me joy, they would just fade, unnoticed, into the background of my life. And I'd go on wanting the next thing, and the next, and the next.

But I really would like that bed frame.

Lord, help me learn to be content with what You've given me.

—DAVE FRANCO

4/ SUN   *And unto one he gave five talents, to another two, and to another one. . . .*   —MATTHEW 25:15

In 1944 I was a nineteen-year-old PFC living with thirty other GIs in a stable near Frome, England. One day the chaplain's assistant, PFC Lauck Crawford, a tall, soft-spoken Virginian who bunked with us, asked, "Can you help me on Sunday?"

"Sure," I said, wondering what I could possibly do for him.

On Sunday morning Lauck and I walked two hundred yards from our stable to a small, stone-walled, thatch-roofed church. Lauck pushed a huge iron key into the keyhole and unlocked the church's iron-hinged door.

Once we were inside, Lauck said, "Up there," and pointed to a hand-carved organ console with worn-down keys at the front of the church. Our combat boots clopping on the flagstone floor, we walked down the nave, which glowed with the light of stained-glass windows.

We squeezed between the ancient organ and the cold stone wall. Lauck pulled a hand bellows from a recess in the organ's back. "When I tap the organ twice," he said, "you pump this bellows. When I tap once, you stop." Then he stepped around to the front of the organ, leaving me and the bellows stuffed between the organ and the wall.

So this is what a one-talent person can do, I thought as I pumped the bellows and put air into the ancient organ. At the keyboard, Lauck accompanied the twenty or thirty soldiers who stood in the straight-backed wooden pews singing hymns. Hidden behind the huge organ, I wondered, as I listened to the music, if they were thinking as I was about the folks gathered at church back home.

It only took a little muscle-power to pump those bellows, but the singing would have been much poorer without them. Many years later, when I was asked to help out at another church and my first reaction was "I don't have the talent for that," I remembered that Sunday morning in England. And the Lord showed me I had two more talents: for pounding nails into wallboard and painting walls for our new Sunday-school rooms.

You've given me a talent, Lord. Help me to discover it and use it in Your service.
—RICHARD HAGERMAN

5/_{MON} *Commit your work to the Lord, then it will succeed.*
—PROVERBS 16:3 (TLB)

I was blinking the sleep out of my eyes and fumbling around the coffee maker when our son Ian came into the kitchen, much too early, and much too energetically for my sluggish 6:00 A.M. disposition. It was his first day on a new job.

"What do you think, Mom? Pretty neat, huh?" He grinned, and my heart skipped a beat in the sheer joy of being "Mom" to this fine young man. His hair was trimmed; his shoes shined mirror-bright; and his new suit was set off by a classy silk tie, a "just right" tie—and I should know, I bought it!

"Absolutely marvelous!" I replied.

Gulping a cup of coffee, Ian turned, as always, to his dad, his hard-nosed, tell-it-like-it-is dad, for assurance and affirmation. *Oh, please, dear Lord,* I prayed, *no critique, no well-meant advice from this man he looks up to and loves so much, not today. Please, Lord, something upbeat from his dad.* I breathed a sigh of relief as my husband put an arm around Ian's shoulder and gave him the words he needed to hear: "You'll ace it, son. You know your stuff."

"Well, here goes!" Ian hugged me just a little too tight, just a little too long. Then with a small, almost imperceptible quiver in his voice, he whispered, "Pray for me, Mom," and I knew he was afraid.

"You've got it, lad!" The Lord must have been smiling; I'd committed this opportunity of Ian's to Him and had been praying for it around the clock for months.

That evening Ian came home smiling ear to ear. "A few kinks to work out," he said, "but Dad's right. I think I'll ace it!"

Lord of the daily workplace, Lord of a job well done, I pray for all those starting a new job today. Settle their shaky hearts. Give them diligence, dependability and a determination to make a go of it.

—FAY ANGUS

6/ TUE
The prudent see danger and take refuge. . . .
—PROVERBS 27:12 (NIV)

Weary from a day of substitute-teaching a large group of rambunctious teenagers, I settled into my seat on the bus, praying, *God, I could use a boost.* Just then I overheard two teenage girls talking about how they used Kool-Aid to highlight their hair. Cherry, they agreed, gave the best red highlights, while blueberry. . . . I was intrigued. Kool-Aid was a lot cheaper than Clairol. Maybe this was the lift I'd prayed about—a new fashion twist.

As soon as I got home, I phoned Kool-Aid's information number. "This really sounds weird, but is it okay for me to use cherry Kool-Aid to color my hair?"

Apparently, this was not the first time the customer service rep had been asked this question. She began reading through a prepared statement that went something like: "We do not recommend using Kool-Aid for anything other than ingestion as a beverage."

I persisted. "Have you ever heard of anyone using it on her hair?"

There was a pause, and then she lowered her voice and said, "Frankly, we get a lot more callers asking how to get Kool-Aid *out* of their hair than about how to put it on."

I laughed—which turned out to be the lift I needed—and hung

up, deciding to stick with Clairol. But then I soberly considered the larger truth in her comment: how much easier it is to get into things than out of them. When I told my co-worker that I couldn't come to her bridal shower because I was "having out-of-town visitors that weekend," I had to invite people over so I wouldn't be a liar. And it was a lot easier for me to put those two pairs of high-heeled black pumps on my credit card than it was to work the seven hours at a substitute job to pay for them.

Over a tall glass of cherry Kool-Aid, I prayed:

God, let me look ahead a bit today and not "put the Kool-Aid in" before I think about how difficult it may be to "get the Kool-Aid out."

—LINDA NEUKRUG

7/ WED   *And God said, "I will be with you. . . ."*
                                     —EXODUS 3:12 (NIV)

I stood in the kitchen and shuddered as blasts of wind shook our house. It was nearly midnight and we were experiencing one of our fierce winter windstorms that sweep across the front range of the Rocky Mountains with gusts up to one hundred and forty miles per hour.

"What's the use of going to bed?" I asked my husband Lynn. "We won't be able to sleep." The words were barely out of my mouth when we heard an explosive crash, tinkling glass and then a huge whooshing sound as dirt and ashes from our fireplace suddenly filled the family room and kitchen. Our floor-to-ceiling corner window had blown in, spreading shattered glass everywhere.

"What shall we do?" I wailed in despair.

Lynn picked up the phone and did what most people do in the face of an emergency. He dialed 911. Unfortunately, the dispatchers were swamped with calls about wind-related emergencies and told us we'd have to "hold tight and wait until morning."

I looked at the awful mess and the gaping hole where dirt and dust continued to blow in and knew I couldn't "hold tight." Then I remembered Mike, the window repairman I'd called a few days earlier because we were concerned about the caulking around this very window. He hadn't come by to fix it yet, but I still had his business card, so I dialed the phone number on it.

To my amazement, Mike answered! So I poured out our tale of woe.

"I'll be right there," he said simply.

I hung up the phone in shock. "He said he'd be right here," I told Lynn.

About ten minutes later, Mike and his wife showed up with a huge piece of canvas, a long ladder, a super-suction vacuum cleaner and can-do smiles. As Mike pounded the canvas into place, his wife and Lynn and I cleaned up most of the dirt and pieces of glass.

"We hardly know how to thank you," we told them about two hours later as they prepared to leave.

"Hey, this is our job," Mike said with a grin.

As Lynn and I fell into bed that night, the wind still howling around the house, we thanked God for bringing comfort into our chaos through a window repairman.

Father, thank You for being "right there" in my moments of fear and helplessness.
                                                        —CAROL KUYKENDALL

8/THU   *Lord, who may dwell in your sanctuary? . . . He whose walk is blameless . . . who keeps his oath even when it hurts.*   —PSALM 15:1-2, 4 (NIV)

For several years while we lived in East Africa, a young man named Ndwati worked at our home. In his early twenties, Ndwati was a quick and willing learner, soft-spoken and eager to please. His endurance seemed a contrast to his slight build. But his heart was as big as the ocean, and his integrity and honesty were unmatched.

Ndwati came from a village six miles up the mountainside, which had no electricity or telephones and was accessible only by a deeply rutted red-dirt road. His recently acquired bicycle made the daily trip down the mountain easier, but it was still a long six miles back up.

We were living in Arusha, a market town at the foot of Mt. Meru in northern Tanzania. One Sunday morning as we emerged from church, someone looked up and noticed smoke coming from the top of the mountain. Was the long-dormant volcano suddenly erupting? In fact, it was a forest fire, and for the next week we watched from our backyard as hundreds of acres of high mountain forest went up in billows of smoke. By night we could clearly see the gigantic orange flames leaping into the black sky, devouring the precious timber and threatening the mountain villages.

That Monday morning, as always, Ndwati appeared at the door. We exchanged the usual greetings, and then with his meager English and my minimal Swahili he managed to tell me, "Our chief has asked that all the men of the village join together in fighting against the fires. I have come to ask your permission to leave my work for as many days as I am needed there." I was stunned. He had come all that way just to let me know why he would be absent from work.

The forest is slowly returning to that Tanzanian mountainside, and eventually most traces of the fire will be gone. But I hope the lesson I learned from Ndwati that day will last a lifetime.

Lord Jesus, help me to keep my word, even when it's inconvenient.
—MARY JANE CLARK

9/ *FRI*   *All these people were still living by faith when they died.*   —HEBREWS 11:13 (NIV)

Several years ago, I met a lady named Joan who was just returning from the funeral of her son. Early in her marriage she gave birth to two handicapped children. Her husband couldn't deal with the situation; he divorced her, and she was left alone with the children. After struggling heroically for several years, and after much prayer, she placed the more severely handicapped child in a facility that could better handle and care for him. She maintained close contact with the school and visited her son as often as she could. At age nineteen, he died.

"Why don't I feel sad?" Joan asked me.

Then she answered her own question. "Dolphus, I gave my children to the Lord years ago, and I did everything that I could do to care for them. I made the best decision that I could, and trusted the Lord for His will to be done."

Joan didn't know why God gave her two handicapped children. She wanted God to heal her son on this earth. When this didn't happen, she kept on living by faith that God would take care of him. And when he died, the eyes of faith showed her God's mercy at work.

There are times when, despite earnest prayer, God doesn't give me what I want. That's when, like Joan, I need to live by faith.

Lord, when You give me a cross, also give me a strong back, a praying spirit and a trusting heart.
—DOLPHUS WEARY

10/SAT *Ye all are partakers of my grace.* —PHILIPPIANS 1:7

I was cleaning out my son William's desk on a Saturday afternoon, while wondering how I would manage the next day's lesson with his Sunday school class. As I went through drawers of old party favors, homework assignments, worn-out pencils, forgotten cards, I asked myself, "How will I explain grace to these kids? It's a little like having your mom or dad clean up your room when you're not home," I grumbled on. "You should do it yourself, but they do it because they love you."

Well, what good is grace then? That was just the sort of question one of my charges would ask. What would I tell him?

Then I had a very clear vision, a memory from childhood: coming home from school with a heavy book bag and walking into my bedroom to see everything spotless because Mom had cleaned and reorganized my desk. I should have done it, but she did it, and I was all too grateful.

"When grace is given to you, you feel more inclined to extend it to others as best you can," I answered my own question.

Or to take William's words when he saw his room all clean, "You spoil me, Dad."

"I have been spoiled myself," I told him.

Lord, as I have been given, let me give. —RICK HAMLIN

11/SUN *Where two or three are gathered together in my name, there am I in the midst of them.* —MATTHEW 18:20

It was raining buckets when I walked through a side door into the Batesville United Methodist Church in Indiana. The rain was a fitting backdrop for the topic on which I was to speak: "Where do we go to draw spiritual water when our wells run dry?"

I had never been to Batesville before, and I didn't know a soul. I was nervous. When I looked through the double doors of the fellowship hall, I saw people everywhere, standing in groups, carrying food to long tables, looking at me. The minister appeared, a friendly man with crinkly eyes and a firm hand under my elbow. I was greeted, smiled at and nudged to the head of the line for a wonderful meal.

By the time I got up to speak, the homegrown friendliness had eased my nerves. I talked about digging deeper into our faith and God's promises and finding hidden streams of water, thunderous even, like the rain hitting the roof.

When I was finished, the minister had the congregation line up in front of a table; on the table were a pitcher of water and paper cups. He poured; I handed out the cups of water. The line inched by me. Hands touched, eyes met, and smiles were exchanged as each person took a cup of water and drank. When the pitcher was empty, someone refilled it. Two people stepped forward to pour and give water to the minister and me: an unbroken circle of pouring, giving, receiving.

This silent, shared fellowship said something my talk hadn't: that the Water of Life also comes to us from each other, not in gushes, but in small cups. In smiles, in touches, in kind words and deeds, in little rituals we do together in Christ's name.

Lord, on this day, help me to give others to You in all I say and do.
—SHARI SMYTH

12/MON
To have a glad heart makes a perpetual feast.
—PROVERBS 15:15 (NEB)

Okay, I'll admit it: I had made up my mind to be miserable even before I entered the store. I had been shopping in this Mom-and-Pop health-food store all the years we'd lived in Nashville, and now a chain had bought the place.

They're all alike, I thought as I parked my car. *Impersonal, the same merchandise wherever you go. I came for flowers and they've taken away the fresh flower bin. Well, I might as well pick up some curry and cinnamon while I'm here.*

"So the new owners have changed the prices from ounces to pounds," I said dolefully to the lady next to me. We were both measuring our spices from the big glass jars that sit on shelves in alphabetical order. "Just their sneaky way of disguising a price hike, I guess."

"Well, actually, no," the woman answered. "I figured it out. Most of the prices are the same, except the cinnamon." She glanced at the scoop of cinnamon I held in my hand. "It seems to be a few pennies cheaper."

Okay, so they haven't hiked the prices . . . yet, I thought. *Oh, great, they've added a food bar and tables. Must be big profit in that. Probably the same old tired lettuce and limp carrot sticks.* I parked my shopping cart and walked over.

Umm, artichoke hearts, tiny pickles, grilled tofu. Wow! African peanut soup? I've never even heard of that.

About two minutes later I was on the phone with my husband. "David, want to dash over to Sunshine and meet me for lunch? They have this really neat food bar and this exotic soup. And you remember that new kind of iced tea we saw on TV? Well, they have that, too. Fifteen minutes? I'll be waiting in the new book department."

Father, it's a lot more fun to be alive when I choose a positive attitude, so today I pray for an insatiable appetite for gladness.

—PAM KIDD

13/*TUE*   *And, behold, the Lord passed by, and a great and strong wind rent the mountains, and brake in pieces the rocks before the Lord; but the Lord was not in the wind: and after the wind an earthquake; but the Lord was not in the earthquake: and after the earthquake a fire; but the Lord was not in the fire: and after the fire a still small voice.*   —I KINGS 19:11–12

"Do you talk to God?" an atheist once asked a believer.

"Oh, yes, all the time," replied the Christian.

"And does He answer you?"

"Certainly."

"In an audible voice?" the doubter pressed.

"No, in a still small voice that I hear with my heart."

"How do you know it's Him and not someone else?"

"Years of listening," the believer answered. "Years of listening."

Recently, I heard about a woman who wasn't sure that God heard her prayers, so she asked the Lord to speak to her.

"What should I do with my life?" she asked.

"Visit the sick," God answered. "Help the poor, live in peace."

Startled to hear God reply so quickly and so directly, she muttered, "I . . . I was only testing."

"So was I," God returned.

Sometimes we pray so long about a problem that we fail to hear God's marching orders. Either that, or we are so intent on what we want that we don't hear what He wants. Spiritual listening requires stillness, faith and obedience. And real communication mandates pauses to let the other party get a word in edgewise.

Remind me, Lord, that my hearing clears
When I remember: one mouth, two ears.

—FRED BAUER

PRAYER FOR MARCH

We have so much,
and we need so little.
Forgive us our excesses, Lord,
and give us generous hearts
with which to share
our many blessings.

—FAY ANGUS

14/WED *But whoever has the world's goods, and beholds his brother in need and closes his heart against him, how does the love of God abide in him? Little children, let us not love with word or with tongue, but in deed and truth.* —I JOHN 3:17-18 (NAS)

I was caught red-handed this morning. I was feeding the birds, pouring seed into the ceramic containers that hang from tree limbs outside our kitchen window. Returning to the kitchen, I washed my hands in the sink and gazed out the window, smiling to see some small finches discover that their breakfast had been served. For a moment I basked in the knowledge of a good deed done. God was in His heaven and all was right with the world.

Suddenly, there was a blur of bright color as a red cardinal came whirring into view. Lighting on a bird feeder not five feet away from me, he thrust himself into the midst of the dull brown finches and started pecking at them. Drawing himself up to his full stature, he forced the finches to fly away. This cocky red baron now had the food to himself.

Indignant, I tapped on the window. "You rascal!" I hissed. "All of that food and you won't even share. You ought to be ashamed of yourself."

At that instant, God's Spirit tapped on the window of my awareness, and I got the message: That cardinal was really me, red hair and all. God has given me so many good things, and I need to share far more than birdseed.

Dear God, I know my selfishness breaks Your heart. Forgive me and transform my greed into love. Amen. —SCOTT WALKER

A WHOLE AND HOLY LOVE

15/THU *He revealeth the deep and secret things: he knoweth what is in the darkness, and the light dwelleth with him.* —DANIEL 2:22

My friends Louise and George invited me for dinner one night and included Kent, a recently divorced mutual friend. A very outgoing person with a sparkling sense of humor, Kent was very attractive and it wasn't long before we were friends. Other chances for dating arose, too. Then one day my best friend Mona and I had lunch together and I shared some of the problems that were showing up in these relationships. She asked a penetrating question: "Do you think you may be unconsciously choosing men who are similar to your former husband?"

That night I sat for a long time in prayer and self-examination, and I began to see that I'd been repeating some of the same patterns that had caused my marriage to fail. Clearly, I had work to do—on myself!

About the same time I was shopping for a dining room table. Louise asked me what furniture style I liked. The only answer I could come up with was, "I don't know!" It was another wake-up moment—in many ways I didn't really know who I was!

Over the following weeks and months, I started each morning with silent prayer, asking for self-knowledge and listening for guidance. After breakfast I spent time writing in my journal, asking such questions as: *What are my priorities? How do I really want to spend the rest of my life? What might I give back to life during my remaining years?* As the insights came and I tried to follow the guidance I received during prayer, my sense of independence grew. Gradually I began to feel more like a whole person.

Then one day I found the perfect dining room set for my house, a cottage-style oak-and-tile table with country-blue legs and matching Windsor chairs that just felt *right*. For me, it was a small symbol of larger inner changes occurring in my life. At last I felt I had a clearer sense of who I was. This new awareness opened me to a deeper trust in whatever life might bring.

Then, just after Christmas 1996, I got a surprise phone call. An old friend, Robert, would be passing through the next day and asked to stop for a short visit to get reacquainted.

Thank You, Holy One, for teaching me that to allow others into my life, I must first know myself. —MARILYN MORGAN KING

16/_{FRI} *However, I consider my life worth nothing to me, if only I may finish the race and complete the task the Lord Jesus has given me—the task of testifying to the gospel of God's grace.* —ACTS 20:24 (NIV)

This morning, I woke up with Craig Virgin on my mind. For the past few months, off and on, I've thought about Craig.

Most of my childhood was spent in East St. Louis, Illinois. In high school, I participated in every activity I could think of and attended school sports events from football to track and field. It was at a track meet in 1973 that I first saw Craig.

It was cold that day, but I didn't feel the chill as I stood on the sidelines cheering for one or another of our school's track stars. Then Craig blazed by. I don't remember much about his appearance except that he was pale and had brown hair.

What I do remember clearly, more than twenty-five years later, is the elegance with which he ran the long-distance race, not his runner's gait, but his style. At one point, he began to dominate the race. I fell silent—all I could do was watch him. With little effort he seemed to pull away from the rest of the pack, first a few steps, then yards. That was when I realized that all the other spectators, who had been loudly cheering for their schools, were now silently watching Craig.

I don't recall whether a whisper sent his name through the crowd, or whether it was the PA announcer. I do remember that we all started cheering for Craig Virgin to pull ahead of the other runners by one complete circuit of the track, to lap the pack. Even though he was yards and yards ahead of them, Craig was running full out right up to the end, when he passed the rest of the group and crossed the finish line.

That day, I knew he was going to the Olympics. He did, three times. This morning I prayed that he is still running full out.

Dear God, help me to do the things you have set before me. Give me strength and courage to run the race to win. —SHARON FOSTER

17 / SAT   *And the light shineth in darkness; and the darkness comprehended it not.* —JOHN 1:5

More than half a million visitors come annually to see the Book of Kells at Trinity College, Dublin, but my hotel's concierge assured me there would be no crowds this time of year. "Ah, 'tis a lovely thing to see, sir," he said, pointing me in the direction of Trinity.

The Book of Kells, dating from A.D. 800, is a copy of the four Gospels. It was painstakingly transcribed and illuminated—that is, illustrated—by the monks of St. Columba on the island of Iona before it was removed to Kells in County Meath to protect it from plundering Vikings.

My eyes took awhile adjusting to the dim lighting of the Old Library's East Pavilion where the manuscript is kept. Tourists were indeed in short supply, but there were several groups of Irish schoolchildren, and I kept bumping into them in the russet gloom. "It's so dark in here I can hardly see my own foot," I remarked to a studious-looking older gentleman bent over one of the display cases.

"Light can damage the paper," he remarked. "None at all would be best but then. . . ." His words trailed off as he gestured to the milling children. My eyes followed his back to the fragile but magnificent pages beneath the glass, bathed in soft light. The breathtaking beauty of the manuscript shone through as if it had light of its own.

The monks labored over their manuscript during what we call the Dark Ages. Their rich and ornate embellishments emblazoned the pages of Scripture, the words of Jesus that lighted the way through the chaos and darkness that followed the fall of the Roman Empire. All these centuries later we are protecting the Light of the World from—literally—the light of the world.

We may not consider ourselves as living in a dark age, but you never know. One Light burns a path of beauty and brightness when all seems dark. And it burns brightest when the world seems darkest.

Lord, Your Word is our light. —EDWARD GRINNAN

18 / SUN

Is not this the fast that I have chosen? . . . Is it not to deal thy bread to the hungry . . . ? —ISAIAH 58:6-7

The sermon had been going on for at least twenty minutes, and four-year-old Elizabeth was getting restless. But she was trying valiantly to be good. In recent months we've instituted a "Star Chart," and good behavior in church is one of the things that counts toward stars.

I handed her a brochure for an organization called Food for the Poor. The speaker was talking about the work they did in the Caribbean and Central America. "He's talking about people who are very poor," I whispered. "Some of them live in houses like this." I pointed to a picture of a makeshift shack.

Elizabeth studied it. "Mom," she whispered back, "the walls are made of cardboard boxes!"

I nodded. Elizabeth was silent for a while. Then she looked up at me with round eyes. "Mom, they would get wet when it rains!"

I quietly explained that there would be a special collection today for Food for the Poor. Elizabeth said, "We should give them some money!" Then she added, "I have money!"

She did. At the end of each week we count up all of her stars, and she earns a penny for each one. In a good week, she might get nearly fifty stars. So far she'd amassed $2.16.

"Would you like to give some of your star money to them?" I asked.

She nodded vigorously. "I think I should give them a dollar." The brochure indicated that a dollar would provide lunch for ninety-two children.

I looked at my daughter in wonder. *Half* of her hard-earned star money? I opened my mouth to say something, but Elizabeth was looking intently at the brochure again. She smiled and pointed to a picture of a little girl. "I think she is going to be happy to have some lunch!" And when the basket was passed, Elizabeth put in the dollar. She remembers it to this day—only because she is pleased that she was able to help.

Lord Jesus, help me to look at my worldly goods as tools for serving You.
                                                                —JULIA ATTAWAY

19/MON   *Break forth into singing, O mountains. . . .*
                                                —ISAIAH 49:13

I gloomily surveyed the thick white powder coating the back of my clothes dryer. At least the fire was out, and it hadn't been my fault. The air vent had been installed backward, trapping lint.

"Remember, don't use it until an appliance repairman takes a look," advised my friendly volunteer fireman. No, I certainly wasn't ready to risk another fire, but with three teenagers in the house, I sure would miss the convenience of a dryer.

Oh, well, at least it's spring, I thought as I ducked under branches to tie one end of a cotton clothesline to a Russian olive and the other to a willow in the backyard. After I had hauled the first load to the new line, I began the classic, rhythmic routine: Bend to the basket; stretch to the line; squeak the clothespin over damp cloth. Bend. Stretch. Squeak. The movement began to lull me.

A light breeze fluffed my hair and set the aspens quivering. Sunlight filtering through their leaves in a dozen shades of green cast dappled shadows along the edge of the swift-running creek near the end of the clothesline. The water lapped at branches trailing in the twinkling stream. As I pegged out each sock and towel, my contentment becoming deeper and deeper, I gazed up at a panoramic view of the Wind River Mountains, snow glistening on the ten-thousand-foot peaks. I took a deep breath of cool mountain air. When puffy clouds drifted overhead in a postcard blue sky, my daily tensions drifted away, too. *I have a better view from my clothesline than most tourists have from their resorts. Who needs a dryer?*

Even after the dryer was repaired, I found myself using the clothesline until snow began to fly. What had begun as an inconvenience had become a refreshing interlude—and a perfect setting for "fresh air prayer."

Father of all Creation, keep my eyes open to the marvelous works of Your hands. —GAIL THORELL SCHILLING

INTO AFRICA

Last year, Eric Fellman spent three weeks traveling through Africa. He wanted to learn about that vast continent and see if he could be useful in meeting its many problems. But something very different happened to Eric: He discovered what Africa could do for him. Join Eric today and from time to time over the coming months to find out how a continent and its people became an abiding presence in his heart. —THE EDITORS

20 / TUE *God is Love. Whoever lives in love lives in God, and God in him.* —I JOHN 4:16 (NIV)

In the Makapa Valley outside Nairobi, Kenya, thousands of homeless families live in a vast shantytown that begins to assault eyes, ears and noses from high atop the surrounding ridge. The ankle-deep mud, open sewers and hungry, hollow-eyed children overwhelmed me within minutes. Sensing my discomfort, my guide, an Ethiopian friend, said to me, "You see only the despair. Come and see the hope."

Down an alleyway and around a corner we came to an open courtyard about ten yards square, surrounded on all four sides by lean-tos. Two of them were for sleeping, one was for cooking and one was a classroom. Small children filled the courtyard. A dozen old women sat on benches along the outer edges.

"What do you see now?" my friend asked.

What struck me the most were the smiles and energy; only a few paces away we had been surrounded by despair and listlessness. "What makes the difference?" I asked.

"Love," he replied. "These children are the outcasts—orphans with no one to care for them. And these old women thought they had nothing to live for until they began to look after the children. The orphans had no hope until they were touched by such love. Look around you. The shacks here are no better than those elsewhere, the ground is no cleaner, the food no more plentiful. The only difference is God's love reaching out through human hands."

Lord, help me to use my hands to show Your love's power over every sort of evil and despair.
                                                    —ERIC FELLMAN

21 / WED

Blessed is a man who perseveres under trial . . . .
                                    —JAMES 1:12 (NAS)

The assignment was proving to be too much for me. Tossing still another attempt into the trash can, I stormed out of my home office and decided to go grocery shopping.

"That caller from Connecticut phoned again," my husband Gene told me when I got home. "Won't leave a number. Fourth time, too." As I set down the grocery bags, the phone rang and I picked it up.

"Is this Marion Bond West of Watkinsville, Georgia?" a small but resolute voice asked.

"Yes. Are you the caller from Connecticut?"

"I am. Did you write about a duck that died?"

"Yes."

"Is it true?"

"Yes."

Pause. "Every single word?" I now realized I was talking to a child. "Yes."

Big sigh. "Oh, I'm so glad! I loved your story. You see, I love ducks, too, and I had pet ducks—three. I raised them from babies. One day after school they didn't meet me at the bus and I found a pile of feathers . . . and sure enough, the neighbor's dog had killed them."

"Oh, I'm so sorry. How old are you?"

"Twelve."

"Won't your parents be upset by your calling down to Georgia so many times?"

"No. I'm paying for the calls myself. I wouldn't dream of letting my parents pay for my calls. I have money. I work in people's yards, plus I sell eggs."

And that's how a determined Jake Hendrickson from Woodstock, Connecticut, and I became friends. After our conversation about ducks, I marched right back to my typewriter and decided to give that impossible assignment one more try.

Thank You, Lord (and you, too, Jake), for teaching me not to give up. Amen. —MARION BOND WEST

22 / THU   *Speak to the earth, and it shall teach thee. . . .*
—JOB 12:8

In March 1938, when I was a college student in Virginia, Mr. Perkins, my math teacher, told the class about the Hoosac Tunnel. "You may feel math is unimportant. But the Hoosac Tunnel, between Greenfield and North Adams, Massachusetts, was built by digging simultaneously from opposite sides of Hoosac Mountain. The engineer's calculations were so accurate that when the tunnels met at midpoint, they were off only a little more than a half-inch."

Later I learned the tunnel had been proposed in 1819, but delays prevented its completion until 1875. The tunnel provided speedy and inexpensive transportation between Boston, western Massachusetts and upper New York State. From 1873 until 1916, it was the longest tunnel in North America.

That July I took my first train ride through the Hoosac Tunnel. I left Williamstown and passed through North Adams on my way to Boston. Then, without warning, I was plunged into pitch darkness! For 4.7501 miles I felt as if I were trapped in an elevator between floors. It was frightening. Finally, the train broke into daylight.

Over the years many significant events in my life were marked by trips through the Hoosac Tunnel. I went through the tunnel from Williamstown to Boston for induction into the U.S. Army in 1944. I returned through the tunnel after my discharge in 1946. I traveled through the tunnel to attend my brother's graduation from Williams College in January 1948 and my sister's wedding in June 1950.

On November 30, 1958, the last passenger train left Williamstown for Boston, ending eighty-three years of service through the Hoosac Tunnel. Freight trains still use it, however, and in 1997 work began to carve an extra fifteen inches of clearance into the tunnel's roof.

Sometimes my life resembles a long, dark tunnel. When illness strikes or I'm burdened with responsibilities, the darkness seems endless. But my trips through the Hoosac Tunnel remind me that there's always light ahead.

No matter how hopeless things may seem, Father, You are the light at the end of all the tunnels of my life. —OSCAR GREENE

23 / FRI   *But I trusted in thee, O Lord: I said, Thou art my God. My times are in thy hand. . . .* —PSALM 31:14–15

The contents of my overcoat pocket on my forty-first birthday:

1. Albuterol bronchodilator, Warrick Pharmaceuticals. For bronchitis. A gift from my children. How thoughtful.

2. Hasco one-year muffler warranty, plus the bill for installation and state inspection from Bob's Service ($209.02). I used to do this kind of work myself—mufflers, brake jobs. I'm getting lazy. Now I pay someone else to do it and complain about the price. At least I still change my own oil.

3. A phone number written on a scrap of paper (no name). Probably a student of mine. I hope he/she got whatever guidance was required. I'm too embarrassed to call and say, "This is Mark Collins. And you are . . . ?"

4. A map of the Pittsburgh Children's Museum. From our last visit. Faith, the eight-year-old, got lost on the third floor. "I thought you left me," she said when we found her. I remember saying the same thing to my parents once. How to explain the depth of feeling I have for this child? Does she know that her mother and I would gladly lay down our lives for her? Or does she only remember the consternation in our voices?

5. A *yarmulke* from the Schugar Funeral Home. From the service for Claryne, my friend Ralph's mom. I didn't feel out of place until they chanted the *Kaddish* around the grave. Then I felt alone. *I don't have the language to say good-bye,* I thought. Of

course, my ignorance of Hebrew isn't the problem. I've been attending more and more funerals as my friends' parents pass away one by one. There is no language for these good-byes.

Five weeks later, the *yarmulke* got recycled: I attended the *bris* of Ralph's new baby boy Caleb—one huge life tailgating another. It's hard not to think in clichés at times like these; I kept remembering Claryne's favorite song from *Fiddler on the Roof*, "Sunrise, Sunset."

Shalom, Clare. Next year in Jerusalem.

6. A coupon for thirty-five cents off instant soup cups. Don't like soup cups. Don't know why I have this. Think I'll throw it away.

Thank You for my birthday, Lord, and for all the years You've given me. I may be fraying around the edges, but I know that the threads, like the times, are in Your hands. —MARK COLLINS

24 / SAT *Charge them that are rich in this world, that they be not highminded, nor trust in uncertain riches, but in the living God, who giveth us richly all things to enjoy.* —I TIMOTHY 6:17

Just across the street from where I live in New York City lies Central Park. I go into the park about four times a day to walk my dog Shep, and I've come to know it in each of its seasons. We've wandered far afield to Belvedere Castle and to Strawberry Fields, to the Ramble, the Dairy, the Sheep Meadow, the Mall and more.

The one walk that is a constant with us is the one around Summit Rock. It's the highest point in the park, 137 feet. We go there early every morning, sometimes in darkness, when few, if any, people are there. Down below, I remove Shep's leash, and she runs while I huff and puff my way up. I sit on a bench, and eventually Shep comes along for me to refasten her leash. We move down and around, the squirrels scurrying out of our way, until we come to the memorable part of the walk, Our Tree.

It isn't much, considering the twenty-six thousand trees in the park, some grand and of great age. It's a simple spruce pine, conical, sitting all alone, with a three-foot fence surrounding it for protection. Of course it isn't ours—how could it be?—it's just that we have silently adopted it ever since it was planted several years ago. We were there at a distance when we saw people gather, and we watched as someone read from a Bible while the people stood reverently. When they had gone, Shep and I went up to the tree. There was no marker for it, nor has there ever been. Who the person was it memorializes doesn't matter; what better way to remember than with a living thing. We silently pay our respects every morning.

We have watched Our Tree grow and prosper. One day soon they will remove the wire fence and it will be on its own, just one more object in the cosmos called Central Park.

Another wondrous thing You have given me, Lord. Let me protect it.
　　　　　　　　　　　　　　　　　　　　　　　—VAN VARNER

25/<small>SUN</small>　*And he said, Abba, Father, all things are possible unto thee; take away this cup from me. . . .*
　　　　　　　　　　　　　　　　　　　　　　　—MARK 14:36

This prayer is a complete surprise to me. A Messiah, whose whole purpose is to die for our sins, is not supposed to pray, "Father, take away this cup." He is supposed to pray something like, "Help me to be brave," or "Make me think only of others." Instead, He wants a parachute to bail out of the Crucifixion.

Three times He begged to get out of the Crucifixion, and I, for one, am glad He did. It's comforting to know that I can tell God exactly how I feel. Too often I'm tempted to pray the sanitized, sweet-smelling, pretty prayer that you might hear in church.

Instead of praying, "Lord, I do *not* want to go to church this morning," I pray, "Bless the services and help me to do my part."

Instead of saying, "Lord, I'm really short of cash. Would it be all right to skip my tithe for a month?" I end up saying, "Bless my stewardship," whatever that means.

I need to learn to trust God with my real feelings. After all, He knows the truth anyhow. If I can learn to be honest with Him, then maybe it will give me the strength to pray, "Thy will be done," as Jesus went on to do.

Lord, You know my most secret thoughts. Help me to trust You enough to talk with You about them.
　　　　　　　　　　　　　　　　　　　　　—DANIEL SCHANTZ

26/<small>MON</small> *You will be enriched in every way for great generosity, which through us will produce thanksgiving to God.* —II CORINTHIANS 9:11 (RSV)

I'd like to take the thousands of you who have sent sweaters to the Guideposts Sweater Project on a journey. It begins when a package arrives in my office.

We receive as many as sixty packages a day, large and small, envelopes and heavy boxes. Some contain fifty sweaters, some just one. Within the confines of the basic patterns, crafters add knitted pictures of dogs or Christmas trees; the crocheters trim the straight edges of the sleeves with shell borders. The color combinations are endless. Many come with messages, prayers or letters. The stories of where and how people got involved are fascinating: clubs formed, chance meetings on airplanes, mothers and daughters, the bereaved and the commuters, all with their needles or their hooks, all answering the questions of the curious—and so the project spreads.

Back in the office, armed with razor blades, we use every spare minute to open the boxes and note the name and address of the senders so we can acknowledge their work. Then we fold and pack the sweaters into large cartons that hold about a hundred garments. Our offices are small, so as soon as five or six cartons are stacked up in the hall, we contact one of the agencies that distribute the sweaters. It might be the New York Foundling Hospital or World Vision or the Salvation Army. The sweaters may go to earthquake victims, starving refugees or victims of poverty.

Sometimes we receive photographs of the children wearing their sweaters, and it's hard not to shed a tear or immediately pick up one's knitting needles. Pictures of Nepalese, Romanian, Native American and inner-city children fill the scrapbook that we keep, along with photos of proud knitters with their finished garments.

Even after handling thousands of the simple T-shaped garments, I still see each stitch as a prayer—a warm, woolen prayer sent out across the world from a knitter in Palo Alto, California, to a child in Istanbul, Turkey, or from a crocheter in New Jersey to a toddler in Mississippi.

Thank You, Lord, for the warmth and generosity of the human spirit. —BRIGITTE WEEKS

EDITOR'S NOTE: For a free copy of the pattern, send a self-addressed stamped envelope to Guideposts Sweater Project, 16 E. 34th St., New York, NY 10016.

27/ TUE

The greatest of these is love.
—I CORINTHIANS 13:13(RSV)

All writers know, or should know, that there is power in simplicity. I was reminded of this the other day when I came across a passage in a book called *Views from the Publisher's Desk* by a Minnesota newspaperman named Elmer Andersen, who also served as governor of his state.

Mr. Andersen told of being at a dinner party where people were asked to guess the world's most popular song. Everyone tried, but no one came up with the correct answer: "Happy Birthday to You." As Mr. Andersen says, it is sung countless times every day. The tune was composed by a Kentucky school teacher named Mildred J. Hill; her younger sister Patty Smith Hill wrote the lyrics.

How amazing that such a simple handful of words and notes has touched and continues to touch so many lives! And the message is simple, too: *We love you and we wish you well, on this day that is so special to you.*

Every minute of every day, all around the world, somebody is sending that musical greeting to a relative or neighbor, colleague or friend.

Comforting thought, isn't it?

Lord, teach us not only to feel love, but to share it.

—ARTHUR GORDON

28/ WED

The earth which drinketh in the rain that cometh oft upon it . . . receiveth blessing from God.
—HEBREWS 6:7

Every time my car turns the corner from my street into the adjoining one, my eyes see the entire yard of the house there. I never noticed it much until last summer, when an ugly mound of weeds and dirt was dumped near the street. My first thought was that the man who lived there would probably use it for fill dirt around the yard. But that wasn't done.

Perhaps he needs some flowerbeds and will remove the weeds and use the dirt for that, I thought as the summer came along. No flowerbeds appeared.

As I watched winter frost cover the unsightly mass, I found myself quietly fuming about that offensive blot on our nice neighborhood. I was tempted to express my feelings to the owner, but decided to keep quiet.

And then it was spring, a beautiful warm morning. I turned the corner expecting to see the same pile of dirt. Instead, the entire mound sparkled with white blossoms, a beauty to behold! I couldn't resist stopping my car and getting out for a closer look. The blooms of wild strawberries bobbed on fragile stems, cushioned by a thick layer of the plant's dark leaves. My heart thrilled at the beauty that had transformed an eyesore, and my soul was filled with praise for God.

Lord, when I make a mess of my life, forgive me and transform me with the beauty of Your love. Amen. —DRUE DUKE

---

29 / THU

Bearing with one another in love. . . .
—EPHESIANS 4:2 (NIV)

Last week, while cleaning the house, I found a pair of my husband Leo's old shoes stashed away in a corner. "I'll just throw these out, okay?"

"Not yet. They might come in handy."

"But look at them!" I protested. "They're turned up at the toes, run down at the heels, there's a hole in the sole, and the laces are broken."

"So? I could still use them for gardening." He grinned sheepishly.

Mumbling and grumbling about useless old shoes taking up prime storage space, I stuffed them back into the cupboard.

The following Sunday, I held the church door open for Alice as she brought her husband to the worship service in a wheelchair. He was smartly dressed in a gray suit, white shirt and maroon tie, but it was his black shoes that caught my attention. They looked so shiny and new, with not even the hint of a crease across the vamps. *That's because he hasn't walked since his stroke ten years ago*, I thought.

The very next morning, I was about to complain about another pair of Leo's old work shoes littering the back entrance when I stopped short in my tracks. *Thank You, Lord, that he has been healthy enough to take thousands of steps in these wrinkled old shoes. He has worn them to carry in the groceries and carry out the garbage. By the look of the mud on them, he has even tilled the garden in them and dug my flower beds. Thank You for the man who wears these shoes.*

I surprised myself by what I said next. "Is it okay," I called to Leo, "if I park your gardening shoes right here on the welcome mat?"

Father God, help me appreciate my loved ones more and fret about their petty annoyances less.   —ALMA BARKMAN

30 / *FRI*   *"Judge not, that you be not judged."*
                                         —MATTHEW 7:1 (RSV)

Outside my dorm room, I have a four-by-eight-foot dry-erase marker board. Every passerby is welcome to embellish it with cartoons or quotes or messages. Doing my part to keep the decorations interesting, I sat cross-legged in the hall one night, marker in hand, writing a silly poem about our quantum mechanics textbook. I was trying to think of a rhyme for the author's name, Cohen-Tannoudji, when someone tapped me on the shoulder. I looked up and saw my friend Andrew.

He was quite a sight that night. His socks were pulled high, his shorts were just a little too short for his six-foot-three-inch frame, his jacket was the loudest red I had ever seen, and he had the strangest hat on his head. "Andrew, what *are* you wearing?" I asked, capping my marker. *At least I won't lose him in a crowd,* I thought.

Andrew looked confused; he had just opened his mouth to speak when our friend Cheryl rounded the corner. She looked at both of us and couldn't stifle her laughter. "Those are some interesting outfits, you two!"

Suddenly blushing red to match Andrew's jacket, I realized I was wearing the same thing he was: my Scout uniform. Engrossed in my poem, I had completely forgotten about our Scout meeting and hadn't even recognized the uniform. I had no more expected Andrew to show up in his knee-high, red and green Scout socks than I expected "Cohen-Tannoudji" to rhyme with "Physics."

My poem on hold for the moment, I wiped the marker board clean with my own red sleeve and stood up. A little embarrassed, I tried to explain to Andrew that his uniform really looked fine. Andrew rolled his eyes and grinned, saying, "Haven't changed gears yet? Still in recovering-from-physics-homework mode? That's okay. I've done it, too. Cheryl, on the other hand . . . well, sometimes there's no accounting for taste."

> *Help me, Father, not to judge;*
> *Next time, they might not laugh so much!*
> *Help me to think before I say*
> *Words that may darken someone's day.*
>
> —KJERSTIN EASTON

31 / *SAT*   *He that is not with me is against me. . . .*
                                                    —LUKE 11:23

Sitting in the bleachers at the Little League ball field on a chilly Saturday, I overheard two mothers talking about a teacher I knew and respected. They were complaining that the teacher wasn't doing right by their children. *The teacher's only trying to do what's best,* I thought. *This world would be a whole lot better place if people realized they were on the same side and pulled together for a change.*

Then a question came into my mind: *And you, Karen, what are you doing to support the Little League team today?*

Well, I'm here, I thought. Then I looked down at my hands. I hadn't been clapping; I was still wearing my gloves. *It's easy to get trapped in your own concerns without even knowing it,* the inner voice seemed to say. *Pulling together takes effort because first you have to pull away from yourself.*

I looked back out at the baseball diamond and decided perhaps it was time I stopped just occupying my spot on the bench and started occupying a place on the team. I began to call out something encouraging after each play. As I yelled, "Way to hang in there!" when our boys finally stopped a runner at third base after dropping the ball at first and second, even the mothers who had been raking the teacher over the coals smiled.

Lord, help me to do something today, no matter how small, to be part of my community.
                                                    —KAREN BARBER

DAILY GIFTS

1 _____

2 _____

3 _____

4 _____

5 _____

6 _____

7 _____

8 _____

9 _____

10 _____

11 _____

12 _____

13 _____

14 _____

15 _____

16 _____

17 _____

18 _____

19 _____

20 _____

21 _____

22 _____

23 _____

24 _____

25 _____

26 _____

27 _____

28 _____

29 _____

30 _____

31 _____

April

For it pleased the
Father that in him
should all fulness
dwell; And, having
made peace
through the blood
of his cross, by
him to reconcile
all things unto
himself . . . .

—COLOSSIANS
1:19–20

S	M	T	W	T	F	S
1	2	3	4	5	6	7
8	9	10	11	12	13	14
15	16	17	18	19	20	21
22	23	24	25	26	27	28
29	30					

WHEN GOD REACHES OUT . . . THROUGH OTHER PEOPLE

1/_{SUN}

He hath put a new song in my mouth. . . .
—PSALM 40:3

My work often takes me overseas. This time the writing seminar was in Singapore, and I was exhausted from the start. The flight had been endless, the thermometer stood at one hundred degrees, and I found my group's Singaporean English hard to follow. When Sunday came, I took a break by visiting a park where, I'd been told, people brought their caged birds for a weekly airing.

I heard the twittering songs as I stepped from the bus. There they were, hundreds of tiny birds in dainty cages hung from long horizontal poles. Singapore apartments are small, and birds are the pets of choice. Exclamation points of green, blue, yellow, they hopped excitedly from perch to perch.

And the cages! Each one was a work of art: bamboo, brass, teakwood, with hand-carved ivory swings and ladders, and exquisite porcelain water dishes. *That must be*, I thought, *why people bring their birds from every corner of the sprawling city to this one spot—to show off these miniature palaces.*

But there was a more important reason, an elderly bird owner explained. "We bring them together," he said, "to learn each other's songs."

Each other's songs. . . .

I'd come to Singapore to share my own song. Now, through this stranger, Jesus was reminding me to listen more closely to the songs of my students. *Every person has a melody of his or her own. When I bring you together, it's to learn new melodies for the universal chorus.*

What new song, Lord, will someone teach me today?

—ELIZABETH SHERRILL

EDITOR'S NOTE: How has God been reaching out to you this year? Take a few minutes to look back at what you've written in your "Daily Gifts" pages, and let us know some of the exciting things God has done. Send your letter to *Daily Guideposts* Reader's Room, Guideposts Books, 16 E. 34th St., New York, NY 10016. We'll share some of what you tell us in *Daily Guideposts, 2003*.

2/ MON
With weeping they shall come, and with consolations I will lead them back. —JEREMIAH 31:9 (RSV)

When Bonnie, my best friend of more than forty years, died in April of 1998, she left me her almost brand-new car. She'd teased me for years about my old car, a 1981 model with more than 150,000 miles on it. She also used to tease me about other things, one of which was how much I cried at the movies we saw together. "You cry at the end of every movie we've ever seen," she insisted.

"No, I don't," I said. "Only at the ones that are sad or touching or joyful."

"You cried at the end of *Seven Brides for Seven Brothers*," she accused me scornfully. That was an exaggeration.

But when we saw *Beaches* together—the story of a lifelong friendship between two women, one of whom dies at the end—I wept buckets, especially when Bette Midler sang "The Wind Beneath My Wings" while Barbara Hershey died.

Bonnie eyed me with a profound forbearance, as if to say, "Well, you're my friend, so I suppose I have to put up with this sort of thing."

After Bonnie died, the lawyer handling her estate told me I would need to fly up to Portland, Oregon, to pick up the car. I had a fairly smooth flight, a quick trip to the lawyer's office to sign papers and a cab ride to what had been Bonnie's condo, where the car waited. I took the keys, started the car and began the two-day, thousand-mile drive back to Los Angeles. As I headed for the interstate, I flicked on the radio. A song was ending. There was a short pause, without an announcer. Then the next song started. It was "Wind Beneath My Wings."

I knew that Bonnie was still teasing me, but I also knew that I would not be making the drive to Los Angeles alone. I thought that she probably expected me to cry, but I called her names instead.

Thank You, Lord, for the friends You give me throughout my life.
—RHODA BLECKER

3 / TUE
"He will turn the hearts of the fathers to their children. . . ." —MALACHI 4:6 (NIV)

We were driving to the Gulf Coast for a meeting one day when Rosie and I noticed that Ryan, our youngest son, in the backseat, was reading a copy of my book, *I Ain't Comin' Back*. He was very intent as he thumbed the pages, and I thought to myself how special it was to see my eleven-year-old reading my book.

Suddenly, Ryan leaned toward us and said, "Dad, why am I not in your book? I've been reading about my sister and my brother, but why was I left out?" I paused for a moment and said, "Ryan, most of the book was written before you were born, but I did mention your name in the dedication." He sat back in the seat and was quiet for about twenty miles. Then with a sad look on his face, he said, "Dad, you have to write another book."

Ryan was feeling left out. *Well,* I thought, *maybe it is time to write another book.* But then I realized that the book itself wasn't the problem. You see, Ryan is thirteen years younger than his sister and eleven years younger than his brother. It's almost as if we have two different families, and the book is about the family Ryan's not in.

Then I got to thinking that being left out of the book might not be the only reason Ryan was feeling this way. I travel a lot these days, speaking in churches and to civic groups, spreading the message of racial reconciliation. I'm not at home as much as I was when Ryan's brother and sister were his age, and he misses me. So whether I write another book or not, I've got some work to do. I've got to take a look at my life and make sure there's plenty of room for Ryan.

Lord, as You use me to reach out to others, help me to listen to the voice of my child. —DOLPHUS WEARY

4 / WED
God gives some the gift of a husband or wife, and others he gives the gift of being able to stay happily unmarried. —I CORINTHIANS 7:7 (TLB)

According to the *Statistical Abstract of the United States,* there are 195.5 million adults in this country. Of these, 116.6 million are married, and 78.9 million have either never married or are divorced or widowed; therefore 40.4 percent of all adults in this country are single.

My current period of singleness began in 1985. At first, I spent my single life waiting for the man of my dreams. But after a dozen or so years I decided the single life is a wonderful way to live. Instead of waiting for Mr. Right to come along, my other single friends showed me how to live my life with as much joy, gusto and fulfillment as married couples by concentrating on being a great friend to all sorts of people.

Since we have Mother's Day in May and Father's Day in June and Grandparents Day in September, perhaps we could have Singles Day in April. If I were in charge of Singles Day, I'd make greeting cards proclaiming the reasons why it's great to be single. Things like:

- You can sleep in the middle of the bed if you want.
- Toothpaste is always rolled up the way you like.
- The car seat is always in the right position.
- You can cook what you want when you want, including having popcorn for lunch or eating your dessert first.
- You can tear whatever you want out of the newspaper, even if you're the first person to read it.
- Your friends can drop into your home anytime without an invitation and nobody's going to get upset.
- No one is going to throw a fit if you put a little dent in the car.
- You can eat cookies in bed and listen to the radio at 3:00 A.M. without bothering anybody.

So to all you other single folks out there, happy Singles Day!

Heavenly Father, be with my single friends and me as we live our single-file life in a two-by-two world. —PATRICIA LORENZ

5/THU *Whosoever shall do the will of my Father which is in heaven, the same is my brother, and sister, and mother.* —MATTHEW 12:50

I walked into my mother's room at Claussen Manor, where she was an Alzheimer's patient, to find her bed surrounded by people I thought were strangers. The night before, my sister had called me from Michigan. "You'd better come," she said, and I didn't have to ask why.

Mom looked unimaginably frail and parched. A woman with blond hair held Mom's hand in both of hers while an aide dribbled sugar water from a dropper through Mom's lips, making rivulets of the deeper wrinkles on her chin. I noticed Mom's buddy Pat standing guard at the end of the bed. I now recognized the blond woman, Colleen Burke, whom I'd met once not long after she'd taken charge of the unit. "Hey, green eyes," she said softly to Mom, "look who's here." My mother turned her head weakly and gave me that goofy Alzheimer's grin that had taken so much getting used to. The movement caused more sugar water to run down her chin as she made a sound that substituted for "Hi."

The hospice nurse and a social worker slipped in, and Mom's eyes brightened even as she tried to fend off the hovering dropper. "Hi, Estelle," whispered the nurse. Mom waved as if she were in a parade.

For an instant, I felt like an intruder. My mom had always been so profoundly devoted to her family. Yet here she was, surrounded mostly by young strangers. Dying.

I made myself go forward. Colleen transferred Mom's hand to mine. Her grip was surprisingly strong, and she was pulling me closer even as she closed her eyes. I knew then that I was exactly where I was supposed to be, surrounded by my mother's new family, the people who cared for her on a daily, hourly basis. They were not strangers but helpers, and in the coming days I was to learn how much they cared.

God, I thank You not only for the help You send but the people who bring it.
—EDWARD GRINNAN

6/*FRI*   *Seek the Lord and his strength. . . .*
—I CHRONICLES 16:11

Even before it sailed into theaters as a multimillion-dollar blockbuster, I had an avid interest in the *Titanic*. I've read dozens of accounts that attempt to solve the riddle of the great ship's sinking. Of course, it struck an iceberg while traveling at a high rate of speed. But questions have arisen regarding the construction of the vessel and the role that construction may have played in its destruction.

So I was particularly intrigued with a recent headline in a Chicago paper: "TWO WEAK RIVETS MAY HELP EXPLAIN 1912 SINKING OF THE *TITANIC*." According to the story, experts believe they have evidence suggesting the *Titanic* may have been done in by two wrought-iron rivets from the hull. The rivets were riddled with unusually high concentrations of slag and, consequently, were very brittle. One theory is that they popped and allowed the plates to separate, letting water in.

I'll remember that the next time I'm tempted to neglect my own "spiritual rivets"—the unseen things like early-morning prayer, solitary walks dedicated to praise, time spent memorizing Scripture. After all, life—like ships—needs to be held together with strong supports.

Support me, God, as I sail the seas of life. Hold me together in the midst of storms. Bring me safely into heaven's harbor.

—MARY LOU CARNEY

TO WALK IN JERUSALEM

How many times have you read the story of Holy Week and Easter, or heard them preached about, or seen them depicted in paintings or on the screen? If you're like most of us, you've known about the Palm Sunday procession, the agony in the garden, the way of the Cross and the empty tomb for as long as you can remember. But where do those old familiar stories fit into your life? How have they been part of your own story? This Holy Week, Kenneth Chafin shares some of the moments in his life that turned the events of the distant past into today's good news. Join Kenneth and find out how city sidewalks and country roads, like the stone-paved streets of Jerusalem, can lead us to Jesus, wherever we are. —THE EDITORS

7/SAT

SATURDAY BEFORE PALM SUNDAY
"Everything that is written by the prophets about the Son of Man will be fulfilled." —LUKE 18:31 (NIV)

For years Holy Week has been my favorite time in the Christian calendar, but this year I come with higher expectations. I want to find in the stories and events of that week insights that will give new meaning and hope in my life in this new millennium. I found a clue to the way I can do that in the most unlikely of places.

Friends invited my wife Barbara and me to a performance of *Tina and Tony's Wedding*, which was playing in a community theater building that had once housed a church. "They serve dinner, and they say it's really funny," our friends reported, so we went thinking it would be standard dinner-theater fare—a nice meal followed by a play. But when we arrived, we were ushered into the former sanctuary with the option of sitting either on the bride's side or the groom's. When the bridal couple and their party walked down the aisle at the end of the ceremony, the minister announced that we were all invited to attend the reception in the church's fellowship hall. We shook hands with the bride and groom as we exited and were ushered to assigned tables. After the normal delay for pictures, the whole bridal party entered and began moving among the tables thanking us for coming. I was a bit uncomfortable at first, but soon realized that those who were allowing themselves to become participants were *experiencing* the play and not just watching it.

That's what I want to do during this Holy Week—not just look at the events of this most significant of weeks, but experience them in my own life, as if they were happening for the very first time.

Lord, let me walk with You through the week that continues to transform my life.
                                                              —KENNETH CHAFIN

8/ sun   *PALM SUNDAY*
            When Jesus entered Jerusalem, the whole city was stirred. . . .   —MATTHEW 21:10 (NIV)

All the emotions that will characterize Holy Week are packed into the events of Palm Sunday. At the center of it all is a Man on a donkey. Those who believe He is Messiah remember that past kings had ridden to their formal anointing on such an animal. On fire with hope, they begin to celebrate—singing messianic songs and laying palm branches and their garments in the road. At the edge of the scene are Jesus' critics, demanding that He hush the crowd, even as they lay traps with their questions and plan His destruction. And lining the roadsides are the Passover crowds, wild with curiosity.

More than thirty years ago I spoke to a New Year's Eve crowd of several thousand students who had gathered in the center of Atlanta to say good-bye to the sixties and to welcome a new decade. As the New Year's Eve revelers spilled into the streets from their parties singing "Auld Lang Syne," the students came from the city auditorium singing their theme song, "Here is my life! I want to live it! Here is my life. I want to give it!" I was moved by the contrast between the two crowds. Standing there in the street, I felt a new sense of hope for the future and a call to a deeper commitment of my life.

Like Jesus' disciples that first Palm Sunday, we were on fire with hope. And although, like the disciples, none of us could have anticipated what the future would bring, the hope that we celebrated made a difference that night and in all the days that followed.

Lord, as I face an unknown future, help me to celebrate Your love and power in my life.
—KENNETH CHAFIN

9/MON

MONDAY IN HOLY WEEK
Jesus entered the temple area and began driving out those who were buying and selling there. . . .
—MARK 11:15 (NIV)

After Jesus entered Jerusalem on Sunday and the people went wild with anticipation, it might have seemed natural for Him to have encouraged them with words of assurance. Instead, He went the next day to the place most sacred to them and began driving out the people who bought and sold there. His action frightened the religious authorities. It was a symbol of the much larger conflict between Jesus and the establishment about the essential character of God. These were differences Jesus thought were worth upsetting people about—and they led to the Cross.

When Barbara and I were first married, it took me awhile to get used to the healthy but animated discussions her parents would have. They would debate almost anything, from the political topics of the day to where we would eat lunch when we drove through Perry, Georgia, on the way to Atlanta. I had grown up in a family where conflict and confrontation were avoided at all costs. When we children sensed that our parents felt differently about something, things got real quiet and we said nothing. Unfortunately, the churches I grew up in reinforced the idea that if something upsets people, it must not be Christian.

But when the church was dealing with issues such as the giftedness and worth of women or the openness of the church to all races, I decided that I had to take a stand, however it upset some people. And when I overheard people insisting that anything so upsetting couldn't be Christian, I remembered our Lord's actions on that Monday of Holy Week and the response He got.

Confrontation is still difficult for me, but if I am to love as my Lord did and live with integrity, I should expect some conflict in my life and be prepared to face it calmly and courageously.

Lord, give me discernment as I look at life's issues and courage to follow Your example.
—KENNETH CHAFIN

10/TUE

TUESDAY IN HOLY WEEK
"She did what she could. . . .wherever the gospel is preached throughout the world, what she has done will also be told, in memory of her."
—MARK 14:8-9 (NIV)

During my first semester in college I preached on Saturday night and Sunday morning at Galey schoolhouse in a rural community about fifty miles from school. I'd catch a ride with someone and wait until church time at the store across from the school. People from the congregation would take me home for the night, providing me with supper and breakfast and a place to sleep.

One Saturday night I was warned that my hosts were very poor and had a small house. When we got there, they lit a lamp and sat me down at the table to my late supper—cold fried chicken, homemade bread, cole slaw, deviled eggs and wonderful apple pie. When I finished eating, they asked me if I would read to them from their family Bible and pray for them. I slept like a log on a feather mattress under a hand-stitched quilt, and awoke to the smell of rich coffee and a bountiful country breakfast. I learned later that they'd given me their own bed and that they'd fasted to provide my two meals.

The story of the woman who poured the costly oil over Jesus' head always reminds me of that couple who anointed my beginnings with their extravagant gift of love. The container of oil was the only thing of value she owned, and she must have been stung by the response her gift provoked in those who witnessed it. But Jesus stopped the criticism, accepted her gift and promised her that what she had done would be remembered—a promise kept today and whenever the story of that first Holy Week is read.

Lord, help me remember the gifts of love that have enriched my life, and help me to give generously to others. —KENNETH CHAFIN

11 / WED

WEDNESDAY IN HOLY WEEK
When he rose from prayer and went back to the disciples, he found them asleep, exhausted from sorrow.
—LUKE 22:45 (NIV)

When I came to, I was in a hospital bed surrounded by stands holding plastic bags of liquids connected to my arms with tiny tubes. When I was able to focus my eyes, I saw my wife Barbara. She touched my shoulder and said, "You're in intensive care, and you're all right. I'll tell you about it later, but right now you need to rest." Later she told me that when the cardiologist was placing the catheter in the large artery in my groin to open a blocked artery at the back of my heart, the artery was punctured and there was internal bleeding. I'd lost half my blood and had been rushed to emergency surgery.

To this day I don't remember a thing about it. My memory loss bothered me so much that I asked my doctor if he could explain it. "It could have been the anesthesia used in surgery," he said. "But with all the things happening so fast in the cath lab, it was probably your system's way of dealing with the overload."

I think that's what happened to the disciples in the Garden of Gethsemane. They had heard friends try to warn Jesus not to go to Jerusalem, had felt the rising animosity of the authorities in their questions and accusations, and had just been told in the upper room that one of them would betray Jesus and that after His death they would be scattered. It was more than their minds could fathom or their emotions could handle. Sleep was their escape.

As I picture the disciples sleeping in the garden, with Jesus praying a short distance away, I know that even in those times in my life when I am overwhelmed by the things that are happening to me, the Lord understands and is with me.

Lord, thank You for being with me in difficult times, even when I'm not aware of Your presence. —KENNETH CHAFIN

12/THU

MAUNDY THURSDAY
Immediately the rooster crowed. . . . Peter remembered the word Jesus had spoken to him. . . . And he broke down and wept. —MARK 14:72 (NIV)

It bothers me when I catch myself remembering the mistakes people have made. I plan and preside over a pastors' conference for Georgetown College in Kentucky, and each year, in the closing session, I have asked for an evaluation of the meeting and for suggestions for future speakers. One year as I read through the suggestions, I was confronted with the name of someone I knew I wouldn't ask to speak. I'd heard him years before, and at the time he had seemed so angry that I didn't think he could make a constructive contribution to the program. But the fact that several people had suggested him made me uncomfortable with my decision.

I thought of that experience when I came to the Gospel passages that tell of Peter's denial of Christ. It's the experience in Peter's life that many people remember more than any other. In his shame, he might have opted for Judas's way out, but instead he went fishing, and the risen Lord came to the seashore. He gave Peter a chance to confess his love for Jesus for each time he had denied Him, then called him to the work that consumed the rest of his life.

I needed Peter's reminder of God's love and grace because I'm often too quick to judge the failure of others, and because in spite of all my good intentions, I fail Him, too—over and over. So I decided to call some people about that speaker for the pastors' conference. Those who knew him best assured me that he would be a good choice. He accepted my invitation, and as I watched the skillful and loving way he spoke to those young pastors, I was glad that I hadn't continued to remember him only by his mistakes.

Lord, thank You for not giving up on me when I fail You or when I disappoint others. —KENNETH CHAFIN

13/FRI

GOOD FRIDAY
"He saved others," they said, "but he can't save himself!" —MARK 15:31 (NIV)

None of my earliest memories of Holy Week are religious. They're of watching my mother sew a new dress for my sister or color boiled eggs with bluing or food coloring. One year I stood on a piece of paper, and she traced the outline of my foot and had our neighbor bring me new shoes from town. They were too tight, but I didn't mention it for fear she would send them back.

When I was nine, my folks moved from the farm to an industrial community in northern Illinois, and my grandmother enrolled me in a Sunday school class at a nearby church. A very caring woman taught it. That first spring she guided my study of the story of the Crucifixion. I remember thinking, *If Jesus had only come today, I'm sure that I wouldn't have treated Him that way.* I think my child's heart was completely sincere, but I've come to doubt that Jesus would have been treated any differently in our—or any—time.

If someone came to us preaching a God Who is defined by compassion, spent time with people we look down on, encouraged people not to keep all the rules religion has developed and demanded that we radically remake our lives, our sins would cry out to silence that one. The Cross was inevitable.

It hurts me to admit it, but it's true: There is a little bit of each of the people of that first Holy Week in me. So when I hear again the words of the spiritual, "Were you there when they crucified my Lord?" I know that the answer is "Yes, I was there. In God's love and in my sin. And that fact makes all the difference in my life."

Thank You, God, for Your love and grace, which continue to be poured out for me, a sinner. —KENNETH CHAFIN

14/SAT

HOLY SATURDAY
When all the people who had gathered to witness this sight saw what took place, they beat their breasts and went away. —LUKE 23:48 (NIV)

My father had died less than an hour before, and my brother, two sisters and I were leaving the room where we had kept a vigil for ten days. A heart attack had starved Dad's brain of oxygen, and he never regained consciousness. We had spent those days remembering him. We retold his favorite stories, remembered things we had enjoyed doing with him and talked about his quaint phrases that were part of our vocabulary. Now he was gone, and we walked out of the hospital with that feeling of cosmic loneliness that losing a parent can bring. We felt numb and empty, with a tiredness sleep would not cure.

Outside the sun was shining, beds of brightly colored flowers were everywhere, people were coming and going as though nothing had happened, and the laughter of children playing on the lawn filled the air. The ordinary signs of life seemed out of place to me.

That's how the disciples must have felt on the day after Christ had been crucified. They were filled with fear and disillusionment. They had stood helplessly by and watched it all. The One on Whom they had pinned their hopes was dead. Many went into hiding, not knowing who might be arrested next. They were too traumatized by all that had happened to think, much less make plans. With a sense of unreality, they stared at people going about the routines of their lives and wondered if life could ever be routine for them again.

Since that day when I said good-bye to my father, I've had other Holy Saturdays in my life, days when I lived in yesterday's pain and with no real hope for tomorrow. It's only later, on the other side of Easter, that I've known that even in those terrible times when I couldn't feel His presence, God was still at work in my life.

Lord, thank You for never abandoning me, no matter what happens.
—KENNETH CHAFIN

15/SUN

EASTER SUNDAY
"Why do you look for the living among the dead?"
—LUKE 24:5 (NIV)

It was my first Easter in my first pastorate—Los Lunas Baptist Church, a congregation with a one-room adobe building located south of Albuquerque, New Mexico. I was a second-semester student at the University of New Mexico and lived with my Aunt Parthy on Rio Grande Boulevard. She had come West to find relief from acute bronchial problems and spent most of her time propped up on pillows in the front bedroom. Over the weeks I'd developed a Sunday-morning ritual: I'd stand a minute at the foot of her bed for her inspection. Then, as I turned to leave, she would say, "I'll be praying for you."

But on this day she said, "It's Easter Sunday. What are you going to say?"

While eating my breakfast, I had recalled one of the members saying, "Easter and Christmas are the only times we'll need extra chairs all year." So I quipped, "I think I'll say, 'See you on Christmas.'"

A pained look came to her face, her eyes filled with tears, and she blurted out, "Kenneth, I'm ashamed of you!" I've spent fifty years discovering all that was in her tears.

Aunt Parthy dried her eyes and, recovering her composure, said with great feeling, "This is the Sunday when you can stand and say to all those people that Christ is risen and that God brings life that death will not destroy."

Though I was crushed by her words, I knew that my aunt was right. As I drove to my little church, I rewrote my message in my mind and arrived with a different sermon than I'd started out with. It was a simple testimony to the fact that in Christ we can all experience life that transcends even physical death.

That first Easter morning Mary Magdelene and the other women brought the news of the risen Christ to the disbelieving disciples. This Easter I look forward to joining them in bearing witness to the Resurrection.

On this day of days, God, let me celebrate the hope that is born through the living Christ.
                                                        —KENNETH CHAFIN

16/MON   *EASTER MONDAY*
"Were not our hearts burning within us while he talked with us on the road and opened the Scriptures to us?"
                                                        —LUKE 24:32 (NIV)

The minister of music had opened the service with a choir and orchestra rendition of the spiritual "The Angels Rolled the Stone Away," and everyone had joined in on the hallelujahs. After the invocation the congregation sang the stirring hymn "Christ the Lord Is Risen Today." The sanctuary was filled with a sense of the presence of the living Christ.

But during a quiet interlude following the offering, I looked into the faces of the people gathered for worship and realized that a number of them weren't getting into the spirit of the service. They were preoccupied with some very heavy loads they were carrying. As their pastor, I knew what most of those loads were, and my heart ached for them.

I have the same feeling each time I read Luke's account of the two disciples from the village of Emmaus who were trudging home after

Jesus' death with "their faces downcast." Though they had heard of the women's report, they had the same response as the apostles—it all seemed nonsense. As they walked and talked, Jesus joined them and asked what they were discussing. They were so involved in their own grief that they didn't recognize Him. They thought He didn't know what had happened, so they opened their hearts to Him. When they arrived at their village, they asked Him to share a meal with them, and that experience changed their lives.

To know the true joy of Easter, I must meet the living Christ in places other than church and on days other than Sunday. I may feel His presence in a thoughtful note when I'm blue or in the counsel of a wise friend when I need help in making a hard decision. But Easter won't really come for me until I know that every day, in all my comings and goings, the Christ of Easter is present in my life.

Lord, help me to be able to celebrate Easter's victory in all of my life.
—KENNETH CHAFIN

PRAYER FOR APRIL

"Take your burden to the Cross
and leave it there."
Glorious advice, and simple;
But how do I comply?
It seems harder to lay the burden down,
Than to limp away,
Still bearing it on my back.
Show me how, dear Lord,
To lay my burden down.
Without Your help,
I cannot do even that much.

—ELLEN GUNDERSON TRAYLOR

17 / TUE   *And Sarah said, God hath made me to laugh, so that all that hear will laugh with me.*   —GENESIS 21:6

"A special cake for a special day," I reminded grandsons Ryan, 9, David, 6, and Mark, 3, as we carefully poured cake batter into the lamb mold on Holy Saturday night. "After it's baked and cooled, you can decorate it." The cake, symbolizing Jesus the Lamb of God, was an Easter tradition. Sharing it as a family always brought us a solemn and special awareness of Christ's sacrificial love.

Perhaps I shouldn't have let small boys decorate unsupervised. The finished cake was Pepto-Bismol pink, except where the blue-gumdrop eyes had combined with the frosting to create purple blotches. The lamb's head wobbled precariously. And someone had put black jelly beans in the coconut "grass" to symbolize ... well, you get the picture.

There wasn't time to make another dessert. I touched up the eyes, secured the head with a dozen toothpicks and picked out the jelly beans. After Easter dinner, I carried the cake to the table, repeating the words from John 1:29 (RSV): "Behold, the Lamb of God, who takes away the sins of the world." But when I set down the cake, the lamb's head toppled off, spraying us with coconut before it came to rest upside down on the tablecloth. The kids burst into peals of laughter; so did their parents.

The moment was ruined. Or was it? As I cleaned up the mess and passed around slices of cake, I remembered that while Jesus was indeed the Lamb of God, He was also part of the everyday world. He helped with refreshments at the wedding in Cana, got Zaccheus out of a tree, and ate and drank with common people. He not only blessed little children, but used them as an example of the kingdom of heaven—a kingdom that surely includes laughter.

Lord Jesus, thank You for showing the heavenly and the holy in the laughter of Your little children.   —PENNEY SCHWAB

A Whole and Holy Love

18/₍WED₎ *No one has ever seen God; but if we love one another, God lives in us and his love is made complete in us.*
—1 JOHN 4:12 (NIV)

We had not seen each other for several years when I suggested to Marilyn that I stop for a visit on my way through western Kansas after spending Christmas with my daughter. I had been divorced for about a year and was looking for ways to reconnect with family and friends. We had known each other growing up, but had little contact during our adult years. We knew we had some things in common— we both liked to write, for instance, and our children were very important to us—but we did not know that we were on a common spiritual journey.

So we spent a day together catching up on each other's lives, a day given over mainly to talk, although there were some periods of silence, meals shared and a walk in the park. Then came a moment that changed my life. It was late in the afternoon, and the sunlight through the living room window put Marilyn's face in deep relief. She was talking about a particularly painful time in her life, and there were tears in her eyes. I was sitting across from her and could feel the pain in her voice. But just as I was about to offer some words of reassurance, I saw her in a new way: I saw her as a complete person, with nothing lacking. In that moment there was no separation between us. For the first time in my life I experienced total, unconditional acceptance of another human being.

I have come to appreciate that, in this precious moment, I was permitted to see with the eyes of love. While we don't see God in this life, I believe we do sometimes see with the eyes of God. In those grace-filled moments God's love shines through us like the afternoon sun, revealing the dark places in our lives, but also bringing out the beauty.

Open my heart, Holy One, that I may see through Your eyes.

—ROBERT KING

19/THU   *All the ends of the world shall remember and turn unto the Lord.* —PSALM 22:27

April 19 is an important anniversary for me. I like to celebrate it with my friend Ray, because it's important for him, too. He calls me or I call him and we schedule lunch. Initially we don't talk about why we happen to be celebrating. Maybe I'll be conscious of it in a noisy restaurant as I try to seat myself close to his right side because he's been deaf in his left ear since his operation. Or I might scratch my left ear and think of it because of the lingering numbness in my nerves there ever since my operation. Otherwise we talk about our kids, our wives, our work.

At the end of lunch, when I'm taking a bite out of his slice of chocolate cake and he's taking a spoonful of my apple pie, it will come up in an oblique way. I'll remember that morning when we were both recovering from surgery, when the best distraction from my discomfort had been to pray for him because I was too afraid to pray for myself. That we both had tumors in similar places and that we both were operated on—in different hospitals—on the same day was the sort of coincidence that we would have been happier without.

But then came the good news. My surgery was successful, so was his. Both our tumors were benign. In the five years since, our other news has been good. So we schedule this annual lunch to remind ourselves of our blessings. We have a lot to be grateful for. No one knows that as well as Ray and I, two guys in business suits at a thanksgiving feast. Just what an anniversary is for.

Let me never forget all the good reasons I have for celebrating, Lord!

—RICK HAMLIN

20/FRI

*I well remember them, and my soul is downcast. . . .
Yet this I call to mind and therefore I have hope: Because of the Lord's great love we are not consumed, for his compassions never fail.*
—LAMENTATIONS 3:20-22 (NIV)

Today marks an anniversary indelibly imprinted in many of our hearts. Two years ago today, the tragic Columbine High School shootings occurred. Two armed students killed thirteen people and injured more than twenty others before killing themselves in the school library. Here in the Denver area, we absorbed many of the painful shock waves because this struck so close to home. I work with a mom whose son hid for hours as a captive in the school that day, and another woman whose teenage babysitter was critically injured.

Where is the hope in the midst of this horror? I wondered.

A few days after the tragedy, while getting some bedding plants at a local nursery, I spied a packet of columbine flower seeds. On the front was a beautiful picture of these blue-and-white blossoms, a hopeful vision of what could grow out of the dead-looking seeds inside. I purchased a packet and placed it on the windowsill above my desk at my office to remind me that the seeds of hope could grow something beautiful out of this tragedy. And sure enough, as the days wore on, I began to see some of those seeds of hope. At local blood banks, people stood in line for hours to donate. Young people all over Denver committed their lives to Christ; church attendance grew and many congregations reported incredible revivals. A high school student in California raised eighteen thousand dollars to help pay for a victim's medical bills. Students broke down the barriers between cliques, and some victim's families lived out amazing examples of forgiveness.

I still have that packet of columbine seeds on my windowsill, and today, as the media again review the horror of that day, I will remember how little seeds of hope can blossom into great blessings.

Lord, today please comfort and bless the families of those touched by tragedy.
—CAROL KUYKENDALL

21 / SAT
"As a mother comforts her child, so will I comfort you. . . ."
—ISAIAH 66:13 (NIV)

My husband Whitney and I had just come home from an overnight trip, and our pet sitter wore a long face. "That wild kitten got in the house," she said. "He's upstairs and won't let me near him. I'm so sorry."

The kitten belonged to a stray named Babe who lived on our porch. She had given birth to him in the woods. He'd never seen a human till the week before, when she brought him home to us. He was as wild as could be, and now he was in the house. I hadn't a clue how to catch him.

I climbed the stairs in dread. There he was, his little yellow face poking around the corner. When he saw me, he hissed and raised his back, unsheathed his claws and sprang for my face. I ducked just in time. He ran to the bedroom; I ran in after him and closed the door.

The kitten was hunched in a corner under the bed, panting with fear. I thought about ways to trap him. *The butterfly net! If I chase him long enough and tire him out, I can put the net over him. Then I'll cover the net with a towel and. . . .*

But, no. The little guy would never get over the trauma if I used such force. *Think, Shari, think. If you were that kitten, what would take away your terror?* I closed the door softly, went out to the porch, picked up the mother cat and carried her up to the bedroom. She sniffed at the rug. "Meow," she called. I heard a rustling from under the bed.

The kitten's taut little face appeared, draped with the dust ruffle. He raced to greet his mother. She washed his ears and talked to him in soft meows. He purred. Ever so gently I nudged them both into the crate I had waiting and carried it downstairs to the porch. When I opened the crate, kitten and mother strolled out.

I bowed my head and said:

Thank You, God, for comfort and comforters. —SHARI SMYTH

22 / SUN
God has surely listened and heard my voice in prayer.
—PSALM 66:19 (NIV)

I've been noticing young mothers with their children lately. Maybe it's because my own children are now in their thirties and forties, and I like to remember what they were like when they were little.

On Easter morning I enjoyed seeing all the children dressed up for church in new pastel colors. The little girls wore hats and the small boys sported new suits. The young fellow who sat in front of us each Sunday wore a solid white suit with short pants. His hair was combed perfectly, and I couldn't help but steal glances at him sitting attentively next to his mother. When we stood to sing, he climbed up on the seat so he could see better. That's when I saw he was wearing very old, but obviously beloved cowboy boots with his new white suit. Had his mother forgotten to have him change shoes? He sang loudly and clapped along with the lively music about a risen Savior. He and his mother exchanged looks of pure love.

Sadly, I knew I would never have allowed one of my sons to wear those boots with a brand-new suit on such a special Sunday. We would have fought all morning, but I would never have relented. My unhappy child would have worn matching shoes to church, probably asking himself what a loving God had against cowboy boots.

As the pastor prayed, I peeked at the little boy. His head was bowed and his hands folded underneath his chin. He didn't move an inch. He may have been only four, but he had obviously come to worship with a happy heart.

Dear Lord, help my inside and outside to match when I come to worship You. Amen. —MARION BOND WEST

23 / MON

A lion which is strongest among beasts, and turneth not away for any. —PROVERBS 30:30

There is a place in New York City that I never go to, or merely pass by, without my spirit being renewed: the massive marble edifice of the New York Public Library at Fifth Avenue and Forty-second Street. It's not that I remember the exhilaration of some successful research I've accomplished there, or the pleasure gained from any number of special exhibitions I've visited. No, I refer to those two stalwart guardians flanking the front steps, on duty in summer's heat and winter's cold, twenty-four hours a day, those two majestic concrete lions.

The lions and I go back to the days when I was a student in college. I would come to the library for special reading and occasionally take a break in the sunshine on the steps outside. I would see them lying there, two creatures at ease, their tails quiet and their front paws stretched out before them, with heads held high and a look of satisfaction approaching a smile on their faces. They were not intimidating, but they were not a child's plaything. They had dignity.

"They seem almost alive," I mused to a fellow nearby, one of many taking the sun for one reason or another.

"They are alive," he replied. "They're alive for me, at any rate. They're here to give me hope. And they have, repeatedly." He pointed to each lion and introduced me. "This one is Fortitude and that one is Patience."

Now, whenever I see a bird alighting on one of the lions' heads, I see that the lion doesn't mind. One Christmas years ago someone set fire to the wreaths around their necks, but the lions retained their composure. (Fortunately, after years without them, the wreaths are back.) And whenever I am near the library, no matter my frame of mind, I look and am invigorated by the fortitude of David and the patience of Job given me by my two friends of the lion heart.

Lord, protect these sculptures as though they were truly beasts of the earth.
—VAN VARNER

24 / TUE *Later Jesus appeared again to the disciples beside the Lake of Galilee. . . . A fire was kindled and fish were frying over it, and there was bread.*
—JOHN 21:1, 9 (TLB)

It's early in the morning, and the lake is veiled from the shore by an April mist. The shadow of a man moves back and forth on the beach as he gathers driftwood and builds a fire. With a simple string he angles a few fish from the waves, then makes a kind of fish-kabob, which he slowly turns over the fire. Taking off his outer garment, he spreads it out on the sand and sets the fish upon it. Out of his knapsack he pulls a thick loaf of bread, a jug of goat's milk and a handful of figs. The gulls fly over to inspect his beach breakfast, and the whitecaps lick the shore hungrily.

Out on the lake, a group of strong, professional fishermen in a boat wrestle with a heavy net, but each time the net comes up empty. Nothing is more humiliating to men than to be defeated by the lowliest and slimiest of creatures. The empty net reminds these men of their spiritual emptiness: Thomas, the doubter; James and John, the hotheads; and Simon, who denied the Lord not once but thrice.

Their eyes are glassy and hot. Their arms are weak and wet. Their lips are parched, and their stomachs as hollow as seashells.

As the boat nears the shore they notice the fragrance of a hot breakfast, and in a few minutes they are seated round their Savior, laughing and feasting on food and forgiveness.

Whenever I sit down at the table to eat, I will remember Jesus the cook, Who understands my hunger and my failures. I will take the time to thank Him for the wheat for my toast, the grapes for my jelly, the oranges for my juice and for His presence at my table.

Our Father, give us this day our daily bread, and forgive us our trespasses.
—DANIEL SCHANTZ

25 / WED *A man of quick temper acts foolishly, but a man of discretion is patient.* —PROVERBS 14:17 (RSV)

It was raining lightly as we trudged home from the subway with one item left on our long to-do list. The bell on the door of the tiny dry cleaner's shop tinkled as we entered.

"I need to pick up my husband's suit, but I don't have the ticket."

The counter clerk went in search of the owner. Two-year-old John whined that he was thirsty. Mary, in the pouch strapped to my chest, began to cry.

When the owner appeared, I explained what I needed. He looked skeptical and asked, "Do you know what the suit looks like?"

I had no idea which suit it was; all I knew was that Andrew needed it for an important meeting the next day. Mary began to screech in earnest. John fussed his way into a tantrum. Elizabeth tugged on my sleeve with one of her endless *whys*.

The man flipped aimlessly through a stack of tickets. He pressed the button to rotate the clothing racks, and touched two or three suits before giving up. "Lady, can't you just go home and come back with the ticket?"

I looked at him as if he had two heads, neither of which was functioning. Eyes blazing, lips compressed, I turned quickly and herded my screaming offspring toward the door. "Don't get mad at *me*, lady!" the man shouted after us. "*You're* the one who forgot the ticket!"

I was not a model of Christian charity at that moment. My words were loud, brief and to the point. Slamming the door felt mighty good. Yet once outside, I caught sight of the faces of my children. They had never seen me angry like this before. They were terrified.

I knelt on the sidewalk in the rain and drew them close to me. "I'm sorry, children. Mommy just did something that was very wrong." I glanced back at the window of the shop, knowing I was too riled to apologize to the owner now. "And tomorrow, we'll come back so I can say 'I'm sorry' to the man who owns this store."

Lord Jesus, no matter what the provocation, You responded in love. Help me to control my anger for love of You. —JULIA ATTAWAY

26/THU *Forgive us our debts, as we forgive our debtors.*
—MATTHEW 6:12

The day was fine, sunny and crisp. After breakfast and morning prayers, I put the kids into jackets and we headed out the door.

"Where are we going, Mommy?" Elizabeth asked as she skipped down the sidewalk.

"To the dry cleaner." I replied.

"Did the man find Daddy's suit?"

"I don't know, honey. We're not going to get Daddy's suit. We're going so that I can apologize for yelling at him yesterday."

"Oh. You mean you'll say you're sorry, and then he'll say, 'I forgive you'?"

I smiled at Elizabeth's simple view of the world. "Well, something like that. I'm not so sure he's going to say he forgives me. He might still be mad. He might even yell at me again." I thought of my anger the day before, and the shop owner's, too. If my kids hadn't been there, if I hadn't seen myself through their eyes, I probably wouldn't be going back to apologize today.

"Why would the man yell at you again?" John wanted to know.

"Well, sweetie, not everyone knows that Jesus wants us to forgive one another. Sometimes people hold on to their anger."

"Then why are you going to go back if he might still be angry at you?"

"Because Jesus wants me to say I'm sorry when I've done something wrong, even if I get yelled at for doing it."

The children fell silent as we walked toward the shop. The bell tinkled on the door as we entered, and the shop owner came out. I braced myself for whatever his reaction might be. He was silent for a moment, and then rather sheepishly he said, "I found the suit after you left."

I smiled. "I didn't come for the suit. My husband will pick it up later. I came to say I'm sorry for the way I behaved last night."

The man took a deep breath and extended his hand. "I'm sorry I got upset, too."

We shook hands. The kids grinned. We closed the door quietly on the way out.

Lord, grant me the grace to forgive others, that I may know the power of Your forgiveness. —JULIA ATTAWAY

27 / FRI *For I am persuaded, that neither death, nor life, nor angels, nor principalities, nor powers, nor things present, nor things to come, Nor height, nor depth, nor any other creature, shall be able to separate us from the love of God, which is in Christ Jesus our Lord.*
—ROMANS 8:38–39

In the final days of his life, William Saroyan joked with a friend visiting him in the hospital. " I always knew that people don't live forever," the famous writer said, "but somehow in my case, I thought there would be an exception made." Like Saroyan, we all have trouble imagining our own deaths. However as we grow older, that reality looms larger and larger.

I suppose I didn't really give dying much serious thought until a life-threatening illness visited me a few years ago. Then my life came into perspective, and time was of the essence. Shortcomings were magnified, mistakes easier to admit, forgiveness easier to ask, estrangements mended, things undone and unsaid acted upon.

Although the crisis passed, I was changed more than a little by my brush with death. Time has become more precious, relationships more important, and God's manifold gifts and grace more appreciated. And a magnificent piece of Scripture more meaningful than ever before. It comes from Paul's letter to the Romans, the incomparable eighth chapter, which concludes with the question: "What can separate us from the love of Christ?" The apostle's answer: Nothing. Not tribulation, distress, persecution, famine, nakedness, peril or the sword. And certainly not death.

Once we have that assurance in our hearts, once we know and believe and trust the One Who died for us, the length of our life becomes far less important than its legacy, its duration far less significant than its donation.

> *Help me discern, Lord, lesser from finer,*
> *Lasting from passing, major from minor.*
>
> —FRED BAUER

28 / SAT

We glory in tribulations also: knowing that tribulation worketh patience. —ROMANS 5:3

My son Ross was on the mound for his Little League team, pitching for only the second time in his nine-year-old life. He walked two, and his confidence was shaken. Then he threw one wild pitch and hit the batter on the foot. Now he was really rattled. He gave up a couple of hits and runs, and the bases were still loaded. Suddenly, he pulled himself together, striking out two and catching a pop-up to end the inning. After the game I told him how proud I was of his tenacity and wondered how he got through that tough spot. He shrugged his shoulders and said, "I don't know, Mom. I just kept throwing the ball."

I've been thinking a lot recently about that beautifully simple philosophy. I'm not a quitter, but I have my limits. A friend and I have been trying for more than a year to work with a local business on an idea we think will help both the company and the community, but a lot of difficulties have blocked our way. I'm trying to use the ideas and the inspiration God has given me to make the project work, but I'm starting to doubt myself and am ready to give up. Then I hear Ross's innocent words. They're akin to Paul's encouragement of Timothy: Forge ahead, strengthened by God's power. Only then will I know, as Paul did, that "I have fought the good fight . . . [and] finished the race" (II Timothy 4:7, RSV).

Win or lose, Paul's aim was to finish the task God set before him. I need to do the same. In my trials I'm learning that while God doesn't promise victory, He does offer a guarantee: If I "just keep throwing the ball," God will be beside me every step of the way.

Give me courage and strength, Lord, to follow through and finish the job. —GINA BRIDGEMAN

29 / SUN *Open the gates, that the righteous nation which keeps faith may enter in. Thou dost keep him in perfect peace, whose mind is stayed on thee. . . .*
—ISAIAH 26:2–3 (RSV)

I used to wonder how prayer could alter our minds and create a state of peace, until I stepped into Rome's Pantheon, a majestic, circular temple built to honor all the gods of Rome, but rededicated as a Christian church in A.D. 607.

I approached the building slowly, admiring the sixteen high granite columns, then slowly passed through the bronze doors, which were ajar. I peeked in. Sunlight fell in a shaft, angling down from the high dome toward the place where I entered. I slipped in softly, barely breathing. A holy place.

Spellbound, I circled the interior, gazing past statues and paintings to the high, open dome and the spill of hushed sunlight. As I circled, I felt almost weightless, and I was not surprised to read later that the building was designed to create a sense of perfect equilibrium.

The startling subtlety was the architect's intent. He wanted all who entered his Pantheon to find a place of perfect balance. And so effective was his work that the roaring bustle of everyday Rome outside was silenced, and tourists and children fell quiet.

And now I know why prayer alters our state of mind. When we pray, we enter a holy place, uniquely designed by the Master, a place designed for perfect balance.

Father in heaven, when life is chaotic and noisy, help me to remember that through prayer there is a place I can go for equilibrium, relief from my burdens and perfect peace. —BRENDA WILBEE

30 / MON *Ye shall seek me, and find me, when ye shall search for me with all your heart.* —JEREMIAH: 29:13

Sometimes my reaching out for God crosses the line between faith and superstition. In my family, we've always been great believers in signs and omens, portents and messages, with an unfortunate tendency to confuse everyday events with signals from God.

But a friend taught me a strong lesson about crossing that line. Shortly after I was diagnosed with malignant melanoma, a friend confided that she, too, had had cancer. This shared confidence opened a floodgate of communication between us. I soon learned that thoughts and terrors I'd feared were only mine, were not. Anne, and probably many others with cancer, had had similar experiences.

I was particularly prone to interpreting dreams. If I dreamed about being swept out to sea, I automatically wondered if God was warning me about an imminent malignancy. If disturbing dreams came at the time of a biopsy, I became even more frightened.

Anne told me she had experienced the same worrisome tendency, until one morning when she was on her way to an appointment to learn the results of a recent test. She stepped out her door to find a perfect robin dead on her steps. Panic-stricken, convinced her doctors would report a malignancy, Anne drove to the office with a dry mouth and a pounding heart. It took a few moments for her to realize that the doctor was congratulating her on her clean test results.

I've kept Anne's story near my heart, drawing it out every time a doctor's appointment or a biopsy looms before me. It comforts me to remember that sometimes God waits for us to find the faith inside ourselves, to see beyond superstition and reach for Him.

Lord, help me to recognize the difference between superstitious searching and faithful reaching. —MARCI ALBORGHETTI

DAILY GIFTS

1 _____

2 _____

3 _____

4 _____

5 _____

6 _____

7 _____

8 _____

9 _____

10 _____

11 _____

12 _____

13 _____

14 _____

15 _____

16 _____

17 _____

18 _____

19 _____

20 _____

21 _____

22 _____

23 _____

24 _____

25 _____

26 _____

27 _____

28 _____

29 _____

30 _____

May

Ho, every one that
thirsteth, come
ye to the waters,
and he that hath no
money; come ye,
buy, and eat....
—ISAIAH 55:1

S	M	T	W	T	F	S
		1	2	3	4	5
6	7	8	9	10	11	12
13	14	15	16	17	18	19
20	21	22	23	24	25	26
27	28	29	30	31		

WHEN GOD REACHES OUT . . . THROUGH OTHER PEOPLE

1/TUE

"I am the true vine and my Father is the gardener."
—JOHN 15:1 (NIV)

A mile from our house is a roadside restaurant in a spectacular garden setting. For years, on my morning walk, I've stopped to gaze over the hedge at beds of roses, peonies, asters, an acre and more of color changing with the seasons. *Who couldn't have a beautiful garden,* I've thought, *with the gardening staff they must have here!*

I'd always gone by too early to see any of them at work. Then one day, when I had to handle a big mailing project single-handedly, I didn't get out to walk till afternoon. As I passed the garden, a stocky middle-aged man came from the restaurant basement carrying a tray of begonias. Seeing me stop, he waved me inside the hedge. He had to spell his last name before I caught it: Joseph Csomor.

"Are you the head gardener?" I asked.

Mr. Csomor shook his head. "Just the assistant."

He'd come here from Hungary twenty-seven years ago, he went on. The restaurant had hired him as a cleaning man, but when he was through sweeping and scrubbing, he'd spent his free time digging around the roots of the potted geraniums that were the only flowers on the place. Seeing the geraniums thrive, the owner had let him plant some rosebushes out back.

My puzzlement grew as Mr. Csomor told how year after year he'd planted a lilac bush here, a marigold border there, until the garden became the showplace it is today. If he'd done all this . . . "Then what does the head gardener do?"

Mr. Csomor pointed a stubby finger skyward. "He makes the flowers grow."

When the job is a big one, Lord, remind me again that I'm "just the assistant."
—ELIZABETH SHERRILL

2 / WED

"Those whom I love I rebuke and discipline. . . ."
—REVELATION 3:19 (NIV)

"If I'm ever in that situation again," I told myself, "I'm going to say something."

Five years ago I had passed by two young men as I entered the subway. One of them seemed to be trying to start a fight with the other. *I should do something,* I thought as I ducked my head and slipped by the pair. But what could I do? They were both a lot bigger than I was.

"I'll do it differently next time," I assured myself. Today I got the chance.

A group of teenagers walked down the sidewalk near where I had just parked my car. It was 11:00 A.M., and they were a mile from school. As I locked eyes with one of the young men, I had a sinking feeling—trouble was brewing.

It's not any of your business, an inner voice told me. *What if they get angry?* But the image of the two young men in the subway was still in my mind. The voice tried to compromise. *Okay, only say something if they're really doing something bad.*

I backed my car out and drove up to the group, rolled down my window and spoke to a young man who looked like one of the leaders. "You know, you're real obvious," I told him. "Other people must be watching you."

"I'm not doing anything," he said. "I'm just waiting for my bus." He laughed.

"Maybe, but you look like trouble getting ready to happen. Be careful." The sound of calm and concern in my voice surprised me. "Just be careful."

His smile was different now. "Thank you for caring," the young man said. By the time I parked my car and looked back, the group was dispersing.

I would be dishonest if I didn't tell you that he laughed as I drove away and yelled after me, "Hey, lady! Can I drive your car?" But I can tell you that I feel better than I did five years ago. And maybe I helped someone avoid a little trouble.

God, give me courage and boldness so that I will display walking, talking faith and love.
—SHARON FOSTER

3/ *THU* *I have called daily upon thee, I have stretched out my hands unto thee.* —PSALM 88:9

My wife Carol has a group of friends on the Internet, most of whom she's never met face-to-face. They are part of a network set up by our college where alumni from different classes get to know each other. In her group the primary bond is parenting—all of the alums are rearing children—and over the years they have come to know one another well, discussing everything from homework problems to soccer camp. Inevitably, they have also talked each other through some tough times.

One of the toughest came when one member was diagnosed with breast cancer. Advice flew through cyberspace—what treatments to try, what doctors had said, which hospitals were best. In this case, the family made the decision to move across the country to be near a fine hospital in Texas. Progress reports kept the e-mail group well informed. But then, at a crucial moment, someone came up with an idea as good as any medical science had provided. "12:00 tomorrow, Central Time, let's meet for prayer," said the e-mail message.

The next day Carol logged on at 1:00 our time, noon in Texas, and opened her e-mail. She scrolled down. "I'm here," "Ready," "Waiting," came the litany of responses, and from office buildings in New York to kitchens in California, people prayed through the great electronic silence. "Amen," they signed out.

No one who first heard Christ say, "Where two or more are gathered in my name," could have guessed at a gathering encompassing thousands of miles. But then again, the mystery and power of prayer is more profound than cyberspace. And our communities of prayer need only be a password away.

May I be tireless, Lord, in Your community of prayer.

—RICK HAMLIN

4/ *FRI* *What man is he that liveth, and shall not see death? . . .* —PSALM 89:48

We have a neighborhood cat, as most neighborhoods do—you know, the cat who makes the rounds of all the houses looking for things to eat, interesting crimes, love, warm car engines, good sunny spots in the garden, children who don't pull tails. Our neighborhood cat is

Missy, and this morning Missy did what cats do with astonishing grace and skill: She killed a bird.

I didn't see the stalk and spring, but I found the evidence first thing in the morning, when I shuffled out to get the paper: a phoebe, very young, probably just fledged from the nest.

I knelt down to examine the bird carefully. Birds are among the most amazingly built and beautiful of the Lord's creatures, and I never tire of examining their intricacies. My children came pouring out of the house to see what brought Dad to his knees. They crowded around—my wise, leggy seven-year-old daughter and headlong, exuberant four-year-old twin sons—and stared at the stiffening bird. And, suddenly, without warning, they prayed.

"God, make the bird better," prayed my sons, who are open to miracles.

"God, kill the cat," prayed my daughter, who is absorbed by justice and vengeance.

"God, let me die before they do," I found myself praying, there on my knees in the wet grass, a bird in my hand. "Let them live healthy a hundred years. Don't make me see them broken and pale and dying before me. Let me die first, and let them weep for me on their knees, weeping for the lost beautiful intricacy of life and heart You gave me. Give me the gift of death before my beloved children. Don't take them from me when they are fledglings from the nest."

Lord, give me the wit and heart to thank You with every breath for the mind-boggling gift of my own life. And I thank You in advance for the whole span of it, however long that will be. —BRIAN DOYLE

5/SAT   *A prudent wife is from the Lord.* —PROVERBS 19:14

I couldn't believe it! After fifteen years of talking about it, my husband was sorting through and clearing out the boxes stacked in the stairwell of the garage.

Then he found the letter. "What about this?" he asked as he came into the kitchen for a glass of iced tea.

"What is it?" I asked.

"You know, Aunt Belle's letter," he said.

How could I ever forget! Aunt Belle lived on a farm on the White Horse Plains, about a hundred miles west of Winnipeg, Manitoba,

Canada. She was a God-fearing, no-nonsense woman; the strength of the prairie ran in her blood. It had to. She took her family through hail, grasshoppers, rust blight and drought, and then through the crippling Depression of the thirties.

Her letter came after we became engaged and John had written telling her about me and enclosed a picture. "Well now," she wrote, "at last you have found someone willing to marry you. She seems like a sensible girl; should make you a good wife."

The only compliment she gave me was that I seemed sensible! I had bristled at the word. What happened to pretty, dainty, graceful or glamorous? Or smart?

"She's given you the best compliment ever," John assured me. "A farm wife has to be sensible."

Unimpressed, I frowned. "Well, I don't like her, and that's that."

Little did I know then how much Aunt Belle's word *sensible* would focus me through my life. As problems came up, I'd think, *Now what would be Aunt Belle's sensible way to solve this?* When the bills kept coming in and our money kept running out, I'd sit down and tell myself, "Aunt Belle says I'm *sensible*. There must be a way to cut the corners." I did.

When our son got engaged, I said to my husband, "Melissa's a pretty girl, and"—with a knowing wink—"she seems sensible. Should make him a good wife."

Aunt Belle is with the Lord now, but maybe she can still hear me say it: "I like you, Aunt Belle!"

Thank You, Lord, for those who through the living of their lives have given me gems of wisdom.
—FAY ANGUS

6/SUN   *For God alone my soul waits in silence; from him comes my salvation.*   —PSALM 62:1 (RSV)

No one else was within five miles of Laity Lodge that night. The lodge was a new Christian conference center, cantilevered over the edge of a canyon deep in the hill country of southwest Texas. The first official conference was scheduled to begin in two days.

The huge tan flagstone floor of Great Hall reflected the full moon beyond the fifteen-foot glass wall where I sat and looked down at the same moon mirrored in the silent lake far below. This lodge was a place to tell people about God, people who might never listen in a church. I was to be the first director.

I was frightened. I didn't know what to do except tell them my own story: how I'd always sought God, but also run from Him, until I ran out of places and ways to run. And finally, one day on a roadside in east Texas, I surrendered to God as I saw Him in Jesus. But that was years ago, and now I was afraid that I was powerless to help anyone. I felt tears coming to my eyes; I wanted to run away, to hide where no one could find me.

I was sitting in a beam of moonlight coming from the sun-roof window in the vaulted ceiling far above my head, with the rest of the cavernous room in shadows. Now I began to feel a reverence, a presence almost, in that beam of moonlight, splayed in an elongated square around me on the flagstones. Excitement, fear, joy flashed through me as I wondered if it could be true, or if it was another trick of my mind. But it didn't matter what my mind thought in that moment: God was with me there, and I with Him. I let go, surrendered, and I was chastened, calmed and filled with a sure knowledge that everything would be all right.

I wept tears of gratitude. Somehow, God had filled that empty place and washed my fears away in a silver beam of moonlight.

Lord, thank You for reaching out to us, even where there is no preacher nor church spire. Amen. —KEITH MILLER

THE LEANING LOG

Three years ago the foundation of Roberta Messner's home and heart crumbled. Her marriage of more than two decades died, and she found herself living alone in an old log cabin she'd bought as a getaway. Recovering from a serious accident and facing permanent

disability, Roberta began the daunting task of rebuilding her life and turning her cockeyed cabin into a home. Come with her for the next five days as she reaches for a new start and discovers new meaning in an old truth: Our only firm foundation is to lean on the Lord.

—THE EDITORS

7/ MON

DAY ONE: THE UNSEEN GUEST
"As for me and my house, we will serve the Lord."
—JOSHUA 24:15 (NAS)

I found the old plaque at a flea market. It was only a dollar; on it was a faded picture of Jesus and the words, "Christ is the head of this house, the unseen guest at every meal, the silent listener to every conversation." I knew I had to have it to hang in the entrance of the log cabin I'd recently bought.

We had a lot in common—that cabin, the plaque and I. In its heyday at the turn of the twentieth century, the cabin had been a fishing camp, alive with the sounds of adventure and tall tales. Now, its walls sagged and its floors were warped. No matter where you stood in it, you leaned. I dubbed it "The Leaning Log."

I was leaning, too. I was barely making it through each day, on my own for the first time in twenty-one years. I faced an uncertain future that included a shattered marriage and almost certain disability retirement. I dared not be hopeful about anything anymore. In recent months, dizziness from a new medication had caused me to suffer a severe fall, resulting in a head injury and a broken shoulder. *Where was God when everything I'd counted on was falling apart?*

When an artist friend tried to touch up the plaque, the image of Christ crumbled even more, making it nearly unrecognizable. Then a thought came to me: *Let Me help you build a new life, Roberta. Paint "The Leaning Log" over the picture of Me. You won't see Me with your physical eyes, but I will be there supporting you just the same.*

My artist friend completed the project with a sense of urgency. I made a little ceremony of hanging the plaque in the entranceway of the cabin before I made any renovations or unpacked the first box. Christ would be the unseen guest in The Leaning Log. I didn't know how, but He would teach me anew to lean on His everlasting arms.

Jesus, You meet us in our brokenness when all earthly structures have fallen about us. Help me to entrust my life to Your care.

—ROBERTA MESSNER

8/TUE

DAY TWO: THE WEAVER'S PATTERN
The bird also has found a house, And the swallow a
nest for herself, where she may lay her young. . . .
—PSALM 84:3 (NAS)

How will I ever make this cockeyed cabin a real home? I thought when I moved into The Leaning Log. I unpacked only the necessities and stored the remnants of the life I'd left behind in the garage and adjoining breezeway, dreading the long cold winter ahead. As the wind whistled through gaps in the logs, I thought of one of the cabin's former owners, who told me how his father had hung quilts on the walls to try to keep Old Man Winter out.

When summer came, I noticed an abandoned bird's nest tucked under the eaves. Something made me reach for it. In the past, I'd used such treasures of nature for Christmas decorations. But this one was different. Some creative bird had woven the most colorful materials into her nest.

Wait a minute! Isn't this the rosebud wallpaper my friend Carole helped me hang in the guest bedroom at my old house? I'd been reluctant to try wallpapering, but Carole was sure the two of us could figure out plumb lines and trimming around baseboards. The industrious bird had woven that twenty-one-year-old wallpaper into her new home. There had been enough remaining on the roll for a craft project, and I'd never been able to throw it away; all these years later, I'd brought it with me. *And isn't that my red-checked kitchen curtain fabric amidst the mud and twigs?* I'd saved some of the scraps to use in a quilt. *Why, that tenacious mama bird even found my duct tape!*

When I'm the General Contractor, I build on your past, Roberta, Christ seemed to say. *I don't discard it. Just trust Me.* Right then and there, I gave Him the shattered, jagged pieces of my past—failures and fears I'd held on to far too long. It was time for the two of us to rebuild *my* nest, *my* life, *my* relationship with Him.

I thank You, Jesus, that no life is so hopeless that it can't be woven back together with Your loving touch.   —ROBERTA MESSNER

9/_{WED}

DAY THREE: JUST AS I AM
"I will give you a new heart and put a new spirit in you. . . ."
—EZEKIEL 36:26 (NIV)

The contract on The Leaning Log plainly stated that I'd purchased it "as is." "Now you know what that means," the real estate attorney had stressed as I signed on the dotted line. But lured by the cabin's fascinating fishing-lodge past, I'd glossed over those two telling words.

I soon learned the reason for them. New wiring and plumbing headed the budget-breaking list of must-dos, closely followed by heating and air conditioning. And did I mention repairing sagging ceilings and replacing decades of peeling wallpaper?

But the warm weather gave new meaning to the words "as is." Daffodils and dogwoods, lilies of the valley and lilacs, redbuds and roses brought color and new life to the once-barren grounds. The previous owner, I learned from a neighbor, had purchased many of the plants from the Audubon Society, unknowingly investing in my future so I would be surrounded by birdsong and blossoms.

Hadn't God accepted me "as is" when He welcomed me into His family? I thought as I looked out over the flowers. He'd taken me, foibles and all, no questions asked, when I showed no signs of promise. It was like that old hymn we sang at church:

> *"Just as I am without one plea,*
> *But that thy blood was shed for me."*

I suddenly felt alive with new purpose for both the cabin and me. From my brokenness and barrenness there was something—lovely, though hidden from view—already in the making.

God, thank You for accepting me "as is" and beginning the work of restoring Your likeness in me.
—ROBERTA MESSNER

10/_{THU}

DAY FOUR: BURIED TREASURES
"The Lord is my rock and my fortress and my deliverer."
—II SAMUEL 22:2 (NAS)

An expert in log cabin restoration paid me a visit one afternoon. "Wouldn't you like to take a peek at the logs hiding behind all these layers of old wallpaper?" he asked. In no time flat, he was swinging a crowbar, filling the air with the dust of disintegrating drywall as he

stripped the old cabin bare. The gaps between the logs were hap-
hazardly stuffed with rags, old newspapers and an occasional abandoned animal's nest. *That explains those long, cold winters,* I thought
with a shiver.

And then I saw them—breathtaking chestnut and pine logs with
the rich patina of a forgotten era. "Knock down another one!" I cried
as he tackled a wall of bowed white beadboard. He returned the next
day and the next, and with each swing of his crowbar, I felt an exhilarating sense of freedom.

There are some walls in your life that need to come tumbling down, too,
the Lord nudged. I knew them all too well. Brick walls of rigid thinking. Thick plaster walls that kept me from being open to this new stage
of my life. Tongue-and-groove paneled walls that held me captive to
me, myself and I.

After installing insulation between the logs, the craftsman nailed in
screening, followed by gray mortar to keep out the elements. Now rock
solid, the mortar and the century-old logs work together to create the
most secure and snug haven ever. The old and the new, working together in harmony, teaching me to do the same as I trust the Solid Rock.

Father, You are my Rock, the Source of my strength in good times
and bad.
                                                    —ROBERTA MESSNER

11/*FRI*   *DAY FIVE: A HOME FOREVER*
           For we know that if the earthly tent which is our
           house is torn down, we have a building from God, a
           house not made with hands, eternal in the heavens.
                            —II CORINTHIANS 5:1 (NAS)

My mother adored my little log cabin, and it was a special place of
refuge for her when her cancer became terminal. When the hospital
discharged her, Mother came to live her last days with me. Those
rock-solid log walls became the backdrop for a hospital bed, suction
machine and oxygen tanks, as friends gathered around with home-
cooked meals and comforting words.

Some months before, I'd designed a sign and hung it in the front
yard by the arbor. It featured an angel and the words, ON THE WAY TO
SOMEWHERE ELSE, communicating the conviction Mother and I
shared, that life is a journey where divine opportunities are often dis-
guised as detours.

The afternoon of Mother's death, as the mortuary staff carried her tired and tattered earthly body through the screened-in porch she so loved, we children followed behind. When we came up the cobblestone path leading back to the house, I saw the words as if for the very first time: ON THE WAY TO SOMEWHERE ELSE.

With the Lord rebuilding my home and heart, my once-frightening detour had become the setting for Mother's ultimate journey: to her eternal home in the heavens not made with hands.

Dear Lord, help me always to make my heart Your home.
—ROBERTA MESSNER

12/ SAT   *"Whom shall I send, and who will go for us?" Then I said, "Here I am! Send me."* —ISAIAH 6:8 (RSV)

One night a few days before Mother's Day 1999, I was in a bit of a whiny, poor-me mood. I e-mailed my brother and sister-in-law, telling them that none of my four children (who all live out of town or state) could be with me on Mother's Day, so on Sunday I was planning to go in-line skating by myself along Milwaukee's beautiful lakefront. "I'm going to go where no one will recognize me and where I can pretend I'm an old spinster who never had any children," I joked.

A few hours later, my sister-in-law called to say that she was going to Japan the day after next to meet my brother, who would be on a five-day layover there on his job as an airline pilot. They wanted me to join them, at very little cost, because Linda works for another major airline and we'd be flying on stand-by passes.

Linda was giving me thirty-six hours notice to drop everything and fly to Japan, only the second time in my life I'd be off the continent! My first reaction was to rattle off all the things I had to do that week. But then I caught myself. I shouted "Yes!" did a happy dance around the house, canceled or postponed everything on my calendar, and started packing.

The trip, the sightseeing, the food and the people were fabulous, but what I will always remember most is that not only was I able to say yes, I did say yes to an outrageous opportunity, and learned once again that *yes* is not only magical, it's almost always a great idea.

Lord, help me always to say Yes! to every one of Your opportunities, no matter how mind-boggling they are.
—PATRICIA LORENZ

PRAYER FOR MAY

Lord, thank You for miracles of every size:
Caterpillar to chrysalis . . . to butterfly;
Bulb to thrusting green spear . . . to full-blown lily;
Child born into life . . . reborn through faith into Life
  Eternal.

Lord, thank You for miracles of every magnitude:
Colorful pebbles found in streambeds . . . to soaring
  ranges of granite peaks;
Squat rhododendron . . . to massive sequoia;
Whispering brooklets . . . to thunderous Niagara.

Lord, thank You for miracles of healing:
Desperation . . . to contentment;
Anger . . . to reconciliation;
Infirmity . . . to wholeness.

Lord, thank You for miracles!

—EVELYN MINSHULL

13/_SUN_ *And Miriam answered them, Sing ye to the Lord, for
he hath triumphed gloriously. . . .* —EXODUS 15:21

Oh, no, here she goes again.

The *she* was my mother, and I was the twelve-year-old boy standing next to her in the pew on Sunday morning. Mom loved to sing in
church. Fortunately, it was the only time she sang, because my mother
couldn't carry a tune to save her life. Yet sing she did, as if there were
no tomorrow. Whatever the diametric opposite of perfect pitch is, she
had it, the uncanny ability not to go anywhere near the right tone.

It was bad enough going to church with your parents (I always tried
to go to a different service so I could sit with my friends), but to have
that kind of attention drawn to yourself was utterly mortifying. And
people did cast slightly alarmed looks in our direction, to be sure.
Even when I decided to attend the "guitar service" (it was the sixties, after all), my mother followed, eager to learn a new sort of music
to mangle.

I was an altar boy, and I remember serving Mass with Father Walling when my mother would launch into song. He'd wince ever so slightly, and I would imagine that he could barely restrain his hands from flying up to cover his patient, suffering ears. Instead, he would quickly summon me with the cruets of wine and water.

All protests from my siblings and me fell on (tone) deaf ears. "You are supposed to be singing, not listening," she'd say, completely un-sympathetic. "Besides, I'm sure God doesn't mind my voice one bit." I envisaged God frantically putting in cosmic earplugs.

Well, today it pleases me to no end that my mother really didn't give a hoot about what anyone thought of her singing. She was singing to God, not to us, and she believed that whatever came out of her mouth came out of her soul, and it was music to His ears. And now that she is gone, I miss her awful caterwauling more than I ever could have imagined when I was that self-conscious boy. But I know she is in heaven, singing, and God doesn't mind one bit.

My praise, Lord, is never on pitch until it reaches You.

—EDWARD GRINNAN

INTO AFRICA

14/MON   *My times are in thy hand. . . .*   —PSALM 31:15

I had to pack lightly for my trip to Africa. We used light planes, four-wheel-drive utility vehicles, and foot travel for short distances. I was pretty proud that my baggage consisted only of a backpack and small shoulder bag. However, I soon discovered that not all baggage is external.

One day we were visiting a rural village and had an appointment scheduled that evening in a distant city. Like many of the people of the world, most Africans are not slaves to their schedules, so I was constantly checking my watch and reminding our African friend and guide of the need to speed things up. Aware that my haste would keep me from really getting to know the people we were meeting, he stopped at one point and asked to see my watch.

Holding my left wrist with his right hand, he stretched his bare left wrist out next to my watch and said, "It is a very nice watch. We have a saying in Africa: All Americans have nice watches, and yet they never have any time, while few Africans can afford a watch, yet we have all the time we need for each other."

I got the point, and soon afterward took off my watch and buried it in my backpack for a few days. Of course, I dug it out again the night we left for home, so we wouldn't miss the plane. But I've found myself going without my watch from time to time since then. Try it sometime. You'll be amazed at how much time frees up when you leave your watch at home.

Lord, help me remember today that my time is in Your hands and I can trust You to make the day move at Your pace. —ERIC FELLMAN

A WHOLE AND HOLY LOVE

15/TUE *While they were talking and discussing together, Jesus himself drew near and went with them.*
—LUKE 24:15 (RSV)

What can I say about how I came to love Robert? For me it wasn't a moment of seeing the beloved through God's eyes, although I felt very much with Robert in his experience. For me love entered quietly, on bare feet. I wouldn't say I *fell* in love. It was more an awakening into love.

In all the years I'd known Robert I'd felt a special affinity with him, but he had seemed rather distant, somehow unreachable. Now he began to let me into his soul. When he told me of the tears he shed when he left his ailing mother, I felt the deep sensitivity and tender-heartedness he'd previously kept hidden. When I mentioned his nervousness the night we first prayed together, he responded, "It's because it's so important." In that moment I knew we shared the same spiritual values. When we attended our first retreat together, I became deeply aware, like the disciples on the road to Emmaus, of Another walking with us, blessing the communion we shared.

Instead of bursting forth suddenly, love took root in me and grew slowly. It was composed of small memories of such moments as the December night when Robert first sat in my kitchen and read to me, and we laughed away our reserve; the sweet-sad loneliness I felt when, having prayed with him, I now prayed alone; love letters from across the sea; two-hour phone calls; long talks about life and death and matters of the heart and soul; and finally, the magical night when he reached across the restaurant table, took my hands in his and said, "When the time is right, will you marry me?"

My answer came quickly, from a deeply rooted certainty: "Yes. Oh, yes!"

Thank You, Lord, for opening our eyes to Your presence, which is the true ground of lasting love. —MARILYN MORGAN KING

16/ WED *I can do all things through Christ which strengtheneth me.* —PHILIPPIANS 4:13

"Take a running start and dive forward, allowing your body to fly headfirst toward the ground. Now, just before you land, pull your chin and feet up and slide to a stop on your chest."

Our high-school volleyball coach was teaching my teammates and me this maneuver so we could dive for balls without cracking our ribs on the gym floor. The only problem was, it was one hundred percent counterintuitive. We'd grown up trying to avoid ever having to hurtle toward the earth upside-down; now we were being told we had to do it. Guys were landing with a thud on their knees, sprawling on their bellies, coming within inches of chipping their metal-braced teeth. Some guys would just stand there for minutes at a time, frozen, without the foggiest idea of how they were going to get their chests to hit the floor before their faces.

Finally, I got the hang of it. And it really wasn't a matter of mechanics; it was a matter of trust. If I listened to the instructor and didn't listen to the inner voice telling me it was impossible, I could indeed experience the freedom of letting myself fly through the air and land like a seaplane on a lake of still water.

I learned a lesson that day. There are some things that seem completely impossible, but with a little trust, I can do them. I *can* forgive somebody who has hurt me. I *can* sit next to somebody I don't know at church and start up a conversation. I *can* extend a hand and a heart of friendship to someone of a different color. It's all in the letting go.

Lord, when I think I'm trapped by my limitations, help me to surpass them by trusting You.
— DAVE FRANCO

17/THU *Therefore shall a man leave his father and his mother, and shall cleave unto his wife: and they shall be one flesh.*
— GENESIS 2:24

As I began helping my daughter Kendall plan her wedding, I needed plenty of advice, so I attached myself to friends who had already been through this experience.

"Beware of the tensions that can flare up in a mother-daughter relationship at this hectic time, filled with so many decisions," one warned me.

"You'll get along better if you just let her make most of the decisions," said another. "In fact, it's probably best if you simply have *no* opinion."

Kendall and I did just fine with cake flavors and flower colors and musical selections. But I was surprised by the passion I felt about one choice. It had to do with the lighting of the unity candle, a part of the ceremony that symbolizes the couple's two lives becoming one. Usually, the mothers come forward before the wedding party enters and light two separate candles, representing the bride and groom. Then, following the vows, the bride and groom take the two candles and together light the single unity candle. Now here's the choice: Do they blow out their individual candles, or leave them burning? "You don't snuff out who you are in your new union," I told Kendall. "You continue to grow as individuals, even when you're married."

"Mom, I appreciate your opinion. David and I will talk about it,"

Kendall calmly answered, which was her tactful way of letting me know this would be their decision.

Later I told one of my mentor-friends about our little conflict.

"Often the tensions have nothing to do with the decision at hand, but with other emotions we're feeling," she said.

Her remark helped me recognize the real fears behind my feelings. It wasn't so much about snuffing out their individuality in marriage, but about snuffing out their connections to their families. It was about learning to let go—about leaving and cleaving. So I composed a prayer to guide me through the rest of our preparations and the up-coming transition in our family.

Lord, I confess that I don't know how Kendall's marriage will change our relationship. Help me to bring my fears to You, and trust Your provisions, for You have ordained this "letting go."

—CAROL KUYKENDALL

18/ FRI

Love. . . .does not boast, it is not proud. . . .it is not self-seeking. . . . —I CORINTHIANS 13:4-5 (NIV)

Up the road from us in Tennessee is an ostrich farm where a proud peacock lives. When I walk my dog Leah, I see him up on a hill, strutting before the ostriches with his tail fanned full, its rich blues and greens shimmering in the sun like the plumes of a king. I look up; he looks down, his long silky body arched for show. "Okay, you're the fairest in the land," I tell him, tugging at my odd-looking mutt.

But one day I thought I saw another side of the peacock. He'd crossed the road and ascended a neighbor's porch. His great train of a tail was dragging and dusty. He was looking through the storm door into the living room, as if he were trying to say hello. "Well," I said to Leah, "our friend's gone calling on the neighbors."

I was afraid he'd get hit going back across the road, so I knocked at the door of the ostrich farm. A woman answered. "Your peacock is visiting the neighbors," I said.

She laughed. "He doesn't give a hoot about the neighbors. He's just looking at his reflection in the glass. He'll go anywhere to see himself." We laughed together about it and she assured me he knew how to cross the road. Then, before closing the door, she added, "My husband and I get a kick out of him. We often say there's a bit of peacock in all of us."

Lord, whenever I'm entranced by my own reflection, help me forget about myself and focus on others. —SHARI SMYTH

19/SAT *"Then I said, 'I have labored in vain, I have spent my strength for nothing and in vain; Yet surely my just reward is with the Lord, And my work with God.'"*
—ISAIAH 49:4 (NKJV)

When should you give up on something that isn't working? For twenty years I have tried to grow asparagus for my wife, who is wild about it. I can get the ferns to come up, but then it dies.

I've read dozens of articles on growing asparagus, and they assure me that "growing asparagus is easy," which makes me feel dumber than dirt. Dozens of friends have given helpful advice, such as "Put salt on it," and "Never put salt on it."

"Danny," my wife consoles, "you don't have to do this. I can get all the asparagus I need at Ritter's vegetable stand. Give it up."

So why don't I just give it up? Maybe I hate to be defeated by things that are lower down on the food chain. Maybe it's my pride or my bullheadedness.

In reality I think it's hope that keeps me going. Not just in gardening but in college teaching and in all my relationships. I keep praying for "impossible" things because deep down I think they just might happen. A few of them have.

I keep trying to overcome my bad habits—overeating, shyness, discouragement—because it would be so wonderful if I could do it. Just because I never have doesn't mean I never will.

It doesn't matter if I give up on asparagus, but it does matter that I keep trying to overcome my temptations. My job is to try, and to leave the results to God Who will give me my just rewards when the time is right.

Father, I believe You when You say that "All things are possible to him who believes" (Mark 9:23, NKJV). With Your help, I will keep trying impossible things. —DANIEL SCHANTZ

20/ SUN *On the Sabbath day he went into the synagogue, as was his custom. . . .* —LUKE 4:16 (NIV)

I had been trying to listen more closely to God, but as I entered church on Sunday, I thought, *Nothing dramatic has come to me this week. Everything's the same old routine.* I followed my husband Gordon and our nine-year-old John into the sanctuary and scooted down the pew to save two seats—one for my teenage son Chris and one for his girlfriend. In a few moments they arrived, and the service began.

The oddest thing happened, though, when I opened my eyes after the morning prayer. I saw our family sitting in the pew together as if I were seeing them for the first time. A startling thought came to me: *Chris brings his girlfriend to church. She didn't attend regularly anywhere until he invited her, and now she comes.* Then another startling thought came: *The same thing happened with Jeff, who's off at college. His girlfriend began attending church with our family and became quite active in the youth group.*

In that moment of clarity, I saw that I had underestimated the importance of a good, ordinary routine. We had made it a simple habit to go to church each Sunday. We expected our boys to continue coming with us during their teenage years and on any Sunday when they were home from college. It was low-key, simple and unremarkable, yet God had done something quite remarkable with it. Every time our hands opened the church door, it made it easier for someone else to come in and join us.

I settled back, knowing that I had been hearing from God more often than I had imagined, for every Sunday our family had answered His invitation, "Let us go to the house of the Lord" (Psalm 122:1, NIV).

Lord, help me to get into such a good, deep rut of Sunday worship that others can't help but follow the well-worn path.

—KAREN BARBER

21/ MON *A word spoken in due season, how good is it!* —PROVERBS 15:23

"Hi, Pam. This is Randy Raider," the voice at the other end of the phone said. "I was just sitting here in my office and all at once it occurred to me that I've never thanked you for being such a good neighbor."

I had to stop and catch my breath before I answered. All morning I had been plagued with unpleasantness. My daughter Keri had called from college to warn me of the huge tab she had just run up in the bookstore. My husband David had put a big pile of papers on my desk and requested that I edit them for him by noon. All this had made me feel stretched, pressured and dull. "Well, that's nice of you to say," I answered Randy, "but I'm afraid I haven't done anything that great."

"Oh, but you have, and that's why I'm calling. Our children are always coming in and saying 'Miss Pam said' this or 'Miss Pam told me' that. You just make Karley and Jase feel so special with all the attention you give them. To tell the truth, not that many adults even bother to talk to them. I just wanted to say thanks, while it was on my mind."

I hung up the phone and sat at my desk for a long moment. My heart had lightened. I knew I could handle the tasks before me in a flash. Funny how a few kind words can change the trajectory of an entire day.

I reached for the pile of papers, then paused. Then, I picked up the phone and dialed. "Janie, this is Pam. I was just sitting at my desk when it occurred to me that I've never told you how much your good work on David's behalf means to me. You are one of the best secretaries that I've ever. . . ."

Father, thank You for showing me the power of thankfulness.

—PAM KIDD

22 / TUE *O my Strength, I watch for you; you, O God, are my fortress, my loving God.* —PSALM 59:9-10 (NIV)

Most of the time I'm the one who puts three-year-old John and five-year-old Elizabeth to bed. After prayers, I brush their teeth, give them a drink of water, tell them stories and tuck them in. Actually, I tuck Elizabeth in. Then I pick up John and take him to the blue chair. We bought the blue chair for my dad when he lived with us. It's an overstuffed velour-covered recliner that now sits in our bedroom next to the window.

Cradling John in my arms, I sit down in the chair. In the light from the hallway, I watch him, eyes closing and breathing slowing, as he settles down. *He's such a big boy now,* I think, *such a guy.* In my mind's eye I can see him at sixteen months, lying on a hospital gurney as an anesthesiologist gets him ready for surgery. I close my eyes and pray: *Thank You for bringing him through the surgery, Lord. Keep him well, help him grow up strong.*

I open my eyes and look at my son. In repose, his face is sweet, innocent. A couple of hours ago, though, there was mischief in it as he teased his little sister. I put my head back and close my eyes again. *Keep his soul as healthy as his body, Lord. Don't let his mischief turn to meanness.*

Carefully, slowly, I get up, lifting my sleeping son. I carry him to his room, put him gently in his bed and give him a good-night kiss.

I know I could easily get John to go to sleep by himself. But for as long as he lets me, I'll be happy to sit in the blue chair and hold my son in my arms.

Lord, thank You for the children who teach me to know the power of Your love.
— ANDREW ATTAWAY

23 / WED   *Their strength is to sit still.*   — ISAIAH 30:7

For days I'd suffered with what I call "a rushing spirit." No matter how fast I thought or hurried, a nasty inner voice insisted, *You're still behind.*

My list of things to do that spring Wednesday included going to our church at ten-thirty in the morning for one hour of solitary prayer. I entered the small, simple room in our church wishing I felt spiritual—like a real prayer warrior. I sat down in a metal folding chair and leaned hard against the heavy wooden table. "You know my heart and mind are rushed," I told God. "I don't even know how to slow down and try to hear You, but I desperately need to." I didn't really believe God would honor such a half-hearted prayer, but then thoughts began to glide into my troubled mind.

Remember the woman sitting alone on the bench outside the grocery store yesterday? You slowed down because she was reading from a small New Testament. You saw her defeated face, and I even allowed you to peek into her lonely heart. You understood that she was hurting. You almost stopped, but then you hurried on with your groceries to the car. I had placed her there just for you.

"Oh, Lord, Lord! Forgive me. Yes, of course I remember. I saw her all the way home in my mind. I still see her! It wouldn't have taken long. I . . . I..."

She was My plan to help you slow down and learn to be still, child. I often reach you through unlikely people. Just sit here for a bit now while I comfort you.

My Comforter, when my life is speeding up, make me attentive to the means You give me to slow it down. Amen.

—MARION BOND WEST

24 / **THU** *For now we see through a glass, darkly; but then face to face. . . .* —I CORINTHIANS 13:12

Several years ago my husband Paul's Aunt Jeanne told us a lovely story about her father, Paul's grandfather, that I've always remembered. Aunt Jeanne had spent a lot of time with Grandpa in the last year of his life, especially after Grandma died. They read the Bible together, and, as Aunt Jeanne told us, he talked about how much he wanted to see Grandma again.

"I reminded him he was going to see Jesus, too," she told us, "and he looked at me in a puzzled way.

" 'You mean I'm going to see the dear Jesus Who died on the Cross for me?' he asked." Then Aunt Jeanne showed him one of several places in Scripture where Jesus makes that promise. " 'Oh, yes,' he said, smiling like a child who's made a wonderful discovery, 'I want to see Jesus' face and be with Him forever.'

"Grandpa had thought about heaven," Aunt Jeanne explained, "but he'd never really contemplated the most beautiful part of the promise—that one day he'd see Jesus face to face."

That's the miracle of the Ascension, God's gift to the disciples who actually saw Jesus rise up to heaven in a glorious cloud and His gift to us today. There can be no mistake: Jesus not only defeated death but sits beside God the Father in heaven. And His sacrifice makes it possible for us to enjoy life forever, not just with those we love, but also with Him.

On this Ascension Day, Lord, I rejoice in the opportunity You have given me to be with You forever.

—GINA BRIDGEMAN

25 / FRI
Every man shall give as he is able, according to the blessing of the Lord the God which he hath given thee.
—DEUTERONOMY 16:17

I graduated from college in May 1941. Earlier that month, I had mailed invitations, knowing that most of my family and friends in Massachusetts would not be able to come to Virginia to attend. On May 25, a letter arrived from Ed and Florence, cousins living in the greater Boston area. They were thirty years older than I, and I had seen them only once. Ed was a red cap at Boston's North Station, where his tips for the day were sometimes less than a dollar. Florence did housecleaning for well-to-do families. They were hard-working, and they were struggling to survive.

I opened their letter, and out tumbled a crisp five-dollar bill I knew they could ill afford to give. Then I read their words: "If your invitation had come sooner, Ed would have gotten passes, and we would have attended your graduation. We are so proud of you! You graduate May 27, and the next day is your birthday. This is your time, your day."

As the years go by, Ed and Florence's thoughtfulness looms larger and larger in my memory. Their kindness to a young man about to take his first steps in the world taught me that no matter how little I have, it's always enough to share. And whatever I give will be received with gratitude, as long as it's given from the heart.

Loving Father, I can't thank You enough for all You have given me. Help me to share it lovingly, according to Your will.

—OSCAR GREENE

26 / SAT
And God saw every thing that he had made, and, behold, it was very good. . . .
—GENESIS 1:31

I had an overgrown shrub bed and got some help from a very knowledgeable man named Bob Chandler. As he was finishing up, he pointed to the telephone lines that run along the east edge of my property, adjoining a county bird sanctuary. "You've got bluebirds!" he said. I looked up and saw mourning doves, pigeons and two small chubby birds I didn't recognize. At that moment, the two little ones took off and I saw how they got their name. In flight their color is a brilliant, deep blue.

Bluebirds have returned to many areas, but Bob explained that development had made bluebirds rare in our neighborhood because they can't find places to build their nests. So he and several other neighbors were setting up bluebird houses on their property—little boxlike wooden houses on tall poles set in the ground. "They like to nest near the fields," Bob said. "That's where they get their food."

The next day Bob surprised me with a bluebird house and a long pole, which he set up along my driveway, looking out on the fields. One morning when I took my dogs out, I saw a bluebird sitting on top of the house, looking as if it owned it.

A few times I saw a bluebird with a twig in its beak entering the small hole in the front, and I assumed it was building a nest. Then one morning as I was passing by, I heard the sound of chirping inside the house. Little ones! And a few days later I looked up at the telephone wire and saw not one, not two, but four bluebirds. I was so excited that I called Bob to tell him the good news.

"That's great!" he said. "You see, all they needed was a little help."

He's right. So many of God's creatures are having a hard time these days because they have to fit in with our way of life. But the story doesn't have to have a sad ending. As Bob says, all they need is a little help.

Thank You, Jesus, for the gift of Your many wonderful creatures. Surely, we can share our space with them. Amen. —PHYLLIS HOBE

27 / SUN *Let brotherly love continue.* —HEBREWS 13:1

Our house is slowly becoming a library. I collect books faster than I can read them, and I never want to part with my "old friends." But this week I decided to select some books to give away.

As I gazed at my shelves, I saw an old Bible concordance. The book had been my father's, and I inherited it when Dad died thirty-four years ago. I have used it often to look up Bible verses I vaguely remembered but couldn't quite put my finger on. The cover of the old concordance is threadbare, and it has a broken spine. Computer software has now taken its place.

I took the book from its shelf to put in my give-away box and opened it one last time. On the flyleaf I saw something I had never noticed before: *Marvin Shipp* was scrawled there in large letters.

Marvin Shipp had been my father's college roommate. Below the name, an old letter was wedged into the binding. Marvin had written it to my father on January 1, 1942, when Marvin was a young army private being shipped off to combat in Europe. He wrote:

> Al, I sure hope they don't drag you into this war. And, while I'm on the subject, things being what they are and all, if something should happen to me, then, of course, I want you to have my books and the rest of the stuff I left with you. It's kind of a grim thought, but we might as well face it.

Marvin Shipp was killed three years later in the Battle of the Bulge. It broke my father's heart. Now I realized why Dad had never thrown away this old book. And I knew that it would have a home with me forever.

I dusted off the old concordance and placed it in a more prominent place on my shelf. Then I stopped and gave thanks for a memory almost forgotten, a treasure nearly thrown away.

Dear God, thank You for friendships that are eternal and continue to enrich us throughout the generations. Amen. —SCOTT WALKER

28 / MON
But let all who take refuge in you be glad; let them ever sing for joy. . . . —PSALM 5:11 (NIV)

Finally. I'd cleaned up the breakfast dishes, a load of laundry was in the washing machine, a batch of granola was baking in the oven. I closed the door of my upstairs study and settled in to do some writing. A few minutes later I dashed down the stairs again for a needed book. An hour passed, and I took a break to hang the laundry out on this blue-sky day.

Back at my desk again, I glanced up and noticed that the calendar page was still on January. *Has it really been that long since I've spent any time up here?*

The first four months of this year were full. After surgery and radiation treatments for melanoma, the work of recovery seemed to require all of every day. Sitz baths, taking naps, adult diapers, remembering which pills to take when, learning to eat lying down—it was an exhausting and often humiliating journey. Every trip off the sofa was an exercise in agony at first, and getting back into a prone position without sitting on my surgical wounds or radiation burns was a special feat.

Those months are a blur of painful, slow-motion memories. Now I can plop myself into any chair without careful calculations or fluffing of pillows. Yesterday we went for a three-hour hike in the mountains, and some days I spend hours working in the garden.

I am thankful beyond words to the God Who brings healing. I'm grateful for the gift of each new day and the energy to enjoy it. And I have a whole new appreciation for those whose lives are bounded by physical limitations, or who struggle with health problems. Never again will I underestimate what it requires of some people just to live through each day.

Keep me from becoming presumptuous, Lord of my life. May my appreciation for Your gifts be renewed every time I climb the stairs or take a walk. —MARY JANE CLARK

29 / *TUE* *He lifted up his hands, and blessed them. And it came to pass, while he blessed them, he was parted from them. . . .* —LUKE 24:50–51

Every morning when Uncle Jack backed out of the driveway to go to work, Aunt Nellie would bustle to the window and wave to him through the lace curtains. I was a teenager at the time, but I just knew there was something special about their little ritual that I wanted to copy some day.

The first few months after Leo and I got married, I waved to him through the cupola window of a big old house in the inner city. Then it was through the hoar-frosted panes of a tiny bungalow in the suburbs. Eventually we exchanged waves through the front picture window of our very own home, I with a baby in my arms and the toddlers jostling for a place at my side.

When our oldest son Lyle bravely strode off down the street on his first day of school, we waved to each other, and on all the schooldays of the twelve years that followed. It was the same with each of the other three children. They expectantly waited until I got to the window for our little ritual before bounding off down the road with their friends. And when our youngest son Glen, on his very last day of school, backed out of the driveway in our '76 Nova, he smiled and waved. I cried. It was the end of an era.

But tradition dies hard. Leo and I still wave to each other when one of us drives away. And we always stand together at the dining-room window to bid farewell to departing family and friends. It has become a kind of unspoken blessing.

These days, when Leo and I go for an early morning walk around the neighborhood, we even find ourselves waving to people as they drive off to work. It's our way of wishing them "Godspeed."

You know something? Even total strangers wave back. And somehow they no longer seem like strangers.

Lord, when people are leaving, they want to feel they still belong to someone, to a family, to a neighborhood, to You. Remind me to "lift up my hands, and bless them."
— ALMA BARKMAN

30/ WED
Yea, they may forget, yet will I not forget thee.
—ISAIAH 49:15

The lilacs were especially abundant that year, so I encouraged my eleven-year-old daughter Trina and her friend Rachel to clip extras. Now we would make our Memorial Day journey to decorate the graves of several friends. Since I had grown up in New Hampshire but relocated to Wyoming twenty years ago, I had no relatives to honor here; however, I wanted my children to understand the eloquent ritual of remembering and blessing loved ones with spring flowers.

The ride to Mount Hope Cemetery took only a few minutes. Many others were there ahead of us. They spoke in hushed voices as they arranged a vase or spray, straightened a flag, or simply stood shoulder to shoulder gazing at a headstone. We delivered jars of dewy lilacs to the resting places of those we had known for all too short a time: Mick, the sheep shearer; Roy the chicken rancher; Loraine and Emmett, godparents of my son Tom.

When we had finished, I walked back toward the van reminiscing, while Trina and her friend lagged behind carrying the leftover lilacs.

"Gee, this one says 'BORN OCTOBER 31, 1903, DIED MARCH 29, 1904.'" Trina squinted, calculating. "She was only a baby! Look, Mom." I retraced my steps to the bleached stone, topped with a lamb.

"And nobody even brought her any flowers," said Rachel disconsolately.

"Well, let's give her some!" said Trina.

"Are there any more babies?" Rachel wondered. Both girls scanned the flowerless plaques, some bearing sentiments like "Budded on earth to bloom in heaven" or "God needs angels, too." The girls continued to put flowers on the babies' graves until the lilacs were gone.

I shouldn't have worried about carrying on the tradition far from home. Our Memorial Day recollection is in compassionate hands.

Dear God, thank You for the gift of children who reflect Your compassion.
—GAIL THORELL SCHILLING

31/THU *He led them by a straight way, till they reached a city to dwell in.*
—PSALM 107:7 (RSV)

New neighbors moved in this week. Very nice people, recently transplanted from Connecticut. I'm glad the house next door is once again full, but new-neighbors-not-from-Pittsburgh require a different approach. This city requires explanation. Pittsburgh is a surprisingly mystical place, except to natives. It's like family. We've grown up with these folks, so we're inured to their eccentricities. Thanksgiving visitors are enchanted by Uncle Fred's stories of the steel mills, until he retells the graphic tale about how some guy's watch once melted into his wrist—and kept on ticking. Thanks, Uncle Fred. Can you pass the gravy?

Pittsburgh's peculiarities put wrinkles in all trajectories. Cross an intersection and Seventh Avenue changes into Ninth Street. Fifth and Sixth avenues run parallel—until they meet. Street names mutate. To get from the north side to Emsworth, just follow one road: California Avenue–Lincoln Avenue–Church Avenue–Center Avenue. What do you mean you got lost?

And if you do get lost, asking for directions is asking for trouble. Ask how to get on the parkway, and the answer will be simple: "Go down to where the J&L Steel Mill used to be, right across from the old Lasek's." Roger, bub. Thanks for the help.

Truth is, I won't tell my new neighbors any of this. They seem on the ball, able to figure it out. But maybe I'll tell them stories of other neighbors, neighbors I sometimes knew only for a few minutes. The fan at the Pirates game who tracked me down when I lost my wallet. The cars that pulled over when I've had a flat. The people who helped out when a storm took down my maple tree. Our grandparents taught us to work hard, to brush the mill soot off our shirts and put our shoulders to the wheel. And come the weekend, stop over, 'cause the Steelers are on and we've got cable.

Lord, thank You for my city, for neighbors, new and old, and the life we have together. And keep me mindful of Your city, not made with hands, eternal in the heavens. —MARK COLLINS

DAILY GIFTS

1 _____

2 _____

3 _____

4 _____

5 _____

6 _____

7 _____

8 _____

9 _____

10 _____

11 _____

12 _____

13 _____

14 _____

15 _____

16 _____

17 _____

18 _____

19 _____

20 _____

21 _____

22 _____

23 _____

24 _____

25 _____

26 _____

27 _____

28 _____

29 _____

30 _____

31 _____

June

Go ye into all the world, and preach the gospel to every creature.

—MARK 16:15

S	M	T	W	T	F	S
					1	2
3	4	5	6	7	8	9
10	11	12	13	14	15	16
17	18	19	20	21	22	23
24	25	26	27	28	29	30

WHEN GOD REACHES OUT . . . THROUGH OTHER PEOPLE

1/*FRI*

"She out of her poverty has put in everything she had. . . .   —MARK 12:44 (RSV)

It was one of those spells when trouble comes in batches. My husband had been hospitalized for ten days with diverticulitis so painful I'd scarcely left his side. I was scheduled for major surgery myself later in the month, and our work projects were on hold. And, of course, this was the moment both the oil burner and the refrigerator picked to break down.

I had no patience for outside demands just then. I had enough problems of my own, I told myself, without taking on other people's. Until, that is, our friend Evelyn Flynn phoned with the news of her son Bob's sudden death. Suddenly my own concerns seemed inconsequential. For Evelyn, in frail health herself, living in a retirement home in Virginia on a tiny income, this was only the latest in a lifetime of recurring tragedy. Thinking to brighten a corner of her room, I sent her a miniature rose bush in a little ceramic pot.

Her thank-you arrived a week later. "I'm so grateful for the gift! It's given me a lovely little rose to share with every one of my shut-in neighbors."

The thanks were from Evelyn, but the message to my self-pity was from God: *When you're feeling poorest, that's the time to give the most.*

Lord, use the difficulties in my life this month to stretch my heart a little wider.   —ELIZABETH SHERRILL

2/ SAT   *I bow my knees unto the Father of our Lord Jesus Christ, Of whom the whole family in heaven and earth is named. . . .*   —EPHESIANS 3:14–15

Though Jessica, our granddaughter, started tennis late, she has improved dramatically, and last year I got to see her compete as a high school junior. For the most part, Shirley and I were bystanders, cheering good shots and looking elsewhere when shots went awry. That is, until an incident late in the season.

Jessica was doing well, leading in the first set of a match with a fairly good opponent, when she turned her ankle while running down a cross-court volley. Though she didn't fall, she gingerly limped to the sidelines where her coach examined her injury. I watched from a distance as the two discussed what should happen next. Jessica obviously wanted to continue, and she did, though not at full strength. Gradually, her rival took the lead and eventually won the match.

Afterward we wandered over to where she sat in the grass with a couple of teammates. She was massaging her swollen ankle, but I could tell by her eyes that the real hurt was losing the match. Putting my arm around her neck, I leaned down and whispered that I was proud of her courage. I felt a couple of sobs under my arm, so I turned my attention to her ankle. "A little ice tonight and you'll be ready for your next match," I predicted, and she was.

But the incident reminded me of how powerless I sometimes felt as a parent. And that feeling revisited me with my granddaughter. What we want to do is make everything all right for our children and our children's children. We want to shoulder their pain, pave over the rough spots, and kiss away all the "boo boos" and "ouches" of life. But, of course, we can't. The best we can do is show our kids we care, and point them to a heavenly Father Who is always there—even when parents and grandparents can't be. That's an important truth to impart to those we love.

> *When I go off half-cocked, Lord,*
> *And overplay my role,*
> *Remind me once again Who's in control.*

—FRED BAUER

3/ *SUN*   *And they were all filled with the Holy Spirit. . . .*
                                              —ACTS 2:4 (RSV)

It's Pentecost Sunday. Our Sunday-school children, from first through sixth grade, are having a birthday party for the church. There are red streamers, balloons, tablecloths and, of course, a cake with as many candles as we can get on it. We sing "Happy birthday, Christian church." The children pull names out of a hat to see who gets to blow out the candles. There is great excitement, much laughter and noise. Meanwhile, standing in the back of the room, I'm trying to relax and enjoy the party I've worked so hard to put together. But I can't. I was up until the wee hours of the morning getting everything ready, and now I'm worn out and cranky.

One of the teachers holds up her hands for quiet. When the room is still, she begins the story: "A long time ago, in the upper room, one hundred and twenty people waited and prayed for more than a week. Finally, it happened. A mighty rushing wind swept through the whole place, and what looked like tongues of fire sat on each one of them. They began to speak in different languages. It was the Holy Spirit, Who had come to fill them with a power that would change their lives."

As I listen to this familiar story, my heart is pierced; I've spent so much time working and so little waiting and praying as the disciples did so long ago. No wonder I'm burnt out and anxious. Closing my eyes, I pray:

Lord, my body is tired and my heart is empty. Fill me with Your Spirit, and make me new.   —SHARI SMYTH

4/ *MON*   *And that these days should be remembered and kept throughout every generation, every family. . . .*
                                              —ESTHER 9:28

Next Saturday my husband Bob and I will attend the graduation of our granddaughter Christy as she receives her MBA degree.

We've shared all of Christy's and her brother Bob's school years. On the first morning of each term, we've telephoned them, wishing them happiness and success. One morning when Bob was nine years old, the time drew near for them to leave their house and start for school. Glancing at his watch, Bob said dejectedly, "Our grandparents didn't call this morning." At that moment, the telephone rang, and he sprang to his feet shouting, "Yes, they did!"

We've been with them at every graduation, even kindergarten. Now, as we learn the details of the arrangements Christy has made for us this time, my heart overflows with love and gratitude. She has borrowed a friend's sport utility vehicle so that my husband Bob, who is handicapped, can ride comfortably from our home in Sheffield, Alabama, to hers in Huntsville. She has provided a wheelchair to assure him good seating during the program. And since we will be staying overnight with Christy and her family, she has outfitted a bed with the special equipment he will need.

What a joyful time we're expecting when we celebrate together!

Dear Father, thank You for the landmarks of life that bind the generations together. Amen. —DRUE DUKE

5/TUE *Let the brother of low degree rejoice in that he is exalted.* —JAMES 1:9

This is how the furor began.

In the morning I'd talked on the telephone with my friend John and told him I had a dental appointment at 11:30 and would come to his house for lunch about 12:30. What was not specified was the day that this was to take place. John assumed it was to be that same day; I thought we were on for the following day. I went off to the ball game with my old friend Harold, who'd come down from Connecticut.

Twelve-thirty came and went. John waited. And waited. He telephoned my apartment; no answer. He wanted to call my dentist to see if I had kept the appointment, but he didn't know the dentist's name. He tried several other people, who didn't know either but were disturbed that I hadn't appeared. Could Van have had an accident, a possible recurrence of his stroke?

John called the superintendent of my building, who went up and let himself into my apartment with a passkey; only the dog was there. Now deeply distressed, John called Harold, with no success. Then he tried my two godchildren, who were in different parts of the country; then friends in Baltimore and New Mexico who might know the name of the dentist; and finally Guideposts, where I had worked for so long. They were quick to respond with an all-points alert. Brigitte and Elizabeth called hospitals, Edward the police station. Everyone was involved. Everyone had desperate thoughts. Celeste eventually went up to my apartment with the key I'd given her when she stayed with my dog Shep.

Six o'clock. Harold dropped me off, and I blithely approached the doorman, who greeted me effusively while saying that Celeste upstairs would explain. And she did, after the warmest hug I have ever received.

The rest of the night was spent on the phone apologizing, but the thing that moved me then, and moves me now, was the heartfelt surge of relief that everyone expressed. There was no mistaking it, I was loved.

Father, help me never to forget those I frightened. I love them.

—VAN VARNER

6/ WED   *O satisfy us early with thy mercy; that we may rejoice and be glad all our days.*   —PSALM 90:14

The look of sheer joy on Mary's face said it all. It was as if no one in the history of the world had ever learned to walk before. Eyes glowing, arms held out for balance, she laughed and gurgled and staggered toward me, in love with life and her newfound ability.

Ah, that look! If I had a dozen babies, I'd still find each one's face in that first week of walking a miracle. Without a word, that look rejoices, *I can do it!* With ecstatic amazement, it proclaims, *I am wonderful!* Above all, it shouts, *God is so awesome and the world is good!* It is not a look you see on the face of most fourteen-year-olds. Or fifty-year-olds. Or me, for that matter.

Why not? It could—it should—be there.

Lord, today let me fling out my arms and run, giddy with joy, into Your loving embrace.   —JULIA ATTAWAY

7/ THU   *You received the Spirit of sonship. And by him we cry, "Abba, Father."*   —ROMANS 8:15 (NIV)

We first met Ravit and her parents Bennie and Erella at my daughter's nursery school, where Ravit and our daughter Jessie quickly became best friends. Just arrived from Israel, they were looking for a place to live while Bennie did some postgraduate work at the university. The duplex across the street from us was available, so we helped them find furniture and settle in there.

Our families quickly became intertwined, sharing everything from child care to a washing machine, and hand-me-down clothes went both ways. They visited our church one Sunday morning, and we went to their synagogue for a Bar Mitzvah. They came for Christmas dinners and Easter picnics, and sometimes we all squeezed into their tiny kitchen for a *Shabbat* meal. When one of us was sick, Erella's wonderful chicken soup appeared on the scene.

Late one afternoon, I went over to Erella's to borrow a cup of sugar. Erella and I visited as she fixed supper, and the girls played in the living room with Ravit's baby sister Hila. Suddenly, Hila sped across the carpet on hands and knees toward the screen door. She had seen her daddy through the window, walking home from work. Pulling herself up, she began pounding on the door, calling out excitedly, "Abba! Abba! Abba!" A moment later Bennie came through the door with a wide smile and scooped her up in his arms.

I immediately thought of Paul's reminder that we are God's children, that He is our Abba. We can run to Him with that same eagerness, with the confidence of a well-loved child. And He takes us in His arms, loving and accepting us just as we are.

Abba Father, may I come to You with eagerness and excitement, and with the childlike assurance that I am welcomed and loved.

—MARY JANE CLARK

INTO AFRICA

8/FRI *How hard is it for them that trust in riches to enter into the kingdom of God!* —MARK 10:24

After being in Africa about two weeks and visiting several countries, I began to be overwhelmed by what I viewed as the abject poverty of most people. In cities, towns and villages, whole families lived without any of what we consider the necessities of life. Poorest of all, to me, were the Masai people we met while visiting the Serengeti Plain. Families of a dozen or so people could be found moving from place to place with all they owned on the back of a donkey or a couple of cows.

One day we met a group of Masai men who had traveled for days dressed only in bright red blankets. Draped across one shoulder, each blanket was knotted at the waist with a piece of rope from which hung a gourd for water. In their hands each of them carried a walking stick and a spear. As we talked, I noticed one of the men pointing repeatedly to me and staring with great interest. Our interpreter said he wanted to know what was in my backpack. So I proudly lowered it to the ground and began to display all the items so compactly crammed into the pouches and pockets: Neatly rolled clothes, toiletries, a miniature flashlight, two books, shoes, emergency rations of raisins and nuts, assorted medicines, and even a sport coat and tie emerged. Proud that I had gotten so much into such a small space, I looked up to see the wonder on the face of the Masai man.

He began an animated conversation with our interpreter, which caused a smile and then laughter to erupt among the group. Finally, the interpreter turned to me and said, "I think this question is some sort of Masai humor, but he wants to know what great evil you have done to be required to carry such a heavy burden on your back!"

As I knelt to reassemble my gear, I wondered if it really was a joke. How much of the stuff I think is essential really is? That's a question well worth pondering the next time I'm hunting for boxes to take things to the attic or looking through the paper for storage space to rent.

Lord, help me remember that my life is in You and not in my things.
—ERIC FELLMAN

9/*SAT*   *Love bears all things. . . .*
—I CORINTHIANS 13:7 (RSV)

My husband Lynn and I celebrated our thirty-third wedding anniversary over a long weekend in a little mountain town in the Colorado Rockies. On Saturday afternoon, we wandered into a gift store. In a jewelry case along one wall were some silver-and-gold rings. For years, I'd been wanting such a ring to wear on my right hand.

"Try one on," Lynn urged. An hour later, we walked out of the store, with a bright and shiny silver-and-gold ring on my finger. "It's perfect!" I gushed to Lynn. "Thank you!"

It wasn't until we were driving down the mountain toward home the next day that I spotted a tiny flaw in the ring, a pin-prick-sized hole in the gold on the front side. "Oh, no," I moaned, showing Lynn the flaw.

"I can hardly see it," he assured me. But all the way down the mountain, I stared at that flaw, and it seemed to grow bigger and bigger before my eyes. "I wonder if it was there yesterday and I just didn't notice it in my excitement?" I said.

For the next several days, I struggled with the imperfection in my ring. When I looked at it, all I saw was that tiny hole.

"We'll just take it back," Lynn finally told me, exasperated with my monomania.

His words made me realize that I had a choice: I could fixate on the flaw or focus on the ring's overall beauty. And with its tiny flaw, the ring was the perfect gift to celebrate the longevity of our marriage and remind me of a choice I face every day.

Lord, in marriage, and in all relationships, help me overlook the flaws and focus on the good. —CAROL KUYKENDALL

10/*SUN* *The one thing I want from God, the thing I seek most of all, is the privilege of meditating in his Temple, living in his presence every day of my life. . . .*
—PSALMS 27:4 (TLB)

In 1999 my brother Joe and sister-in-law Linda invited me to join them on their trip to Japan. One day, after visiting a breathtakingly beautiful temple and seeing some of Japan's amazing parks and gardens, we stopped for a sit-on-the-floor lunch at a small restaurant nestled among the shops on a winding, busy street in the small town of Narita.

As we finished our meal, we heard drums pounding and music playing in the street. We looked up to see rows and rows of women dancing in perfect unison, all wearing festive black and white kimonos with different colored sashes.

We quickly paid our bill and stepped out onto the street to catch what we figured would be the tail-end of a short parade. But instead, the happy procession continued. Row after row of women of all ages, arms and legs moving in unison to the music, danced past us. The magnificent parade went on for at least thirty minutes.

"Where are they going?" I asked a shopkeeper.

"They're going to the temple. Once a year all the women in the town process to the temple in this way."

As I watched the women, joy on their faces and a bounce to their perfectly choreographed steps, I started to feel a little guilty. *I've never ever felt that happy on my way to church back in Wisconsin.*

When the parade of women was over, we walked through the market shops where Linda and I each purchased a lovely cotton kimono. Now, whenever I see it hanging in my closet or slip it on over my shoulders, I try to pursue everything I do that day with a little more energy, a little more excitement and a little more joy. Just like the thousand dancing women of Narita, Japan, on their way to the temple.

Lord, help me to be joyful as I make my way to Your house each Sunday and to keep the joy I find there in my heart all week.

—PATRICIA LORENZ

11/_{MON}

To every thing there is a season, and a time to every purpose under the heaven. . . . A time to weep, and a time to laugh; a time to mourn, and a time to dance.
—ECCLESIASTES 3:1, 4

My wife Beth and I were rushing to catch a plane to the Philippine Islands where I would be delivering a series of lectures. As I drove madly toward the airport, a torrential rain beat down on the windshield, and I prayed that traffic would not become congested.

Careening into the airport parking lot, I parked in the first available space. Grabbing our luggage, we sprinted to the ticket counter and then on to the gate. If we had arrived two minutes later, we would have missed our flight.

Five weeks later we returned. As we walked through the long-term parking area, I could not find my car. Looking intently at my parking ticket stub, I discovered my mistake: In my haste to make the flight, I had missed the long-term parking exit and had instead parked in the short-term lot. The short-term parking fee was seven dollars a day; my blunder had cost me two hundred and fifty-two dollars! I was fit to be tied.

As I drove slowly home, I fumed in silence, like a smoking volcano ready to explode. Suddenly, Beth started giggling and then burst into laughter. And before I knew it, I was laughing, too. Our sense of humor had caught up with our ridiculous plight. I could hear the voice of my mother repeating her favorite maxim: "Well, you can laugh or you can cry!"

Sometimes I have a choice as to whether my own mistakes will spoil a wonderful occasion and erase a happy memory. At that point, I really do have to count the cost. The memory of five wonderful weeks with Beth was worth far more than an expensive taste of humility. And laughter is better than anger any day.

Lord, You changed water into wine. Transform my anger into peals of laughter. Amen. —SCOTT WALKER

12/ *TUE* *Not unto us, O Lord, not unto us, but unto thy name give glory. . . .* —PSALM 115:1

I have a secret admirer. Well, it's not quite like the time in eighth grade when I received an anonymous Valentine with only a typed *?* for a signature. This nameless person sends me Bible verses or thoughtful quotes carefully typed on postcards. I'm guessing he or she is a *Daily Guideposts* reader, because that's just the kind of encouragement readers often send. But instead of a signed letter, these are short, simple spirit-boosters. "Life is ten percent what you make it and ninety percent how you take it." Or the one I've taped to the door of my laundry room where our dog Cookie sleeps: "One reason a dog is such a lovable creature is that his tail wags instead of his tongue."

I've often thought how unusual it is that someone whose name I don't even know can so frequently make me smile. But even I didn't realize the power of these messages until the day I received a disappointing letter telling me I would not be included in a book project I was hoping to work on. I was crushed, barely thinking as I flipped through the rest of the mail. Then I stopped at the familiar-looking postcard with this message: "God never closes one door without opening another." That old line had never held such power for me, healing my hurt with the balm of hope. Now the rejection didn't feel so bad.

I began to wonder why my anonymous friend wants no credit for these small kindnesses that have meant so much. Then it occurred to me—because the credit belongs to God. As God is the Source of all good things, everything we do, whether or not it has a name on it, is His. No act is truly anonymous. I may never know *who* sends me those day-brightening little cards. But I know *where* they come from: from the Spirit of God from Whom all good things flow.

God, let Your Spirit inspire me to help others, in simple ways, along the path.
—GINA BRIDGEMAN

13 / WED
Deliver me from mine enemies, O my God: defend me from them that rise up against me. —PSALM 59:1

There are verses of the Bible that I would rather skip, whole passages that I would like to believe simply don't apply to me and my modern-day circumstances. "These words probably meant something to believers hundreds of years ago," I tell myself, "but for me, they don't count." The verses I stumble over are the ones that ask for God's vengeance, like this from the Fifty-ninth Psalm: "Consume them in wrath, consume them that they may not be."

"I don't have any enemies," I said to a friend. "Or at least not enemies on whom I would wish such harm." I like to consider myself a mild-mannered, easygoing person.

"Okay," my friend said, "maybe you don't know any people you'd wish vengeance upon, but what about spiritual enemies? Do you have any of them?"

"Sure," I said. "Things like sloth, envy, anger, pride. They drive me nuts."

"Spoken honestly," he said. "Then look at the Psalms as your chance to ask God to wreak havoc on them. The language is strong because that's just how we should speak to our enemies. Especially spiritual ones."

So I went back to the Fifty-ninth Psalm and looked back at passages like, "Let them make a noise like a dog and go round about the city. Let them wander up and down for meat, and grudge if they be not satisfied." How about that for sloth? Why not that for pride?

Strong words for some terrible foes—and just what they deserve. The Psalmist knew exactly what he was doing. Some things we shouldn't be mild-mannered about.

Consume my spiritual enemies, Lord, that they may not be.

—RICK HAMLIN

PRAYER FOR JUNE

Father, a bright red ladybug just landed on my hand. I wonder, as I stare at the perfectly symmetrical pattern of black spots on this tiny body, how You, Who created the stars in the immense universe, cared enough to create the intricacies of this little ladybug. How awesome of You, God. Thank You.

—CAROL KUYKENDALL

14/_{THU} *Blessed is the nation whose God is the Lord; and the people whom he hath chosen for his own inheritance.*

—PSALM 33:12

Bring out the flags! On this day two hundred and twenty-four years ago, our Congress adopted the Stars and Stripes as the national emblem of the United States. My heart still thrills when I visit a school and stand with the students to face the flag and say the Pledge of Allegiance, which ends with the words, "one nation under God, indivisible, with liberty and justice for all."

It's interesting that the words *under God* were not added until 1954, sixty-two years after the original pledge was written. President Eisenhower said that the addition of those words represented "the transcendence of religious faith in America's heritage and future."

So today I think about America's future and the meaning of patriotic emblems and pledges, and particularly about what liberty means to me:

1. The liberty to worship as I choose.
2. The liberty to vote for the candidates of my choice.
3. The liberty to attend school and study different subjects.
4. The liberty to travel freely from state to state.
5. The liberty to assume responsibility as a citizen for the protection and preservation of all our freedoms, including freedom of speech and justice for all.

On this Flag Day, why not take a moment to list some of the things liberty means to you?

Almighty God, You stand above all nations. Today I pledge my foremost allegiance to You.
—MADGE HARRAH

A WHOLE AND HOLY LOVE

15/*FRI*   *"If I do not wash you, you have no part in me."*
—JOHN 13:8 (RSV)

We have been told that it is more blessed to give than to receive. What we have not been told is that it is also safer.

When Marilyn and I began to make a life together, we discovered we had many wonderful things in common. We like to take walks together in the evening, listen to the sound of a mountain stream, read aloud to each other and sometimes just sit in silence together. We also like doing things *for* each other. I like to do the dishes after Marilyn has prepared a meal; she likes to reassure me whenever I express a momentary disappointment.

But our desire to help each other eventually became a point of contention. I didn't always want to be reassured, while she would frequently respond to my offers of help by saying, "You don't need to do that." It soon became evident that both of us were more comfortable in the role of giver than receiver.

I was reminded of the story of Jesus washing His disciples' feet on the eve of His death. Peter objected, saying, "You shall never wash my feet." But Jesus replied, "If I do not wash you, you have no part in me." Like Peter, Marilyn and I each wanted to be the giver. It was a safer position, one in which we were less likely to be hurt. Yet it also kept some distance between us—and kept us from being fully receptive to God's love.

We are gradually learning to be receivers as well as givers in expressing our love. In the process, we have found that we are more vulnerable, but also more at-one with each other. While we continue to delight in the many ways we are alike, we have come to realize that in this regard we both needed to change. We needed to allow the One Who came in the form of a servant to wash our feet, so that we could in turn wash each other's.

May I be like the transformed Peter, Lord, graciously receiving, authentically giving.
—ROBERT KING

16/SAT *The labourer is worthy of his hire. . . .* —LUKE 10:7

"Are you sure you can do it?" I asked my husband John. "I'd feel a whole lot better if we called the tree service."

"No way! It'd cost a fortune, and besides, Ian can help me. I've already got it all figured out." I watched uneasily as he propped the ladder against the huge oak tree. The limb that needed to be trimmed overhung a bed of particularly prickly cacti. Our son Ian followed, a saw in one hand and a coil of rope in the other.

It took the full extension of the ladder to reach the limb, probably twenty feet or so up in the air. John double-twisted the rope around the branch to be cut, then threw the end down to Ian. "Now, when it starts to break, pull hard. Put your whole weight behind it."

I sat on a rock and held my breath. Within minutes the branch was cut nearly through. "Pull!" yelled John. Ian pulled. The branch broke with tremendous force and spun the ladder completely around. One corner of the top rung caught on a small stub on the tree.

John dangled by one hand from the ladder. "Help," he said in a strangled voice.

"I'm coming, Dad," said Ian as he pushed through the bushes. "What'll I do?"

"I don't know," croaked his dad. "If I move, I could jostle the ladder off the stub."

"Just drop, Dad," said Ian. "It's not that far down."

"I'll fall in the cactus," growled my husband.

"I'm getting the camera!" I said. "Don't come down till I get a picture." I raced into the house, but by the time I got back out, John had slowly inched his way to the safety of the ground.

The fellows were furious. "All you could do was laugh!"

"Sorry, darling. But you didn't get hurt, and it *was* funny. Wish I'd gotten my picture."

We call the tree service now. As expensive as it sometimes is, as the Scripture says, "The laborer is worthy of his hire."

Thanks, Lord, for those with the expertise to do the jobs we can't.

—FAY ANGUS

17/SUN *Hear, ye children, the instruction of a father. . . .*
—PROVERBS 4:1

My interview for a security clearance was going well. The interviewer and I liked each other. Then she asked, "Tell me about your father."

Without thinking, I answered, "I never knew my father." The interviewer blushed and passed quickly to the next question.

Perhaps it was my hunger for warmth, attention and companionship that triggered my blunt response. Mother and Father divorced before I was two. Mother remarried when I was seven. My stepfather was an excellent provider who felt that giving encouragement and praise was silly and unnecessary. From time to time I wondered about my "real" father, but this was curiosity rather than yearning. Over the years I made no attempt to find him. Now I wrote to my mother to let her know about my angry feelings.

I received my security clearance; I also received a letter from Mother. "I can understand your anger, son," she wrote. "Try not to be too critical. Try to remember all the fine people who reached out to help you."

My thoughts raced back to the Reverend Gardiner M. Day, our minister, who gave me a job during the Great Depression; to Edward

Welch, my high-school English teacher, who nurtured my talent for public speaking while teaching me the joys of reading and writing; to John B. Clark, my high-school principal, who helped me get into college with a much-needed scholarship; to Herbert Kenny, arts editor at *The Boston Globe*, who hired me to be a book reviewer; to Dave McKinney, the aerospace engineer who selected me to serve in the Project Gemini space program.

Suddenly, I was aware that I had many fathers, caring men who guided and encouraged me, each in his own way. So on this Father's Day, I give thanks to my Father in heaven, to the father I never knew, to my stepfather and to all the fatherly men who have touched my life.

Heavenly Father, thank You for opening my eyes to see and to appreciate the gifts of my many fathers.   —OSCAR GREENE

18/MON *O that my people would listen to me, that Israel would walk in my ways!*   —PSALM 81:13 (RSV)

I had phoned my elderly friend Ossie Mobley for a short chat. Just before we hung up, she said in her quiet voice, "Marion, would you have time to say something to Donnie? He just wants to hear your voice. Doesn't matter what you say."

Donnie is sixty-plus, and due to an injury at birth, he's in a wheelchair and isn't able to speak normally. He can make sounds that Ossie understands from a lifetime of caring for her only child. I could hear Donnie in the background, and I pictured him happily anticipating my voice, listening with all his might as his mother held the phone to his ear.

"Oh, yes, Ossie! Of course. I'd love to speak to Donnie. Put him on."

I heard Donnie breathing, waiting, listening for my voice. I had the distinct feeling I was about to learn something. "Hey, Donnie! How are you?" I said. "Did y'all get rain today? We did. I'll bet you went to church Sunday. I need to stop by and see you."

"Ummm," he agreed excitedly. *I'd really like to see you.*

"We love you and Ossie, Donnie."

"Ummm!" *We love you, too.*

"Well, bye Donnie. Thanks for talking to me. Bye-bye."

Then Ossie came back on. "Thank you so much, Marion. Donnie sure enjoyed talking to you."

Lord, it doesn't really matter what You say—I yearn to hear Your voice. Teach me how to listen. Amen. —MARION BOND WEST

19/*TUE* *Let your eyes look directly forward, and your gaze be straight before you. Take heed to the path of your feet, then all your ways will be sure.*
—PROVERBS 4:25–26 (RSV)

When my husband and I visited Maui last year, we took a bike ride down the face of a volcano—thirty-eight miles of winding, hairpin turns. Before we began the rather intimidating journey, our leader talked to us about "visual reality."

"You will tend to go wherever you look," he said. "You must, of course, be cautious about glancing back over your shoulder to talk to your mate. But also be careful about looking at the spectacular landscape along our route." He pointed to the sides of the road, where lava rock fell away thousands of feet without the support of even a guard rail.

As we rode, I stole furtive glances over my shoulder once or twice to say something to my husband. I managed to take in much of the scenery. But, mainly, I focused on our leader. I kept his brightly striped bike helmet in my line of vision. As he careened around a curve, I imitated his lean and waited expectantly for him to come into view again: mile after mile, through lava rock, pine groves, pineapple fields and, finally, to the edge of the ocean itself.

I had made it! And I'd done it by going exactly where I had been looking: in the direction my guide intended for me to go. It was a lesson I'd remember long after I left Hawaii.

You, Lord, are the Guide of my life. Help me keep my eyes fixed on You. Become my "visual reality," all day, every day.

—MARY LOU CARNEY

20/ WED *So the descendants of Aaron were given Hebron (a city of refuge)....* —I CHRONICLES 6:57 (NIV)

I had been talking to the director of a ministry in Jackson, Mississippi, about coming down to take a look at some of the things they were doing for the outcasts of the community. Finally I gave him a call and set a date to tour the ministry's homes for homeless men and women. As we drove down the street where the ministry is located, I was encouraged to see how much work was being done. Old houses were being torn down and replaced with new ones, and other houses were being remodeled.

At the end of our tour we walked into a small, hot room where thirty people had gathered for chapel. A man walked in who seemed disturbed and was talking loudly. The song leader quietly left his place up front and gently said some words to the disturbed man. He became quiet and the service went on. As the singing came to an end, the man said that he wanted to sing a song, and the ministry's director assured him, "You and I will sing a song together at the end of the service."

I had been asked to give a short message at the service, and after I finished, the director and the disturbed man sang "Do Lord, Remember Me." They were way off-key, but that didn't matter at all. Here, in the midst of a city filled—like so many—with poverty and indifference, was a real city of refuge for the poor and hurting.

Lord, thank You for cities of refuge that reach out to mend broken lives.
—DOLPHUS WEARY

21/ THU *Mary...sat down at the feet of the Lord and listened.* —LUKE 10:39 (GNB)

I'm a compulsive helper. No sooner does a friend mention a problem, then I have a solution.

Recently, my good friend Kathy faced a particularly difficult time with a sick daughter, a looming mortgage payment and an out-of-work husband. Of course, I was at the ready with doctor referrals, job applications and offers of a loan. My efforts were stubbornly, if affectionately, ignored.

I was mulling over Kathy's problems during a walk yesterday when I noticed a boy and his younger sister riding bikes. They sped around their driveway. Suddenly, the little girl's bike turned over, and she fell with a thud. She looked mournfully at her brother, uncertainty and the beginning of a wail on her face. I started to rush over to see if she was hurt and, if not, encourage her to avoid unnecessary tears.

Her brother, however, knew what she really needed. He studied the woeful expression on her face for a split second before deliberately spilling his bike in the exact same way. They sat there, an arm's length apart, gazing at each other for a few moments. I had enough grace to stop in my tracks.

She said something, too softly for me to overhear, and he nodded. Eventually, without another word, they got up and began to ride their bikes again.

That evening, I invited Kathy to visit a local park with me. "What for?" she asked warily, preparing for my usual deluge of helpful suggestions.

"Just to sit together," I replied.

We sat together, not saying much, absorbing the scent and sight of just-blooming roses, and watched the sun set. I think it helped.

Lord, help me recognize when it's best just to step back and listen.

—MARCI ALBORGHETTI

22 / FRI *The wise heart will know the proper time and procedure.* —ECCLESIASTES 8:5 (NIV)

"I did it, Mom! I found an apartment, and got the phone, the water and electricity all turned on in one day. They should have the air conditioning fixed by tomorrow, and we have a microwave, so I don't have to buy one!"

Dave's phone call left me as breathless as he was. Our last son was out on his own, an Army officer at his first base, near Dothan, Alabama.

"Dave," I said with a grin, "I bet you don't remember when you were about four years old, and you and I had just ridden up the elevator to Dad's office. He showed you his computer and phone and how he worked there every day. Suddenly, you looked up at me with your lip quivering, 'When I grow up can I stay with you?' Tears swam in your brown eyes.

"I knelt down and wrapped you in a hug. 'Why, sweetheart, when you're grown, you'll want to be out on your own. What has frightened you?'

"'Oh, Mommy,' you wailed, 'how will I know which buttons to push?'

"I assured you that as you grew, you would slowly learn how to be an adult, how to understand and affect the world around you properly, which buttons to push on phones and computers, for microwaves, in elevators and cars. Obviously, you've learned!"

We laughed.

But recalling David's small-child concerns about how he might survive in the adult world made me think of my own worries for the future. How will I handle growing older? Can I adapt to changes in my life? How will I know which buttons to push?

Then I smiled to myself. Just as we reassured David that he would know the proper procedure to succeed in his daily circumstances, so my heavenly Father will grant me the same grace and learning.

Heavenly Father, remind me often that You give me Your grace and wisdom step by step, each in its proper season, all my life long.

—ROBERTA ROGERS

23/ SAT *Walk in love. . . .*   —EPHESIANS 5:2

It was my sister Keri's wedding day, and my job was to walk her down the aisle. It was hard to believe that my baby sister was getting married, much less to Ben, my best friend and college roommate. I could hardly get my mind around the idea.

I thought about our family's trip to the Grand Canyon the summer before. It had been wonderful, the way things had been in our family pretty much my whole life. Now it was all changing; nothing would ever be the same.

I pulled the crisp white collar of my formal shirt away from my neck as I waited for Keri to come down from her dressing room. I was standing up as straight as I could, my legs trembling slightly. I checked my tie in the mirror and adjusted my cummerbund.

All of a sudden, Keri was there. She was beautiful. I swallowed hard as I looked into her eyes. This was the little girl I had watched over as a child—playing in the creek, running through sprinklers, sledding down snowy white hills—and I was about to give her away.

Just before the sanctuary doors swung open Keri wrapped her arms around me and whispered, "Brock, thanks for everything you've done throughout our lives together. You'll always be my hero."

The rest of that walk was like a dream. I remember the hundreds of smiling people, Keri and I giggling as we made the slow approach to the front of the church and the look of appreciation on Ben's face as I gave him a wink. I remember my dad standing there, eyes brimming with tears, waiting to conduct the ceremony. But most of all, I remember how I felt as I lifted Keri's veil, kissed her on the cheek and made my way back to the front pew where my mother waited.

God was in this place. I knew that He had put Keri and Ben together. I knew that many wonderful memories lay ahead of us. And I knew that the trip that I had just taken down that long church aisle had been a walk of pure love.

Father, help me learn to trust You completely and always to walk in Your love.
—BROCK KIDD

24 / SUN   *The eyes of all wait upon thee; and thou givest them their meat in due season.*   —PSALM 145:15

Every time I spent a day with Grandma Ellen, she offered me a peppermint. She always had a plastic bag of them in her purse. Though I rarely ate them, it seemed as if every time we went to the store she bought another package. If I asked her if she really needed more, she'd just add a bag to her cart and say, "Well, they're on sale."

After Grandma Ellen died, I helped sort through some of her papers. I was working at Grandma's desk when I heard Mom groan. Turning to look, I saw her pull a plastic bag from Grandma's purse. "What in the world am I going to do with all these peppermints?" she asked. A few minutes later, I heard a louder groan. Several more bags of mints waited in a drawer. Mom had found Grandma's stockpile! "How am I going to get rid of them?" she asked.

At church that Sunday Mom had an idea. A lady sitting in the pew in front of us seemed to be having some trouble with a cough, so Mom tapped her gently on the shoulder and handed her a mint. The woman smiled and unwrapped the mint quietly. Soon her cough was soothed, but the wrapper's crinkling had caught the attention of a small child down the row, so Mom passed a peppermint that way, too. The next week, Mom gave a mint to another coughing friend and two more children. After the service, several ladies enjoyed mints with their coffee in the social hall. Mom left a handful in the Sunday school candy dish.

A couple of months after Mom's "mint ministry" began, we went grocery shopping, and as we approached the candy aisle, I asked Mom if she had given away most of Grandma's mints. She chuckled, but didn't answer. Somehow, I wasn't surprised when I saw Mom reach for two bags of mints. She looked at me, grinning, and said, "Well, they're on sale."

Father, thank You for Grandma's peppermints. Though I don't like to eat them, they're wonderful to share! —KJERSTIN EASTON

25/ MON *Talk no more so very proudly, let not arrogance come from your mouth. . . .* —I SAMUEL 2:3 (RSV)

Some years ago I saw an ad on television for some sort of cosmetic product or shampoo. The ad began with a model saying, "Don't hate me because I'm beautiful." While I am not beautiful, I never had any inclination to hate her. I thank God—if not every day, then when it occurs to me—that I do not conform to the media's idea of beauty. Believe me, I have enough problems.

When I first came to Los Angeles, I had a roommate who was classically beautiful. She devoted at least half of her energy trying to ensure that she stayed that way, another quarter of it worrying about what it would be like if she lost that beauty, and the last quarter fretting that all men ever saw in her were her looks and that she would never be loved for herself.

I have been blessed with many things. If I were beautiful, too, I think I would have fallen into arrogance, thoughtlessness and self-ishness. But my looks have kept me, not humble, but humble enough. And I know for certain that I am loved for myself.

So I have to be grateful that God knew what He was doing when He decided to give me a roundish body, a narrow forehead and pouchy eyes. He knew I'd need them to find my way from myself and closer to Him.

Thank You, God, for the imperfections in myself that remind me of Your care for me. —RHODA BLECKER

26/TUE

The swift of foot shall not . . . deliver himself.
—AMOS 2:15 (NKJV)

She looked at me as if I had just crawled out of a cave with a club in my hand. "You mean you still write with a typewriter?"

I smiled, thinking of all the writers who "still" use a typewriter, a pencil or even a fountain pen.

She shook her head. "But a computer is so much faster and easier."

I'm sure she's right, but my computer tempts me to do the "quick fix" instead of the total rewrites that are necessary. After all, writing is not like microwaving a ham sandwich. It's more like sculpting in marble.

Writing is only one of many things that I can't seem to hurry. The beautiful garden outside my window tends to bloom when it's good and ready.

"And don't forget marriage," my wife reminds me. "That takes time to create."

In an age that seems to worship the gods of "Speed" and "Convenience," it gets harder and harder for me to pace myself. I feel swept along by a riptide. I know, there is a time to pour on the steam and get a job done fast. But the older I get, the more I relish the *process* of writing, gardening, relating, and the less I'm interested in setting speed records.

My friendship with God has not been about speed or convenience but about wrestling with angels all night long. I am a block of marble, and God is sculpting me, but I keep resisting His chisel. My character is taking shape slowly, with many setbacks, and I have no choice but to be patient with the Sculptor.

These days I often find myself rehearsing a little prayer I memorized in my teens:

Not so in haste, my heart. Have faith in God and wait.
The feet that wait for God are soonest at the goal that is not gained
*   by speed.*
So hold thee still my heart and wait His lead.   —DANIEL SCHANTZ

27 / WED *Ye were sometimes darkness, but now are ye light in the Lord: walk as children of light.* —EPHESIANS 5:8

It is early morning. The day is clear, and the green of early summer is a sight to behold. The neighbor's cat is lolling on a concrete bench, enjoying a spot of sun. Minutes later, as the day unfolds, the cat moves lazily to a brighter patch of light. The cat reminds me of a lesson I learned awhile back, a truth of light and shadow.

Several years ago I had a friend named Eva. We took care of each other's children, exchanged meals and planned outings together. But every time I was with her, I ended up talking negatively about others and being disgruntled with life in general.

"Pam," my husband David said one night as we drove home from dinner at Eva's, "I can't believe how down you were on everything tonight. I've never heard you criticize old Miss Laney before, and you acted as if you were totally against that new kids' program at church. What's wrong?"

The answer was simple: Being with Eva brought out the worst in me. I'm not saying that my behavior was Eva's fault. For all I know, I had an equally negative influence on her. But I knew I had to remedy the situation. So I began to spend less and less time with Eva, and more time with people who brought out the best in me.

The same principle holds true in other areas of my life. If driving on a stacked-up freeway makes me angry, I can find another route. If I end up in a church group where the emphasis is on criticizing some of God's children, I can step out of the shadows cast by judging others and find a brighter patch of light. The way I see it, the world is a little like my front yard—patches of darkness, islands of light. Like my neighbor's cat, all I have to do is get up and move over to where it feels best to be alive.

Father, good springs from Your presence, and You grant us freedom of movement. Let me be wise enough to choose the bright spots where the light of Your love waits. —PAM KIDD

28 / THU *The desire of a man is his kindness. . . .* —PROVERBS 19:22

Like many people, I don't like to stand in line, especially when I'm in a hurry, so I do my food shopping at a market known for its fast checkers. You load your cart, pay your bill, and you're out of there! But one day the line was moving slowly, and when I looked ahead I saw that the checker was talking to a customer. I was annoyed. I wanted to go home, cook dinner and get to a meeting, and this woman was holding me back.

As I inched forward and began to unload my cart, I could hear what she was saying. She greeted the customer ahead of me with a smile that looked genuine and said "Hello" as if she meant it. She mentioned the weather (it was a nice day) and said she was looking forward to a camping trip with her family that weekend. The customer ahead of me actually began to relax and responded with some remarks about her garden. Then they exchanged a few words about their children. It was all very pleasant, and it rubbed off on me. I felt the stress begin to lift from my shoulders. I even hoped the checker might say a few words to me.

She did. Her smile made me feel welcome, and when she mentioned her cat, I told her about mine. The whole conversation took only a few seconds, but it made a difference in my day. I remembered that I was more than someone who got things done. I was a human being. I mattered.

On the way to my car, I thanked God for reminding me that "small talk" is a pretty big part of our daily lives. Sure, it takes a few seconds of our precious time, but in our busy world, it accomplishes something essential: It connects us to each other—like a handshake or, better yet, a hug. And it's so easy to give.

Dear Lord, when time becomes so important to me that I start putting people last, help me to remember that You always find time for me. Amen. —PHYLLIS HOBE

$29/_{FRI}$ *"The hope of the godless man shall perish. His confidence breaks in sunder, and his trust is a spider's web."* —JOB 8:13-14 (RSV)

Last summer I lost my Social Security disability status. My fragile finances toppled, and I found myself feeling hopeless and depressed. With nothing else to do, I headed back down to the Social Security office to file an appeal, took my number and waited in line. Beside me sat a tall, wiry man with an interesting sort of hound-dog face. He wore a faded baseball cap, and a long pencil-thin gray ponytail hung down his back. We got to talking. He lived on Lummi Island, near Bellingham, Washington, he told me, in a blue school bus he called "Recess."

I smiled and told him a little of my troubles. He sat listening with his long, lean frame hunched over, legs crossed, an elbow resting on one thigh, his chin propped up by his thumb. "You ever think about praying?" he suddenly asked, peeking at me from under his cap and waggling his index finger in my direction, thumb still holding up his chin.

"God doesn't seem to be answering these days."

"Maybe you've got to pray more."

"Yeah?" Another smile.

"You believe in God, don't you?" he demanded.

"Sure, I believe in God!"

"Tell me then," he suddenly whispered, leaning in close and briefly glancing at the bored clerks on the other side of the room. His long finger swept clean down the line like a pointer. "Who'd you rather trust?" he whispered, pointing his finger back up the line. "God? Or these folks?

I burst out laughing.

He thrust his big hand at me. "Name's Briggs. What's yours?"

I told him.

"Well, Brenda. Nice to meet you."

Thanks, dear Lord, for introducing me to Mr. Briggs and for reminding me that for real security I can depend on You.

—BRENDA WILBEE

30/_{SAT} *"I will pour out my Spirit on your offspring, and my blessing on your descendants."* —ISAIAH 44:3 (NIV)

To the west of our country property, separating our backyard from a field of neatly groomed raspberry bushes, stand five enormous poplar trees. My husband and I planted the saplings when our five children were small—one for each child. Now as I look at the sturdy trees reaching for the sky I wonder where the time has gone. The youngest of our children left home to get married two years ago.

Our children's interests take them far away from home, to Africa, Europe, China. Often I don't hear from them for months at a time. I worry about their safety. I worry that my imperfect mothering has not prepared them adequately for life's pitfalls. Sometimes I'm perplexed at the decisions they've made or the direction in which their lives are going. I want to shield them from trouble. But I can't.

At times like these, I like to read the promises God has given me concerning my children. I've highlighted them in my Bible and typed them out separately for easy access—three pages, single spaced. They include the following:

"All your sons will be taught by the Lord and great will be your children's peace" (Isaiah 54:13, NIV).

"My eyes will watch over them for their good, and I will bring them back to this land. . . .I will give them a heart to know me, that I am the Lord" (Jeremiah 24:6–7, NIV).

"Your descendants. . . .will spring up like grass in a meadow, like poplar trees by flowing streams" (Isaiah 44:3–4, NIV).

As I gaze at the sturdy poplars in our backyard, I reflect how little I had to do with their growth. Beyond their initial nurturing, I simply committed them to the Master of trees.

Father, into Your gentle, capable hands I commit my children.

—HELEN GRACE LESCHEID

DAILY GIFTS

1 _____

2 _____

3 _____

4 _____

5 _____

6 _____

7 _____

8 _____

9 _____

10 _____

11 _____

12 _____

13 _____

14 _____

15 _____

16 _____

17 _____

18 _____

19 _____

20 _____

21 _____

22 _____

23 _____

24 _____

25 _____

26 _____

27 _____

28 _____

29 _____

30 _____

July

Come unto me, all ye that labour and are heavy laden, and I will give you rest.
—MATTHEW 11:28

S	M	T	W	T	F	S
1	2	3	4	5	6	7
8	9	10	11	12	13	14
15	16	17	18	19	20	21
22	23	24	25	26	27	28
29	30	31				

WHEN GOD REACHES OUT . . . THROUGH OTHER PEOPLE

1/SUN *This is the day which the Lord has made; let us rejoice and be glad in it.* —PSALM 118:24 (RSV)

Ahna Fiske was my mother's closest friend. A brilliant woman, a pioneer in the education of learning-disabled children, Ahna also had a lovely singing voice. With Mother accompanying her on the piano, she often gave concerts in hospitals and nursing homes.

So it seemed particularly poignant when Ahna, in her eighties, entered a nursing home herself. Mother warned me, when I went to visit her old friend in a pleasant facility in Sudbury, Massachusetts, that Ahna would not know me. Sure enough, that accomplished woman had lost all of the past, even events only minutes old. Over and over—always graciously, but each time as though greeting a total stranger—Ahna welcomed me into her room as though I'd only then arrived.

Otherwise her observations were as keen as ever. She was clearly aware that her memory no longer served her, for she kept asking, "Have I just told you that?" Just as clearly, she was determined not to let forgetfulness spoil her zest for life. As I stood up to go, she apologized for not remembering the name I'd repeated a dozen times.

"I can't recall much of anything these days," she said. "I just enjoy the moment I'm in and don't worry about the other ones."

I walked down the chlorine-scented corridor with a wisdom more than human ringing through Ahna's words. *Don't live in the past. Don't live in the future. Right now, this present moment, is My loving gift to you.*

Father, let me find You in the fleeting moments of this day.
—ELIZABETH SHERRILL

2 / MON

$2/$ MON   *Let a good man strike or rebuke me in kindness. . . .*
                                    —PSALM 141:5 (RSV)

A few years ago, a *Daily Guideposts* reader wrote to me about my devotionals. This is the letter I wrote back to him.

> E. G. Alridge
> Fort Smith, Arkansas

> Dear E. G. Aldridge,
> Thank you very much for writing to me about my essays in last year's *Daily Guideposts*. I was especially struck by your comment that my writing "portrays an individual who is self-sufficient." At first I was confused by this—*of course* I'm self-sufficient. It's almost un-American *not* to be self-sufficient. Then I realized what you meant: that I wasn't dependent on God. So I'm writing to . . . I don't know, to *explain* myself, I guess.
> I *am* dependent on God. Problem is, I don't always realize it. For whatever reason (selfishness? pride?) I often believe I can do things myself, only to find that I cannot, that I must rely on prayer, on self-examination, on humility, on God. I don't think pride is my greatest sin; I think my greatest sin is my short memory, which allows me to forget how much I've been given, how blessed I've been—and what I owe in return.
> One last, important note. I take a risk every time I write. I take a risk that people will judge me—not just agree or disagree, but actually judge the entire content of my character based on the words in front of them. It's a risk I accept; it's part of the territory. But you, on the other hand, were careful *not* to judge. You took the time to write, to ask more questions, to withhold opinion. Do you realize what a gift that is? You said in your letter how much you rely on *Daily Guideposts* for guidance. In this case, it is the reader who is the wise teacher.
> Thanks again for writing.

Lord, thank You for the people who, with love and concern, challenge me to be truer to You.
                                    —MARK COLLINS

3 / TUE *Now faith is the substance of things hoped for, the evidence of things not seen.* —HEBREWS 11:1

As I drove along a rural road in New Mexico on a hot summer day, I wrestled with the problem of what to do about my parents and Larry's mother, all of them terminally ill back in Missouri. They wanted to live out their last days in their own homes, yet they were becoming increasingly helpless, and good home health care was hard to find in the small towns where they lived. They resisted the idea of coming to live with us or going into a nursing home, but Larry and I, with our own family and jobs, couldn't keep flying back and forth to Missouri to care for them. I felt lost and confused as I tried to come up with the best solution. If only I could look into the future and see what lay ahead, maybe I'd know what to do.

In desperation I prayed, "Lord, please, give me an answer!"

A couple of miles ahead the road slanted up a hill and vanished, dissolving into the sky. The trees on either side of the road shimmered and danced on air, while a lake suddenly appeared, drowning the valley in front of me.

I knew, of course, that I was viewing a mirage, but I wondered what a child who had never before seen a mirage might think as we drove toward apparent disaster. In my mind I started explaining about mirages and how things aren't always what they seem.

"Sometimes," I said to my make-believe child, "you have to keep going on faith even when you can't see the end of the road."

And I laughed out loud.

"Okay, Lord, I get the message," I said. "All I can do is keep on keeping on, trusting that You will pave the way."

Father, today I will set aside my fear for the future as I move forward, placing my faith in Your guidance and vision.

—MADGE HARRAH

4 / WED *He hath sent me to bind up the brokenhearted, to proclaim liberty to the captives, and the opening of the prison to them that are bound.* —ISAIAH 61:1

My wife Joy and I took a whirlwind trip to India to participate in a conference and visit some friends. We spent several days in places where it seemed that nothing worked. The electricity would fail, the phones wouldn't connect, the water wasn't drinkable, the bathrooms were broken, and the trains ran hours late on poorly maintained track. I was more than ready to get back to hot water, cold soda and my cell phone.

On our way home we had a six-hour layover between flights. Finally we boarded, settled into our seats and waited for takeoff. And waited. And waited. After almost an hour, the pilot told us, "We have an unusual problem. Security has discovered a man in a maintenance uniform hiding in the baggage compartment. All your luggage must be unloaded and reinspected while they question the man."

Fears of hijacking or worse ran through my mind. In a little while the pilot reported, "It looks like everything will be okay, folks. Our maintenance man was trying to smuggle himself into the U.S. He has been begging security not to send him home, but to let him go to America and freedom."

As we took off, I couldn't get the unknown stowaway out of my mind. He was willing to endure twelve hours in a cold baggage compartment and risk imprisonment to come to America. He wasn't, like me, anticipating the creature comforts of our consumer society; he longed for freedom.

In the last couple of years I have visited many countries, and everywhere people want to know about America, to know if I can help them get there. Do I really understand the great gift of freedom, divinely given and so easily forgotten?

On this Independence Day, I have decided to say a prayer for those who long for the great gift I almost take for granted. Won't you join me?

Lord, You sent Your Son to "set the captives free." Help me never to take my freedom for granted and to pray for oppressed people everywhere.
—ERIC FELLMAN

5/*THU*   *God setteth the solitary in families.... —PSALM 68:6*

There is something very reassuring about a summer's twilight walk around the neighborhood. Lights are being turned on, families are getting ready for dinner, and before the drapes are drawn, I can see people bustling about. Sometimes a child is at the window, nose squashed against the pane, waiting for Mom's or Dad's car to pull into the driveway. I smile and wave and, eyes wide with surprise, the child waves back.

With windows open, sounds and scents drift through the evening cool. Music, laughter, a baby's cry, voices calling to each other and then the tantalizing aroma of someone's dinner.

"*Ummm*," I tell my husband, whose long-legged stride I try to match, "roast chicken there!" Or, "Barbecue—fabulous! Stop. Smell. That's about all we'll get of it tonight!"

"Rats!" he says. "Salad again for us?"

I nod my head. "Yup. But a bowl of soup as well for lucky you."

We've walked around our neighborhood for almost forty years. We know each house as though it were our own. Some are repainting, remodeling, replanting the walkways, with people moving in and out, and some, like ours, remain much the same.

> O little homes, set forth on every hand,
> You little walled-in worlds of joy and fears,
> Built on the common place of smiles and tears,
> You are the strength and sinew of the land.
> *(Author unknown)*

As we walk, I pray for the families in the homes on our route. We've all been through earthquakes, fires and floods. We've shared the joy of our celebrations and the sadness of our bereavements in a continuum of life that makes each one of us an integral part of the whole. We are indeed the strength and sinew of our land.

Be with me in this place I call home, dear Lord. Keep my family and the families around me in Your love, and help us to reach out to one another. —FAY ANGUS

6/ *FRI*

When thou hast eaten and art full, then thou shalt bless the Lord thy God for the good land which he hath given thee. —DEUTERONOMY 8:10

A summer blackout. New York is famous for them. People trapped in elevators, subways, high-rise office buildings in the sweltering heat. When one happened last year, we were lucky. We were trapped at home with plenty of flashlights and candles. "It's kind of nice," I said to my wife Carol, "the quiet, without everyone's air conditioners running." Neighbors poured out of their apartments and congregated on the sidewalk, exchanging information. How long would the power be out? What had caused it? How far did the blackout area extend?

Back inside, I opened the refrigerator to get something to drink. *Why is the light* out? I wondered, and then remembered. Of course, the power outage. I wandered over to the computer. No, that wouldn't work. Nor would the television. *If I could listen to a little music on my CD player. . .* impossible. Absentmindedly I flicked the switch for the ceiling fan. I would lie in bed and stay cool—but naturally the fan wouldn't work, either. I opened the windows wide, grateful for the breeze. Just then Carol came into the bedroom. "There's not much water coming out of the faucet," she said. Of course—the pumps run on electricity.

That night I read in bed by flashlight, feeling like a kid on a camping trip. The next morning, as I sadly emptied soured milk down the drain, I was grateful for official promises of power by midday. (I could only read about it in the newspaper.)

Sometimes you don't realize how good things are until they go. For the time being I thanked God for sunshine, candlelight, batteries and the breeze. And I would never take a glass of cold water for granted again.

Thank You, Lord, for my well-fed life. Forgive me for taking it for granted.
—RICK HAMLIN

7/ SAT
"No plan of yours can be thwarted."
—JOB 42:2 (NIV)

I'm not sure exactly why I decided to take Amtrak to see my family in New York City. A plane would have gotten me there in a few hours rather than the train's two and a half days.

Restless after the first day in my seat, I decided to visit the lounge car where I could stretch my legs. I sat down next to a mother with twin girls who were about four years old. Chattering and lively, the girls pulled at their mother's legs as she read *God's Plan for the Single Parent.* Touched, I prayed, *God, let her find a partner to help her raise these children.*

"Can you draw a cat?" one of the girls, Becky, asked me.

My mixture of circles and dots and lines must have passed muster, because her sister scampered over and the next hour was spent with the three of us drawing while their mother read her book. Then the three of us sang a few choruses of "The Wheels on the Train" before I told them that I'd better head back to my seat.

I shrugged off the mother's thanks and nodded toward her book. "I'll pray that God's plan is revealed for you," I said. "I hope you meet Mr. Right," I added with a grin.

She grinned back. "Actually, I'm sure you were part of God's plan for me today. I've been on this train for three days already, and—well, I adore my kids, but I prayed for some peace and some quiet time to read. And there you were."

My jaw dropped. Me? A part of God's plan? But I wasn't important enough, was I? Maybe that's why I'd decided to take the train. Maybe it wasn't *my* idea at all! I'd keep my eyes open during this long trip for others who might need my help. As part of God's plan, of course.

God, today let me consider how I may be a part of Your plan.

—LINDA NEUKRUG

8/ SUN *For this reason he had to be made like his brothers in every way. . . .* —HEBREWS 2:17 (NIV)

Perhaps it wasn't so, but I couldn't help thinking people were staring as I wheeled my mother into the crowded fast-food restaurant after church that Sunday. It was Mom's first outing since she had been released from the rehabilitation hospital following a serious stroke. She was slumped in her wheelchair, her hands quivered, and a black patch covered her drooping eye. To cover my embarrassment, I busied myself settling Mom at the table while Dad ordered.

In the wheelchair bag I found a nice purple-checked bib with lace edging that Aunt Josie had made. As I tied it on Mom, I sighed. Even the lace couldn't disguise the fact that the bib was as big as a bath towel, big enough to cover Mom's torso and fold down into her lap to catch the large amounts of food she spilled.

Dad came over with a tray of food, sat down and quietly said the blessing. Then he rummaged through the wheelchair bag and got out a second bib. This one was a faded, ratty-looking terry cloth affair, with just a hint of blue left from the constant washing at the rehab hospital. Dad draped the bib over his suit, vest and tie, tied it around his neck, and then took a bite of his hamburger.

My tense shoulders relaxed at once. In a busy fast-food restaurant full of onlookers, my father had just shown me that the best cure for self-consciousness is a self-forgetful act of love.

Dear Lord, help me do something loving today that will have people staring—and smiling.
—KAREN BARBER

9 / MON
Rejoice with the wife of thy youth. . . . be thou ravished always with her love. —PROVERBS 5:18–19

First, there was the number I found affixed to the sole of her foot one summer night, as she slept, her hair cascading, her face calm in repose, the faraway hollow ringing of a bay buoy in the night air, the ocean seething far below our room high in an old house: 75365, printed on a tiny slip of paper. After a moment I realized that it was the number of the person who had inspected the new sandals my wife had worn that day, but for an arresting instant I thought I had found her secret number, her mathematical name, the parade of numerals that had worked its way to the surface of her skin finally after many years.

I have since become a collector of her numbers. They come to me in bunches, herds, gaggles, most often when I am paying bills: Social Security number; license number; the identification number of her foster child in Egypt; account numbers.

I turn back to terser numbers: my wife's weight (105); her height (63 inches); the number of her teeth (32); her children (3). I think of what is innumerable about her: kindness; wit; courage; grace. I think of her sad numbers: beloved fathers dead too young (1); nephews dead before they could flower (1). I try to decide what single number would sum her up best.

But she is unaccountable in this fashion, and numbers slide off her like rain. No number catches her quick grin, the high-beam flash of her eyes, the leap of her mind, the utter absorption with which she rocks her children in the blue hours of the night, the grace of her hands, the elegance of her neck, the whip-crack of her anger, the calm mathematics of her limbs when she is asleep on a summer night, her hair cascading, the buoy bell silvering in the night, a sea breeze sifting through the screen door.

Dear Lord, thank You, with all my heart, for love—and wonder.
—BRIAN DOYLE

10/ TUE   *Nevertheless he left not himself without witness, in that he did good . . . filling our hearts with food and gladness.*
—ACTS 14:17

I'm not a food person. I don't relish new recipes, and I don't enjoy cooking and baking. My favorite food as a skinny child was a banana Popsicle. So it's been next to impossible for me to accept that, for some people, food is synonymous with love.

On a recent hot July day, my son Jon phoned from work, asking in an almost reverent tone, "Have you tasted those tomatoes I gave you, Mom?" I hadn't. "I'm eating one now," he explained excitedly. "Mom, they're incredible. Get one and taste it while we talk, okay?" When I didn't, his voice gradually took on a ho-hum tone and the conversation wound down.

Later in the day I was suddenly really sorry I hadn't sampled the tomatoes, so I called Jon back and invited him to supper the next evening. "What are you having?" he asked cautiously.

"Country fried steak, gravy and mashed potatoes," I sang out. "Fresh stewed corn, fresh squash, biscuits, cantaloupe, some of those marvelous tomatoes you brought us and . . . ta-dah . . . fresh peach cobbler!"

"I'll be there!" he shouted.

Jon *ooh*ed and *aah*ed throughout the meal, speaking in a mellow, tender tone. As I packed up some of the food for him to take home, he looked at me long and hard, then burst into an incredible, impromptu smile that conveyed unmistakably, *I love you!*

Lord Jesus, whether You were feeding thousands by the Sea of Galilee or a handful of friends in the upper room, You always did it gladly. Show me how. Amen.
—MARION BOND WEST

11/ WED *But the Lord has been my stronghold, And my God the rock of my refuge.* —PSALM 94:22 (NAS)

Don Garner and I have been good friends since we met twenty-five years ago in seminary. While I have been a pastor, Don has been an Old Testament professor. Don is a gifted biblical scholar and has a love for archaeology and the ancient Jewish world.

This summer while on an archaeological dig in the Middle East, Don received word that his twenty-year-old son Aaron had been killed in an automobile accident. Stunned by grief, Don faced a grueling forty-eight-hour trip home—by himself, but never alone.

I telephoned Don as soon as he got home. As the phone rang, I struggled with what I should say. Then I heard Don's voice, and I knew the words didn't matter. What mattered was the sound of a familiar voice, a human touch across the vast expanse of miles and distance.

As Don described his journey, he said a curious thing. "Scott, you and I have studied the Bible for years. We've taught it and preached it. But I've got to tell you, I don't think I really knew what it's all about until now. And what I've discovered is that this thing we call faith is real. It will hold you up and get you through."

I know from my own experience that Don is right. You can read all the books about theology, quote Scripture from memory, preach lofty sermons and teach great Sunday school lessons, but until you chart your own personal pilgrimage through pain, you cannot fully fathom that God is with you.

Some years ago while struggling with the pain of my father's death, I scribbled these words by the Scottish preacher James Stewart in the back of my Bible: "It is when you have sunk right down to rock bottom that you suddenly find you have struck the Rock of Ages."

Father, thank You for the times when You have taught me that faith is real. Amen. —SCOTT WALKER

12/ THU *Look not only to your own interests, but also to the interests of others.* —PHILIPPIANS 2:4 (NIV)

If you've ever visited the island of Maui, chances are you've driven the Road to Hana. Almost every tourist does! My husband and I made the fifty-four-mile trip in a rented convertible. As we slowed for the curves (there were six hundred of them!), we could hear the *whooshing* roar of waterfalls crashing into lush undergrowth. And the scenery was spectacular! But the thing that impressed me most about that trip was the bridges.

Fifty-two bridges. And all of them one-lane. At the entrance to every one was a YIELD sign—on both sides. Both approaching cars were supposed to yield! No one had the right of way. So what happened? Politeness. Chivalry. Charity. And an occasional laugh as both parties kept motioning for the other one to cross first.

No one has the right of way. It made for a good drive through paradise. It might be a good way to live my life, too. Suppose I surrender my right to that prime parking space (even if I saw it first)? Or how about I take the piece of pie that got squashed in the cutting process? And why shouldn't I be the one to have the middle seat (elbows in, please!) on my next business flight?

I may find that when I don't insist on my own way, I help create paradise no matter where I am.

Forgive me, Father, for the times I insist on having my own way at the expense of others. Humble me that I might know the joy of yielding.   —MARY LOU CARNEY

13/FRI

For God loveth a cheerful giver.
—II CORINTHIANS 9:7

Late one afternoon a white pickup truck pulled into our drive. In it was Mario, a new neighbor. We'd met him shortly after he and his wife moved in.

Mario jumped out of the truck, and we exchanged greetings. "I just wanted to give you my card and let you know I have a business painting and staining houses. I'd be glad to give you some references if you need anything done," he said, glancing at our porch and deck, both of which desperately needed work. In fact, just that morning I'd been dreading that I was going to have to find someone.

Before I committed myself, I wanted to check out his work. It was top quality, so I called him back for an estimate. The figure he gave me was way too low, and in addition, he volunteered to repair our fence for nothing. "Mario," I said as we stood in the driveway, "I'm always looking for a bargain. But this is really too low."

He shuffled around, hands in his pockets, looking back toward his house. Finally he said, "Well, I'll tell you. Usually I'd charge two hundred dollars more. But a few days after we moved in, our driveway was blocked by a tree, and your husband loaned my wife a car so she could get to work. Remember?" I did remember.

"But it wasn't worth all that, Mario," I said. "You could have rented a car for less."

"Yes," he said, his face flushing, "but it gives me great happiness to pay back with interest!"

Lord, when I pay back favors, help me to remember Mario's attitude—and Yours.   —SHARI SMYTH

14/*SAT*   *I will trust, and not be afraid. . . .*   —ISAIAH 12:2

I woke up feeling troubled. It was Sunday morning, July 14, 1996, and Hurricane Bertha was gone. Her punishing winds had diminished to a tropical storm by the time she limped into Medford, Massachusetts. Her visit brought four inches of much-needed rain. Although we had suffered no damage and the day was sunny and bright, I still worried. On Saturday, Hurricane Bertha had ripped through Wilmington, North Carolina, where my recently widowed friend Margaret lived. I'd tried to call her, but got no answer.

On Sunday I ushered at church. Things moved smoothly, yet I was still worried about Margaret. Then, as I was helping with the collection, I heard the congregation softly singing.

> Breathe on me, Breath of God
> Fill me with life anew,
> That I may love what Thou dost love,
> And do what Thou wouldst do.

The words were soothing. After the service, I rushed home and called Margaret. Still no answer. Then I remembered receiving a letter from a friend of Margaret's who lived in Massachusetts. I called, and she said, "Margaret is just fine!" Suddenly, I was fine, too. I had finally gotten through to someone.

Later, a letter from Margaret arrived. "We are well," she said. "Had trees down and debris, but no damage to the house."

With my mind fixed on Bertha's ferocious winds, worry had troubled my heart even at church, and I couldn't think clearly how to reach Margaret. I had forgotten that the gentle breath of God's Holy Spirit is always with us to sustain and uphold us, and to fill us with life. We'll be just fine . . . we just have to remember how to get through to Him.

Father of Comfort, never let my worries break my connection to You.
—OSCAR GREENE

A WHOLE AND HOLY LOVE

15/<small>SUN</small> *Unless the Lord builds the house, those who build it labor in vain. . . .* —PSALM 127:1 (RSV)

Like our new home, Robert's and my marriage is built on a mountain. That mountain is strong and tall and absolutely dependable. Its name is Shared Prayer, and it's a solid place we enter together every evening. This daily practice started the evening Robert first visited me, and it has continued into our marriage.

We've discovered that it's much easier to be faithful to our daily prayer commitment if set aside a special time and place for it. It's so important to us that in our new home we've provided ourselves with a small room that we use only for prayer.

We planned that room from our hearts. It's furnished with a small table, covered with a white cloth, above which hangs the needlepoint cross that was given to me by a *Daily Guideposts* reader. The room has an oak floor, a softly glowing amber light with a dimmer and two kneeling cushions. It's the place where we come together before God, sometimes praying aloud, sometimes singing, often just sitting together in silent prayer and always concluding with a warm hug. It's this daily prayer time, as much as anything in our lives, that creates the deepest bond between us.

We haven't always had the luxury of a separate room for our home sanctuary, but we've found that it's possible to have a "place apart" for prayer even in a crowded home. For many years, my sacred space was simply my green prayer chair, with my Bible and a notebook on the table next to it. All that you need is a quiet corner of any room, faithfulness to your prayer commitment and a heart that longs for communion with God.

Tonight, Lord, when the busy day winds down and the last lights flicker out, may couples, families and friends stand together on the mountain called Shared Prayer, in houses all over the world.
—MARILYN MORGAN KING

16/MON *Seek, and ye shall find; knock, and it shall be opened unto you.*　—MATTHEW 7:7

The milky computer screen seemed out of place in the Emigration Room of the Irish National Library in Dublin. On vacation last fall in Ireland, I had dropped by the stately old Georgian building to see an exhibit on Jonathan Swift when I spotted this little room set aside principally for Irish Americans like me who are curious about their ancestors.

My mother's father's family, the Rossiters, came over from County Wexford before the Revolutionary War. The McBrides, my mother's mother's people, were from Wicklow. My paternal grandmother's family, the Daleys, were said to be from Cork. But Grinnan? No one could figure out Grinnan.

Except now, after a few clicks of the computer mouse, here I was staring at a page from a genealogical database, looking back in time to the records of the parish of St. Sebastian in County Offaly in the mid-1840s—to a family by the name of Grinnan. There were Mary, Seamus, Liam, Thomas, Elizabeth, Patrick, living not far outside the town of Tullamore. Yet no sign of them after that. Nothing.

I was perplexed until I consulted a dusty collection of ship's manifests—famine ships, embarking from Liverpool to the U.S. There I found a few of those same Grinnans listed as passengers. Not all of them made it to Liverpool in 1845, the beginning of the Great Hunger that killed more than a million Irish and drove twice that many from their homeland. Most of the Grinnans had been wiped out by the famine, it seemed, and there was no telling who out of those who'd made it onto ships actually survived the horrific crossing. But someone had. Someone whose name I still carried. Closing the manifest, I felt a wonderful shiver of unexpected recognition.

I'd come to Ireland for the museums and bookshops, for the Abbey Theatre and Bewley's Oriental Café, for the land and the sea. But almost by accident, with a click of the computer mouse, I'd been connected to a misty past and a historic tragedy, and found a piece of myself.

Family is the road You give us to travel in life, Father, each generation another step in the journey to You. —EDWARD GRINNAN

PRAYER FOR JULY

Here in my garden,
    hushed in Your peace, Lord,
You give Your pardon
    from the loud world.
Lost in the beauties
    of meditation,
Free from life's duties
    with You alone.

Rainbowed by flowers,
    lulled by a dove song,
Through sunlit hours
    sorrows are gone.
Heaven comes nearer,
    death does not threaten,
Visions grow clearer
    when we are One.
        —MARY A. KOEPKE

17 / TUE *Let your conversation be as it becometh the gospel of Christ. . . .* —PHILIPPIANS 1:27

I was flying back home from a business trip, trying to watch the in-flight movie, but the elderly man next to me kept interrupting the movie to ask a smattering of unrelated questions. I took off my head-phones to answer him, but in order not to miss anything, I put them back on immediately afterward. Each time, however, I felt a little more guilty. I had been trying to be more open to people, and now I was intentionally doing the opposite.

Finally, I gave my seatmate my undivided attention. He was from Nebraska, traveling with a tour group of seniors. The next day was his wife's birthday. In 1948 he was supposed to go to New York, but he never made it. He was quite sure that Orville and Wilber Wright would faint if they saw what had become of their grand invention.

As the southern tip of Manhattan appeared outside our window, I pointed out as many sites as I could. "Golly!" he said with amaze-ment. "And what might that building be over there?"

"That's the Empire State, sir."

"Oh, my," he said, "there it finally is."

The plane landed, and when it came time for him to get up to leave, my new friend turned and offered me his hand. "Nice to meet you, young man. I'm sorry I interrupted your show."

As he made his way down the aisle, his wife moved toward me and said, almost in a whisper, so that no one else could hear, "Years ago, while they were in the service, stationed in Virginia, he and his bud-dies got passes to go to New York City. His buddies got into some sort of trouble and they weren't allowed to go. He was so disap-pointed. You just gave him the tour he never had."

Then she whispered, "He's not doing too well."

I looked ahead and watched his labored walk and thought to my-self, *Lord, without even knowing it, I just gave a dying man a gift. And I almost missed the chance.*

Lord, thank You for the blessings given and gained in simple conversation.
—DAVE FRANCO

18/ WED *Thou openest thine hand, and satisfiest the desire of every living thing.* —PSALM 145:16

Do you sometimes wonder if the prayers of a mother's heart are answered?

Recently I've been praying that our twenty-five-year-old daughter Lindsay would know God's love in a special, tangible way. Two nights ago, she called from California; her voice broke as she said, "Mom, my bird flew away." Her bird is a cockatiel that is more than a bird because of the way it responds to Lindsay. Sometimes she lets it fly around her apartment, and when she whistles, the bird echoes the sound and lands on her shoulder.

Lindsay said the bird flew out her patio door that afternoon, flopped around on the roof and then disappeared into the trees. She blamed herself and spent three hours scouring the neighborhood, looking up into treetops and whistling. She saw and heard nothing. "When these birds get stressed, they are apt to keep getting farther away, and I know it won't be able to survive long outdoors," she said.

The next morning, Lindsay got up early and looked again before going to work. At noon she decided to drive home and try one more time. As she whistled at the trees around her apartment, a woman appeared and told her she thought she had heard the bird at the swimming pool several blocks away. Off Lindsay went, and as she neared the pool, she began whistling. Way in the distance, she heard a faint echo. Again she whistled. Again the faint echo. She kept following the sound, which got a little louder, until she came to a tall wrought-iron fence, and there on the other side, hopping along the ground, was her bird. Lindsay whistled as she stuck her arm through the wrought-iron fence and the bird jumped on to it, crawling up to her chest where it snuggled down, whistling in response.

"I found my bird!" Lindsay told me gleefully when she called later.

The song in my heart is still singing with praise.

Thank You, Lord, for answered prayers. —CAROL KUYKENDALL

19/ THU *"The Lord turn his face toward you and give you peace."* —NUMBERS 6:26 (NIV)

As I reach for the light switch, the narrow strip of paper with the pink typing catches my eye: "Your life will be peaceful and fulfilling." When I first pulled it out of a Chinese fortune cookie more than a year ago, my response was, "Yes! I like my life! I feel happy, peaceful, fulfilled." And so I tucked it into a corner of my bathroom mirror where I glance past it every day, mostly not noticing. But this morning it gets my attention and I have to ask, "Can I still say this about my life?"

These last few months have been full of painful surprises. In late

January I was diagnosed with melanoma. Because it's such an aggressive cancer and in a very unusual site, we opted to go to a large cancer center in Texas for treatment. By mid-February I was back home, recovering from major surgery. The day after we got home we watched in horror as the surgical wound slowly opened up, stitch by stitch. The doctors assured us that sometimes this happens and not to worry, but we panicked. After many weeks it did heal up, and in early April we returned to Houston for a course of radiation therapy. A bladder infection complicated that recovery experience. It was easy to admit that often in these last months my life has felt anything but peaceful and fulfilling.

This morning I used my Bible concordance to find verses about peace. I was surprised that most refer to God *giving* us peace—it's a gift, not a feeling I can manufacture for myself.

These past months have been filled full of unexpected, often frightening and painful adventures. My illusions about my own good health have been shattered, along with any ideas that I have any real control over the events of my life. But even in the midst of this I see glimpses of God's peace. And that's a gift.

Loving Father, in spite of the unexpected turns my life may take, help me to receive Your gift of a peaceful heart. —MARY JANE CLARK

20/*FRI* *"You are the world's light—a city on a hill, glowing in the night for all to see."* —MATTHEW 5:14 (TLB)

The Old Point Loma Lighthouse sits high atop a bluff overlooking the Pacific Ocean and San Diego Bay. I can see it clearly across the water, miles away from our summer vacation spot on Coronado Island. I feel irresistibly drawn to it, as well as to another lighthouse I've visited, Marblehead Lighthouse on Lake Erie, in the Ohio town where my husband's parents live.

I've never really understood my fascination with these beautiful nineteenth-century structures. Is it the connection to the past, to the solitary lighthouse keepers who lit the oil lamps nightly to guide far-off sailing ships? Something more struck me when I visited both landmarks last summer.

I gazed at the Old Point Loma Lighthouse silhouetted against the sky, and thought of safety, security, a beacon in the dark that offers guidance and comfort. A few weeks later, when our family visited the

Marblehead Lighthouse, I climbed the dozens of steps to the top and looked out at the boats dotting the water. It occurred to me that each of these views points to God's expectations for different times in my life. Looking toward the lighthouse reminded me of when I was a new mother, constantly seeking help and advice from others more knowledgeable, reaching out for a beacon to guide me. Now that I'm older, the view is different. Others look to me for leadership, and I feel God's urging to take on new tasks. I've always found a beacon to guide me when I've needed it, in helpful friends and loving family, and in God Himself. The lighthouse is always in view. Now it's my turn to be the light.

God, strengthen me to shine a guiding light for others as You have always done for me.
                                                    —GINA BRIDGEMAN

21 / SAT   *Thou shalt not take the name of the Lord thy God in vain; for the Lord will not hold him guiltless that taketh his name in vain.*   —EXODUS 20:7

Among the headlines in today's newspaper is one reporting the sentence of a minister convicted of a felony. He will serve time in prison for his offense. But more serious than the crime he committed against society is the one he committed against God's law. He broke the commandment that warns us against taking God's name in vain.

When I was a kid, I thought that swearing was what was meant by taking God's name in vain. And though such expletives are disrespectful, there are much more serious violations: employing God's name for personal vanity or gain; maliciousness or misrepresentation of our Christian commitment. One of the most odious things to Christ was people pretending to be pious. Where I grew up, pretending to be something you weren't was called "playing possum."

Once a possum tried during the night to get a drink out of my birdbath. In the process, he tripped the heavy concrete bowl over and trapped himself beneath it. The next morning I saw his wiry tail wiggling out from under the birdbath. Not wanting to get bitten, I fetched a rake and used its handle to free him, but instead of running off, the bedraggled ball of gray fur went into a swoon. *Was he seriously injured or dying?* I wondered. Leaving him for a moment, I went inside and watched. Slowly, he gathered himself up on his front haunches and looked around until he was sure the coast was clear. Then, he hiked off lickety split into the woods. He had indeed been playing possum.

Abraham Lincoln said that you can fool some of the people all of the time and all of the people some of the time, but you can't fool all of the people all of the time. One that we can't fool any of the time is God, because He looks on our hearts and knows our inner thoughts. That's why it's folly to use God's name in vain.

> Teach us, Lord,
> To say what we mean and mean what we say,
> To let our yeas be yea and our nays be nay.
>
> —FRED BAUER

22 / SUN

But the Spirit itself maketh intercession for us. . . .
—ROMANS 8:26

A police siren sounded just as my friend Pastor Elsie Crickard and the bell choir finished playing at Pleasant Valley United Methodist Church. A few seconds later there was another siren, this one even closer.

Fearing that a parishioner might have fallen in the parking lot, Elsie asked an usher to check, then called for prayer. "The Lord wouldn't want us to continue the Order of Service when someone is in need right outside our door," she said. "Let's pray for the person, the need and for guidance on how we can help."

The usher returned just after the "Amen." "It's a car fire," he told Elsie. "Your family car just burned up."

After they viewed the remains, Elsie thanked the congregation for their prayers. "I thought I was praying for someone else, yet I was really joining the prayers you prayed for me!"

Two weeks later Elsie took me for a ride in a lovely lilac sedan. "This is a wonderful car!" she said. "I'm convinced that the prayers of my congregation gave my husband and me a peace that helped us find a reliable car at a price we could almost afford."

I'm convinced, too! I thank God for the people of Pleasant Valley who prayed when the siren sounded and for everyone who prays for people and needs unknown to them. Most of all, I thank God for the Holy Spirit Who prays for us and with us when we can't find the words.

Thank You, Holy Spirit, for the power of intercessory prayer in the lives of those who are prayed for—and those who pray.

—PENNEY SCHWAB

REHAB FOR THE HEART

In 1998 Guideposts *Roving Editor John Sherrill discovered that he had suffered a "hidden" heart attack—a cardiac event that goes undetected but leaves telltale scar tissue on the heart. To minimize the risk of another episode, John's doctor put him on a rigorous diet and exercise program, including six mornings a week at a nearby cardiac rehabilitation center. Go with John this week as he steps— reluctantly—into a brand-new experience.* —THE EDITORS

23/ MON
DAY ONE: GETTING UP TO SPEED
I know thy works, that thou art neither cold nor hot: I would thou wert cold or hot. —REVELATION 3:15

My first days at Cardiac Rehab were not promising. I didn't want to spend time doing a lot of boring exercises on a collection of shiny, chrome machines.

And besides, there was Carl.

Carl was a temporary employee, and he gave subtle messages that he was not interested in his job. Carl was bored. He kept sneaking glances at his wristwatch and looking out the window toward his red convertible.

How different was Tom, another Rehab employee. From the moment this young man stepped through the door until the minute he signed out, he gave the message that he was stimulated by his work. His first focus was on us. He called us by our first names, and if his familiarity took some getting used to, it soon became clear that his interest was real.

"Hi, Johnny," to me. No one has called me Johnny since I was a boy.

"Hello, Margaret," to a woman in her eighties who had recently come to Rehab and was awkward and timorous as she mounted the strange machines. "Warm up slowly, now. That's right, I'll be back in a minute to see how it's going."

When he wasn't checking our progress, Tom was looking after the equipment, tightening a bolt here, loosening some webbing there. Tom even went around cleaning the chrome with metal polish so the machines looked more inviting.

"You're never bored, are you?" I commented one day.

Tom seemed surprised by the thought. "Bored!" he said. "You guys are really interesting. How could I be bored?"

Months later, when we learned that Tom was taking a new job down in Virginia, we lined up to wish him the best. Tom had taught us a lot about enthusiasm. The root meaning of the word is "God within us." Whether or not Tom thinks in these terms, his enthusiasm makes me ask myself: When I walk into Rehab day after day, whom do *I* resemble? Carl or Tom?

Lord, help me to show Your presence to those I meet today.

—JOHN SHERRILL

24 / TUE *DAY TWO: PEDAL PUSHING*
Do ye look on things after the outward appearance?
—II CORINTHIANS 10:7

I was disappointed when Arnold stopped coming to Cardiac Rehab a few months ago. It took me awhile to discover it, but he was one of the most interesting guys I've met there.

For weeks I avoided exercising next to Arnold. He stood well over six feet tall, weighed two hundred and fifty pounds, and had the word HOG tattooed on his right arm. When Arnold flexed his huge biceps, the bright blue letters popped up and down. Arnold came to Rehab on a Harley-Davidson, and I instinctively disliked motorcyclists. All too often I'd met them roaring down the highway flaunting their hostility with skull and crossbones helmets, black gloves, studded leather jackets. I was always glad when they zoomed past.

Then one day I was working out on a stationary bicycle when Arnold climbed up on the machine next to me. "Not the same as riding a bike," Arnold said cheerfully, and before I had a chance to reply, he started to tell me about his Harley-Davidson. He'd fallen in love with Harleys, he said, when he was twelve years old and had been riding them since he was sixteen. Later in the year he planned to attend the HOG rally in Milwaukee.

"Hog rally?" I asked

"Harley Owners Group," Arnold said. "People from all over the world who love Harley-Davidsons. I've been a HOG since the group was founded, back in eighty-three. We've got half a million members, everybody from little old grandmothers to those lunatics you see riding in packs down the highways.

"You had a heart attack?" he asked unexpectedly.

Arnold and I became friends. I owe him a lot, not only for introducing me vicariously to the excitement of riding free-to-the-wind on a bike, but more importantly for showing me how shortsighted it is to form snap judgments. This particularly pernicious form of prejudice almost cost me the friendship of a most unusual man.

Father, teach me always to look at people with Your eyes.

—JOHN SHERRILL

25/WED **DAY THREE: WORKOUT AND WORSHIP**
And thou shalt love the Lord thy God with all thy heart, and with all thy soul, and with all thy mind, and with all thy strength. . . . —MARK 12:30

Every Wednesday at 6:45 A.M., a group of parishioners gathers in the Resurrection Chapel of St. Mark's Church in Mount Kisco, New York, to celebrate the Eucharist. The exquisite Gothic chapel has Tiffany windows, fresh flowers, a dedicated spiritual purpose. The prayers of generations are in the walls.

Immediately after the service, I go to Cardiac Rehab. What a contrast! Rehab's atmosphere is totally secular. Chrome machines, fluorescent lights, the morning news on television. And in this setting, men and women row and climb and run and pedal until their workout suits are drenched in sweat.

One Wednesday as I was leaving St. Mark's for Rehab, I commented on this contrast to my friend Mary Lynn Windsor, one of the 6:45 regulars. The Resurrection Chapel was holy ground, I said, but Rehab certainly was not.

"Oh, I don't know," Mary Lynn said. "Doesn't Jesus tell us to love God with all our heart and soul and mind and strength? At Rehab you're loving God with all your strength."

What a difference that remark made to me as I walked through the door of Rehab! Yes, my nostrils still smarted with the smell of disinfectant and my eyes narrowed against the glare, but I knew now that, incredible as it seems, I was stepping onto holy ground.

Always and everywhere, Father, You are there.   —JOHN SHERRILL

26/THU   *DAY FOUR: AN EVEN PACE*
For my yoke is easy, and my burden is light.
                    —MATTHEW 11:30

My friend Matthew Zenos, who came to the rehab center each day at the same hour I did, threw himself enthusiastically into his program. He used the treadmill, the bicycle, the StairMaster, the rowing machine, and three days a week he struggled with weights. Soon he was feeling so well, he added jogging to his routine.

One day I noticed that Matthew was limping. He shrugged it off. "No pain, no gain," he said with a laugh.

The limp grew worse. At last Matthew went to see a specialist in sports medicine. To his astonishment, the doctor told him that the muscles in his left leg had begun to atrophy.

"Atrophy!" Matthew said. "But I work out every single day for a couple of hours."

"Well, that's the trouble then. If a muscle is pressed too far too soon, it will shut down."

Amazed, Matthew cut back to a more gradual regimen, and with time the damaged muscle in his thigh repaired itself.

Matthew's experience resonated with me in an unexpected way. Last year I took on a number of extra activities—each one worthwhile in itself, I felt. Apart from my job and the needs of my family, I'd been involved in half a dozen community and church activities, some requiring evening sessions, travel or long phone calls, and one that included an ambitious Bible-reading program. There wasn't a day or evening on my calendar unscheduled.

About a month ago, I began to experience symptoms of spiritual malaise. Prayer seemed hollow. I no longer read my Bible with a sense of immediacy. Matthew's experience came to mind. Could I be suffering a sort of "spiritual atrophy" brought on by trying too hard?

Sure enough, as I slowed down, my damaged soul began to mend. The activities that did remain in my schedule took on new life. Jesus is my model in this, as in all things. His schedule was never crowded. Though His mission was nothing short of saving the whole human race, He didn't dash from one appointment to another. He didn't run. He walked. And if I am to be yoked with Him, as He asks, then I must learn to walk, too.

Help me to walk at Your side, Lord, not race ahead of Your gracious rhythm.
—JOHN SHERRILL

27/ FRI DAY FIVE: HEAVY LIFTING
The Lord is . . . my strength. . . . —PSALM 18:2

It was my first day on a machine I had not tried before. The equipment required special instructions from the staff. You climb onto a seat, the instructor told me, and lean into the backrest. The backrest moves. You are lifting a system of weights.

But there was a problem. "You can strain yourself if you don't keep your back straight," the instructor said. "The trick is to point your chin up. That will prompt you not to bend forward."

He left me to experiment with the clumsy apparatus. I pushed slowly backward, raising my chin. It was then that I noticed a small sign the instructor had placed high on the wall in front of me. LOOK UP HERE, the sign said.

Clever. As long as I kept my eyes on that sign I was automatically aligning my back correctly.

Over the months that little notice has taken on another meaning for me. Recently, for reasons of scheduling, I have had to come to rehab late in the day when no one is there except an instructor who is busy with paperwork. I've started to use the otherwise lonesome, boring exercise routine as a time for petition and intercession. I bring various concerns before God: my own health, the needs of others.

And each day the sign reminds me not to carry these needs alone—not to overestimate what my own back can support—but to keep looking upward to the Lord.

When problems arise today, Father, remind me that help is just a glance away.   —JOHN SHERRILL

28 / SAT   *The crooked shall be made straight, and the rough places plain.*   —ISAIAH 40:4

If you've ever watched a square dance, you know that a square of dancers must listen to the caller. If the dancers don't listen, the square is broken and becomes eight people milling about. And if each of the eight dancers tries to restore order on his or her own, the broken square looks like a bargain basement full of pre-Christmas shoppers looking for a good buy. It's only when the dancers stop and follow the caller's directions that order is restored and the dance continues.

It wasn't long after my wife and I became square dancers that I decided square dancing was a lot like life. A broken life, like a broken square, becomes frenetic and disorganized when I try to correct the problem by myself. It's only when I listen for the Lord's directions that order is restored in my life.

The more I dance, the more I learn that if I want to enjoy square dancing, I have to listen to the caller. The more I live, the more I learn that if I want to enjoy living, I have to listen to the Lord.

Lord, when my life seems to be getting out of hand, open my ears to hear Your call.   —RICHARD HAGERMAN

29 / SUN   *"Will a man rob God? Yet you are robbing Me! But you say, 'How have we robbed Thee?' In tithes and offerings."*   —MALACHI 3:8 (NAS)

It was more money than I'd ever held in my hand, and I'd found it folded to the size of a postage stamp underneath the big maple tree in front of our house on Madison Avenue. Ten dollars! By the time I ran to Mother with it, I'd spent it a dozen times in my mind: Barbie clothes; Nehi grape sodas and Mallo cups; Nancy Drew mysteries.

But Mother put a fast end to my dreaming, and instead of shopping, I was tacking a sign to the maple tree to ask if anyone had lost anything in our neighborhood. After a long week of no inquiries, Mother agreed that I could keep the money.

Sort of. "This is as good a time as any to learn about tithing, Roberta," she said. "The first dollar belongs to God. When you tithe with a willing heart, I think you'll be amazed at how far the rest of your money goes."

Why is it that every time something good happens, some adult comes up with a plan to ruin it? I groused. But that Sunday as I dropped a dollar bill in the collection plate, I felt joyful, a part of something bigger that I didn't quite understand.

And it was amazing. The department store downtown announced a sale on Barbie clothes. Then a lady at church asked Mother if her girls liked to read Nancy Drew. Nine dollars stretched further than ten would have.

In my teen years, as I earned money babysitting and selling cosmetics, Mother continued to stress the principle of tithing, of offering God the first portion of my earnings, not what's left over. By the time I graduated from nursing school and had a real job, tithing had become a part of who I was.

My mother is gone now, but that lesson from childhood is with me still. "Give God the first dollar, the first part of your day," I hear her say. "And watch Him take care of things."

And you know what? He's done just that.

Thank You, Lord, for stretching my skimpy resources beyond my wildest imaginings.
                                                    —ROBERTA MESSNER

30/ MON   *A cheerful heart is good medicine, but a crushed spirit dries up the bones.*   —PROVERBS 17:22 (NIV)

Even though major-league baseball isn't my favorite pastime, I jumped at the chance to take my son Andrew to a Milwaukee Brewers game in July 1999. Just four weeks earlier he'd had surgery. He hadn't been out of the house except for short walks and, quite frankly, I was getting impatient with him.

At Milwaukee County Stadium that night, we watched the game, we watched the people, we ate junk food. Then suddenly, just after the seventh-inning stretch, around 9:30 P.M., there was a power failure and the enormous lights that lit up the field suddenly went out. The stadium and field were left in a hazy darkness, and within a few minutes all the players retreated into the dugouts.

Because the score was Milwaukee 10, Kansas City 3, many people got up and left for home. Others blew bubbles, headed for the refreshment stands or sang songs in groups. I finally pulled a book out of my backpack and started to read under the few dusky lights that were still on in the grandstand.

Twenty minutes later, when I looked up to see that the field was aglow with bright lights once again and the game was ready to resume, I couldn't believe my eyes. I hadn't even noticed when the lights came back on. Andrew said they'd come on very gradually over the entire thirty-minute period.

Gradually, huh? They went from total darkness to bright enough to play ball and I hadn't even noticed?

I started to think about Andrew's healing. He'd gone from major surgery to cheering for the Brewers in four weeks and I hadn't really noticed that he'd been getting a little better each day . . . gradually. I'd been too concerned about pushing him to exercise harder, sleep less, take fewer pain pills, do a few chores and call his friends to notice that he was walking tall, eating normally and anxious to get out to see his beloved Brewers.

Lord, help me to be patient and loving when my loved ones are healing. Keep me mindful that it's a gradual process.

—PATRICIA LORENZ

31 / TUE *The fear of the Lord is the beginning of wisdom. . . .*
—PSALM 111:10

My mother was out back hanging up the wash, so I was all alone in the house, playing war with some lead soldiers in my parents' upstairs bedroom. I had an old brass tray that I used as a gong and a battered tablespoon to strike the tray at the start and the end of each battle.

Suddenly I thought I heard a strange noise. A monster was coming out of its hidden lair in the closet or the attic or the basement! My heart beat so loud I knew the monster would hear it and come to devour me or, worse, carry me away—like some winged older brother—to torture and torment me forever.

In terror, I began to sing and beat the gong. I cried a river of tears and sang at the top of my voice for an eternity of long seconds. I could almost see the shadows of the fangs and beak of the monster projected in the designs of the flowered wallpaper in front of me.

Then the distant "bang"—the back screen door slamming, the signal that my cavalry was going to charge over the hillside against the dragon.

"Mother!" I screamed. I knew the monster could hear me, too, so I beat the gong twice as hard. I heard running footsteps on the stairs. *Dear God, let it be my mother!*

The door burst open. My mother looked bigger than my dragon/beast, and she sent it scurrying back into its dark lair as she pressed me to her bosom and let me sob. Suddenly, a new dread filled me with terror. "What if you died, Mother? What if God took you away? Who would save me then?"

She smiled and held me close. Then she walked through the doorway of my fear and brought me the story of Jesus and His love.

Lord, thank You for reaching out to us in the arms of those who have helped us through the terrors of growing up. Amen.

—KEITH MILLER

DAILY GIFTS

1 _____

2 _____

3 _____

4 _____

5 _____

6 _____

7 _____

8 _____

9 _____

10 _____

11 _____

12 _____

13 _____

14 _____

15 _____

16 _____

17 _____

18 _____

19 _____

20 _____

21 _____

22 _____

23 _____

24 _____

25 _____

26 _____

27 _____

28 _____

29 _____

30 _____

31 _____

August

By love serve one another. For all the law is fulfilled in one word, even in this; Thou shalt love thy neighbour as thyself.

—GALATIANS
5:13–14

S	M	T	W	T	F	S
			1	2	3	4
5	6	7	8	9	10	11
12	13	14	15	16	17	18
19	20	21	22	23	24	25
26	27	28	29	30	31	

WHEN GOD REACHES OUT . . . THROUGH OTHER PEOPLE

*1/*WED

Then the Lord opened the servant's eyes, and he looked and saw the hills full of horses and chariots of fire. . . . —II KINGS 6:17 (NIV)

He sat on a stool beneath the stone overpass just north of the zoo in New York's Central Park, a favorite spot with street musicians because the arch makes a natural sounding board. I'd often paused there to listen to a trumpet or a guitar or an accordion. This young man, however, was playing an instrument I didn't recognize, a kind of long-necked, two-stringed violin held on his knees. The bow, positioned between the two strings, produced a haunting nasal melody, ephemeral and melancholy.

I stopped, enthralled and puzzled. I could see only one man, one instrument, yet the echoing space swelled with a great chorus of sound—flutes, gongs, plucked strings, drums. Stepping closer, I saw a small tape player at his feet. An entire orchestra was creating the music, the young man adding his single melodic line. I read the placard propped against the tape player:

> HELLO! HERE IS THE NATIONAL PEOPLE'S ORCHESTRA OF BEIJING (AND ME).

In smaller print the placard explained that the young musician, from China, was a student at Columbia Medical School, supporting himself with these street performances.

It had taken courage, I thought, to come alone to a strange land far from home—the kind of courage, in fact, needed on every journey of faith. God reached out to me beneath a bridge in Central Park to remind me that on my journey I never need to feel alone. When the road ahead is dark and threatening, I can tell my fears:

HELLO! HERE ARE ANGELS AND ARCHANGELS AND ALL
THE HOST OF HEAVEN (AND ME).

*Father, remind me on my journey today that mine is the name in
parentheses.*
—ELIZABETH SHERRILL

2 / THU   *"I have been your leader. . . ."* —1 SAMUEL 12:2 (NIV)

When I was traveling back east on Amtrak to see my parents, I thought
I could get off the train at every one of the fifteen or so stations between Martinez, California, and Penn Station in New York City.

"How long do we stop in Albany?" I asked a woman in a gray skirt
and blue blazer.

She shrugged. "About two hours, I'd guess."

You'd guess? I thought, annoyed at her vagueness.

"Can I get off the train there?" I persisted.

"I think so."

What kind of an answer is that? I wondered. Dissatisfied, I went off
in search of another employee, who said confidently, "Twelve minutes. And if you're not back in time, you'll be looking at the train's
caboose."

"But that other woman said about two hours!" I protested.

She looked in the direction of the woman I'd just asked, and then
she started laughing. "She's wearing a blue blazer, all right, but she's
not an employee! You need to go to the source!"

As I sat on the train in Albany (I didn't want to risk "looking at
the train's caboose"!), I mulled over the times I'd made similar mistakes. I asked all my friends for advice about breaking up with a
boyfriend, instead of praying about it. Their conflicting answers drove
me crazy, and I just prolonged my decision-making time.

And when I was thinking about a career change to substitute
teaching, I talked to co-workers and people at the temp agency where
I was working, but I got no closer to making a decision. It wasn't till
after I'd prayed and spoken to other substitute teachers that I decided
to go ahead.

*God, is there a question I need answered today? Let me go to You,
the Source of all answers.*
—LINDA NEUKRUG

3/ *FRI*   *Be still, and know that I am God. . . .* —PSALM 46:10

As I was walking to the office one morning—a luxury I treasure after years of commuting—I passed a young woman going in the opposite direction. I watched her with fascination. She was struggling to pull a cigarette out of a pack while holding a phone between her shoulder and her ear, all while crossing a busy Manhattan avenue. I held my breath, hoping that she wouldn't become involved in a fourth simultaneous activity by being hit by a car.

She crossed safely and was soon out of sight, but I began to think about the activities of my own hours and days. Anyone who has raised a family, held a job and kept house at the same time knows how to do many things at once. But while I have no cell phone and don't smoke, I began to see that "multitasking," as the techies call it, had become almost an addiction in my life. Setting the table while watching the news while opening the mail may not be as hazardous as crossing the street talking on the phone, but by the time I sit down to dinner the rhythm is set. Eat fast. Clean up. Move on. But to where?

I decided to learn to sit still and be quiet for five whole minutes each morning before leaving my apartment. It wasn't at all easy, but I clung to that wonderful and reassuring phrase from Psalm 46: "Be still, and know that I am God." I'm not perfect, and I still fidget and tend to cram in too many things, but I'm better, and those five minutes have had an extraordinary influence on my day. If I listen carefully, mysteriously and clearly, I realize what will really count in the day ahead. And that never means picking up the dry cleaning or planning errands for my lunch hour.

God, let me learn to listen to You at least once a day without interruption.   —BRIGITTE WEEKS

4/ *SAT*   *And all the days of Methuselah were nine hundred sixty and nine years. . . .*   —GENESIS 5:27

Last summer when my eighty-seventh birthday rolled inexorably around, I reminded myself hopefully that I was just a youngster compared to the ancient biblical character Methuselah. But one of the grandchildren had another idea when she sent me a birthday card.

"Congratulations on your special day, Granddad," she wrote on it, "but what about all your yesterdays? I don't think they should be left out. So here are thirty-one thousand, seven hundred and forty-three more congratulations just to take care of them!"

More than thirty-one thousand yesterdays! Whether or not she included leap years I don't know, but that's an astonishing number of sunrises and sunsets. This year, when Thanksgiving Day comes around, I'm going to remind myself that each yesterday was a gift from the Creator of all things . . . and be truly thankful!

Father, when You send another day, teach us not to take it for granted but make it count in the pattern of our lives.

—ARTHUR GORDON

5 / SUN   *Yet I will rejoice in the Lord, I will joy in the God of my salvation.*   —HABAKKUK 3:18

The older I get, the more I am trying to learn, or relearn, how to relax. Recently my wife Rosie and I found the perfect place: Laity Lodge, a Christian retreat and conference center in the west Texas hills, two and a half hours north of San Antonio.

On our first day at the lodge we were introduced to the many activities available to us, including swimming, horseback riding, art, tennis and—unexpectedly—signing, the finger language used by many hearing-impaired people. My first choice was tennis, but on second thought, I decided to give signing a chance. I thought it would be worthwhile even if I went to only one session and learned the alphabet.

At the first class the teacher told us that we would stand together as a group at the final service and use our hands to "sing" a song with the piano accompanying us. My first thought was *No way! I'm not going to embarrass myself.* But she patiently encouraged us to let go of our inhibitions, relax and allow God to use us.

As we finished the first day of practice, I was still awkward. My hands and fingers were not moving with the best rhythm. I was still self-conscious, imagining how silly I thought I'd look, trying to make the proper signs in time with the music. Then I remembered just what I would be doing—participating as best I could in a worship service to praise the Lord.

That Sunday morning, we stood before the group of worshipers signing the song "I Surrender All." As I moved my hands, I lifted my spirit in praise, and my heart was filled with joy and thanksgiving.

Lord, help me to follow You joyfully despite my fears.

—DOLPHUS WEARY

6/_{MON} *God . . . causes the growth.*

—I CORINTHIANS 3:7 (NAS)

I felt very little joy that Easter morning. Just a few days before, the doctor had told me my only sister had terminal cancer, and I was grieving for her. Not only that, but so far she had shown little interest in God's offers of hope and peace. What could I possibly do to help her?

Preoccupied with my thoughts, I wandered into the kitchen. On the windowsill was a hibiscus plant; it had been given to me as an expression of sympathy when my mother passed away. I had been diligently nurturing it along ever since, and in God's perfect timing, a large coral blossom shaped like a trumpet greeted me that Easter morning. It was both a glorious message of resurrection hope and a beautiful reminder of my mother's faith.

As I stood there admiring the bloom, God seemed to say, *For several months now you have been concerned about the soil and the sunshine and the water for this plant, and that is good. But remember, the budding and the blossoming are My business. You do the possible. I will do the impossible. You tend to your sister's physical needs with loving patience and diligent care, but leave the flowering of her soul to me.*

At that moment, the anxiety I had been experiencing disappeared. I simply resolved to reach out to my sister with love that was "rooted and grounded" in God (Ephesians 3:17, NAS).

As I write this a few months later, I can see some tiny buds of belief beginning to swell. They give me hope that my sister will eventually blossom out in faith—resurrection faith.

Lord, as I watch a soul slowly open like a flower in the light of Your presence, I can only say with Paul, "How . . . unfathomable [are Your] ways" (Romans 11:33, NAS).

—ALMA BARKMAN

7 / *TUE* *At thy right hand there are pleasures for evermore.*
—PSALM 16:11

I was on hold on a pay phone on Exit 87 outside Jackson, Tennessee.

A few minutes earlier, my husband David and I had been riding happily down the interstate, talking about all the places we hoped to travel to someday. David was at the wheel of an eighteen-foot rental truck loaded down with stuff for our daughter Keri's graduate school apartment in Memphis.

The blowout came quickly: a pop, then a low hiss. We were lucky to make it to the exit.

I had called the rental agency's toll-free number for assistance, while David trekked off to look for help. Now, on the other end of the phone line, a recording droned on: "And for fifteen dollars you can get an extra copy of your rental contract sent. . . ."

I spotted a moth in the gravel by the phone. Its wings were white with black spots. The spots formed a lovely pattern, the same on both wings. Its legs were cobalt blue. The moth seemed to be having a bit of trouble. I looked around and my eyes fell on a tree that seemed to offer a nice shelter for the moth's recovery. I lay down the phone long enough to scoop up the moth with the original rental contract (which we got for free when we rented the truck) and transported it to the tree. Back at the phone, the voice of a real, live person told me a road service representative would be along to fix the tire in fifteen minutes.

A few minutes before, I had set my sights on traveling out into the blue horizons of someday—completely oblivious to the view along the way. Now, I watched the moth fly over to a patch of dew-drenched grass, hover for a moment, then fly away.

On hold, on a pay phone, on a nondescript exit of the interstate, I had learned a timely lesson: Someday is now.

Father, You plant the potential for pleasure all along the road of life. Give me the wisdom to enjoy all that is close at hand. —PAM KIDD

8 / *WED* *I will restore health unto thee, and I will heal thee of thy wounds, saith the Lord.* —JEREMIAH 30:17

The news from home had me worried. Dad was in the hospital for a torn Achilles tendon. After surgery he wouldn't be able to walk for six weeks. I could picture him trapped upstairs in the bedroom, Mom shuttling up and down, bringing him his meals, mail, newspaper. If I were closer to home, at least I could run errands for her, or help Dad with his physical therapy. But they were in California, some two thousand miles away, so I had to content myself with phone calls and letters. What else could I do?

Then my friend Gary had a seizure. He lives in an apartment across the street. The doctors weren't sure what the cause was, but they didn't want him going to work on his own. "Rick," he asked me one evening on the phone, "could you accompany me on the subway in the morning? My doctor doesn't want me to be alone, in case I have another seizure."

"Sure," I said. "No problem."

The next day I met Gary outside his building and we walked to the station together. "I know you like to pray in the mornings," he said, "so go ahead. I have something to read." On the train I took out my Bible and he took out his newspaper. When I closed my eyes, I had a lot on my mind. *Lord, be with Mom and Dad back home. I wish I could be there.* Then it occurred to me that God had given me something good to do right here. *Be with Gary as the doctors help him.*

Later when I talked to Mom, she told me about all the people who had been giving them a hand. "I'm sorry I can't be with you," I said.

"That's all right," she said. "I know there are things you need to be doing there." Someday I'd tell her the half of it.

Let me serve You, Lord, wherever I am.   —RICK HAMLIN

*9/**THU*   *You have planted them, and they have taken root; they grow and bear fruit. . . .* —JEREMIAH 12:2 (NIV)

"And these," our Hawaiian guide said with a flourish of his hand and a wide smile, "are pineapples!" Gentle laughter rippled through the bus. Every tourist knew that! But then he proceeded to tell us something we didn't know: Pineapples will grow bigger if they're given room. "Could be very big!" the guide continued. "But they are deliberately grown small so they will pack into cans that fit on your grocery store shelves."

As we drove on through the huge fields of sweet-smelling fruit, I felt a twinge of sadness that they were forced to fit into a predeter-mined space. *Glad it's not like that with people,* I thought. Or was it? What about the people "growing" near me—co-workers, family members, fellow churchgoers, friends. Was I allowing them to reach their potential? Giving them space to try their ideas, express their opinions? Was I allowing them room to make mistakes, to take risks that would enable them to grow?

The bus lumbered toward its next attraction, but I looked back at those pineapples. "Grow," I whispered softly. It was what I planned to do—and help others to do, too.

Use me, Father, to cultivate all that is fine and noble in others. And don't let me cramp their growth in the process!

—MARY LOU CARNEY

10/ FRI *When the morning stars sang together, and all the sons of God shouted for joy?* —JOB 38:7

All I have to do is walk out into the evening and look up into the sky, and the memory returns: I was five years old. My dad stood over my bed, gently shaking me awake. "Come with me, Brock. I have a sur-prise for you."

He carried me out into the yard where my mom had spread a big quilt. I realized that it was way past my bedtime. Why had my par-ents awakened me, and why were we outside in the warm summer night?

"God is going to give us a special show," my father whispered to me.

For the next few hours we lay side by side on the quilt. We watched the shooting stars flare across the sky one after the other, sometimes two at once.

I had a unique feeling that night, one that to this day I find hard to describe. I was receiving a gift, a revelation of God's wonder. This gift was given, I felt, exclusively to me and my parents by the Lord God Himself.

This show, the Perseid meteor shower, returns to the summer sky every year in August, and I have seen it many times since. I have seen it from a canoe on a rural lake in Alabama and from the roof of my college fraternity house in Knoxville, Tennessee. I have even seen it over the Grand Canyon. But no meteor shower will ever match the one my parents awakened me to see from an old quilt in the backyard that summer night.

Lord, let the star's song be heard and let us all shout for joy!

—BROCK KIDD

11/_{SAT} *Though I walk in the midst of trouble, thou wilt revive me . . . thy right hand shall save me.*

—PSALM 138:7

We've had our share of extraordinary pets, but when it comes to determination and sheer instinct for survival, Gussie tops the list.

My husband was the first to spot her. "What on earth?" he mused as he peered out the kitchen window. "Is that a small gray rock moving out there?" Both our daughter and I looked. Then, quick as lightening, our daughter was out the door and racing across the lawn. She came back in holding a baby possum.

We filled a basin with warm water, then made a solution of antiseptic mixed with shampoo. As I gently sloshed the little creature through the water, hundreds of fleas rinsed off her. We changed the water and did it again. And again, until she was completely clean. She didn't seem to mind, perhaps because she was barely alive. Dehydrated, she kept sucking on an eye dropper filled with liquid nutrition. Then, wrapped in a soft washcloth, she fell asleep in our daughter's hand.

"Because it's August, we'll call her Gussie," decided our daughter. "Do you suppose we could keep her?"

I frowned, not comfortable with the prospect of a possum in the house. "Better check with the Humane Society. Possums are wild creatures, and they could be dangerous pets."

Our daughter was put in touch with the Opossum Society, which rescues little creatures such as Gussie. Soon we were deep in the world of possum rescue, a world that has reached into our hearts and enriched our lives as we have learned the gentle ways of these small wild creatures.

"The secret was she kept moving, or I wouldn't have seen her," my husband observed, obviously impressed.

"That little creature didn't give up!" I agreed. "She's given me an example I'll never forget."

Dear Lord, when I'm consumed by worries and troubles, help me to trust that Your gentle hand will reach out to rescue me, Your mercy heal my wounds, and Your love revive me and hold me forever against Your heart.   —FAY ANGUS

---

12 / SUN

Be strong and of a good courage; be not afraid, neither be thou dismayed: for the Lord thy God is with thee whithersoever thou goest.   —JOSHUA 1:9

After the recessional every Sunday, our minister stands in the back of the sanctuary and in his rich preacher's voice delivers a stirring benediction: "God is with you. Therefore, go out into the world and fear nothing."

The words fill me with courage. *Yes! I can do anything!* At least until I hit the glare of the noonday sun in the parking lot. *Fear nothing? Not the confrontation I must have with a friend? Not the talk on storytelling I'm supposed to give? Not the overloaded schedule I can't possibly keep? How, Lord?*

My mind goes back to a long-ago summer day. I'm about ten, a scrawny child standing on a platform twenty-five feet above our local swimming hole. The courage to jump has drained out of me; the bottoms of my feet seem cemented to the hot wood. Behind me, a line of impatient kids is yelling at me to jump. Finally, an older boy steps close and whispers, "The first time you have to jump scared." I close my eyes, release my sweaty grip and fall. My stomach dives to my ankles; I feel the cold shock of the water. It swallows me, and down I go until I feel slimy plants and mud against my bare legs. Then I begin to rise upward. I emerge from the water spitting victory.

Now, as I pull out of the church parking lot, I hear the pastor's challenge as it was meant to be heard: The "go" comes first. The "fear nothing" comes after.

Lord, thank You for meeting me as I step out into my fear.
      —SHARI SMYTH

PRAYER FOR AUGUST

Within my spirit, nothing stirs or wavers.
Becalmed and motionless, I quietly wait.

Lord, send Your whispered breeze,
to reassure and comfort . . .
Your sweeping wind,
to cleanse, refresh, reorganize . . .
Your gale-force blast,
to overturn, reshape, uproot, reclaim . . .

Send *anything* to stir my stagnant soul . . .
to fill and move me.

—EVELYN MINSHULL

13/ MON   *"All nations will call you blessed, for you will be a land sparkling with happiness. . . ."*
—MALACHI 3:12 (TLB)

There's something magical about this place. On a rented bike, I glide along the waterfront of South Haven, Michigan, a small resort town on the eastern shore of Lake Michigan. I held a ministry internship here thirty-nine years ago, but the town is not the same unspoiled paradise. Now it's a tourist magnet. The church building now houses a bank. The once placid harbor is packed with sailboats, and the beach is a swarm of seagulls and swimmers.

And yet something about this town sparkles.

At the bicycle shop the bearded salesman is so entertaining that I urge him to start his own sitcom. He laughs. "Thanks, and don't worry about getting this bike back right on time. Enjoy yourself out there."

When an ATM machine balks on me, the bank teller actually crawls inside the machine and fixes it. "There," she says, sweetly, "now you can enjoy the rest of your vacation without money worries."

When I accidentally leave my toolbox at the motel, I go back for it, but it's gone. *Oh, great, two hundred dollars worth of tools just vanished!* But when I tell the manager, he sends out a search party. A young groundskeeper, wearing an "I Love Jesus" T-shirt, finds the box in the laundry room, and he hands it to me, glowing with joy at his success. "I know how it is," he says. "You can buy new tools, but they don't have the same feel as your own tools."

Now I remember why I'm drawn back to South Haven in the summers. It's not just the cool breezes and blue waters. It's that small-town spirit of joyful service.

The town of Moberly, Missouri, where I live, is unremarkable. Deep inside I know it's up to me to make this place sparkle by wearing a smile and being ready to lend a hand to those in need.

May the happiness of the Savior shine through me and touch those I meet today.
—DANIEL SCHANTZ

14/ **TUE** *And Agrippa said to Paul, "In a short time you think to make me a Christian!"* —ACTS 26:28 (RSV)

In the days of the Model A Ford, outdoor advertising signs had much longer messages than today. The reason is simple enough: When people were driving down the road at forty miles an hour, they could read a lot more words than at sixty or more. Speed, I'm told, doomed my all-time favorite outdoor ads, those five-sign rhymes posted by Burma Shave. Readers of a certain age will recall those entertaining fence-post sayings. I'm not sure I can quote it exactly, but one of the rhymes quipped:

> He saw her beauty
> And made a bum's rush
> She saw his stubble
> And gave him the brush.

What brought this all to mind was a series of recent outdoor ads attributed to God. An anonymous Florida resident commissioned a Fort Lauderdale agency to create some billboards that would call people's attention to spiritual matters in a provocative way. What started out to be a local campaign turned national; at last count, thanks to the Outdoor Advertising Agency of America, the pithy sayings have appeared on more than ten thousand billboards. Among my favorites: "Loved the wedding. Invite me to the marriage." "Let's meet at my house Sunday before the game." "What part of 'Thou Shalt Not. . .' didn't you understand?" "Do you have any idea where you're going?"

Isn't it amazing what can be communicated in a few words? Our mistake sometimes is thinking that we need to set aside a whole hour to reach God, when in fact we can talk to Him on the move, in short takes, day or night. Something like a billboard.

> *Lord, when I'm stressed and my day is peaceless,*
> *Help me live a prayer that's ceaseless.*

—FRED BAUER

15/WED *The pride of thine heart hath deceived thee. . . .*
—OBADIAH 3

As I scrubbed the spines off the dozens of green-and-white-marbled pickling cucumbers in my kitchen sink, I was pleased with my first attempt at gardening. Bulbs of garlic and pungent dill waited on the draining board. This morning my seventyish rancher friend Margaret Norman was teaching me how to put up dill pickles. I longed for them to be as tasty as hers and had often joked that I would always choose a jar of her dills over any of the stunning silver, turquoise and jade jewelry she made.

"Now first, honey, you steam the jars." I felt myself tensing. I wanted to boil them.

"Try to pack 'em like this." I listened politely, but felt I had a better idea.

"Then you mix up the brine, boil it, and seal 'em."

I'd had enough.

"But, Margaret, I read that you're supposed to *boil* the jars."

Margaret had had enough, too. "Okay, kid," she sighed, "I can see you've got your own ideas. Go ahead and do it your way, and tell me how they come out." She hung up her potholder and walked out the kitchen door.

Too busy to feel upset, I continued working in the steamy kitchen. Later I admired my beautiful pickles, a filigree of dill and pearly garlic at the bottom of each translucent jar. Several weeks later, I was ready to taste my handiwork. *Yuck!* No vinegar! My beautiful pickles were nothing more than boiled cucumbers in jars of water.

I sheepishly confessed to Margaret. She smiled gently. "Well, honey, I knew you weren't about to listen to me. I had to let you learn on your own." She patted my hand and gave me a jar of dills from her root cellar.

To this day, I can't make dill pickles like Margaret, but I do know a little better how to listen.

Lord, give me the sense to recognize my pride and friends patient enough to teach me in spite of it. —GAIL THORELL SCHILLING

A WHOLE AND HOLY LOVE

16/THU

Search me, O God, and know my heart. . . .
—PSALM 139:23

"Sometimes you treat me like a child!"

Marilyn's words came unexpectedly and went straight to my heart. We were on our way to an appointment, and I asked her if she had remembered to bring some papers we needed. What was so wrong with that? Of course, I didn't think she was a child; I saw her as an extremely intelligent, exceptionally competent person. But she was telling me that I didn't always treat her that way, and that was hard to hear.

Her words cut into my image of myself and exposed a contradiction between what I thought and what I did. I thought I respected her independence and valued our relationship as equals, yet, as her words revealed, I could, on occasion, assume the role of a parent and treat her like a child.

This is my "dark side," a part of me I don't want to acknowledge, even to myself. It comes out in my relationship with Marilyn because we are committed to being open with each other. And it's good that it does come out, because it's only as I'm fully known that I can be fully loved.

The Psalmist knew that when he called upon God to "search me and know my heart." Nothing, after all, is hidden from God, and yet

God loves us unconditionally. By allowing myself to be known, even the dark and unacceptable parts of myself, I open myself for love, the kind of love I most long for, unconditional love.

One of the great blessings of our marriage is that Marilyn and I can be mirrors to each other. It has been painful for us to see ourselves reflected in one another's eyes, but it also has been healing. We have found that this is one of the ways God's grace enters our lives and transforms us.

All-knowing God, may I allow myself to be known, even as I am known by You.
—ROBERT KING

17 / FRI

The Lord is my strength and my shield; my heart trusted in him, and I am helped. . . . —PSALM 28:7

The good news about the hurricane was that it might have killed off the encephalitis-bearing mosquitoes that had invaded New York City. The bad news was that it left my husband Andrew stranded in Cleveland, Ohio, while I was sick at home with three small children.

"Mommy, Mary has clay in her mouth." I opened an eyelid and stumbled to my feet. I knew I needed another adult in the house, but finding someone who could come over in the middle of a hurricane was more than I could manage. *Lord, You've got to keep my children safe for me!* I took the clay out of Mary's mouth, mumbled something about not letting her have any more and curled up again on the sofa.

"Mommy, I'm hungry." I pried myself out of a fetal position and, surprised at how much time had passed, staggered to the kitchen to make some dinner. *Lord, they are Yours. Take care of them.*

"Mommy, can we have a bath?" I couldn't sit up long enough to supervise, so the answer was no. They galloped off to their room to go on with whatever game they'd invented. *God, thank You for such good children.*

At last it was bedtime, and everyone went to sleep. The wind howled outside, the rain hammered at the window. Yet even with two storms raging—one outside and one within me—I was at peace. God had provided. My children were safe.

O Lord of all creation, even though the whole universe is Yours, You care for me and my family as if we were the most precious things You've made.
—JULIA ATTAWAY

18/ SAT

There are friends who pretend to be friends, but there is a friend who sticks closer than a brother.
—PROVERBS 18:24 (RSV)

"Hi, Pat."

"Oh, hello." Pat looked at me blankly for a second, holding a lunch tray, her handbag slung over her arm.

"Estelle's son," I added. Pat smiled and said, "Oh, yes," then sat down with me at the table in the dining area of the Alzheimer's unit at Claussen Manor, where my mother was a resident. Every morning Pat dressed to the nines, meticulously and tastefully. For each outfit she had a matching handbag, and she took it everywhere.

"How's Estelle doing?"

"She's pretty weak. She's sleeping now."

"Oh, I love your mother. We go way back. We're best friends, you might say. Once in high school we were both interested in the same fellow, even though I think he liked Estelle better than me. It was that red hair of hers, like bronze. Made the boys crazy. Then we decided that we'd rather stay friends than fall out over some dumb boy, so we got rid of him! That was us, inseparable.

"We used to go to church together a lot, too, every day. The nuns made us. Boy, could Estelle sing—not very well, but loud! You couldn't miss it."

It gave me great comfort to know that Mom had a lifelong friend like Pat with her at Claussen. Except the term *lifelong* is relative. Pat and my mother had known each other only a short while. They met at Claussen, though you would not have known it to hear them go on about the old days, the good times they had together as the best friends they swore they were. It made perfect sense to them that they were together. And when I happened upon Pat the evening before, standing at the foot of Mom's bed, her old friend slipping farther and farther away, it didn't surprise me to see a tear slip down her cheek and hear her say, "I'm praying for you, Estelle, just like always."

At first I had been afraid my mother would be lonely at Claussen. But God saw to it that she wasn't. He sent Pat, in her daily best, my mom's temporary lifelong friend.

God, You give us miracles at every turn. And by the way, how did Pat know Mom's hair was once bronze?
—EDWARD GRINNAN

19/_{SUN} *A bruised reed he will not break, and a smoldering wick he will not snuff out. In faithfulness he will bring forth justice. . . .* —ISAIAH 42:3 (NIV)

For a couple of years I volunteered three days a week at our tiny church office, where they have given me the title Director of Communications. This meant that I wrote and edited the monthly newsletter and updated the weekly bulletin. It also meant that I heard many of the joys and sorrows of the church family.

One week, many of our families seemed to be struggling. Financial loss, severe illness, a breaking marriage, a miscarriage, a death in the family—the list went on and on. I knew that behind each of the prayer requests lay people who were hurting, struggling to let their faith grow in adversity and uncertainty.

I was absentmindedly typing the prayer list for Sunday's bulletin as I concentrated on praying for the various people and their needs. When I looked up at the computer screen to check my work, I found I had typed the phrase "each member" as "each ember."

The image of an "ember," something burning low, brought to my mind the "smoldering wicks" of Isaiah 42. As I corrected my mistake, I smiled and thanked God that His promise was sure: Not one of these "embers" would be snuffed out. He would sustain them and bring forth a good result in His own perfect way and time.

Lord, bless and sustain those whose faith candle burns low today.

—ROBERTA ROGERS

INTO AFRICA

20 / MON *The heavens declare the glory of God; and the firma-ment showeth his handiwork.* —PSALM 19:1

After a day of bouncing over rock-strewn four-wheel-drive tracks until my tailbone ached, I was beginning to feel that Africa was a long way from home. I'd had two weeks of strange foods and a different bed every night, and I missed my family, my recliner, pizza and interstate highways. Everything familiar seemed remote, even God.

We began climbing a long, winding switchback track, and suddenly we were at the rim of the Ngorongoro Crater in Tanzania. Nothing in my experience had prepared me for the wonder of this place we dubbed "God's workshop." The crater is perhaps twenty-five miles across and a mile or two deep. Its floor is filled with rich soil, and a lazy river winds across the level valley, emptying into a small, quiet lake. A lush forest rings the valley, while its center is dominated by a grassy plain.

As if Noah had opened the Ark here, the crater seems filled with every kind of animal. In the space of four hours driving the winding tracks on the crater floor, we saw elephants, giraffes, lions, rhinoceroses, water buffaloes, zebras, gazelles, wildebeests, monkeys and cheetahs. It was like watching a nature film, except we were close enough to touch these magnificent creatures.

Instead of adding to my feelings of being out of place, seeing so much of God's creativity in one place gave me a renewed sense of His presence. It was as if we were arriving around each bend just after God had been there, preparing a new discovery, each more wonderful than the last.

Lord, thank You for all the signs of Your presence, whether in the wonder of wild Africa or the beauty of a flower in an urban window box. —ERIC FELLMAN

21 / *TUE*   *"Give to everyone who asks you. . . ."*
—LUKE 6:30 (NIV)

I love ice cream, which is probably why I cheerfully gave the pan-handler outside my favorite ice cream shop a dollar. I hardly glanced at him when I gave him the money, avoiding the touch of what I imagined was a hand unused to soap. Barely acknowledging his garbled thanks, I was through the door and in line for my favorite flavor.

Within moments, the familiar, rather sullen teen behind the counter had packed my German chocolate cake. I already had the money out—exact change to save time—when she put down the container and ambled over to the cash register. She looked just beyond me and broke into a huge grin, something I'd never seen her do before. Then she asked the customer behind me, "Single scoop cone, right? And what's today's flavor?" As she waited for an answer, I began to fidget and fume, finally turning around to aim an outraged glance at the indecisive offender.

It was the panhandler. As he struggled to name "today's flavor," I saw that he was disabled. He worked to help the girl (clearly his friend from similar past encounters) understand his choice.

My shame deepened when she exclaimed, "German chocolate cake? Is that it?"

As she turned to fill his order, I murmured, "Here," in a voice more strangled than the one he'd thanked me with, and shoved my pint into his hand, the hand that still grasped the dollar I'd so coolly handed him outside. Leaving the money for the pint on the counter, I fled.

I sat in the car, remembering how smugly I'd congratulated myself for being so generous a few moments earlier. I had a lot to learn about giving.

Lord, help me to give with a heart as open as my hand.
—MARCI ALBORGHETTI

22 / *WED*   *"As I was with Moses, so I will be with you. . . ."*
—JOSHUA 1:5 (NIV)

Tonight I had a "Moses Moment," one of those times when I tell God, "I can't. . . . I don't want to. . . . I won't!" It struck me about 6:00 P.M. as I began the final preparations to teach a 7:30 P.M. Bible study at our church. Weeks earlier, when I agreed to fill in for this one-night stand, it had sounded like a fine idea. But now I was filled with dread and fears of inadequacy. "I'm not a Bible study teacher, Lord. Surely there will be people there who know more about this passage than I do. I'm tired. My stomach is filled with flutter feelings. I can't. . . . "

I call it a "Moses Moment" because Moses voiced similar fears when God told him to go somewhere and speak. "Who am I that I should go? What if they don't believe me or listen to me? O Lord, please send someone else to do it. I can't. . . . "

Then I remembered the gist of what God told Moses: "Go, and when you get to the place where you feel afraid, I will be with you. I will give you what you need."

In spite of my flutter feelings, I forced myself to read over the text and study my notes. Then off I went to teach the class. Two hours later, as I drove home, I felt pretty sheepish because none of my fears had materialized. I led the class through the study of the Scripture passage. And my feelings of dread disappeared as soon as the class started.

I also felt pretty sheepish because I've endured many "Moses Moments" in my life when I dread the challenge before me, and I should know that my flutter feelings are merely part of the preparation. Enduring them helps me trust God's promise that when He calls me to do a task, He'll provide what I need. Always.

Lord, when I face another "Moses Moment" and say, "I can't," remind me of Your promise that together, "We can."

—CAROL KUYKENDALL

A WEEKEND AWAY

As we get ready to enjoy these last few summer weekends, Van Varner is boarding the train for one more weekend away. Let's join

Van in his compartment. We're not sure where he's going, but we know there will be sea spray somewhere on his travels!

—THE EDITORS

23/THU

DAY ONE: A JOURNEY BY RAIL
And he shall not judge after the sight of his eyes. . . .
—ISAIAH 11:3

The train was crowded—and late—leaving New York. Luckily there was a seat, and I grabbed it, stowed my baggage overhead and plopped down. I nodded to my seatmate, a young man, and took out my book. The volume, *The Oxford Book of the Sea,* had everything from a long quote from *Moby Dick* to a brief eight lines of Emily Dickinson, proper reading for me since I was heading to an island off New London, Connecticut—that is, if the train didn't lose more time. I worried a little. What would I do if I missed the last ferry of the day? There was a plane from Groton, if I could afford it. A hotel, somewhere? No, I had better not think about it.

Suddenly my seatmate began to talk, not to me but into an instrument he held in his hand—a cell phone. "Hello, Margie, it's me, calling from the Hell Gate Bridge. I'm heading to Boston on Amtrak." The one-sided conversation did not get more electrifying than a list of the towns we passed. And it was loud, loud enough to keep a fellow awake five rows away. "Hey, Ronnie. Guess where I am?" The second call was equally edifying, and with the third and fourth, I was properly irked. But I kept quiet. Cell phones are a curse of modern society.

By the time we reached Old Saybrook, I was definitely concerned about the time. I was telling the woman conductor of my plight when my seatmate burst in. "Use this," he said, offering his phone. "Call the ferry. Tell them to hold it a minute." I must have stared, my mouth open. The ferry left on time no matter what, but that wasn't the point. That this stranger had volunteered his "curse of modern society" flustered me.

"Thank you," I said meekly.

I made the ferry with ten minutes to spare.

I know he should have been more mindful of others, Lord, but I am too quick to judge. Help me. —VAN VARNER

24 / *FRI*

DAY TWO: AN EVENING ON THE FERRY
They shall abundantly utter the memory of thy great
goodness, and shall sing of thy righteousness.

—PSALM 145:7

I knew the ferry ride to the island would take forty-five minutes, for I'd made the trip countless times. I knew, too, that my old friend, in spite of her recent surgery, would be there to meet me. On board the passengers settled down. Some chatted and some took to reading, while the children ran to the soda machine and the dogs sniffed at their surroundings.

I went out on deck and leaned over the forward railing. It was the place I always came to, where the waters churned against the prow and the mainland seemed to wash from me. I felt different here, as we made our way to sea. With each lap of the water I felt—what should I say?—an exultation, like the poem I had just read on the train. Where was it? I scurried back for *The Oxford Book of the Sea* and there it was, by Emily Dickinson:

> *Exultation is the going*
> *Of an inland soul to sea,*
> *Past the houses—past the headlands—*
> *Into deep Eternity.*

Emily Dickinson had likely never been to sea, but she understood it, and more than that, she comprehended the soul. Right then and there, looking deep into the sea, I was profoundly grateful for that wondrous essence that God had breathed into our nostrils with the breath of life—a living soul.

The poem was only eight lines long, and I reread the closing:

> *Bred as we, among the mountains,*
> *Can the sailor understand*
> *The divine intoxication*
> *Of the first league out from land?*

The answer from this poor sailor was "Yes." And as I was thinking about it, we pulled into the dock.

For all those years of memory, I thank You, Father. —VAN VARNER

25 / SAT

DAY THREE: BACK ON THE ISLAND
The Lord is good to all: and his tender mercies are over all his works. —PSALM 145:9

She was there at the ferry landing as usual, her movements a little slower, but you'd never guess she was a month from her ninetieth birthday. She drove the automobile with care through the island's tiny shopping center (three stores) and past the two churches. I wondered if time had ceased; the island seemed not to have changed at all. How many years had I been coming? Thirty-five, maybe. Then we came to the familiar lane of green thicket and suddenly her house—low-lying, simple, isolated from other habitations—and a vast green lawn stretching down to the sea.

"Just the same old faces," she said before listing the events of the days ahead. "I'm afraid you'll be bored."

"Not on your life," I said, and I couldn't have been more honest, for I was about to settle into a routine I looked forward to: breakfast with her, a trip to get the newspaper, a swim in the sea, a delicious lunch, a selection of good books, a heavenly dinner with people I knew and liked, and early to bed. Bored? On the contrary, utter contentment.

One evening over dinner, just the two of us, I spoke of my contented state. "I, too," she replied. "It's a luxury to admit it, when others have so many troubles." I reminded her of her recent major surgery. "Yes, and you endured a stroke, but we are still here. Relish life while you can, dearie."

As we talked, I felt as though I were David all those centuries gone by, strumming his harp and composing a song of praise and love for the Lord.

For each and every year I am grateful, Lord. —VAN VARNER

26 / SUN

And the Lord God planted a garden eastward in Eden. . . . —GENESIS 2:8

The Butchart Gardens of Victoria, British Columbia, enjoy a world-wide reputation. Begun in 1904 in Mr. Butchart's abandoned stone quarry north of the city, the gardens now contain fifty acres of year-round blossom and sculptured greenery.

I first visited the Butchart Gardens as a child. My grandfather knew Mr. Shiner, the head gardener, and one summer day Grandpa took me to visit his old friend. Lest I get lost in the sea of people *ooh*ing and *aah*ing and bending over to sniff the endless varieties of flowers, Mr. Shiner took me by the hand. I traipsed alongside, mesmerized.

As we traveled the pathways, Mr. Shiner explained flower rotation, bug infestation and his ideas for irrigation along the high rockeries. He showed us the greenhouses, where spent flowers could rest and recuperate, and he spoke of expansion plans. He pointed with pride to a new kind of rose he'd developed. Mr. Shiner knew every flower in the garden, and it was he who made sure they stayed healthy and beautiful and always growing. What a privilege, I thought, to know the head gardener!

On a recent visit to the gardens, I recalled with pleasure that magic day so many years ago. As I thought back on my walk with Grandpa and Mr. Shiner, it occurred to me that God protects and nurtures us in much the same way. Like the gardener, God provides all that we need. He tends us when we suffer infestations of ill-will, poor health and other woes. He creates within us a new spirit; He expands our horizons with new goals.

Truly it is a privilege to know the Head Gardener!

Whether I'm withering or flourishing, let me remember it is You, Lord, the Head Gardener, Who always nourishes and protects.

—BRENDA WILBEE

27 / MON   *As the appearance of the bow that is in the cloud in the day of rain, so was the appearance of the brightness round about. This was the appearance of the likeness of the glory of the Lord.* . . . —EZEKIEL 1:28

This morning, between 7:30 and 8:00, God created a wonderful spectacle: a brilliant rainbow that stretched from the land up to the sky, across the heavens and down to the earth again. It was radiant with colors—red, orange, yellow, green, blue, indigo, violet—and lasted a long time.

How often am I so absorbed in my schedule, my responsibilities and duties for the day that nature does not touch me? How many beautiful rainbows, glorious sunsets, spectacular cloud formations or skies full of stars have happened around me that I haven't taken the time to notice?

And how many times will God speak to me as I go through this day? Just as I ought to keep my eyes open for His gifts of beauty, I ought to listen as He calls me to praise Him by helping those around me.

Here is my list of some of the ways I can respond to God's call: I just heard that a dear friend is celebrating her fiftieth birthday next week. A letter must go out to her today. My neighbor is recovering from a heavy cold and has been confined to her house for more than a week. I will take her a special casserole dish. My daughter Margaret is overwhelmed with settling into a new home. I will take her and her husband out to dinner. Finally, I will take my two-mile walk to keep my spirit and body in top condition and aware of God's presence.

Dear God, open my eyes to see Your glory in the world You have made, and open my ears to hear You call through the voice of my neighbor's need.
—RUTH STAFFORD PEALE

28/ TUE *I am sending him to you for this very purpose . . . that he may encourage you.* —EPHESIANS 6:22 (NIV)

My husband Gene and I are both people-watchers. One night we were enjoying a late supper at a fast-food restaurant in the seaside town where we'd vacationed for years. As we ate, we noticed a man and a boy, maybe thirteen years old, sitting on stools at the counter. They seemed to know the waitress and the other people at the counter, so we assumed they lived in the town.

The boy was tall and well-built. After a while he stood up to leave, reached down and gave the man a hug, resting his head on the man's shoulder for a few moments. Over the wailing music on the juke box, we heard him say, "I love you, Daddy." The man, only slightly surprised, returned the hug and said something softly. Smiling and more confident-looking now, the youngster walked out of the restaurant, calling over his shoulder, "Bye, Daddy. I'll be home real soon." The father turned and waved, then turned back smiling to his cup of coffee.

Gene and I stared at each other in shock. Do teenagers really do such things in public? "Wasn't that just marvelous?" I whispered to Gene.

"Yes, and you must tell him so," Gene insisted.

I was uneasy about barging in on the stranger's life, but as we stood to leave, I gathered up all my courage and said, "Excuse me, but we couldn't help but notice your son. What a fine young man. You surely are doing something right as a father."

The man smiled a somewhat weary smile and then said, "I sure hope so. His mother left us a year ago and I'm really trying. Thanks for the encouragement."

Lord, never let me withhold encouragement—not even from a stranger. Amen.
                                                    —MARION BOND WEST

29/ WED   *It is more blessed to give than to receive.*
                                                    —ACTS 20:35

Twenty-five years ago I was a newly married man. Three days after our wedding, Beth and I moved from our childhood homes in Georgia to attend seminary in Louisville, Kentucky. We opened a joint checking account and deposited all of our financial resources: a grand total of one hundred and ten dollars. As seminary classes began, we both frantically looked for jobs. Our checking account dwindled to nothing after our second trip to the grocery store.

Two weeks later I trudged dejectedly to the campus post office, worried about the mounting bills I was receiving. In my mailbox I found an envelope from my home church. In the envelope was a check for a thousand dollars and a note from some people who loved and supported me. As I stood there in stunned amazement, I began to cry. I was learning the joy and the grace of receiving a gift.

Tonight, twenty-five years later, I am writing a check to send to a young woman attending Yale Divinity School. She was a member of our church during her undergraduate days at Baylor University, and Beth and I are very fond of her. This is her first experience of living away from Texas, and her finances are extended to the breaking point. Now Beth and I have the opportunity to give, just as we had the opportunity to receive.

The Bible is right when it says that "it is more blessed to give than to receive." I always thought this verse meant that it is better to give than to receive. What I'm discovering now is that it means it's more joyful. Nothing has made me happier this year than to send this money to someone I love. And nothing has made me more grateful than to realize that the God Who takes care of my needs also enables me to meet the needs of others.

Dear God, thank You for allowing me both to give and to receive. Amen.
—SCOTT WALKER

30/_{THU} *Jesus . . . said to him, "Follow me."*
—JOHN 1:43 (NIV)

In these months since my surgery and radiation treatments for cancer, my husband Harry and I have been learning all we can to make our lifestyle even healthier. We thought we were pretty good before (some of my family refer to me as the Earth Muffin), but now we're motivated to try even harder. As we explore some of the alternative approaches to health and wellness, we're finding a whole spectrum of ideas, from seriously weird to very reasonable. We're going for balance and moderation: Get regular exercise; eat good, real food (more fruits and veggies, some soy, whole grains); and reduce stress.

Even the mainstream medical community is increasingly recognizing the healing connection between our bodies and our minds. On one visit to our local hospital's Wellness Center, we were given two loaner tapes of exercises to aid in relaxation, stress reduction and strengthening the immune system.

The day I went back to purchase one tape and return the other, I was helped by a pleasant young woman named Janet. She asked how I liked them.

"I found them helpful," I replied, "but I confess I'm always a bit reserved about things like this unless I know more about the person who did them."

With a smile she said, "I made the tapes."

A bit hesitantly I asked, "Well, would you mind if I ask where you're coming from spiritually?"

She paused for only a second and then said, "I'm a follower of Jesus Christ." No ambiguity, no defensiveness, just a clear and simple statement of her commitment.

I bought both tapes. And I took something else with me that day as well: a reminder that I am called to live and speak in this world as a follower of Christ, with love and boldness.

My Lord Jesus, may I learn to express my faith in You confidently, boldly and graciously. —MARY JANE CLARK

31 / FRI *Lead me in thy truth, and teach me: for thou art the God of my salvation. . . .* —PSALM 25:5

This past year our daughter Elizabeth's obsession was numbers. Our nightly game was a pretend circus; in the center ring, the one, the only "Elizamath." Julia and I would call out problems, and five-year-old Elizabeth would do them in her head. At bedtime it was "number stories." No cuddly animals, no shining knights. Just numbers.

"Once upon a time, there was a number sixty-four. He lived in a big house in a little forest, and he was very lonely. So he went to the King of Numbers and asked for some friends. 'Well,' said the king, 'I have some very nice sixteens here. Would you like to adopt them?' 'Oh, yes, please!' said the sixty-four, and he took the sixteens home with him.

"When he got home, he had the sixteens stand on each other's shoulders, one on top of the other. And they were exactly the same height as the sixty-four! How many sixteens were there?"

Elizabeth began to jump up and down on the bed with excitement. "Four! Four!" she shouted. "Four sixteens are sixty-four!"

"Settle down, honey," I said, trying to get her ready for sleep. She stopped jumping and paused to think for a moment.

"There were also some eights at the sixty-four's house," Elizabeth said.

"How many, honey?" I asked her.

"Eight!" she crowed, and she began jumping all over again.

Elizabeth enjoys solving math problems because their answers are either true or false. When she's right, she knows she's right—there's no uncertainty here; whatever form the problem takes, four sixteens are always sixty-four. I hope that simple joy in knowing the right answer will follow her throughout her life. And when she's older, and grappling with problems more difficult than arithmetic, I hope that her desire for truth will keep her faithful to Him Who is Truth itself, and that she will know God's goodness and glory with the same assurance and enthusiasm as the times tables she learned at five.

Lord, help my children to grow in Your truth. —ANDREW ATTAWAY

DAILY GIFTS

1 _____

2 _____

3 _____

4 _____

5 _____

6 _____

7 _____

8 _____

9 _____

10 _____

11 _____

12 _____

13 _____

14 _____

15 _____

16 _____

17 _____

18 _____

19 _____

20 _____

21 _____

22 _____

23 _____

24 _____

25 _____

26 _____

27 _____

28 _____

29 _____

30 _____

31 _____

September

Blessed are the
merciful: for they
shall obtain mercy.

—MATTHEW 5:7

S	M	T	W	T	F	S
						1
2	3	4	5	6	7	8
9	10	11	12	13	14	15
16	17	18	19	20	21	22
23	24	25	26	27	28	29
30						

1/ *SAT*

Then Jesus told his disciples a parable to show them that they should always pray and not give up.
—LUKE 18:1 (NIV)

I covered my ears at the yapping. It was Junior, the gangly, brown boxer dog across the street. I adored him and welcomed his friendly visits to my porch, his pug face pushing into my lap. But when he was locked in his pen, his bark had a pitch that could shatter glass, not to mention a peaceful summer morning in the yard.

I knew what ailed him: He wanted to go inside. So today, instead of railing and wishing him laryngitis, I tried a new approach—I rooted for him. "Atta boy, Junior," I called, sitting on my steps. "Anytime now. Don't give up."

It seemed to go on forever. But finally, the door opened across the street. "I'm coming, I'm coming," said Junior's master, striding to the pen. When he unlatched the gate, Junior bounded out, jumping up on him, licking his face and wagging his stub of a tail as if to say, "I knew you were in there and that you'd answer if I didn't give up."

In the sweet peace following Junior's victory, I thought how easily I give up on God when I'm asking for something and the only answer is a closed door. Where is my patience? My persistence? My faith that my Father hears and will answer in due time—His time?

Lord, thank You for turning a morning's annoyance into a lesson on prayer.
—SHARI SMYTH

2/ *SUN*

"He will do everything I want him to do."
—ACTS 13:22 (NIV)

Years ago, when Chinook salmon still returned to breed in Idaho's streams, I stood in a wilderness place called Dagger Falls and watched the mighty fish circle in a deep pool ten feet below a vertical rock bank beside the falls. They were tired. They had left the Pacific Ocean three months before to battle the raging currents of the Columbia, Snake and Salmon rivers to reach this point. Now they were dying.

Every so often a fish would accelerate around the pool, then leap up into the water, spilling over the ten-foot-high wall. I shuddered when a fish flailed and fell onto the pool's surface with a crack louder than the noise of the rushing water. I cheered when a fish ignored the pain of the fall and leaped again and again until it reached the top edge of the rock wall, then flipped and flapped until its tail disappeared into the river.

They have restless hearts, I thought. *They're willing to do everything God wants them to do—return home and bring life to another generation.*

Their example gave me a restless heart. And when I returned home, God led me to teach Bible classes to twelve- and thirteen-year-olds. There were times I was tired. I had three active daughters and a busy dental practice. I struggled—and sometimes failed—to make the classes interesting. But it seemed that I was doing what God wanted me to do. And, years later, when one of my former students thanked me for helping him to find Jesus Christ, I knew I had helped bring life to a new generation.

Lord, give me the will to do Your will in bringing the young to new life in You.
                                                        —RICHARD HAGERMAN

3/ MON   *In all labour there is profit. . . .*   —PROVERBS 14:23

My first real office job came the summer after my freshman year in college. I worked in the mailroom of an architectural firm, making blueprints, photocopying, binding specs, wrapping packages, taking them to the post office. In two days I figured I had mastered everything. "There's not much else to learn," I said to my dad.

"Try learning people's names," he suggested.

That took another week, matching the faces with names and knowing where everybody sat. Just when I thought I'd mastered that, Dad asked, "What do you know about their jobs? How about their families? Do you know their kids' names and what they do?" This was a whole new assignment. On my rounds I began to study family photographs and ask a few questions. There was a lot to absorb.

"I hear people make suggestions about what we can do better in the office," I said.

"Good," Dad said enthusiastically. "Pass on what you hear to your boss."

That took a lot of courage, but I did it, and my boss seemed appreciative. Then, at the end of summer, I heard someone praise the work of another colleague. "Pass that along, too," Dad said. "You can never do wrong by passing along praise."

The job ended with a handshake and a check. The money disappeared very fast, along with my knowledge of how to make a blue-print. But what I discovered about working in an office has lasted. Learn people's names, find out more about them, listen to what they say, and never, ever hesitate to pass along some words of praise.

Thanks, Dad.

Help me see in my work, Lord, that caring for other people is the most important part of the job. —RICK HAMLIN

WHEN GOD REACHES OUT . . . THROUGH OTHER PEOPLE

4/TUE *Behold, you are beautiful, my love; behold, you are beautiful. . . .* —SONG OF SOLOMON 1:15 (RSV)

Visiting our grandson's school for the first time, I was startled to discover that his second-grade teacher had a disfiguring birthmark covering nearly half her face. A dark purple discoloration spread from her left ear across her cheek and lower lip to her jaw line.

Warm and welcoming, the woman herself had obviously come to terms long since with the burden of an unusual appearance. It was I who felt awkward, conscious of the effort neither to look away nor to stare. *If it was hard for me as an adult, how,* I wondered, *did our seven-year-old grandchild handle it?*

I found out when he got home from school that afternoon. "Your teacher seems like a very nice lady," I ventured.

The youngster nodded. "She doesn't look like other teachers," he said.

I nodded, waiting to hear how he would handle the situation.

"Yes," he went on, "even when we're noisy, she has a smiley face."

It was said in a child's piping voice, but the message I heard was God's. *I don't look at your blemishes either,* I heard Him say. *I look at you with the eyes of love.*

Let me see through Your eyes, Father, the beauty in each person I meet today.
—ELIZABETH SHERRILL

5/ WED   *I am the rose of Sharon. . . .* —SONG OF SOLOMON 2:1

I was walking briskly out of the shopping mall, trying to remember where I had parked my car, when a young girl with bobbed blonde hair came up to me, smiling. "Here," she said, handing me a beautiful long-stemmed rose, "I want you to have this."

"How lovely," I said, and before I could thank her she had spun around and was weaving through a line of parked cars to join a couple of other girls at the entrance.

"The strangest, nicest thing happened to me, honey," I told my husband when I got home. "Look, a complete stranger gave me this gorgeous rose."

"Why?"

"I don't know. She just gave it to me, then was gone before I could even thank her."

"Hmmm, well, just enjoy it."

Enjoy it I did, for several days as I watched its deep crimson leaves slowly unfurl, and I prayed for many blessings for that sweet young girl.

It was months later, when I was sharing the joy of it with a friend, that I learned the reason for the rose. She explained that the florists in our area had started a new tradition. Late in the summer they chose a special day on which to give away a dozen free roses to anyone who would care to come in and get them. One catch: The roses had to be given away. Thousands of roses were given away that day; thousands of hearts joyfully blessed. One bus driver passed his dozen out to the passengers who rode with him.

Next year, as soon as the florists choose their day, I'm running down to get a dozen of their give-away-roses to pass along. But I don't have to wait to do something nice for someone. I don't have roses blooming, but I do have glorious purple iris. Today I'll take some to the market, and maybe a lady will go home and say, "The strangest, nicest thing happened to me, honey. Look, a complete stranger gave me this gorgeous iris."

There's nothing quite like flowers to remind me of Your beauty and goodness, dear Lord. I praise You as the rose of Sharon, filling my life with the fragrance of Your presence. —FAY ANGUS

6/THU *Teach them to your children, talking about them when you sit at home and when you walk along the road, when you lie down and when you get up.*
—DEUTERONOMY 11:19 (NIV)

After thirty years of parenting, most of them as a single parent, my nest was suddenly empty. In August 1998 I said good-bye to Andrew on the campus of Arizona State University. But even though my nest was empty, my mothering days weren't over by a long shot. Andrew still needed me. Not to send care packages with cookies, clean underwear and extra dollars stuffed inside a few magazines; no, he needed me to teach him the College Commandments:

I. *Thou Shalt Not Bring Thy Dirty Laundry Home to Mom.* Nothing ruins a perfectly good weekend visit more than the thought of five loads of your jeans and T-shirts languishing on the floor in the laundry room.

II. *Thou Shalt Not Call Thy Mother on the Phone Collect.* If I accept your collect calls, it doesn't teach you anything about fiscal responsibility.

III. *Thou Shalt Not Spend Money Frivolously.* Since your brother and sisters (and now you) got through college with grants, scholarships, loans, work-study programs and two to three part-time jobs each, in addition to the money I've saved for all of you, it seems that your education is the most important part of these four years and not a car, expensive clothes or exotic vacation trips during spring break.

IV. *Thou Shalt Have Thine Own Checking Account to Pay Thine Own Bills.* Checking account good; credit card bad. A checking account teaches you the value of having money in the coffer to pay for the item before you buy it.

There are days when I still miss Andrew desperately. But there's one consolation. My daughter Julia said it best in a letter she wrote me not long after Andrew started college. At the top she'd typed, "A parent is not a person to lean on, but a person to make leaning unnecessary."

Lord, help my children become strong, hard-working, independent adults so I'll know I did Your work well. —PATRICIA LORENZ

7/ *FRI* *Lift up now thine eyes, and look from the place where thou art . . .* —GENESIS 13:14

You can see Camelback Mountain from all around Phoenix, Arizona (a bit of it even from my backyard), and it really does look like a camel lying on its stomach. But seeing its most interesting feature is a tougher trick. There's a chunk of rock near the camel's forehead that looks like a prayerful figure trudging up the mountain clothed in a dark brown robe.

Because of the surrounding rock formations, you can see the Praying Monk only from certain angles. Driving my son Ross home from school, I catch sight of the monk as I approach from the west, but within a few blocks he disappears as I face the camel head-on. More than once I've heard Ross's frustration as he's tried to show the monk to out-of-town visitors. "Wait," he'll say, "you have to be in just the right spot to see him." And as promised, the monk suddenly pops into view.

Just the right spot to see him. Lately I've been thinking that's a clue to what can go wrong in my spiritual life. When my days are hectic, with prayer and devotional time cut short or even cut out, I start to feel disconnected from God. I'm simply not in the right place to see God clearly. God's always there, as steady as the familiar Praying Monk, but I'm driving down the road too busy with life's distractions to notice.

It's probably not a coincidence that this rock formation is a praying monk. When I spy the monk in prayer, he's a perfect reminder of what I must do when my priorities slip. I need to slow down, pull off the road if necessary, and make time for the things that bring me closer to God, especially peaceful time alone to talk with Him. I need to get myself back in just the right spot to see God unmistakably before me every day.

Lord, help me put all distractions aside, to see and hear and be with only You.
—GINA BRIDGEMAN

8/ *SAT*

This also comes from the Lord of hosts; he is wonderful in counsel, and excellent in wisdom.
—ISAIAH 28:29 (RSV)

Every Saturday afternoon for the past two years, I've gone to an hour-long class to study Torah (the five Books of Moses) with a rabbi. Recently, I had to attend a conference on Saturday. I felt bad about missing the class, but the conference was very important to my career.

At one of the conference sessions that Saturday morning, the panelists asked for questions from the audience. One of the questioners introduced himself as a rabbi who had stayed overnight at the hotel to attend the conference (to avoid traveling on the Sabbath). After the panel session I greeted him, and we talked about the questions he'd asked and the panelists' answers. We compared notes and discovered that we each had a free hour, so we sat in the hotel lobby and continued our discussion.

As the hour drew to a close, the rabbi said, "You know, I was feeling really guilty about coming here instead of going to my normal Torah study group, but you've made me feel as if I've done my Sabbath study anyway. Thank you."

I was caught openmouthed, because I'd been just about to say the same thing to him. Instead I said, "I guess God just wanted to make sure we didn't miss our classes, so He put us in the same place at the same time."

He nodded. "It looks that way in hindsight," he said, "but then I suppose human beings are in charge of hindsight, and God is in charge of foresight."

Lord, thank You for the moments when I can catch a glimpse of Your plan for my life.
—RHODA BLECKER

9/SUN *Rejoice with me; for I have found my sheep which was lost.* —LUKE 15:6

Through circumstances none of my family knew or understood, my mother was separated as an infant from her own mother. I grew up with an ache in my heart for this missing grandmother of mine, and longed for the day when I might find and meet her. Through happenstance, my mother discovered she had a half brother, and for several years we enjoyed getting to know my uncle. From him, we learned a little more of my missing grandmother, for she lived with Uncle Dale six months of every year. But, sadly, she made it clear she didn't want to revisit the past.

The year I turned forty, I felt desperate to meet her; neither of us was going to live forever. Uncle Dale suggested I come for a visit and be introduced as a friend of the family. I'd at least get to see what she looked like, learn what her personality was like and maybe, if we got on, I could plumb her for stories of her growing-up years.

I talked it over with my children. Phil, then fifteen, gave me a startled look. "But, Mum, if you go as a *friend* of the family, you'll never meet her as *family*!"

Hope deferred makes the heart sick, and in my desperation I'd nearly committed a terrible blunder. Because, of course, Phil was right. I wanted to meet my grandmother, not some old lady.

But if hope deferred makes the heart sick, so is "desire fulfilled a tree of life" (Proverbs 13:12, RSV). Five years later (and just six months before she died at age ninety-three), Leona Bagley Goodfellow Bent was at last ready to meet me. A miraculous meeting; I found the grandmother I'd been looking for, and she found closure after seventy years of grief. And to think we both nearly missed each other by my giving way to discouragement.

Dear Lord, help me to await steadfastly, and in anticipation, everything I hope for. Amen. —BRENDA WILBEE

10/MON *Make me to know thy ways, O Lord; teach me thy paths.* —PSALM 25:4 (RSV)

I wandered through the store, mulling over my grocery list. *If Elizabeth were starting public school tomorrow, I'd be here wondering what to pack for her lunch.* It was a jarring thought. Ever since we decided to home-school, I'd pretty much put aside all the mundane aspects of school-at-home vs. school-at-school. Now, as everyone else prepared for the first day of school, I realized how different our first day would be. We didn't have new clothes or shoes or backpacks. Elizabeth wouldn't be spending much time learning how to stand in line, or how to raise her hand to ask a question. There wouldn't be the excitement and anxiety of going someplace completely new. It made me feel a tiny bit sad. Not for me, but for Elizabeth.

Suddenly, it seemed as if the path we were taking was going to make Elizabeth's life experience very different from what mine had been. *Some day she's going to ask me what Twinkies are, because she's never had one in her lunchbox,* I thought wistfully. Then I laughed at myself. Andrew and I hadn't made our decision about schooling Elizabeth on the basis of Twinkies and lunchboxes. We are educating our daughter at home because we think it is the best way for her to grow in knowledge and love of the Lord. If that means her experiences will be different from ours, so be it.

I put a box of cheese crackers into my shopping cart. In some ways school is school, no matter where it is. After a hard morning's work, surely Elizabeth would need a snack.

Teacher of teachers, bless all schoolchildren today. May they learn that knowledge of You is the most important knowledge of all.

—JULIA ATTAWAY

11/*TUE*   *I will not fear what flesh can do unto me.*
             —PSALM 56:4

"Pam, I just got a call from the hospital," my husband David was saying, as he walked ashen-faced into the kitchen. "They have Aunt Kate in the emergency room and her doctor says this is it. She can't go back to her apartment. He's talking about a nursing home."

The next morning I began the six-hour drive that would take me to Kate. I had first made this trip as a new bride, twenty-eight years earlier. David had seemed so proud as he introduced me to his Aunt Kate, a tall, genteel matron who played cutthroat bridge and enjoyed working under the hood of her 1968 Mustang.

Years passed, and our visits became islands of comfort for me. Perched on one of her ancient needlepoint chairs, I would drink coffee from an old Wedgwood cup and float in Kate's unqualified acceptance of life as it was. She adored my children, my husband, even me! She was my safe place.

Now I found Kate leashed to a hospital bed by an oxygen machine. "Pam," she said as I leaned over her, "don't look so distressed. This can't be helped. So the only thing to do is make the best of it."

In the next days I emptied her apartment, distributing her treasures to friends and loved ones as she directed. When her possessions were gone and we were alone, Kate talked matter-of-factly of heaven. Her faith filled my head with visions: her husband running to meet her; her mother spreading a banquet cloth for the last, best homecoming. Then, just as matter-of-factly, she picked up her little plastic radio, held it to her ear and switched on the baseball game. "Don't you think it's time you were getting home?" she said. "Your family needs you."

I had seen Kate's home—and her hope—as something tangible, something she could lose. Yet, being old, alone and homeless hadn't even scratched the surface of this woman's spirit. *Fear not*—Kate showed me what those words mean by living them.

Father, help me to live knee-deep in today, trusting always that You are my true home. —PAM KIDD

12/ WED   *And I will bring the blind by a way that they knew not. . . .* —ISAIAH 42:16

Some years ago I used to take my German shepherd for long walks in Philadelphia's Fairmount Park. I'd park my car and take one of the trails that went far up into the hills where I could walk Kate off-leash. After a while I got to know the trails by heart.

One day a friend of mine came along with us, and the two of us were so busy talking that we didn't notice where we were. Finally, Pat looked at her watch and said, "Gosh, I have to get back and make dinner! Which way do we go?" That's when I realized we were lost.

We were surrounded by woods and couldn't see far ahead of us. After trying several times to retrace our steps, we lost all sense of direction. "Wait a minute," I said. "If anyone knows the way back, it's Kate."

I looked at Kate, and in a commanding voice I said, "Kate, take us home!"

Kate brushed past us to lead the way. But after a little while both Pat and I knew it wasn't the way we had come. Kate had taken us off the trail and was leading us up and down some pretty steep hills. She was full of confidence and kept looking back at us as if to reassure us. But the farther we went, the more nervous we got.

Then, suddenly, we came out of the woods and into a huge meadow. At the end of the meadow we looked down a slope and saw the parking lot far below us. "We're home!" I shouted and threw my arms around Kate. So did Pat.

"She knew where she was going all the time," Pat said. "It just wasn't the same way we came."

"No," I agreed, "it was a better way."

Since then I've always tried to remember that when I ask God for guidance—and I do it often—I have to trust Him to know which way is best for me. Even if I haven't gone that way before.

Lead me, dear Jesus, because Your way is always better than mine. Amen.
—PHYLLIS HOBE

13/*THU* Greater love hath no man than this. . . . —JOHN 15:13

"Oink, oink" was the familiar message on the phone. It was September 13 again, and Joe had called me to "celebrate" the Bay of Pigs. Not the CIA's disastrous invasion of Cuba, but the anniversary of the off-Broadway opening of his play *Cockeyed Kite*. Both happened in 1961. Both events had similar fates.

Why, you might ask, has he taken me to dinner every thirteenth of September since then? Because one evening he was despondent when his co-producer dropped out and Bill Nichols had said he couldn't manage the play alone. That's when I, with the confidence of youth as well as a firm belief in Joe as a playwright, blurted out, "I'll be your co-producer."

Bold words; I didn't have more than a couple of cents to my name. Still, I had said I'd co-produce, and I had to start learning how. From then on I tackled everyone I knew, slightly or well, and a host of people I didn't know, for a share, half a share, even small partial shares in the production. I squeezed enough money out, somehow. And there were other matters, like casting and dealing with the director, and the play itself, which centered on a thirteen-year-old boy with a weak heart who managed to accomplish one meaningful thing before dying. It never entered my mind that I, too, was performing one meaningful act—giving the play a chance at life before it met its own destined fate.

So the critics turned their thumbs down. Joe was discouraged, but it turned out that the published play has had performances (not many) all over, and that publishing it led directly to the novels that attest to his brilliant talent. The thing that both embarrasses and pleases me is Joe's unending gratitude. It is, above all else, an example of his sincere love, something that I feel every thirteenth of September.

Father, let me be the kind of man that Joe is.   —VAN VARNER

14/FRI   *Christ also suffered for you, leaving you an example, that you should follow in his steps.*
—I PETER 2:21 (RSV)

Marla was one of the kindest, gentlest, most compassionate people I'd ever met, which made it all the more dismaying that she was so intent on causing me pain. Marla was my physical therapist after I broke my arm last year playing softball. Her office was across the street from mine, so I made my thrice-weekly appointments for early in the morning before work.

The first couple weren't so bad. She kneaded my arm and stretched it a bit while we chatted amiably. *This person wouldn't hurt a fly*, I reassured myself. Then, the second week, we got down to business. Marla would slowly twist my arm in one direction and murmur, "Tell me when it hurts."

"Yow!" I'd yelp.

But rather than stopping, she would twist it further.

"*Yow!*"

Then she would hold it there.

"Count to three," she'd say in her soft, soothing voice. I'd make it to three in record time.

"What you are feeling," Marla explained, "is good pain. Healing pain. You get better by going through it, not around it. It's the only way." Still, as the weeks passed, more and more I found myself playing hooky from PT.

It was during this time that I lost my mother after a long battle with Alzheimer's. When all the postmortem rituals were done, I was left in a kind of emotional fogbank, trying not to dwell on the darkening pain. I put in longer hours at the office and pushed myself harder at the gym. Then Marla called. "I haven't seen you for a while," she said. "Don't you want to get better?"

Her question was still running through my thoughts as I lay on the therapy table the next morning. Marla carefully manipulated my arm, tugging it in a direction I swore it would not go. When she said to count to three, I did—slowly. It was the only way.

Lord, teach me to trust You to be my Guide from the darkness to Your eternal light, step by sometimes painful step. —EDWARD GRINNAN

PRAYER FOR SEPTEMBER

Lord, thank You for this September morning.
The crisp coolness in the breeze reminds me
that this is a new season.

In fact, Father, September feels more like
a New Year than January.
This "new beginning" feeling has been printed into
  my soul
since childhood,
Because September begins a new school year.
New socks and underwear.
New crayons and notepaper.
New teachers, new classrooms,
new books, new challenges and a new clean slate.

Thank You, Father, that the excitement
and anticipation of that fresh new beginning
is born again in my soul on a September morning.
                —CAROL KUYKENDALL

15/*SAT*   *Remember not the sins of my youth and my rebellious ways. . . .*   —PSALM 25:7 (NIV)

On Saturday nights the "Gothics" hang out at a local restaurant after an evening of malling. The Gothics, or "Goths" for short, are teenagers who dye their hair black and paint their faces ghostly white. Several of them came into the restaurant one night and stood in the waiting area near where my daughter and I were eating.

"Oh, no, Mama, let's get out of here!" said twenty-three-year-old Lanea. "They make me uncomfortable." I smiled. Lanea has always dressed and thought somewhat conservatively. She plans to be a lawyer.

I reminded her that there are still some people who don't want to eat with us because we're African Americans. "I think, at least in part, these kids are trying to force us to see that we still too often judge character by outward appearances." Lanea's expression said she was not convinced. "They're just kids," I added. "They may look bizarre, but they're still someone's children."

"Let's go, okay?" Lanea said. She wasn't going for it.

As we stood in line to pay, a young man who had been sitting in the back of the restaurant came up and greeted the group of Goths. "When are you guys going to sit down?"

The spookiest member, a threatening and imposing figure well over six feet tall, all done up in Dracula attire, spoke. "They won't seat us. We've been standing here a long time and they just won't seat us." He sounded hurt. He must have been all of fifteen.

Lanea looked shocked as we approached the manager to pay our check. Very civilly, but assertively, she reminded the manager that the young people had been waiting a long time and had yet to be served. The manager dispatched someone to seat the strangely painted group.

"Don't smile, Mama. I still don't like the way they look, but they should have been seated," Lanea said as we walked out to the parking lot.

"I'm not smiling, baby," I said. I turned my head away so that she wouldn't see the pride on my face.

God, give me a heart that loves and encourages youth, however they may be clothed.
                                                    —SHARON FOSTER

16/_{SUN} *But I am like a green olive tree in the house of God: I trust in the mercy of God for ever and ever.*

—PSALM 52:8

Yesterday a storm whipped through and took down a thirty-foot Australian pine between our house and the beach. Though the wind was strong, the tree had survived much heavier Gulf of Mexico blows during its lifetime, and I was puzzled as to why this tree, seemingly full of life, fell and some other larger, older pines that stood sentinel alongside it did not.

Today I got out my chain saw and began dicing up the branches and trunk that lay across our stairs leading to the water. It was then that I discovered why the tree had toppled. About four feet up from its base, buried in the bark, was a rope that someone had wrapped around it. I have no idea what purpose the rope had served or why it was left, but the rope had cut off the pine from its nourishing roots, and the impediment became its Achilles' heel.

As I carried away the pieces of wood, a conversation I had had a few days earlier with a repairman came to mind. In the course of our exchange, he told me that he no longer attended church because "I don't need it to worship God." I acknowledged that we can worship God anywhere, pray by ourselves and study His Word alone, but that I would miss the support and succor of a church community. "I'm afraid that skipping church and the lessons I learn there would stunt my spiritual growth," I added.

Something like the rope tied around my fallen pine tree. When we cut ourselves off from the Source of Life, we die, too.

Teach me, God, when I grow too independent
How much I need Your love transcendent.

—FRED BAUER

17/_{MON} *Do all things without murmurings and disputings.*

—PHILIPPIANS 2:14

On Monday, September 13, 1937, I entered college and I was thrilled! But within days, I learned the results of my entrance examination. I had scored high in math, but I had failed English composition. My instructor said my sentences ran on and on. I was enrolled in remedial composition.

I worked hard, hoping to enter a freshman English class by midterm. By February I was recommended for English 101, but there was a conflict with my work schedule; I would have to complete the year in remedial English. My heart was broken.

Our teacher was Miss Elliott, a four-foot-ten-inch professor from Ohio, who conducted the class like a Marine drill instructor. She demanded a written theme for each day of class, and an extra one for the weekend. For a young man who had problems with sentence structure, six themes a week was mental torture! I grumbled, felt sorry for myself and considered leaving college. But I was too ashamed to quit.

Near the end of my freshman year something happened in that English class. I was learning to write! Family and friends were astonished at the improvement in my letters. I fell in love with words. Six themes a week, although a challenge, became a joy. By June I had passed remedial composition with flying colors. In September I would be taking sophomore English.

That year, filled with self-questioning and doubt, was difficult. Yet through prayer, hard work and acceptance, change came. Sometimes God has His own way of teaching, through a step backward that can be a source of strength. Thank you, Miss Elliott!

Father, thank You for the joy of accomplishment. —OSCAR GREENE

A WHOLE AND HOLY LOVE

18/*TUE*   *Come ye yourselves apart . . . and rest a while. . . .*
—MARK 6:31

In June, following our January marriage, Robert and I moved into my family cabin in Green Mountain Falls, Colorado, while awaiting the completion of our new home. One evening, after we'd been living in the cabin for several weeks, we found ourselves bickering over whether to set the alarm for 5:50 or 6:00 A.M. in order to make an early meeting the next morning. By the time we went to bed, I was feeling tearful and somewhat unstrung, and I asked myself what was going on.

The next morning on our drive down Ute Pass, it occurred to me why I'd been feeling so contentious. My soul was crying out for private time! When I don't provide myself with some time apart, I tend to become annoyed at little things or take offense when none was intended or feel the need to prove myself right. Our argument had brought me a valuable lesson in maintaining good relationships. But would Robert understand?

As I pondered the question, I looked out the car window and saw the sun painting a triangle of pure gold on the top of Pike's Peak. I breathed in the scene and felt its calmness enter my heart. Then I told Robert what I'd been thinking. He understood completely! We both agreed that it's essential for the health of our relationship to build in some private time.

A couple of days later I packed a lunch and took my yearly trek up the side of the mountain behind the cabin, where I sat on my favorite boulder, listened to the sound of the falls and renewed my personal relationship with God. I felt the Holy Spirit's presence in each pine and aspen, in every chipmunk and blue jay. By noon I was eager to return to my beloved Robert.

Since then we've each made a point to take time apart on a regular basis to renew our souls. How much more we enjoy our time together, now that we're following Jesus' advice to "Come ye yourselves apart . . . and rest a while."

Dear Lord, help us to enrich our time together by spending time alone in Your presence.
                                                    —MARILYN MORGAN KING

19/ WED   *Study to be quiet, and to do your own business, and to work. . . .*
                                                    —I THESSALONIANS 4:11

I work in advertising, and my work knocks around in my brain even when I'm not at the office. When I have a TV commercial to write, I try to come up with new ideas any time I get the chance.

Late one night my baby daughter Noelle needed someone to hold her to help her calm down. So I picked her up from her crib and held her close. Her crying stopped. Instead of putting her back in her crib, I lay down with her on our bed and kept a hand on her so she could feel me near. It worked perfectly. While I waited until her sleep was deep enough to move her back to the crib, I thought about the commercial I was trying to write.

After about five minutes, Noelle's hand, which had been above her head, moved down the sheets and rested just in front of my face, her index finger falling gently across my lips. It was as if God was saying through my sleeping baby, "Shhh . . . don't miss this moment."

I looked at Noelle, silhouetted by the lights of New York City just outside our window. And I listened to her soft breathing, the only sound in the room. Her little eyelids were closed and her stomach slowly eased up and down in a soothing rhythm. She was such a beautiful gift to her mother and me. Yes, this was indeed a *moment*. Dad. Daughter. And silence. Without her hand in front of my mouth, I would have surely missed it.

I closed my eyes and thanked God for the reminder. And kissed Noelle's tiny finger.

Lord, help me to put away the work of the day and take time to enjoy Your gifts.
—DAVE FRANCO

20 / THU

Even a child is known by his doings. . . .
—PROVERBS 20:11

I slumped at the kitchen table fighting back tears. The hieroglyphics in my huge college math book made absolutely no sense. How could I ever become a teacher and provide a better life for my children if I couldn't learn? And as if one math class weren't enough after a thirty-year interval, here I was trying to take two in the same semester!

Just then my son Greg burst through the front door. "Yo, Mom! What's up?" he demanded, blue eyes twinkling with mischief. As he devoured a brownie and made goofy faces, I composed myself. Then I explained that I just couldn't figure out this math problem, fully expecting his sympathy. Greg had always wrestled with school work and never pretended to like junior high.

Instead, he grabbed a pencil and said, "Here, do it like this." I compared the exercise answer in the back of the book with his computation and stared at him in respectful amazement. He was right! I couldn't even match wits with a twelve-year-old!

"That does it!" I growled in a fit of self-loathing. "I'm quitting school!"

For perhaps the first time in his life, Greg stopped clowning and said very solemnly, "You can do it, Mom. I know you can do it. Besides," he looked at me levelly, "if you can quit, I can quit." The challenge was on.

Well, I didn't quit school. By studying extra-long hours and visiting my professor regularly for help, I slogged through those frustrating math courses and earned respectable B's in both. And now that I'm a teacher, I'm a lot more understanding of students who can't catch a concept the first time around.

Greg would still rather skateboard than buckle down to homework. He isn't a perfect student, but then, neither is his mom.

Thank You, Lord, for children who teach us and challenge us to be our best selves. —GAIL THORELL SCHILLING

21 /FRI *I would not write with paper and ink: but I trust to come unto you, and speak face to face, that our joy may be full.* —II JOHN 12

It's the calm after the storm. John and Elizabeth are in bed; Mary, who still hasn't learned how to sleep on her own, is napping in the baby car seat on the living room rug. The floor is strewn with blocks, toy trucks, books, dress-up clothes and wooden train tracks, but neither Julia nor I have the energy to pick up any of it. We sink back into the pink sofa, put our feet up on the ottoman and begin to talk

Julia tells me about Elizabeth's music class, about their trip to the museum with Alex and his mom, about how many new words Mary has learned and how many new friends John has made on the playground, about the books she's put on hold at the library and the new members of her Bible study for moms. I tell her what's new at the office, how *Daily Guideposts* is coming along, what kinds of problems we're praying about at Prayer Fellowship. Usually Julia has the most to say; she wants me to know what the children have been up to while I've been at work, and there's almost no end to the things a five-year-old, a three-year-old and a one-year-old can be up to. If we've spent a Saturday or a day off together, we compare notes on what we've both observed at the park or the botanical garden or the zoo.

That's how most of our evenings go; no matter how tired we are or how late it is, we take the time to talk. It's a good habit, and it helps us to have a good marriage.

And it's a habit I need to develop in my relationship with God. No matter how tired I am, I need to sit down for a few minutes every evening and tell Him about my day. And then I need to be quiet, and in the stillness I need to listen to Him.

Lord, help me never to end a day without talking it over with You.
—ANDREW ATTAWAY

22 / SAT   *Cast thy bread upon the waters: for thou shalt find it after many days.*   —ECCLESIASTES 11:1

Every year on September 22, I give a special present to my grandfather, Pa. It will be a gift offered in secrecy, and the person who receives it will not be my grandfather, but some unsuspecting soul who will never know the reason for the gift.

You see, September 22 is my grandfather's birthday, and although he died in 1983, I still have a reason to celebrate his day. Pa was always a giver. Every year when his birthday rolled around, he was more excited about the unbirthday presents he gave to me and my sister Keri than he was about anything he might be getting.

It was easy for me to see that living that way brought him a lot of joy. So it was only natural that I have the urge to continue his work. Last year on Pa's birthday, I gave a homeless man a bag full of hamburgers. The year before, as I was leaving my office late in the evening, I noticed that one of the cleaning men was younger than the rest. I struck up a conversation with him, and it turned out that he was attending my old high school during the day and working at night in order to help his struggling family. The next morning I called the principal and arranged for an anonymous "alumni award" to be given to the young man.

As for this year . . . well, I'm not going to say what my present to Pa will be, but I know it will bring me joy. Pa always did find a way of turning his birthday into a happy unbirthday for me!

Dear God, help me to remember the happiness that giving to others brings.
—BROCK KIDD

23 / SUN

There was a man named Zacchaeus who was a chief tax collector, and he was rich. And he sought to see who Jesus was, but could not because of the crowd, for he was short of stature. So he ran ahead and climbed up into a sycamore tree to see Him. . . .

—LUKE 19:2–4 (NKJV)

Nature often points the way to God. The river valleys of central Missouri are guarded by magnificent sycamore trees, whose marble-white trunks are lightly burnished with pewter. As big as baseball gloves, the sycamore's leaves catch the slightest breeze and applaud their Maker. Like giant fingers, the trees roots clutch the limestone and loam riverbank, looking for nourishment. These white-robed beauties lift their limbs to God as if praying for mercy. They remind me that all of creation longs to be delivered from the troubles of the earth.

Like Zacchaeus, I, too, long to reach higher to see Jesus, because I am short. Short on joy. Short on patience and energy, short on hope and enthusiasm, and sometimes short on holiness.

Neither Zacchaeus nor I can change our stature, but I can put myself where I have a better chance of glimpsing God. On Sundays that means going to church for organized prayer and praise. Last night, it meant getting up at 3:00 A.M. to witness a glorious meteor shower. When I'm fixing a faucet for my mother-in-law or counseling a student or making breakfast for my wife, at such times I feel God's arm around me.

Everywhere there are sycamore trees to help me, when I look for them: people in need; a quiet park where I can pray; a special sunset I can applaud.

> *Lord lift me up and let me stand,*
> *By faith on heaven's tableland,*
> *A higher plane than I have found;*
> *Lord, plant my feet on higher ground.*
> ("HIGHER GROUND" BY JOHNSON OATMAN, JR.)

—DANIEL SCHANTZ

24 / MON   *The Lord's mercies . . . are new every morning. . . .*
                                        —LAMENTATIONS 3:22-23

Water Tower Place in Chicago has seven floors of shops, selling everything from electric back-scratchers to four-poster beds. One of my favorite stores is FAO Sweets—a smorgasbord of tasty treats, all displayed in huge, see-through bins. One of the clerks is always stationed by the door, handing small, empty plastic bags to everyone who enters this sweet-tooth paradise.

"Here you go, ma'am," he said to me as I stepped inside the door.

"Does everyone who comes in here fill these bags?" I asked, laughing.

The young man smiled back. "Well, we expect them to!"

Next morning, I stuffed the small bag of candy into my briefcase as I headed out the door for work. "Bless me today, Lord," I prayed on automatic pilot. Suddenly, I saw the face of that young clerk. Was I expecting God to bless me as confidently as the clerk had expected me to buy candy? Or did I thwart God with negative attitudes and grumbling? With expressions as sour as lemon drops?

I still like to visit that candy store. But I know that the real sweetness in life comes from being open to God's everyday blessings: a warm muffin; a child to hug; an unexpected phone call from a friend; a "well done!" from my boss; a chance to help in our local blood drive. And a gumdrop at the end of the day!

You, Father, are the Giver of every good thing. Let me hunger for the sweetness of Your presence in my life—every day!
                                        —MARY LOU CARNEY

25 / TUE   *Teach and admonish one another in all wisdom. . . .*
                                        —COLOSSIANS 3:16 (RSV)

I always felt that I had an assignment to fight the fiery dragons—the deep pains and problems of life—wherever I was, at home and school, in marriage and business. I had to fight other people's dragons as well as my own, because I'd survived so many dragons in my own life.

When I became a Christian, I was told that it was God's job to kill the dragons. I was to submit my whole life to Him and learn how to listen to Him, love His people and do His will. And that advice worked for a while. But then, apparently out of nowhere, my life filled up with the raging dragons of overcommitment, pride, angry blaming, unkept promises, isolation and loneliness.

I have a dear Christian friend who used to be as frantic and compulsive as I am. But now she looks peaceful and serene—even though she still lives a very busy life and helps others. Finally, I asked her, "As busy as you are, how do you manage to be so serene and peaceful?"

"Well, one day I just got tired of fighting dragons," she said. "I'd had enough of the chaotic overload, and..." She looked very thoughtful and then said simply, "I just quit feeding the lizards."

"What do you mean?"

"Well, one day I quit dwelling on those small lizards of doubt and fear that develop into huge and fearful dragons for me if I don't deal with them when they first show up. I quit nursing the overcommitment, jealousy and resentment in my life as soon as I saw them beginning. And after a few months of not feeding the lizards, there simply weren't any dragons left to battle!"

Lord, I'm so grateful You told me through my friend that if I confess my problems sooner, You will slay the terrifying dragons in my life and I won't have to run from them anymore. Amen. —KEITH MILLER

26/ WED   *And he led them forth by the right way. . . .*
—PSALM 107:7

I arrived at La Guardia Airport after a long and tedious meeting, wishing I could wave a magic wand and be home, or at least take a direct flight. Only there aren't any direct flights to our farm south of Copeland, Kansas. I had to go from New York to Denver, catch the 9:30 P.M. shuttle plane to Garden City, then drive fifty miles. With luck, I'd be asleep in my own bed by midnight.

The ticket agent checked the computer monitor, then shook his head. "Your plane is still on the ground in Denver. We're looking at a five-hour delay."

"I'll miss the last shuttle!" I wailed. "Can't you route me some other way?"

The agent worked for fifteen minutes. "Ma'am, it is impossible to get you to Garden City tonight. Is there any other destination that would work?"

Another destination? A light turned on in the dark room of my mind. My real destination wasn't Garden City, it was home! Twenty minutes later I boarded a plane to Chicago, where I caught a connecting flight to Wichita. My husband Don met me—and didn't gripe about the long roundabout trip! I tumbled into my own bed only an hour later than originally scheduled.

My life is often like that trip. Plans go awry, there are detours on the road, and the timetable changes without notice. But God graciously leads me every step of the way. I know I'll reach my heavenly home, my final destination, in His good time.

> *"All the way my Savior leads me;*
> *What have I to ask beside?"*
> (FANNY CROSBY)

—PENNEY SCHWAB

27/THU

"Remember the days of old. . . ."
—DEUTERONOMY 32:7 (NAS)

Recently I asked all of my grown children to tell me their happiest childhood memory. Three of them had to think about it, but not Jeremy. "You'd just come back from a writing workshop in New York," he said with a smile. "The laundry was piled up and the phone kept ringing and you needed to go to the grocery store, but you kept typing. I stood right by you and tried to explain that I needed poster paper for a contest at school. Seems like I stood there all day. All you ever said was, 'Mmm.'"

I remembered that day clearly. I had wanted to write so much it was like a physical pain. I could feel Jeremy breathing right beside me. His shadow fell across my paper. I prayed, *Please, Lord, don't let him ask me again to get poster paper.* And he didn't. What he murmured under his breath was, "Contest ends tomorrow, anyway."

I hit the OFF button on my typewriter and grabbed the car keys and Jeremy's hand. I think I may have even managed a smile. We stepped over spilled orange Kool Aid and piles of laundry. I caught a glimpse of his face. There was a ring of orange punch around his mouth. Whatever he'd eaten for lunch stained his shirt. His shoes were untied. On the way to the store, he told me all about the contest—it was about fire prevention. I tried to listen to him as intently as I've ever listened to anyone in my life. He worked on the poster way into the night.

"Remember, Mom?" my now-thirty-three-year-old son asked. "I won the school prize—five dollars, and I even placed in the state finals! What a memory!"

Father, would You help a very busy young mother to take time today to make a memory? Amen. —MARION BOND WEST

INTO AFRICA

28/_{FRI} *Peter . . . walked on the water, to go to Jesus. . . . He was afraid; and beginning to sink, he cried, saying, Lord, save me. And immediately Jesus stretched forth his hand, and caught him. . . .* —MATTHEW 14:29-31

Our group was visiting Ethiopia, where believers in Jesus were persecuted during the Communist era of the 1970s and 1980s. Sitting at breakfast one morning, we heard story after story of people who had suffered for their faith. One man in particular had been in jail for several years. His devotion to the Lord touched me so deeply that I found tears flowing freely down my face. Then the thought hit me, *I have never even been laughed at for my faith. Maybe it isn't a real faith.*

Seeing my tears, the man asked what was troubling me. When I told him, he smiled somewhat sadly and said, "My story is not one of constant victory. You see, one night I felt a strong urge from God to tell an old man lying next to me about the hope and strength my faith brought me. However, it was a very cold night. He had a fine warm blanket and I had none, and my envy of his blanket kept me from sharing my faith.

"Early in the morning guards came and seized a dozen prisoners. They were to be shot to strike fear into those who resisted the regime. Horrified, I watched as the old man was taken. As he was dragged from the cell, a guard pulled the blanket from his shoulders and said, 'You won't be needing this anymore,' and threw it into my lap. It was as if the Lord were saying to me, 'You didn't care for his soul, but you wanted his blanket. Here it is.'

"So friend," he continued, "that memory is a pebble in my shoe that keeps me from being proud. Never think we who suffered for the faith always emerged victorious. Be faithful in following where God takes you. That is enough for Him."

Lord Jesus, when I fear that my own strength will fail me, teach me to keep my eyes on You.
                                                            —ERIC FELLMAN

29 / SAT

Do not interpretations belong to God? . . .
                                                        —GENESIS 40:8

I was cat-sitting for my friend Mabel Tendler, who has two and a half cats. Well, they're really two indoor cats and an outdoor orange cat who picks up food from several kind neighbors, including Mabel. "Make sure to feed him," she had reminded me. "I don't want the poor thing to go hungry. Here's his special dish." No sooner did I fill the bowl and set it down than I got a hungry customer. I heard the noise of dry food being crunched, and I turned to see a big Doberman wolfing down the entire bowl of food.

"Hey!" I shouted. "That's not yours! Leave that alone!" He gave me a big doggy leer and ran off with the orange plastic bowl clenched firmly between his teeth.

The orange cat never showed up the whole week I was there. And Mabel's special bowl was gone, and I was responsible! I agonized all week. Would she cry? Would she yell? My mind conjured up Technicolor versions of how upset she'd be that I hadn't carried out her instructions correctly.

Well, Mabel came home, I confessed—and she laughed! "Oh, that happens all the time. Look in the left corner of the yard and you'll see where Dingo left the bowl."

"But what about the orange cat?" I asked. "The poor thing must have gone hungry."

"I think the orange cat mooches off about six neighbors besides me."

"Oh," was all I said, and then I had to laugh, too—at the doom-and-gloom scenario I'd created in my own mind.

God, is there some "cat dish" in my life I've been blowing up out of all proportion? Let me live calmly today and not in a frightening— and imaginary—future. —LINDA NEUKRUG

30 / SUN *For we ourselves also were sometimes foolish. . . .* —TITUS 3:3

It was early Sunday morning and I was in my car, rushing to church, late for the 8:30 A.M. worship service. My first clue that something was wrong was when orange juice began cascading down my windshield. I glanced in the rearview mirror and saw pieces of paper flying all over the street behind me. Horrified, I realized that the swirling ticker tape was the pages of my sermon. In my hurry, I had put my Bible, my sermon and my glass of orange juice on the car roof and promptly forgotten them. Now my sermon was strewn over five city blocks.

Muttering angrily to myself, I pulled to the curb, got out of the car and ran back down the roadside, collecting the pages. I blushed and waved brightly as a church member drove by, honking her horn and waving. I felt like a fool.

I managed to find all but one page of the manuscript, and gathering them up, I hurried on to church. The choir was in its place and the Scripture was being read as I crept into the sanctuary. I slid into a pew as people bowed their heads in prayer, and paused to catch my breath and gather my thoughts.

A few minutes later as I walked to the pulpit, I was chuckling. On impulse, I told the congregation what had happened to me. They erupted into laughter, and so did I. That laughter united us in a spirit of fellowship, and in the warmth that followed, I felt a special attention to my sermon, despite the missing page.

I make some pretty silly mistakes from time to time, and it is often that foolishness that endears me to others. On those days, the best that I can do is to laugh at myself.

Lord, let me not take myself too seriously today. —SCOTT WALKER

Daily Gifts

1 _____

2 _____

3 _____

4 _____

5 _____

6 _____

7 _____

8 _____

9 _____

10 _____

11 _____

12 _____

13 _____

14 _____

15 _____

16 _____

17 _____

18 _____

19 _____

20 _____

21 _____

22 _____

23 _____

24 _____

25 _____

26 _____

27 _____

28 _____

29 _____

30 _____

October

The Lord hath
anointed me . . . to
comfort all that
mourn.

—ISAIAH 61:1–2

S	M	T	W	T	F	S
	1	2	3	4	5	6
7	8	9	10	11	12	13
14	15	16	17	18	19	20
21	22	23	24	25	26	27
28	29	30	31			

When God Reaches Out . . . Through Other People

1/_{MON} *"Lord, show us the Father and that will be enough for us."* —JOHN 14:8 (NIV)

It was with misgivings that I'd signed up for the art class at our local Continuing Education center. Described in the brochure as "The Natural Way to Draw," the session was offered "for those with no previous art training."

That certainly described me. I hadn't tried to draw since grade school, when I had struggled in vain to reproduce the pictures the teacher pinned to my easel. Comparing my smudgy efforts with the cat or the house I was copying, I would rip my drawing paper into a dozen despairing pieces.

Stepping into the Continuing Ed classroom now, I felt the old certainty of failure sweep over me. There on a high stand sat a pineapple, an orange and a banana that were evidently to be the drawing assignment. I'd never be able to capture those complex shapes!

"There are only two rules tonight," the young instructor announced. "Never look down at your paper. And never lift your pencil from the page. Keep your eyes on the fruit and draw with a continuous line. When you've finished," she went on, "throw the drawing on the floor and start a new one. Don't worry about the results. Just keep looking at the fruit."

It was a wonderfully freeing exercise, I discovered, drawing lines and loops with no concern for how the finished picture turned out. Only at the end of the session were we permitted to retrieve our efforts and look at them. I'd produced some wildly abstract designs, and a few that actually looked like a pineapple, an orange and a banana.

It didn't matter. I was strangely exhilarated, not only because for the first time in my life I'd enjoyed an art class, but because I'd sensed God reaching out once more through words that meant more than the speaker knew. My service to Him falls so short of what I mean it to be! I get so discouraged when I compare my great intentions with the feeble results! *Don't look at results,* I heard Him say. *Keep your eyes on Me and leave the finished picture in My hands.*

Lord, show me Yourself today.　　　　　　　—ELIZABETH SHERRILL

2/TUE　　"*Learn to do right! Seek justice, encourage the oppressed. . . .*"　—ISAIAH 1:17 (NIV)

Several years ago my wife Rosie and I watched a TV special about all the starving children in the world. Needless to say, we both felt overwhelmed. As is so often the case when we're confronted with overwhelming need, we asked ourselves, "How can our small loaf make a difference to a hurting world?" And when we couldn't see the answer to that question, we were tempted to sit back and do nothing.

We heard part of the answer at a spiritual renewal conference we attended recently. The speaker said, "The Lord says, 'You do the feeding; I will do the supplying.'" A light came on in my mind and relief came over my spirit. I don't have to feed everyone in the world. I don't have to help everyone in the world, and I don't have to try to meet the needs of everyone in the world. I just need to be honest about my gifts and the resources that God has given me, use them faithfully when I can and where I can, and allow the great God of the universe to do the rest.

By the way, at the end of that TV show, the narrator said, "You can sponsor a child for just pennies a day." I can't feed all the hungry children in the world; surely feeding a hundred is beyond my means, and maybe even feeding ten. But surely, from what God has given me, I can feed just one.

Lord, help me today to understand that You have asked me not to count the loaves and the fish but to share whatever I have to reach out and touch the lives of others.　　—DOLPHUS WEARY

3 / WED

That you may love the Lord your God, listen to his voice, and hold fast to him. . . .
—DEUTERONOMY 30:20 (NIV)

The phone rang last night as I loaded the dishwasher after dinner. I was glad to hear the voice of an old friend I hadn't spoken with in several months.

"How are you?" I asked as I climbed up on a stool at the kitchen counter and settled down for our talk. We had lots to catch up on, and she chatted on and on about her family, her job and a few concerns about some personal challenges. When I hung up the phone nearly half an hour later, I felt a bit forlorn, and then realized our conversation had been pretty one-sided. She'd done most of the talking and I'd done most of the listening. She hadn't even asked me, "How are *you?*" By the time I turned out the lights in the kitchen, I felt a little irritated with my friend for her insensitivity.

Early the next morning, I sat at the same kitchen counter, talking to God in prayer. I chatted on and on, telling Him all about my concerns for my family and job and some personal challenges, and was about to say "Amen" when I sensed a nudge from the Lord—because our conversation had been totally one-sided. I had talked on and on about myself, but I hadn't praised God or listened to Him.

So I started back into prayer again. "How are *You*, God?" I asked, and then began to listen to the answers. *I am loving. I am kind. I am always with you. I have a plan for you. I am a promise-keeper. I am your provider. I am your source of strength and comfort. I am your Father. I am Lord.*

When I was done listening, I added a P.S. to my prayer:

Father, forgive me for being quick to blame others for carrying on one-sided conversations, and thank You for the reminder that great blessings come from good listening.   —CAROL KUYKENDALL

4 / THU

Let the words of my mouth, and the meditation of my heart, be acceptable in thy sight, O Lord, my strength, and my redeemer.   —PSALM 19:14

The waiting room in the doctor's office is divided into two sections by a four-foot-high wall. Today few patients were waiting. In fact, I was alone on one side of the wall while my husband Bob was in the examining room.

I scanned the tall bookcase against one wall. A book of children's Bible stories was on the very top shelf. I noticed it because a group of identical ones were lined up on the bottom shelf. I took another book for myself and settled down to read.

Just then a little girl came around the wall and stood on tiptoes to take the Bible storybook from the top shelf. Ten or fifteen minutes later, she returned with the book in her hand. She stretched to replace it on the top shelf, turned to leave, paused, then reached up to retrieve the book. She squatted down at the bottom shelf and lined up the book beside the others like it.

"That was very nice of you," I told her as she stood up.

She gave me a one-tooth-missing grin and said, "Thank you. It was out of place."

She disappeared around the wall, and I heard her mother ask her, "What did that lady say to you?"

The child's voice did not carry enough for me to hear her reply, but soon a young woman carrying a baby in her arms rounded the wall, wearing a big smile.

"Thank you for your kind words to my daughter," she said. "We try very hard to teach our children to do the right thing, but we can't help but wonder if they remember when we're not around. You made my day!"

When she had left, I sat quietly, thinking about what she'd said. I hadn't done much—I'd just said a few words to a child. But how often do I let a like opportunity to make someone's day slip by?

Dear Lord, help me to reflect Your love in someone's life today. Amen.
                                                            —DRUE DUKE

5/*FRI*   *Lay not up for yourselves treasures upon earth . . .*
          But lay up for yourselves treasures in heaven. . . .
                                            —MATTHEW 6:19-20

When I was a child during World War II, many commodities—butter, sugar, coffee, gasoline—were rationed for the "duration." That word puzzled me when I saw signs reading "closed for the duration" posted on the doors of businesses whose proprietors had gone off to war. Then someone explained that it meant *until*—until the war was over and those in the armed forces came home.

Meanwhile, people on the home front learned to live by that old motto "Use it up, wear it out, make it do or do without." One thing shortages did was make people more appreciative of previously taken-for-granted things. I remember seeing a long line outside a clothing store one day and getting in it because I knew people were queuing up for something scarce. "What are they selling?" I asked a grandmotherly type in front of me.

"Nylons," she answered. "Do you need a pair?" Everyone laughed, and for a moment I was embarrassed. Thinking quickly, however, I answered that I was there to get some for my mother. Which is what I did. I don't know if I got the right size or color, but I do recall that Mother was overjoyed with my purchase.

Shortages make things more valuable—in the short run, at least. Abundance produces the opposite effect. And people sometimes act like lemmings, slaves to supply and demand. The Bible advises us not to be anxious about material needs; they will be met. And Paul, who counseled Christians to be content whatever state they were in, assured the Philippians from a prison cell that "my God shall supply all your need according to his riches in glory" (Philippians 4:19). That's a promise the Apostle knew from personal experience, and one that you and I can bank on—today, tomorrow and for the duration.

> *When our needs leave us despairing*
> *Remind us, God, Who's ever caring.*

—FRED BAUER

6/ *SAT* *When thou walkest through the fire, thou shalt not be burned; neither shall the flame kindle upon thee.*
—ISAIAH 43:2

I was driving to one of my favorite hiking trails in Ohiopyle State Park. Near the top of the hill, I noticed an amazing amount of smoke. I stopped beside a parked fire truck and offered to help.

A park ranger looked at me. "Okay," he said, "but *please* stay in the back somewhere."

Who knew he would say yes?

The next three hours were beyond description. A yellow line of fire—no more than four inches in height in most places, but extending a hundred yards across a jagged line—was coming right for us.

One of the volunteers sighed. "Start the break here," he said, drawing an imaginary line in the air that paralleled the fire's advance. He then picked up his heavy metal rake and began pulling at the leaves and small twigs. He bared the ground in an eight-foot swath, then moved a foot and began again.

I thought, *Surely we're not going to fight this fire by raking?*

We were. The high, dry brush and the steepness of the hill made raking awkward and slow. When the wind kicked up, overhead branches caught fire, carrying the flames right past our newly dug break. At one point we had to bail out altogether because no one could work through the smoke.

The fire finally slowed. We beat out the hot spots with shovels or stamped them out with our feet. After hours of backbreaking work, the fire retreated. I hadn't thought it possible, but a couple of capable, creative men had directed a band of willing volunteers to stop acres and acres of stubborn flames.

All over our country, volunteer fire companies are fighting for their very survival. You see them riding on their shiny red trucks, and it looks like fun—right up to the point where you clear the first few feet of earth with your rake and understand the awesome, dangerous task before you. And you hope that you're not there alone, that these strangers at your side will be there for you, as heroic and generous as the moment demands.

Lord, bless and protect all those who risk their lives to fight fires.

—MARK COLLINS

7/ SUN *And God said, "Let the earth bring forth every kind of animal. . . ." And God was pleased with what he had done.* —GENESIS 1:24–25 (TLB)

On the first Sunday in October the Episcopal Church of the Ascension in our town has a service called the "Blessing of the Animals." People, children especially, are invited to bring their pets to church, and in memory of St. Francis of Assisi, who dearly loved animals, there is a special time of blessing.

This year we didn't make it, my little dog and I. For close to fourteen years, she's been my constant companion, confidant and most devoted friend; the one I trust implicitly. She's always ready to listen when I ramble on and on about this or that, or shed silent tears, sharing corners of my heart with her I wouldn't dare to share with any other. She's the only one I know who agrees with everything I say and urges me on to tell her more.

When I leave the house, her large dark eyes watch me from the window, and when I return she greets me with ecstatic joy. She asks so little and gives so much, and now she's getting old. She's getting deaf, going blind, sleeps a lot and just can't make it up the stairs. I dread the day, the coming day all too soon, when she will no longer be here beside me.

So on this day of blessing the animals, I hold my own service. Quietly, I kneel in the garden beside my faithful friend, and with gratitude, I thank the Lord for the loyalty, devotion and special gift of comfort of this small dog, and ask Him to give her His blessing.

Thank You, dear Lord, for the animals who are our comfort, who serve us so well and ask for so little in return. I ask You to bless them. May we pet them often, feed them well and show them that we love them. —FAY ANGUS

A Birdsong at Sunset

Sometimes God calls us to reach out farther than we think our arms can stretch. That's what happened to Mary Brown awhile ago when a friend's husband lay dying of cancer. How could she reach out past her insecurities, her lack of training in caregiving and her uneasiness about intruding on another family's pain? Over the next five days, we'll find out how God used Mary's prayer, her friends and even her children to help her overcome her fears. —THE EDITORS

8/ MON

8/ MON

DAY ONE: REACHING OUT . . . IN PRAYER
In all their affliction he was afflicted, and the angel of his presence saved them; in his love and in his pity he redeemed them; he lifted them up and carried them. . . . —ISAIAH 63:9 (RSV)

Last Thursday our friend Ruxandra, or "Ruxy" as she is fondly called, brought her forty-nine-year-old husband Donald home from the hospital to die. Donald had fought cancer valiantly for more than a year; now he knew his departure from this world would be a matter of a few days or weeks.

This Monday I found myself constantly thinking of them. I yearned to help, but I didn't want to intrude on their last days together. Although I had talked and worked with Ruxy at church, I hardly knew Donald. I had spoken with him only a few times. Besides, what could I possibly do?

Then I remembered something I'd once heard: "When the only thing you can do is pray, then that's the most important thing to do—and it will make a difference!"

So I began praying for my friends and found myself asking God to send His angels to help them. I pictured invisible heavenly beings whispering comfort to them, easing Donald's pain and strengthening Ruxy to care for him.

On Wednesday my nurse friend Barb said that Ruxy had called her with several questions. "I've got tomorrow off," said Barb, "so I'm going to visit them." *Ah,* I thought, *one of God's angels!*

That evening our friend Mary phoned and said that she had called Ruxy. "She's been getting very little sleep, so I'm going over now to take the night shift."

"Oh, Mary," I said, "you're another angel God is sending them!"

"Oh, no," she protested, "you know I am no angel. But please pray for us—that I'll be able to care for him alone and Ruxy will be able to sleep."

"I will," I promised, grateful for a way to help.

That night as I prayed, I pictured Mary ministering to Donald and Ruxy sleeping peacefully, watched over by God's angels.

Lord, use my prayers today to reach out Your loving arms to those my own arms cannot reach.
—MARY BROWN

9 / *TUE*

DAY TWO: REACHING OUT . . . WHEN I FEEL INADEQUATE

"I called on thy name, O Lord, from the depths of the pit; thou didst hear my plea, 'Do not close thine ear to my cry for help!' Thou didst come near when I called on thee; thou didst say, 'Do not fear!'"

—LAMENTATIONS 3:55–57 (RSV)

The next day Mary told me she had stayed with Donald all night. Ruxy had slept for the first time in a week.

As Mary described how she had cared for Donald, I was thankful that God had sent him someone so capable. But then she stunned me. "Barb and I wondered if you could come tomorrow and help."

"Well . . . I guess so..." I mumbled. "But I'm no nurse. And I've never been with a dying person before."

"You'll do fine," Mary said. "It was such a privilege to care for him. He was so grateful." She began talking about his IV, drainage tube, oxygen and medications. My mind reeled. *Lord, I can't do this!*

"Mary, I don't know . . . ."

"You can do it. It's like taking care of a child. And Ruxy will show you everything."

"Okay," I said at last. Somehow, I sensed it was not just Mary asking, but my Father calling me to go to my brother and sister in Christ. And if the call was from Him, He'd give me whatever I needed to answer it.

Lord, even when I'm anxious and my hands tremble, help me to reach them out in service.   —MARY BROWN

10 / *WED*

DAY THREE: REACHING OUT . . . WITH THE CHILDREN

Things we have heard and known, things our fathers have told us. We will not hide them from their children; we will tell the next generation the praiseworthy deeds of the Lord, his power, and the wonders he has done.   —PSALM 78:3–4 (NIV)

Although I'd promised to help care for Donald, I still had to make arrangements for the children. After school I explained to Elizabeth and Mark where I'd be the next day and who would be looking after them.

Elizabeth cried. "But I don't want Donald to die. Can't we pray for him to get better?" We had a talk about death and heaven, and how we could pray for God to help Donald in whatever way He thought best.

"It seems to be Donald's time to leave us and go be with Jesus," I said. "Let's ask God to show us how to love Donald." The children prayed, asking God to take Donald at His best time, to help Mom care for him tomorrow and to help Ruxy.

Afterward they made cards, colorful and cheerful, for me to take to Donald. But Elizabeth wasn't satisfied that they'd done enough. She wanted to give Donald a present. She was heading off with her neighbor friend Lizzie to buy school supplies and was determined to look for something for Donald. Elizabeth and Lizzie came home with a small stuffed toy. They had chosen a robin. "We think Donald will really like it!" the girls exclaimed. "He can cuddle it in bed like we do with our toys!"

So the next morning, still with some trepidation, I set off. But I was armed with the children's prayers and cards and little gift, and I felt I had more to offer these friends in need.

Thank You, Father, that my children can be a source of joy for others as well as for me.   —MARY BROWN

11/_THU_ *DAY FOUR: REACHING OUT . . . GOD'S WONDROUS PROVISION*
With everlasting love I will have compassion on you, says the Lord, your Redeemer.   —ISAIAH 54:8 (RSV)

Donald was awake when I arrived. He squeezed my hand tightly and murmured, "Thank you so much for coming." Immediately I knew what Mary meant—I felt privileged to be there.

"Thank you for having me!" I whispered. When I presented the children's cards and little gift, Donald's eyes lit up with joy. "Oh, tell them thank you. Tell them I love them." He clutched the small stuffed robin to his cheek, stroking it softly, asking, "How did you know, how did you know?"

Ruxy explained, "This is amazing. He loves sitting outside listening to the birds. He was just saying yesterday he wanted a bird, how he wished he could have one in the room!"

"And now you've brought me one I can hold." His voice trembled with gratitude. He began telling us about birds and how to approach them so they are not afraid, all the while gently stroking the soft stuffed robin.

My nervousness melted away. As God had guided the children and worked through their earnest efforts to touch Donald so profoundly, He would guide me today.

Lord of mercy and compassion, when I make the tiniest effort to reach out, You provide. Thank You for tenderly reaching out to us.

—MARY BROWN

12/FRI *DAY FIVE: REACHING OUT . . . FRIEND TO FRIEND*
"For the mountains may depart and the hills be removed, but my steadfast love shall not depart from you, and my covenant of peace shall not be removed, says the Lord, who has compassion on you."

—ISAIAH 54:10 (RSV)

When I got to their house, Ruxy showed me how to care for Donald, and the morning went smoothly. She managed to take a shower and a nap. Later a hospice nurse came to check Donald. He had been awake most of the night and morning, but now he seemed exhausted. Hearing voices in the living room, I went to greet Donald's friends Jim and Cathy, who had come from Cleveland, Ohio.

When the nurse left they went in. Donald had fallen asleep, but when he heard Cathy's voice, he was suddenly alert. He grasped her hand and spoke with amazing strength. I left them alone to visit, and could hear them chatting, even laughing.

Awhile later I showed Jim and Cathy how to give Donald water through a sponge on a stick. "Wow, Donald," I said as he gratefully sucked the sponge, "it sounds like you're having a great visit!"

His face was radiant and his voice trembled with joy, "Yes, it's wonderful! My very best friends are here!"

While Donald rested, Jim, Cathy and I ate dinner together and they told story after story of times they'd spent with Donald and Ruxy— parties and picnics and even building a house together. "Such good times," said Jim wistfully. "Now it's so hard to see him like this. We had no idea the cancer was this bad."

Donald slipped away peacefully the next night, surrounded by friends. During the funeral service I kept thinking of his voice trembling with joy. I imagined him arriving in heaven, being greeted by our Lord and His angels and loved ones. I could just hear Donald exclaiming, "It's so wonderful! My very best friends are here!"

Dear God, Your love encompasses heaven and earth and embraces us everywhere—here, on our journey and when we come home to You.
                                                                    —MARY BROWN

*13/*SAT   *Thou shalt teach them diligently unto thy children....*
                                                        —DEUTERONOMY 6:7

In many ways the long-term substitute teaching job was a dream-come-true. I enjoyed a month with the same sixth-graders, friendly colleagues—but someone else's agenda. Though the regular classroom teacher urged me to use my own techniques, we planned lessons together. I sought her approval on all new materials and assessments. Since I was a guest in her classroom, I didn't even feel comfortable changing the month-old bulletin-board display without permission.

As the weeks wore on, I felt less and less like a professional educator and more and more like a clone. One Saturday morning I fumed to Dixie, a church friend of lively faith. "I don't know why I bothered to sell my house and give up three years of my life to go back to school. Why did I go into teaching, anyway?"

My wise friend listened sympathetically. "Sometimes we don't quite know why we do the things we do. We feel we've been led, then feel we aren't getting what we ought to. But you just keep at it! Remember, during those unsatisfying times, you don't know what you're giving, either."

A few weeks later at a coffee shop, I bumped into the mother of one of the pupils in my class.

"Gail! Thank you for helping Missy raise her math grade!"

"But I can't take credit," I said. "I've been with her only a few weeks."

"Yes, but she had a C before you came."

"Oh, she was probably just rusty from summer break."

"No, she had C's all last year, too."

Still bewildered, I mumbled, "Well, I'm glad she's doing well."

As I sipped my cappuccino, I thought about what Dixie had said.

Perhaps I had been so obsessed with feeling successful as a sub that I had failed to recognize small successes in my students. Once again, the kids were teaching me: Even a temporary teacher can achieve some permanent results.

Lord, give me the faith and courage to do my best, even when I feel I make no difference. —GAIL THORELL SCHILLING

PRAYER FOR OCTOBER

Dear Lord, spare Your children from wounding one another when they are already split open with grief from losing someone they love. Keep us from too quickly spouting Bible verses as a form of comfort, rather than simply opening our arms to hold a friend while he or she cries. "They are in heaven now" feels of little consequence—even though it may be the truth—when the giant void of their empty favorite chair fills a room.

God, help us grieve simply with our friends. Embrace them through us and allow us to be Your arms and strong presence. Give us words to pray for them and courage to do it aloud, when Your spirit leads. But spare us from handing out clichés and Scriptures when what is truly required is our genuine heart.

—CHARLENE ANN BAUMBICH

14/*SUN*

"Exalted be God, the Rock, my Savior!"
—II SAMUEL 22:47 (NIV)

It was my favorite Sunday of the month: the Sunday the children's church worshiped with us. I always love their exuberance, their smiling faces, their incessant wiggles. But today I was almost too tired to enjoy them. It had been a week of deadlines and late nights, of worrying about a sick friend and hassling with a troublesome neighbor. I was exhausted!

But as the congregation sang the praise chorus "The Lord Liveth," I noticed one child in particular belting out the words. Each time we came to the chorus, he loudly sang, "Let the God of my salvation be exhausted." *Exalted,* I thought. *It's supposed to be exalted. Imagine God being exhausted!* And in that instant I knew: God didn't want me exhausted, either. He wanted to exalt me, to lift me up in His love and strength. To help me mend fences, meet deadlines, cast my cares on Him.

I sang as loudly as my little friend the next time the chorus came around: "Let the God of my salvation be EXALTED!"

You are exalted above all creation, Lord! I come to You with my weariness and worrisome ways. Draw me into Your presence. Exalt me! —MARY LOU CARNEY

15/ MON *Man looketh on the outward appearance, but the Lord looketh on the heart.* —I SAMUEL 16:7

In February 1964 I attended a men and boys' Communion service at a church in the greater Boston area. As I went into the parish hall for a breakfast of scrambled eggs, ham, hash browns, toast and coffee, I glanced at the guest speaker seated at the head table and my thoughts raced back to October 15, 1946.

It was the seventh game of the World Series between the Boston Red Sox and the St. Louis Cardinals at Sportsman's Park in St. Louis, Missouri. Each team had won three games. Today's winner would take the Series.

At the bottom of the eighth inning, the score was 3–3. Then Enos "Country" Slaughter, the Cardinal right fielder, playing with a broken elbow suffered in game five in Boston, led off with a single. The next two batters were retired. Harry Walker, the Cardinal left fielder, drilled a two-out single into center field. Leon Culberson gunned the ball to Red Sox shortstop Johnny Pesky. Slaughter raced from first base to third, then unexpectedly headed for home plate. Pesky instinctively held the ball for a split second. When he threw to the plate, Slaughter slid safely home. The score was 4–3, and the St. Louis Cardinals were the world champions.

Johnny Pesky was the featured speaker at that Communion breakfast. I don't remember what he said in his speech, but I do remember the questions that followed. The first question was, "Johnny, why did you hold that ball?" Nervous laughter filled the parish hall. In eighteen years that play hadn't been forgotten.

Johnny smiled and shook his head. "Let me tell you a story," he said. "I was at a University of Oregon football game during a downpour. The home team kept fumbling the ball. Then a fan recognized me. He stood up and yelled, 'Give Pesky the ball. He'll hold on to it.'"

Everyone laughed. But within that self-deprecating story was an important message. Despite the World Series record books, Johnny Pesky was a hero. His humility graced us all.

Gracious Father, help me to accept my failures as graciously as my successes. —OSCAR GREENE

A WHOLE AND HOLY LOVE

16/_{TUE} *Daniel had understanding in all visions and dreams.* —DANIEL 1:17

Robert and I have a wonderful way of deepening the intimacy of our relationship. It began very early in our long-distance courtship, when I received a letter from him with a photocopy of a page from his journal in which he described a dream he'd had a year before we reconnected with each other.

In the dream he met a woman at a retreat who shared his spiritual path. He sensed he had known her all his life, though he had no name for her. He inquired about her health, seeming to know she'd had a physical problem. Then, as they stood together, she surprised him by saying, "I love you." And he replied that he loved her, too.

Now, as he reviewed the dream a year later, he saw that many details indicated that the woman in the dream could have been me: We'd known each other since childhood and he'd heard I'd recently had back surgery. Since I've long believed that dreams can be messages from God, I took Robert's dream as a blessing on our relationship.

We've continued our practice of dream-sharing, and it has now become a part of our breakfast-table routine. We enjoy helping each other decode the marvelous symbols of the unconscious, and we've discovered that disclosing our inner lives helps us to know each other better and to love more authentically.

We share our inner lives in other ways, too, such as reading bits from our journals to each other, talking about our childhood memories and being open with each other about our feelings. It's the soul-bonding element that, when added to our physical, mental and spiritual connectedness, makes for a full and rewarding relationship.

Now I'm going to reveal something to Robert that I've never told him before: Yes, my beloved, I feel sure I was the woman you saw that night in your dream, a year before we came together. You see, I loved you even then.

Great Creator, let me never lose my sense of holy wonder!

—MARILYN MORGAN KING

*17/*WED   *Fear hath torment. . . .*   —I JOHN 4:18

When Shakespeare wrote that "Cowards die many times before their death," he was talking about me. Thanks to a busy imagination, I am a person who tends to dread the future. When I see dark clouds ahead, I'm sure they are tornadoes.

For example, I lived for years in dread of an income tax audit. Math is not my middle name, and I just knew I must have made some multiplication error that would land me on The Rock for the rest of my life. Then one day it happened. The audit took half an hour, cost me an additional seventeen dollars, and the auditor complimented my record-keeping.

Then there was the curriculum meeting I dreaded for a year. *I can't handle any more courses in my load,* I thought, *and I don't want to get stuck with a course I just hate.* It turned out that the committee took away two courses I hated, and gave me one new one that I always wanted to teach.

No, it doesn't always turn out this well, but it's seldom as bad as I imagine it's going to be.

In order to cope with these forebodings, I've written myself some mental memos to rehearse whenever I feel my stomach tighten.

1. Don't listen to rumors. Get the facts before you start worrying.
2. Take a "wait and see" attitude. Your fears have lied to you before.
3. Be ready to submit to whatever God wants you to do.

These guidelines don't take away my fears, but they make them manageable. I still have to talk it out with my wife and seek God's assurance in prayer.

Often I find comfort in an old hymn by William Cowper:

> *Ye fearful saints, fresh courage take;*
> *The clouds ye so much dread*
> *Are big with mercy, and shall break*
> *In blessings on your head.*

Lord, I'm a coward. But if You help me, I'll not run from the future.
—DANIEL SCHANTZ

18/ *THU*   *I will sing to the Lord, because he has dealt bountifully with me.*   —PSALM 13:6 (RSV)

As my husband Larry and our two teenage children Eric and Meghan climbed out of our travel trailer in the Zion National Park campground, I stopped and inhaled deeply. Apples! Piles of windfall apples under dozens of trees, filling the air with a sweet cidery odor.

"We'll cook fresh applesauce for supper!" I announced enthusiastically.

Eric looked at me askance. "Can we do that? Will the park ranger allow it?"

"Sure!" said Larry, but he decided to check, nonetheless.

"Take all you want," the park ranger said. "Every year these apples go to waste. It's as if people think apples that don't come from stores aren't any good." He explained that the trees had been planted by early pioneers, long before the area became a park.

That night we ate cinnamon applesauce beside our campfire while gazing up at a golden gibbous moon. "This is cool," said Meghan. "God has made some really neat stuff, hasn't He?"

"He has," said Larry. "Maybe we should say thanks." We paused while Larry said simply, "Lord, thank You for this bounty."

To which we responded, "Amen!"

Lord, today I will look with grateful eyes at the abundant gifts You have bestowed upon this world. —MADGE HARRAH

19/_{FRI} *I waited patiently for the Lord; and he inclined unto me, and heard my cry.* —PSALM 40:1

This is a tale of answered prayer. I call it that, even though God took almost a lifetime to respond.

When I was a boy, there was one prayer that I made over and over again: "Oh Lord, help me not to bite my fingernails." It was an addiction over which I seemed to have little control. I carried my fingers in a tight fist when they weren't in my mouth, and though nobody said anything (at least to my face), I was always aware of my problem. I was in my late sixties (now I'm closing in fast on eighty) before the nails began to grow strong and the cuticles became solid.

Once I made a pact with my mother that if I stopped biting for a month, she'd let me go to the movies on a school night. I don't know how I did it (with gloves, I think), but I succeeded. She took me to the Uptown Theatre on a Thursday night to see George Arliss in *Disraeli* and, as a special bonus, she arranged for me to have a professional manicure. It was a double loss. The movie was talky and the manicure was in a "beauty parlor," something thoroughly embarrassing—especially when the other kids found out. And I soon went back to biting my nails.

Fast forward to the near-present. Given the wear and tear of the years, my teeth were beginning to go. After much consultation, Dr. Karnofsky, my periodontist, suggested replacing the entire lower set of teeth with implants. I agreed, and went through weeks on the rack. The implants were a grand success, but the only thing they couldn't do, in my mouth at least, was get a hold on my fingernails—I could not bite my nails!

Nowadays, I flash my gnarled hands whenever possible, am proud to use a file on the least provocation and thank God for His answer, no matter how late.

Things have a way of working out, Lord, if I have enough patience. —VAN VARNER

EDITOR'S NOTE: A month from today, Monday, November 19, 2001, will be our eighth annual Guideposts Family Day of Prayer. We'd like to include you in our praying family. Please send your prayer requests to Guideposts Prayer Fellowship, PO Box 8001, Pawling, NY 12564. If you can, enclose a picture with your letter.

20 / SAT

The wolf also shall dwell with the lamb . . . and a little child shall lead them. —ISAIAH 11:6

When he was three, my grandson Caleb loved to play "wolf." He would stand in the corner of the playroom and build a tower of cardboard blocks around himself. I would crawl back and forth in front of the tower, growling, "I'm a big, bad wolf! I'm going to eat you up!" Every time Caleb tried to come out, I'd snap my teeth. Finally he'd burst through the blocks and run into the living room, laughing all the way.

One Saturday, after my knees ached from prowling and I'd growled myself hoarse, I changed the rules. I sat down and pretended to cry. "I'm a big, bad wolf! No one likes me! No one will play with me! Won't anyone be my friend?"

Caleb's laughter stopped abruptly. For a moment I thought he would burst into tears. Then he grinned. "Me!" he shouted, tapping his chest. "Me! I will be the wolf's friend!" And he launched himself into my arms.

A silly game? Yes, but one that demonstrated a profound truth: Love can often turn a growling wolf into a gentle friend.

Lord Jesus, thank You for the transforming power of Your Love.

—PENNEY SCHWAB

21 / SUN

He healeth the broken in heart, and bindeth up their wounds. —PSALM 147:3

I longed to get to know the fifteen men and women my husband Gene and I met with each Sunday morning for a Bible study before the worship service at church. I wondered what the diverse group had in common beyond the Sunday clothes and pleasant religious faces we were all wearing. What had brought each of them to the class? So I was elated when our leader announced that those wishing to do so could share a brief testimony about how they came to know and experience God. Without any pressure, every single person contributed. It took five Sundays.

Underneath the proper clothes and smiling faces were some terribly wounded people. Tears became commonplace, but there was laughter, too, and impromptu hugs as the room seemed to fill with God's unconditional love. People spoke, haltingly but truthfully, about behavioral and chemical addictions, pride and arrogance, rebellion, deception, violation of marriage vows, unforgiveness, promiscuity, violence and abuse, divorce, pretense, worry and depression, unwise relationships, love of money, obsessive thought patterns and habits, broken hearts, loneliness, lust and uncontrollable anger.

When the last person had finished, we sat unmoving in total silence, now bonded together by the shared stories of our fierce struggles and amazing survivals, like shipwreck victims who have been miraculously rescued. At last, I understood what we had in common—desperation. Every one of us, limping badly emotionally and spiritually, had finally run, many of us literally for our lives, into the open arms of Christ the Healer.

O Lord Jesus, Your healing is as unfathomable as my wounds are deep! Amen. —MARION BOND WEST

22 / MON *Be not thou afraid when one is made rich. . . .* —PSALM 49:16

We've worked hard, but money-wise, it's been a tough year. So the phone call was the proverbial straw that broke the camel's back.

"Pam, did you hear about Paige? She just inherited over a million dollars from an aunt she never knew existed!"

Okay, God, I thought after I hung up, *this is a bit hard to understand.* Paige has never had to work, never taken her children to church, never helped with community projects. In fact, her biggest concern seems to be her golf game. Why her, God?

After that, my anger came in odd ways: Writing a check for groceries, an unfamiliar bitterness tightened my heart. In a parking lot, my eyes fell on a red convertible and I gritted my teeth in hopelessness. *We'll never be able to give our daughter Keri a car like that.*

Finally, late one sleepless night, I went out to sit on the porch. It was dark, and a breeze rustled in the trees. I thought about my life.

It's a very good life. I thought of our son Brock's progress in his job, the people he's been able to help, the way he's careful to tithe his money to church. I thought of Keri, focused on becoming a psychotherapist for the right reasons. She's always doing something to make life better for someone else. I thought of my husband David, who never says no when I come up with some idea for a project that will ultimately cost him time or money. I thought of my mother, happy and secure with her husband Herb. The truth is, I am very, very rich in all the things money can't buy. I wouldn't sell a single one of my blessings for a million dollars. "So why am I so angry?" I whispered to the night. And I knew exactly what I needed to do.

God, tonight I am so ashamed. I know that You always find a way to fill my family's needs. Yet, something good happens to my friend and I get angry and afraid. For a long time, I've been telling You that I want to be a person who feels joy in the good fortune of others. First, I'm going to hand my future over to You, Father. Then I'm going to show You the kind of person I want to become.

That night I slept like a baby. The next day I called Paige to tell her how happy I was for her. The words came from a light and joyful heart—and from one very rich friend to another!

Father, You have given me so much. Give me a grateful heart to share in the joys and sorrows of my neighbors. —PAM KIDD

$23/$ _TUE_ *So then, while we have opportunity, let us do good to all men. . . .* —GALATIANS 6:10 (NAS)

As I sat at my desk reading my mail, I absently flipped through the pages of yet one more magazine. Turning to throw it away, I noticed an article about the plight of Russian orphans. It was illustrated with a picture of a pretty seven-year-old girl with blonde hair and blue eyes. The caption said her name was Julia and that she had been deserted by her mother on the streets of Moscow in the midst of a winter storm. For a few brief seconds, I gazed into Julia's eyes, and then I dropped the magazine into the trash can.

As I got up to put on my coat and go home, I thought about Alan and Susan Nelson, a young couple in our church. The Nelsons had often talked with me about their desire to adopt a homeless child. *Russia is a long way off,* I thought as I shut and locked my office door. But as I walked to my car, Julia's eyes kept staring at me. Finally, I turned and went back to the office, retrieved the magazine from the trash can, circled Julia's picture and mailed the article to the Nelsons.

That happened more than a year ago. Tonight my wife Beth and I drove with the Nelsons to the Dallas/Fort Worth airport to meet the plane bringing their newly adopted daughter Julia from Russia. Watching that little girl walk off the plane and into her new parents' arms was one of the most moving experiences of my life. And it would never have happened if I hadn't listened to that inner voice nudging me.

I guess I'm slowly learning not to throw away the opportunities that God sends my way, not to doubt God's ability to make good things happen in the most far-fetched of situations. Julia will always remind me of what God can do if we give Him an opportunity.

Father, let me see the opportunities You put before me this day and allow You to work through me. Amen. —SCOTT WALKER

---

24 / **WED** *I plead with you to be of one mind, united in thought and purpose.* —I CORINTHIANS 1:10 (TLB)

In 1999 I got to attend my friend Winnie's wedding in Kuala Lumpur, Malaysia. I took a bus from Milwaukee, Wisconsin, to Chicago, flew from Chicago to Narita, Japan, caught a plane to Singapore, was met in Singapore at midnight by Sreela, a friend of Winnie's whom I had never met, and taken to Sreela's uncle's home to spend the night. At nine o'clock the next morning Sreela and I took the bus from Singapore to Kuala Lumpur, where at long last I met up with Winnie.

The whole week was filled with meeting people from India, China, Japan and London who'd come in for the big wedding. Winnie's mother (who is Chinese and doesn't speak English) and I communicated with hand motions, pidgin English and lots of smiles. She told Winnie it was like a duck talking to a goose, but somehow we managed to communicate.

I made friends with Nilo, a young Indian woman, Muslim by religion, who was raised in Malaysia, married to an Englishman and for the past ten years had been living in London. Nilo and I, who were both staying at the bride's apartment that week, laughed our way through a day of shopping at the Central Market and Chinatown. We attended the wedding together, enjoyed the eight-course Chinese dinner at the reception, then joined the dancing in the two long lines of folks so diverse in their ethnic backgrounds that it looked like a gathering of the United Nations.

I'm planning a trip to London to visit my new friend Nilo, and I'm encouraging her and Sreela, as well as the bridal couple, to visit me in America. And these days I strike up conversations with people of all nationalities. I meet them in restaurants, shops, the theater or at church. I figure if I could have so much fun with strangers who live nearly ten thousand miles from me, I could surely get to know a few people right here in America who hail from other countries.

Lord, give me courage to reach out to people who may seem very different from me but are my neighbors just the same.

—PATRICIA LORENZ

25/ THU *"Son of man, look with your eyes, and hear with your ears, and set your mind upon all that I shall show you. . . ."*
—EZEKIEL 40:4 (RSV)

I got into the office extra early this morning so I could work on this devotional before the business day began. As soon as I turn on my computer, I get an e-mail from my sister-in-law Toni in Michigan, asking if I would mind looking for a first-edition Steinbeck novel she wanted to give my brother for his birthday. "Sure," I type back. "No problem."

Now to get to work. I'm not a line into it before the phone rings: a subscriber complaining that she keeps getting billed even though she has a canceled check proving she's paid up. I explain that I'm just the editor and supply her with the number of someone I know in customer service. "I wouldn't go to all this trouble if I didn't love the magazine," she says before hanging up.

All right, back to work. But, no. Colleen, one of our editors, storms through my door with her coat still on. Her three-year-old, Louisiana, bit another child this morning at day care and Colleen is beside herself. "I can't believe my daughter is a biter!" she sputters. I make her sit down and tell her about how I bit a dog when I was about Louisiana's age. "I didn't turn out so bad, did I?" Colleen casts me a wary look, but I know she feels better.

No sooner has Colleen left than my assistant Tina arrives. She's dying to tell me a joke she heard at dinner the night before. I don't normally go for jokes, but this one truly surprises me and I laugh very hard—so much that I have to call my wife Julee at home and tell her.

Of course, my devotional time is shot. Another morning wasted by interruptions!

Yet look: Toni reminded me that my brother's birthday was around the corner. A subscriber offered an unsolicited compliment about the magazine. I was able to help calm down a dismayed mother and friend. To top it off, I actually heard a funny joke. Not a half-bad way to start the day.

And who knew I would actually get a devotional out of it?

God, thank You for all the wondrous details of life all around me, clamoring to be noticed and overflowing with grace.

—EDWARD GRINNAN

26/ FRI *But where shall wisdom be found? and where is the place of understanding?* —JOB 28:12

The past several weeks have found me again taking my number at the local Department of Social and Health Services office. Frustrated and demoralized each time, I've come home and recounted to my mother the red tape I've encountered. Yesterday, describing yet another bureaucratic runaround, I suddenly remembered something my son said thirteen years ago.

We were in the process of moving from Seattle to Bellingham, Washington. To ease the transition, a friend bought each of my children a new outfit to wear on their first day in their new school. A couple of items, however, were too small or too big, and because I was swamped with the many details of the upcoming move, my sister Tresa volunteered to take them back to the store and find something that would fit.

A few days later we were all driving to the Seattle Center for the last time—my sister, myself and my three children. Tresa, sitting in the front passenger seat, got to telling me how irritated she'd been while trying to get the clothes exchanged. If it wasn't one thing, it was another! She was getting herself all worked up, reliving the ordeal, when suddenly eight-year-old Phillip popped up from the backseat. "Auntie Tresa," he said quietly, "it sounds like you're still there, standing in line at the store."

There was stunned silence from the passenger seat. Then Tresa burst out laughing. "You're so smart, Phillip! I am still there, aren't I? I'm holding on to those silly old clothes when I should just be happy it's over!"

All this came back in a rush when I heard myself going on and on to my mother, except I could hear Phillip talking to me this time. "Mum, it sounds like you're still there, standing in the line at DSHS."

But I'm not there, am I? Thanks, Phil!

Dear Lord, when I wear myself out going over unpleasant things, remind me I can choose to let the misery go and move on.

—BRENDA WILBEE

27 / SAT

He kept him as the apple of his eye.
—DEUTERONOMY 32:10

We were visiting our friends Jen and Rob in their New York City apartment, *ooh*ing and *aah*ing over their new baby, who'd just been christened. I noticed their four-year-old, Rebeka, standing to the side, her arms folded across her "I'm the Big Sister" T-shirt. She wasn't smiling. As an older sister myself, I could relate to that feeling of not being the center of attention. So I knelt, draped a hand over Rebeka's shoulder, looked her in the eye and said, "You know, when you were a tiny baby like that, we all *ooh*ed and *aah*ed over you, too."

She flashed me a skeptical look. Tilting her head, she said, "Oh, I was never tiny like that."

Surprised, I said, "Of course you were! Everybody in this room was created by God, and we all began as tiny babies."

"Even you?" She still looked unconvinced.

"Sure." I lowered my voice. "Even your parents were tiny babies once."

At that she laughed loudly and said, "Oh, I can't believe *that.*" As she ran off, I could hear her murmuring, "Linda's telling stories, Linda's telling stories!"

I chuckled at Rebeka's skepticism, but it reminded me of just how amazing that particular story is. There's no better time than at the beginning of a new life to marvel at the changes we all go through.

Dear God, thank You for Your love that follows us throughout our lives. May I never lose my sense of wonder at how wonderfully You bring us from babyhood to adulthood. —LINDA NEUKRUG

28 / *SUN*

Jesus said, Suffer little children, and forbid them not, to come unto me: for of such is the kingdom of heaven.

—MATTHEW 19:14

Jonathan, an insatiably curious, skinny, sandy-haired ten-year-old, frequently buzzed into my Sunday-school kindergarten class from his classroom next door. On this particular Sunday he stopped in front of Hannah, who was drawing a picture, her long, dark braids touching the table. "What's this?" he asked, peering over her shoulder, tapping the paper with his finger.

"This is Billy, my cat," Hannah said solemnly. "He died and went to heaven. He's waiting there for me."

Jonathan scrunched down over the table and, in a moment of uncommon quiet, studied the picture. "That's good," he said, and buzzed on out of the room.

Billy, who'd been run over by a car a month earlier, was frequently the subject of Hannah's pictures and prayer requests. Knowing he was still hers in heaven bridged the gap his passing had left in her life here.

Some weeks later I received terrible news: Jonathan had died suddenly of a brain aneurysm. That Sunday our class gathered somberly. We talked about Jonathan. I asked the children if they'd like to draw pictures of heaven. They nodded and went to work.

Fifteen minutes later, Hannah handed me her finished picture. Amid green grass and yellow flowers, a gray-and-white stick-figure cat bounded toward a stick-figure boy with familiar sandy hair. "I gave Billy to Jonathan," she whispered, "so he has his own pet up there."

Lord Jesus, help me to prepare for Your kingdom by generous giving. —SHARI SMYTH

29 / *MON*

Awake thou that sleepest, and arise from the dead, and Christ shall give thee light. —EPHESIANS 5:14

I lay on my left side, stretched out on the edge of the precipice. Desperately, my fingers clutched at the stems of the plants that were growing on the cliff. I have a fear of heights, and my head was spinning as I gazed down to the canyon floor. My shoulders and back felt like a mass of bruises.

A sharp impact spread pain through my right shoulder. *No, no,* I thought, *I can't stand another blow like that. I'll fall, I can't hold on any longer—*

I put out my hand to brace myself as I slowly opened my eyes and tried to turn over on my right side. I felt a little knee under my back and heard a sleepy squeal. *Mary again!* Our one-year-old was stretched out across the bed, her head resting on Julia's belly and her feet forcing me to the edge of the mattress. When she stirred in her sleep, she unleashed a flurry of kicks. *Amazing how powerful her legs are,* I thought.

I looked up at the clock: 6:30. *Maybe I can just lie here for another half-hour,* I thought. *I can't get up now.*

Another night of fitful sleep, punctuated by dreams of cliff edges and charging mountain goats. It seemed I'd always slept like this, dragged myself through a day of intermittent attentiveness at the office, ridden home on the subway in a semitrance and faced another endless night. I hadn't had a full night's sleep since we all had the flu and slept in separate beds last fall.

I closed my eyes. When I opened them it was 7:00. I slid off the bed and went into the bathroom to take a shower. When I came out, Mary was up. She toddled over to me and grunted, lifting up her hands to tell me she wanted me to pick her up. When she was resting in the crook of my elbow, she put a hand on my shoulder and looked into my eyes. And smiled.

Lord, thank You for giving me a foretaste of heaven in my baby's smile.
—ANDREW ATTAWAY

*30/*TUE   *. . . Having been firmly rooted and now being built up in Him and established in your faith. . . .*
—COLOSSIANS 2:7 (NAS)

I was admiring the beautiful hardwood pews that a carpenter friend builds for places of worship. He told me he personally selects the trees from which the pews are made. "The cost is considerable," he said. "First of all, I have to travel by plane halfway across the continent to where the trees grow. Then I must hike for days through hardwood forests on the stormy side of the slopes."

"Why the stormy side?" I asked.

"That's where trees develop deep roots and firm cell structures because they must grow strong enough to withstand the prevailing winds. By comparison, the trees on the sheltered side of the slopes have shallow roots and a coarse grain."

Last year the prevailing winds were blowing rather fiercely on my side of the slope. There were family decisions to make, problems complicating my course of action and upheavals in my work schedule. My inclination was simply to give in to self-pity and wait for the pressures to slack off. But they didn't.

Instead, I found myself praying—really praying—for the courage to meet problems head-on, for the grace to confront difficult situations, for guidance in establishing a time-management plan.

At the end of the year, I was not only standing a little taller and a little straighter, I had gone down a whole lot deeper with God.

Lord, You not only created trees, You were raised here on earth by a carpenter and know the value of growing on the stormy side of the slope. Use the winds in my life to help me grow strong in spirit.

—ALMA BARKMAN

31 / WED *Submit yourselves therefore to God. Resist the devil, and he will flee from you.* —JAMES 4:7

We were walking across Manhattan from the library toward Elizabeth's music class. About ten yards from the corner I saw it: an eight-foot-tall monster handing out circulars for Halloween supplies. Not just your average monster, either. This one was truly menacing. I pulled nightmare-prone John close to my side, hoping he wouldn't see. Too late. John froze, petrified. I put my arm around him, hid his face in my skirt and hurried around the corner to the bus stop.

On the bus, John was full of questions. "Why was that monster there, Mommy?" I explained that someone dressed up like that to let people know they could buy costumes at a store nearby.

"But why was he dressed up so scary, Mommy?"

"Because sometimes people like to scare other people, especially around Halloween."

"But why, Mommy?"

"Because sometimes we like to be just a little bit frightened, because it's exciting that way."

"But why so scary, Mommy?"

Good question. I had to stop to think about it.

"Do you remember how scared Elizabeth was when she was learning how to ride her bicycle?" Both children nodded. "After a while, she got used to it. Even though she was afraid of a little hill at first, it would take a very steep hill to frighten her now. The same thing could happen if you listened to lots of scary stories or watched scary videos. After a while, it would take even scarier things to make you frightened." While the children mulled that over, another thought came to me. "It's like doing something bad so often that you get used to it. What might happen?"

"You might do something worser, because it wouldn't seem that bad!" exclaimed John.

"Exactly. And sometimes we like to do things that seem just a little bit bad, don't we? Because it's kind of exciting that way." The children grinned. "But do you think it's a good idea to do that?"

"No," said John, " 'cause some day it might turn into a monster!"

Lord, no sin is so little that it does not hurt You. Forgive me for even the small ways in which I depart from Your will. —JULIA ATTAWAY

DAILY GIFTS

1 _____

2 _____

3 _____

4 _____

5 _____

6 _____

7 _____

8 _____

9 _____

10 _____

11 _____

12 _____

13 _____

14 _____

15 _____

16 _____

17 _____

18 _____

19 _____

20 _____

21 _____

22 _____

23 _____

24 _____

25 _____

26 _____

27 _____

28 _____

29 _____

30 _____

31 _____

November

Whatsoever ye do in word or deed, do all in the name of the Lord Jesus, giving thanks to God and the Father by him.

—COLOSSIANS 3:17

S	M	T	W	T	F	S
				1	2	3
4	5	6	7	8	9	10
11	12	13	14	15	16	17
18	19	20	21	22	23	24
25	26	27	28	29	30	

1 / THU

*As for the saints who are in the land, they are the glo-
rious ones in whom is all my delight.*

—PSALM 16:3 (NIV)

It was the first All Saints' Day after my first husband Jim's death, and
I was keenly aware of "the saints who have gone on before." I was
also becoming well-acquainted with "the saints who are in the land."
Alongside my tears and memories of Jim, I began to think about some
of the people whose thoughtful, loving gestures were helping me to
cope with life.

There was my sister Lin, who came to live with us that first year,
helping with my three young children, doing everything from plumbing to bedtime stories. And Ann, my friend, who listened to my grief
by the hour and seemed always willing to lend a hand. Ted, who spent
an evening helping the kids carve pumpkins and, a few weeks after
their daddy died, took them shopping for Mother's Day gifts. There
was Stephanie, who in those early weeks of our enormous loss, appeared on my doorstep every Friday noon with a hug and a simple
bouquet of flowers.

The saints in the land; the glorious ones, in whom God delights—
my life has been full of people like that, and I'm grateful for an
opportunity to remind myself that the saints of God are many, and
surround me today.

*O Lord of the everyday details, I'm grateful for all those saints who
have touched my life. Help me today to see and to do those small
things for others that so delight You.* —MARY JANE CLARK

2 / FRI

*Let a man so account of us, as of the ministers of
Christ, and stewards of the mysteries of God.*

—I CORINTHIANS 4:1

I've been writing for *Daily Guideposts* for more than twenty years, and
every time I begin a piece I pray it may speak to someone in a helpful way. Most of the time I have no way of knowing whether or not
my prayer is answered. Yet just about the time I begin to doubt it, I
receive a letter from a reader, such as the one from Maris Underwood
of Grand Junction, Michigan, that reminds me of Who is really in
charge of what I write.

Maris's story of amazing grace really began five years ago when my dear friend and prayer partner Carolmae Petersen whispered to me some words based on her favorite hymn, shortly before she died. Those words that meant the world to me were, "I'll meet you at the river, Marilyn." I wrote about that special moment in *Daily Guideposts* two years later.

Maris's letter told me that for Christmas in 1996, her mother had given her a copy of *Daily Guideposts, 1997*. On June 1, 1997, Maris's ill mother told her she knew she was going to die that night. Maris read her mother's favorite Scriptures to her, and the two of them sang hymns together and said their last good-byes. Yet five months later, when Maris opened her copy of *Daily Guideposts* on her birthday (November 2), her mother spoke to her once again. At the top of the page she had written, nearly a year before, "Happy birthday, honey. I love you!" The devotional for that day was the story of Carolmae's parting words to me, "I'll meet you at the river." Maris felt her mother had sent those words to comfort her.

How could I possibly have known, when I wrote about Carolmae, that my dear friend's words would speak comfort to a woman unknown to her, two years after she spoke them? Yet there is One Who knew, One Who moves in mysterious ways and uses all that we offer.

Comforter, I offer You the work of this day. Let me never doubt the wonder of Your ways! —MARILYN MORGAN KING

WHEN GOD REACHES OUT . . . THROUGH OTHER PEOPLE

3/SAT *He asked life of thee, and thou gavest it him, even length of days. . . .* —PSALM 21:4

The dinner party brought together various branches of the family. The seats of honor at the ends of the long table went to the two eldest, my grandfather Papa, then in his mid-eighties, and Grammy, my brother-in-law's grandmother, age ninety-four.

Isolated by deafness, Papa had become almost morbidly interested in the details of illness, both his own and other people's. The table was buzzing with lively conversations when he shouted to Grammy, above the chattering voices, "How's your heart?"

Grammy beamed down the long table at him, a beatific smile that encompassed the entire gathering and seemed to take in all of struggling humanity as well. She answered his question with a single word, "Enlarged."

Papa did not hear, and "enlarged" was relayed to him along the seats. Sitting beside him, I shrieked into his ear, "Her heart's enlarged."

Medically, of course, a serious condition. But as I said the words, I thought they also summed up God's will for all of us as our years increase. Grammy's answer has become for me a kind of shorthand prayer. Like Grammy, let me carry my aches and ailments lightly as I grow older! Each year let me care a little less about myself, a little more for others.

Father, enlarge my heart.   —ELIZABETH SHERRILL

4/ SUN
I have fought a good fight, I have finished my course, I have kept the faith: Henceforth there is laid up for me a crown of righteousness. . . . —II TIMOTHY 4:7-8

Recently my son Daniel ran and completed the New York City Marathon, all twenty-six miles, 385 yards of it. Though I have seen many long-distance races, this was the first marathon I had watched up close and personal, and what an education it was.

Most of the thirty thousand runners were amateurs there to test themselves, hoping, not to win, but to finish the course. They were interested in their individual times, trying to improve on their previous marks. Because this was Daniel's first attempt, he had no prior times to compare himself to, but his aim was to finish in three and a half-hours.

How in the world do race officials keep track of all the different times? I wondered. They do it with computers, I learned. Because there is such a crowd at the start of the race and not all runners can get off the mark at the same time, a specially numbered computer chip is taped to a shoe of each runner. That way, his or her exact time—when the starting and finishing lines are crossed—is recorded and printed out minutes after the race. Daniel's official time: 3:54.53, not bad for a neophyte. And Shirley and I, proud parents, were there to greet him after the race. His prize was the same as thousands of others: a pewter medal testifying that he had finished the course.

Afterward I marveled at the similarities between a marathon and our race as Christians. We may get to the starting line later than others, but we aren't penalized; God's grace takes that into account. And more important than how fast we run is that we complete the course. At the finish line, I expect loved ones will be there to greet us, and the One Who has cheered us all the way to reward us with His approval. "Well done thou good and faithful servant. . . . Enter thou into the joy of the lord" (Matthew 25:21).

> *Teach us, God, that You're our strength*
> *Whatever the race, whatever its length.*

—FRED BAUER

INTO AFRICA

5 / MON *"This man is my chosen instrument to carry my name before the Gentiles and their kings. . . ."*

—ACTS 9:15 (NIV)

When a change occurred in my work life a few years ago, I struggled with a loss of identity. When I lost my title, office, car, company credit card and secretary, it felt like I had lost myself.

In Africa, I discovered a better identity. Everywhere I went, I had to fill out visa or customs forms. Each one asked for name, address, birth date, birthplace, nationality and, always, occupation. I didn't really have one, and I decided I'd rather be known for who I am than what I do. All the changes in my life had drawn me to focus more deeply on my relationship to God and my desire to make that relationship first in my life, however I earned a living. So on the first form in Nairobi, Kenya, I put down the word *disciple*. All across East Africa, I was stamped in and out of country after country as a disciple, with never a comment.

Then it came time to leave for home from Dar es Salaam, Tanzania. The immigration officer looked twice at my answer to occupation and frowned. "What is 'disciple'?" he asked.

I had been thinking about all the new ways I had seen God in Africa, so I replied, "I am a student of a great Teacher Who gave a message of hope to all the world."

"Who was that?" he asked.

"Jesus of Nazareth," I replied.

"Oh," he replied, stamping my passport and handing it back with a smile, "the Palestinian carpenter who became a great prophet. I thought maybe you were doing missionary work without permission."

We talked for a few minutes, and I was surprised by how much he knew about Jesus. His name is revered around the world; He fascinates people and opens their minds to new possibilities. So, even if I get another real job someday, I've decided to keep my occupation of disciple.

How about you?

Lord, no matter what else You have given me to do in life, make disciple my number-one occupation. —ERIC FELLMAN

6/ *TUE*   *The king's heart is in the hand of the Lord. . . .*
—PROVERBS 21:1

Years ago I became enthusiastic about a presidential candidate. A friend and I did some grassroots campaigning locally. We organized prayer groups, gave out bumper stickers and made phone calls. On Election Day I woke up so excited I couldn't stop smiling all the way to the polls. That evening I settled down cross-legged in front of the television to watch the returns, confident of victory.

Hours later my candidate conceded defeat, and I shouted back to the television the way my husband often did when his team lost a football game. Maybe the tide would turn, I reasoned. Maybe the morning paper would announce a miraculous win after all. But there was no such miracle the next day. Unless, of course, you count the one that arrived by telephone.

It was my campaigning friend. "Hi, Marion," she piped with all the eagerness of Mother Goose to her goslings. I sighed heavily and shifted the phone to the other ear. "Listen," she insisted, "God is still God. He's not even surprised, and the Bible admonishes us to pray for everyone in leadership. Have you prayed for our President-elect yet?"

Sitting there on the tall kitchen stool, my hand still on the phone I'd just hung up, I bowed my head and prayed for the man I hadn't wanted to win.

Lord, may Your holy presence abide in the hearts of everyone elected to office today. Amen. —MARION BOND WEST

---

7 / WED *Don't you know that a little yeast works through the whole batch of dough? Get rid of the old yeast that you may be a new batch without yeast. . . .*
—I CORINTHIANS 5:6–7 (NIV)

For days I had been testing and retesting a unit that adjusted the air intake on aircraft engines. The performance of the unit was erratic, and the test results were inconsistent. At the time I was a working leader in development testing, where troubled parts were returned for observation. These parts had passed inspection, but now they weren't working normally. Engineers with complex instruments joined me, and for one week we tested without an answer.

Finally a gentleman with tousled hair and a crumpled suit entered the test lab. He appeared to be deep in thought as he examined the errant part. After a few minutes of silence, he said, "Do you have one that works?" I nodded. "Let's try it," he said. I did, and it worked perfectly.

Then the man reached down to the floor and gathered some lint between his fingers. The amount was so small I could hardly see it. He sprinkled the fibers into the unit. "Give it a whirl," he said. I did, and the part functioned as erratically as the rest had. The man turned and left without introducing himself. Later I learned he had a doctorate in engineering design.

When I find myself angry or sad as I go about my tasks, or if my prayer life seems to be drying up, I think back to our problem with that errant part. Sometimes the source of my problem isn't an obvious error or a structural flaw. Sometimes it's as simple as a cross word with my wife Ruby or a quiet time I've skipped or a bad night's sleep. As simple as a pinch of lint.

Dear Father, help me to avoid the little things that lead me away from You. —OSCAR GREENE

8/ THU *The trash cans in the Temple of the Lord will be as sacred as the bowls beside the altar.*
—ZECHARIAH 14:20 (TLB)

For three years I was a student janitor at the college where I am now a teacher. To some people this might seem like a social leap, but not to me. I think that making a living with one's hands is just as honorable and holy as using one's mind or voice.

I'm surprised at how often I use my hands in teaching—fixing a stubborn projector, or making posters, or working on a student's car. A lot of my work as a teacher is a kind of janitoring: opening doors to knowledge; sweeping out old ideas; turning on lights in students' minds.

Jesus Himself was a blue-collar laborer for most of His life, and how would He have ministered without the help of laborers? The manger was made by carpenters, and so was the Temple and the synagogue where Jesus taught. Craftsmen made the upper room and the table where Jesus broke bread with His disciples. Even the Cross and the tomb were fashioned by skilled hands.

Often Jesus made reference to manual labor in His talks, thus imparting a luster to the blue-collar life. He talked about farming and construction, sewing and cooking, shepherding and fishing. He included potters and pruners and musicians in His talks, and most of His audience was made up of such people.

I think there will be a lot of janitors in heaven, polishing the pearly gates and sweeping gold dust off the twenty-four-karat streets.

No matter what you do for a living, you can always use your hands to extend a friendly greeting or to applaud those who have done exceptional work. If my work as a teacher does not pass the Final Examination, I'll just show God my hands, and I think He will know what I mean.

Thank You, Lord, for all those who minister to us with their hands.
—DANIEL SCHANTZ

9/ *FRI*   *Let us not become weary in doing good, for at the proper time we will reap a harvest if we do not give up.*   —GALATIANS 6:9 (NIV)

When my father had emergency gall bladder surgery, I stepped into the temporary role of running the household and caring for Mom, who was confined to a wheelchair. There was so much to remember—feed the dog, water the plants, exercise Mom's legs, cancel the hair appointment, switch Mom's eye patch every few hours. I fell into bed exhausted, then remembered that I'd forgotten to brush Mom's teeth. *I'll never be able to keep this up,* I thought wearily.

The next day I noticed that one of Mom's medications was running low. Dad had managed to tell me that he orders medicine by mail and that the necessary forms and instructions were in a file marked "Medical." I pulled open the file cabinet in my parents' bedroom, searched through it three times and found only files for the organizations Dad supports.

"I give up," I muttered in frustration as I stumbled out of the bedroom and down the hall. Then I noticed another file cabinet in a small spare bedroom. I went through it eagerly, but I didn't see the "Medical" file. Then I yanked open the top drawer again, and my eyes fell on a file marked "Perseverance." Curious about the odd title, I pulled out the file. It was a talk Dad had given at a retreat. I flipped to the last page and saw these underlined words: "We can persevere because Christ and the Holy Spirit will enable us."

I put the "Perseverance" file back in the drawer; almost immediately I found the file I was looking for, right there in the top drawer where it had been all along. "I guess I *can* do this job, Lord—if You'll enable me," I said. And I closed the file drawer, having found what I was searching for—and also something I desperately needed.

Lord, thank You for the strength You give me to accomplish the hardest tasks.   —KAREN BARBER

10/ *SAT*   *She is clothed with strength and dignity; she can laugh at the days to come.*   —PROVERBS 31:25 (NIV)

At ninety-seven, my great-aunt Anna is enthusiastic about life. Born in Russia twelve years before the Revolution, she's survived three terrible wars and a flight for her life that took her across Europe and ended in a pioneer settlement in Paraguay. Then in her early fifties she emigrated to Canada, where she started over again. "I've had a good life," she exclaims.

Anna had not lived in Canada long when one day, on her afternoon off work as a cook in a nursing home, she and her friend Lena walked three miles to my mother's house. After a delightful visit and the usual *vaspa* (evening meal), they were ready to walk back. "It's too dark for you to be walking," my mother said. Anna and her friend allowed my mother to call a taxi.

The two women were huddled in the backseat when they suddenly heard a man's voice. After a few moments, the driver answered.

"Who's he talking to?" Lena whispered in her native German.

"Another man," Anna whispered back. "He's got another man in this car. They're up to no good!"

As the darkened countryside flitted by and nothing looked familiar anymore, the women became convinced that these men had evil intentions. Why else would one of them be crouching so low that they couldn't see him?

"When he slows at a stop sign," Anna whispered, "be ready to jump."

Suddenly the car stopped. The driver got out and opened the passenger door.

"Here you are, ladies, safe and sound at the Menno Home," he said in perfect German.

"Later I learned about two-way radios," my great-aunt laughed. "I also found out the taxi driver goes to my church."

Instead of being embarrassed, Aunt Anna saw humor in the situation. And come to think of it, many of her stories end with a good laugh. Laughter is a great way to get over the potholes of life. My great-aunt seems to know that.

Dear Lord, send me on my way today with a sense of humor.

—HELEN GRACE LESCHEID

11/*SUN* *Ye are bought with a price....* —I CORINTHIANS 7:23

I'm sad to say that I didn't even realize it was Veterans Day until my daughter Keri and I came upon a roadblock in downtown Memphis, Tennessee.

"What's going on?" we asked the attendant at the entrance to the parking garage.

"Why, the parade's coming," he answered. "You know, it's Veterans Day."

I don't suppose we would have ever thought to stay if it weren't for this man perched atop a doorstep. He was looking down the empty street as if something very important was about to happen. "Keri, how would you feel about staying for the parade?" I asked.

"Sure, Mama, I love parades."

So we chose a sunny spot on the edge of the sidewalk and waited. Others gathered around us: a group of preschoolers, an elderly couple, several men wearing VFW caps. Then came the crash of a cymbal, the roll of a drum, and finally the parade spread out before us. A band marched by, then another. Girls twirled batons and drum majors pranced. Next came convertibles marked POWS and PEARL HARBOR SURVIVORS and PURPLE HEART HONOREES, followed by rows of robust wheelchair vets who tossed candy to the cheering crowd.

Then an old sailor came by, all alone. He marched with such purpose that he might as well have been a one-man parade. A survivor of World War II, he was dressed in an old, blue wool uniform with bell-bottom trousers. Something in his face said he was marching for other sailors, the ones who never came home. Overcome by his silent testimony, I couldn't suppress my tears. I caught Keri's eye. She was crying, too.

Later that evening I heard Keri tell her new husband Ben, "When we have children, let's make a pact always to take them to a parade on Veterans Day. I think it's important."

Father, today we come to You remembering the sailors and soldiers and all the rest who willingly gave their lives for our country, and in the process assured us the freedom to turn toward You.

—PAM KIDD

12 / MON

Be still before the Lord and wait patiently for him. . . . do not fret—it leads only to evil.

—PSALM 37:7–8 (NIV)

The morning started badly. I slept through my wake-up call at my hotel in Los Angeles, leaving little time for the mad dash to the airport in the pouring rain. I nearly rear-ended a shuttle bus trying to figure out how to work the rental-car phone so I could check on delays and see if there was any hope at all that I would make the meeting I had foolishly insisted on scheduling in New York that afternoon. Then I couldn't find the car return lot and ended up trapped in orbit around the airport. I finally spotted a sign that was obscured by construction equipment; I made a furious mental note to track down the people responsible and lodge a formal complaint when I got back home.

When I finally arrived at the lot and checked in, I missed the departing shuttle, then languished on the next one as the driver chitchatted with passengers. *Is he trying to network a screenplay or something? Let's just get moving here!* When he finally got around to putting the bus in gear and announced that my airline was the last stop on the run, I felt my mushrooming anger turn to despair.

I glanced around for another passenger who was as frenzied and desperate as I was, someone else whose existence was poised on the brink of chaos if all did not go precisely as planned. Everyone seemed quite relaxed, especially the man sitting across from me. He was reading his pocket Bible. A feeling of embarrassment and relief passed over me. He was doing what I had neglected to do—take a few minutes for God. And here I was again, trying to control things only God can control, and driving myself temporarily insane.

I made my plane, I made my meeting and, most importantly, I made it home to my wife Julee and the dogs. But first, bouncing along on the rental car shuttle, I had closed my eyes and done what I should have done to begin with—found a few minutes for a God break.

Is it any wonder, Lord, that when I force myself in front of You, my way becomes so difficult?
—EDWARD GRINNAN

13/ *TUE*   *But solid food is for the mature, for those who have their faculties trained by practice. . . .*
—HEBREWS 5:14 (RSV)

"Mom, let's take cooking lessons." That suggestion from a twenty-four-year-old guy more likely to be listening to rap than spending time in the kitchen came as quite a shock.

"Why would you want to do that, lovey?" I asked.

"Well," he answered bluntly, "you can't cook and neither can I, so

Dad cooks for you, and I just eat expensive junk food. We should both give it a try."

So we did, taking an eight-week course in basic cooking techniques. I was definitely the oldest student, and my son was the only male among bright, energetic young women. I was skeptical at first, but Daniel loved every minute of it, energetically carving up a raw chicken with a vicious eight-inch chef's knife. The only part he didn't like was chopping garlic cloves, until the teacher told him lemon juice would remove the pungent aroma from his hands. I enjoyed learning about different foods and listening to the witty and talented teacher. But even more I enjoyed watching my son.

After about half the classes were over, Daniel actually cooked dinner for some of his friends and invited me. As he brought the platter of chicken Marsala out of the kitchen to the astonishment of the assembled youth, there was such a look of pride on his face that tears suddenly stung my eyes. My troubled, angry, disaffected teenager had turned into a self-confident young man who was proud of his achievements and actually enjoyed his mother's company.

"We had fun, didn't we, Mom?" he said as he set the platter down. "And, by the way, I'll make the pies for Thanksgiving—and the pastry."

Thank You, Lord, for young people who bring light and laughter into my world.
                                                              —BRIGITTE WEEKS

14/ WED   *And having ears, hear ye not? . . .*   —MARK 8:18

Though I had played trombone with the band for years, it was a new thrill to thread through the audience after my jazz-singing debut, voices coming from all sides: "Nice job!" "Loved your singing!" "When's the next show?" When a small, shrill voice called out, "That was a great Peggy Lee impression!" I paused. Abandoning my thankyous and waves, I stepped toward the voice.

Three older women, still in their seats, smiled up at me. The nearest put her hand on my arm and sighed. "I loved how you did 'Why Don't You Do Right.' You sounded just like Miss Peggy Lee!"

I smiled, flattered, but a part of me was disappointed. I wanted to sound like *me*! I had worked hard to develop my own style, my own sound. "And I so look forward to the next concert," the woman said.

"Will you sing 'Fever'? I just love 'Fever.'" I shook the ladies' hands and thanked them for attending.

When my next concert rolled around, I was indeed slated to sing "Fever." As I was mingling with the audience afterward, I heard that voice again: "Dear, we just loved your impression!" The same three ladies sat in the same three seats, and the one nearest me said, "You do sound just like Peggy Lee! And the way you talk to the audience—just as she did!" I tried to explain that though I admire Miss Lee, I try to sing the songs my own way. But they wouldn't hear it.

After each concert, there they were, always in the same seats. I learned that two of them had seen Peggy Lee perform on many occasions and the other was a singing teacher. The one nearest me would always say, "I loved your songs, dear, but you should really do more Peggy Lee material!"

Finally, I gave up protesting. Peggy Lee was and would always be their favorite. And to compliment me on my "imitation" was their sincerest form of flattery.

Dear Lord, help me pause and listen not only to what others say, but also to what they really mean. —KJERSTIN EASTON

A WHOLE AND HOLY LOVE

15/THU   *And all the crowd sought to touch him, for power came forth from him and healed them all.*
—LUKE 6:19 (RSV)

There wasn't much touching in my family when I was growing up. My parents were both loving people who took wonderful care of me, but they seldom expressed affection openly.

Because of my upbringing, I haven't, until recently, felt comfortable touching or being touched—even by someone I love. But that began to change when Marilyn and I started seeing each other. The first time we ate together, we decided to begin the meal by holding hands in a silent grace. In this silent touching, something profound was communicated. A field of love formed between us so that we were no longer two, but in some mysterious way, one. Suddenly, my fear of touch dissolved.

Since our marriage, we've continued our silent, handholding graces, and we've found other ways to communicate through touch—with a gentle caress, a back rub or a reassuring hug. And we have found that touch—simple, everyday touch—has healing power.

The crowds of people who were drawn to Jesus knew this. That's why they sought to touch Him; they wanted to experience His healing power. Through my relationship with Marilyn, I've come to appreciate as never before the significance of Jesus *touching* those He healed. It was a way He had of communicating His love, God's love, for us all. As Marilyn and I continue to live and grow together, I hope we will always be "in touch."

Loving God, may I never be afraid to show affection by reaching out to touch those I love.
—ROBERT KING

16/FRI

Now I know in part; but then shall I know even as also I am known. —I CORINTHIANS 13:12

Across the crowded hotel lobby, I saw the pastor of the church I had attended as a child. I had last seen him in 1969, when I was eight years old. But even though it was now three decades later and his face had been altered by the passage of time, he was unmistakable.

I knew he would need help to remember who I was, so I began to rehearse an introduction: *My name is Dave Franco. My mom and dad were part of your congregation at Alamitos Friends Church during the sixties. Their names are Ruben and Sally Franco. My sisters Laura and Karen were friends of your daughter's, and I knew your son Mickey.*

Feeling sufficiently prepared, I made my way across the lobby to say hello to my dear old pastor. As I approached him, his eyes caught mine, and before I could open my mouth, he said, "David! How wonderful to see you!"

Thirty years had passed. He had looked into thousands of different faces since then. I had changed from a boy to a man nearly forty years old. And still he knew me. What a welcoming feeling that was!

I think that's something like what it will be like when I get to heaven. The Lord knows me even better than I know myself, and when I finally approach Him, He'll give me the warmest welcome of my life.

Lord, I can't wait to feel Your arms around me. —DAVE FRANCO

17/ SAT   *Encourage one another and build one another up. . . .*
      —I THESSALONIANS 5:11 (RSV)

"Does anyone know what this kind of monster is called?"

Elizabeth's hand shot up, but not before the words were out of her mouth. "It's a griffin!" As usual, my jump-right-in daughter was answering all of the questions; none of the other children on the museum tour could get a word in edgewise. Elizabeth's zest for learning is a wonder, but in group situations it's a bit much. I tapped her on the shoulder and whispered that she needed to let the other children have a turn. She scowled, but was quiet.

I winced awhile later when Elizabeth's nonstop questions and answers resumed. This time I gently pulled her away from the front of the group and had her stand next to me. Sometimes simply keeping my hand on her shoulder helps her restrain herself. *I'm going to have to have another talk with her*, I thought to myself, and spent most of the rest of the tour thinking about how best to do it.

Back at our house, I chatted with the friends who had come to the museum with us. "Elizabeth is irrepressible in class settings," I admitted with embarrassment.

Mary Ellen looked surprised. "Yes, but I was impressed that when you corrected her, she listened." My train of thought came to a sudden stop. I'd been so absorbed in thinking about my daughter's lack of self-control that I'd overlooked the positives in her behavior.

That night I had my talk with Elizabeth as I tucked her in. "I was very proud of you today, honey. I know how hard it is for you when you want to answer all the questions. But you did a good job of letting other children have a turn, and I know that took a lot of self-control." Elizabeth smiled and snuggled under the covers. I smiled, too, and thought, *Thank you, Mary Ellen. Thank You, God.*

Light of the World, when I see the shadows in someone else, help me remember that I can't see shadows if there is no light.

—JULIA ATTAWAY

PRAYER FOR NOVEMBER

Hallelujah!
You open Your hand
Cascading light upon the earth,
Illuminating our days.

So may our acts prolong Your light.

Hallelujah!
You open Your hand
Spilling radiance upon the night,
Safeguarding darkness.

So may our deeds echo Your nightsong.

Hallelujah!
You open Your hand
And sculpt billowing rain clouds,
Nourishing Your creations.

So may we give succor in Your Name.

We remember Your kindnesses
In every hallelujah;
We recall Your creation
When we create goodness in our lives.

So may we be privileged to sing hallelujah!
Praise the Eternal!
Hallelujah!

—DEBBIE PERLMAN

18/SUN *Thou hast known the holy scriptures, which are able to make thee wise unto salvation through faith which is in Christ Jesus.* —II TIMOTHY 3:15

I parked the truck at the back of the auction barn and waited as the auctioneer approached. He was a short, stocky young man with a brown, curly beard.

"What do you have?" he asked.

"A couple of cabinet sinks from the office," I replied.

He pointed to a wire fence. "Drive over there, and let's unload them."

The job was easy with each of us lifting one side of the sinks. After we finished unloading them, he wrote out a receipt and asked me to sign it.

"Hope that does it," I said as I signed.

He looked at my name, lifted his face and asked, "What's the good news?"

"All's well with the world" was my innocuous and somewhat puzzled answer.

He smiled. "And the Lord's in charge."

"You're a Christian," I said.

"That's right," he replied. "And it's your daughter's fault. A few years back at Bible study, your daughter Anne gave me her Bible because I didn't have one. It was old and worn, but it led me to accept Jesus as my Savior. Now I use it to teach a youth Bible study in my church."

Lord, I prayed silently, *if a gift of a Bible can lead someone to You, I can be a giver, too.*

Since that day, I've helped to give Bibles to people in my town and in places all around the world. And with each gift, I've prayed:

Lord, open the hearts of all who open the Bible so that they may receive Your words of life.
—RICHARD HAGERMAN

19/MON

The Lord is nigh unto all them that call upon him . . . in truth.
—PSALM 145:18

The most important weekly meeting I attend at the office has no formal presentations, no overhead projectors, no budget proposals. People don't argue their positions or make impassioned justifications for their departments. Those of us who come to the conference room sit around a large table and pick up a handful of letters. In silence we read.

"My grandson needs a raise at work," a grandmother writes. "Even with overtime he's not able to support his family. Please pray for him."

"Last year I was in the hospital for five and a half weeks," says another letter. "I now have an apartment, but it does not allow pets. My twelve-and-a-half-year-old dog has been with a foster family for over a year. Please pray for me as I speak to my landlord. Wiggles is very well-behaved."

The greeting on one note makes me smile. "Hi, Spiritual Siblings!" it says. Another letter is painfully succinct: "Keep my mind intact." I find myself moved by another's plea: "I'm so lonely. I haven't met anyone who wants to date or take out a 53-year-old woman. Help me to pray."

The ideal words come from a cheerful soul who says, "I live on two acres and love to mow the grass. (I have a rider.)" I read her prayer aloud: "I have faith in Jesus. For He's there on my good days; He's there on my bad days; He's there all the time." What a reminder for starting out my week!

By now you might realize I'm writing about the Guideposts Prayer Fellowship. We gather in our offices on Monday mornings at 9:45 to pray for others. With every letter, I find myself fortified. It's a meeting of spiritual siblings worldwide.

Lord, be there on my good days; be there on my bad days; be there all the time.　　　　　　　　　　　　　　　　　　　—RICK HAMLIN

EDITOR'S NOTE: Today is Guideposts Family Day of Prayer. Please join us as we join in prayer for all the needs of our Guideposts family.

$20/$ _TUE_　　*But I trust in your unfailing love; my heart rejoices in your salvation.*　　　—PSALM 13:5 (NIV)

For many years of my life my dad helped and looked after me. And for the past several years I have looked after him. He has Alzheimer's disease and lives in a nursing home near me. He no longer knows me, but I visit with him anyway, although it's difficult to find things to say. He has no memory of his life at all. When he catches a glimpse of himself in a mirror, it frightens him because he doesn't recognize the man he sees.

During the past year, my dad has had pneumonia three times. This last time has been especially difficult for him. He's very weak and occasionally needs oxygen to help him breathe. He has a living will, so nothing drastic will be done to keep him going. All anyone can do is try to make him comfortable.

At first I had a hard time dealing with the fact that I couldn't do anything to help my dad. All I could do was hold his hand and pray as I watched him drift off into sleep. Finally, just the other day, I realized that I had a problem: My will was struggling with God's will. What I needed to do was let go and turn this over to God—because my father's life was in His hands, not mine. At that moment I prayed again, but this time for myself. I asked God to help me release my dad into His loving hands. And almost immediately I felt at peace. I still do.

I know now that when I sit beside my dad's bed, I am not supposed to do anything. God is his caregiver—and mine.

Dear Lord, there are so many of us caring for loved ones who are ill. Be with us in our helplessness and comfort us with Your love. Amen.

—PHYLLIS HOBE

21 / WED   *In her tongue is the law of kindness.*

—PROVERBS 31:26

The other day in a conversation with one of our grandchildren, I used an old phrase. I said, "Have a T.L. for you."

She looked puzzled. "A what?"

"A T.L. That means I heard someone say something nice about you. A compliment, in other words."

"Aren't you going to tell me what it was?"

"Eventually, perhaps. But first you're supposed to pass along a compliment to me. Those initials stand for *Trade Last*. That means we'll exchange pleasantries, but you have to go first, and I'll trade last. We used to play this game when I was your age."

She gave me an impish smile. "What if I can't think of a compliment for you?"

"Then the game ends right there," I said, and we both laughed.

But that little game from years ago is not as foolish as it sounds. All of us crave admiration. All of us need the reassurance that comes from approval. And it's so easy to pass a compliment along if we can just train our memory to retain it until the opportunity presents itself.

There's an old proverb that says, "Blessed is he who speaks a kindness; thrice blessed who repeats it." In many places the Bible urges us to love our neighbor. Isn't this one way to do it?

Father, let the law of kindness rule my life, not just my tongue.

—ARTHUR GORDON

22 / THU *Since my youth, O God, you have taught me, and to this day I declare your marvelous deeds.*
—PSALM 71:17 (NIV)

Last Thanksgiving my children and I joined my friend Portia and her new family, and reminisced over past Thanksgivings, including the year we ate beans and rice in our trailer in rural North Carolina. Several days later, alone in our hotel room, my daughter Lanea, my son Chase and I made a list of the things we had to be thankful for.

It was quite a list: Chase had healed with no visible scars from the head and face wounds he received in a skiing accident. Lanea had started graduate school and had her first apartment and car. Our Chihuahua Punkin had been returned to us after three weeks of futile searching. I had completed my first novel. Portia had celebrated her first anniversary as the wife of a widowed minister and stepmother to his children. Our extended family was well and blessed. My brother Newton was thriving after surviving a bout with cancer, and my mother was recovering from hip replacement surgery. And finally, the lingering grief that we had felt since the death of Chase's father seemed to leave us.

After we finished our thanksgivings, we sang a song in which the singer professes that he came to God and got just what he wanted. He sings about miracles, healing and deliverance. It's a simple chorus, and we sang it over and over. As we sang, a look of surprise came over fifteen-year-old Chase's face. "I just realized," he said, "we really did get what we wanted!"

I smiled and added one more thing to the thanksgiving list: My children have grateful hearts.

It's true—we got just what we wanted.

God, thank You that every day truly is a day of thanksgiving.
—SHARON FOSTER

23 / FRI *Bear ye one another's burdens, and so fulfil the law of Christ.* —GALATIANS 6:2

My seventeen-year-old son Drew is growing up quickly in so many ways. Now a senior in high school, he recently spent a week in Mexico City working in an orphanage. Today he showed me some photographs he had taken of the kids with whom he worked.

One of the photographs captures the playful delight of children in every city and culture. It's a picture of a twelve-year-old boy giving his ten-year-old friend a piggyback ride. Both boys are thin and ragged, but are smiling from ear to ear.

Gazing at the photo, Drew said, "Dad, you don't understand this picture. That's Juan and Mario. Juan is the kid who's giving Mario a ride. Juan was born blind, but he can walk. And Mario, who is on his back, is paralyzed. He can't walk, but he can see. So Juan gives Mario rides and Mario gives Juan directions. They've worked out quite a system. They're a team."

As I looked up at my son, I knew that he had been initiated into the sad world of human suffering. But I also knew that he had discovered the beauty of the human spirit, of one person helping another.

All of us are handicapped in some way. We have our weaknesses and limitations. But all of us have the ability to give what we have in the service of others. We can help the lame to walk and the blind to see and feed thousands with a few fish sandwiches. This is the spirit of Jesus. And this is the source of miracles.

Dear Father, take my strengths and my limitations and use them to help others. Amen. —SCOTT WALKER

24 / SAT *Whatsoever ye do in word or deed, do all in the name of the Lord Jesus, giving thanks to God. . . .*
—COLOSSIANS 3:17

I'm in the basement, radio on, folding laundry. It's a contemplative act, with its own rules.

First rule: Look for towels, sheets and blankets to fold quickly into squares. In the hands of a master, the folds fairly fly. You want to get off to a good start, to have the feeling of work being done efficiently and the towels build up into an impressive stack of folded stuff.

Next: kid stuff. Might as well concentrate on what is most plentiful, and with three small children there is an eye-popping number of shirts, pants, socks, hats, sweaters, sweatshirts and diapers. With baby stuff you enter the dream zone, when your mind sails to Italy and walks the sunny rows of the vineyard contemplating the exact right day to begin harvest while your hands lift the shirt, snap it straight, fold sleeves in, fold belly up, reach for next shirt.

Then wife's stuff. Mostly shirts and jeans, but hey, here's a bra! How do you fold a bra?

My stuff: A hundred years ago, when I was young and single, I didn't wash anything; I'd actually leave things out in the rain on purpose. Then I started washing unmentionables. Then everything else. But what self-respecting guy folded his own stuff? Now I fold my own stuff, with affection and respect, savoring each hardworking garment, some of which have been with me half my life.

This is the prayer of the laundry room, which is really the prayer of the small daily act. And what are our days but a whole motley pile of small daily acts—each a prayer, if only we can keep attending to its inherent holiness.

Lord, give me the sharpness of eye and width of heart to spy Your grace and humor in what seem to be the smallest and most insignificant corners of my days. Yea, even unto the finding and folding of socks hot from the dryer. —BRIAN DOYLE

25 / SUN

"Unless you change and become like little children, you will never enter the kingdom of heaven."
—MATTHEW 18:3 (NIV)

On the wall above my desk, I've taped a wonderful snapshot of a chubby-cheeked, three-year-old cherub, wearing a fluffy pink tutu and confident smile. Her name is Gracie, and her mother sent me the picture because I told her that Gracie had become my symbol of what it means to keep a childlike heart.

I was attending a Sunday after-church brunch with a bunch of adults I hardly knew. We all seemed a bit self-conscious as we sat knee-to-knee, balancing paper plates of food on our laps and making small talk. Then Gracie arrived in her pink tutu.

"It's her favorite outfit right now," her mother explained as Gracie paused at the door, and then floated into the room, totally free from self-consciousness or self-centeredness. Everywhere she went, she created a pink space for herself. When she reached the food table, she squealed with delight at the sight of the gooey cinnamon rolls.

As I watched Gracie that day, I admired the way she responded to the world with such joy and exuberance. And now, as I look at her picture above my desk, I vow to do the same, especially now that I'm past the fifty-year mark in my life. "Maturity is the process of becoming childlike," someone once said. Part of my vow is to be more playful. Though I probably won't show up in a pink tutu, I do have a collection of hats I can sometimes wear for fun, including one that has flashing lights, another with clapping hands and one that has a halo.

I also vow never to lose a *wow!* response to evidences of God's goodness, like arching rainbows, fluffy snowflakes, exquisite little ladybugs or gooey cinnamon rolls.

And I don't want to let self-consciousness grow bigger than self-confidence, so I vow to trust that where I am and who I am is delightful in God's eyes. If I start forgetting any of these childlike goals, I have that picture of Gracie, my heroine in her pink tutu, right above my desk to remind me.

Father, show me how to keep a childlike heart in this aging body.

—CAROL KUYKENDALL

26/MON
He who conceals his sins does not prosper. . . .
—PROVERBS 28:13 (NIV)

Last fall, when I needed a new car, I found a good buy on a low-mileage model that had been used as a rental car. The interior looked brand-new, its impeccable gray velour upholstery made even more convincing by that new-car smell.

But after I'd driven the car for a week or so, I noticed a cigarette burn in the driver's seat. *Impossible,* I thought. *No one who smokes has been in my car.* When I went to an upholstery shop for an estimate, the repairman nodded knowingly. "Yep, one of the oldest tricks in the book. When one of these babies gets a cigarette burn, they just shave some of the nap from underneath the seat and glue it in the hole. The only problem is, when the glue patch pops out, you've got an even bigger hole. Barely lasts till you drive her home."

The car has served me well in every other respect, although I'm a little hesitant to refer friends to that dealership. And it's also made me take a closer look at my own life and work ethic. Am I doing a job truly worthy of Christ's name or am I merely keeping up appearances if I think no one will know?

Dear Lord, help me to do all my work for You. —ROBERTA MESSNER

27 / TUE *Truly the light is sweet, and a pleasant thing it is for the eyes to behold the sun.* —ECCLESIASTES 11:7

Driving the Southern California freeways during rush hour is a test of true grit and something to be avoided if at all possible. I had deliberately timed my return home from a conference in San Diego to miss the traffic. I was whizzing along, making good time when, suddenly, coming around the turn that feeds 57 North westward onto the 210 freeway, I found myself caught in a hideous backup. *Bother!* I thought. *Now what?*

By the time I had inched my way around the bend and was driving west, I had my answer. The long line of cars had all slowed down and were crawling along so that their drivers could see one of the most magnificent sunsets I have ever experienced. I joined the drivers who had moved their cars over to the right shoulder to stop and catch the wonder, mesmerized by the brilliant light that filled the sky with reds and gold and surreal electric pinks.

It didn't last long, probably no more than five or ten minutes. Then came the gray of dusk. As suddenly as we had been caught up in the glory of a celestial light show, we were once again earthbound. Those of us parked on the shoulder revved our engines, turned our wheels and jostled our way back into the rush of the traffic.

I didn't think a sunset could get any better than the ones I'd seen over the ocean in Hawaii, but here in midst of the stress-filled California rush-hour traffic, God splashed a canvas across the sky of such dazzling glory that freeway drivers slowed, pulled over and bestowed the accolade of a pause that, in our best Hollywood tradition, applauded "Bravo!"

How magnificent is Your handiwork, Lord God of creation! And how much more will be Your glory when I see You face-to-face!

—FAY ANGUS

28 / WED *They helped every one his neighbor; and every one said to his brother, Be of good courage.* —ISAIAH 41:6

I love getting e-mail, especially when it's like the one my husband sent me recently. "Thanks for being my parachute packer," was all it said.

Attached to the e-mail was a story about a Navy pilot whose plane was blown apart in Vietnam. He was able to eject from the plane, and his parachute settled him slowly to safety on the ground. Years later, as he was dining in a restaurant, a man wandered over to his table, called him by name and said, "You flew jet fighters in 'Nam and were shot down!"

"How did you know that?" the ex-pilot said, startled.

"Because I packed your parachute!" the other man said with a grin.

The ex-pilot grabbed the man's hand and thanked him profusely. "If that parachute hadn't worked, I wouldn't be here today!"

The story made me think about those who, largely unseen, provide the emotional, physical and spiritual "parachutes" that we all need every day. My husband's six-word e-mail was sweet recognition of the little things I do for him that most of the time go unnoticed, but that keep his life from crashing out of control.

Who packs your parachute?

Lord, I'm praying today for the people whose words or deeds help keep me afloat, especially _____.
(FILL IN NAME)
Help me to show how much I appreciate them. —ROBERTA ROGERS

29 / THU   *Two are better than one. . . .*   —ECCLESIASTES 4:9

While we were preparing for my sister Keri's wedding, people kept asking about my own plans. My answer was always the same: "Ask me again in the year two thousand!" I was happy with my career as a financial consultant, I had plenty of friends in town, and I enjoyed the laid-back life of a bachelor.

But seeing Keri and her fiancé Ben together, I found myself beginning to look at things differently. Long weekend nights out with my buddies began to lose some of their appeal. Parties began to seem dull. I could feel a life change coming down the pike.

There was one pretty blue-eyed woman in particular who was having a big influence on my feelings. Her name was Candy Johnston. Candy had been my date for several of Keri's parties, and every time I was with her, her eyes got bluer and her smile grew sweeter.

But the thought of giving up my bachelorhood was, well . . . scary. I had been on my own since I had graduated from college five years before. I had bought a house and was renting bedrooms to two of my old frat brothers. I did anything I wanted to do: I could take trips with friends or go hunting and fishing anytime, and I didn't have to take care of anyone but myself.

But there was something about Candy, a brightness that made my shining bachelorhood appear dim in comparison. Then one day the brightness overcame me. We were sitting on the back porch of her parents' house, the sun was disappearing over the horizon, and we were laughing together. I looked into those beautiful blue eyes, and right then I realized that Candy was "the one."

A few weeks later she had a ring on her finger, and we were on our way to a new life—because by now, I was convinced that, as the Bible says, two really are better than one!

Father, thank You for Your surprises—the ones that keep turning our lives in new and better directions.   —BROCK KIDD

30 / FRI *Yea, the stork in the heaven knoweth her appointed times; and the turtle and the crane and the swallow observe the time of their coming. . . .* —JEREMIAH 8:7

My husband and I were driving to the Grand Canyon for a much-anticipated long weekend in late November. As we were driving east across the Arizona desert, Keith asked me, "What time is it?"

I looked at my watch and said, "Eleven-ten. Unless..."

"Unless what?" he said.

"Is Arizona in the same time zone as California?" I thought I remembered something about its being different, but I hadn't looked it up.

"I think it is," he said.

"Or maybe it has something to do with Standard Time versus Daylight Saving Time," I said. "Part of the year they're the same time zone we are, and part of the year they're not. I don't know which part this is."

We turned on the radio and began looking for stations that would give us the time. We found all sorts of music and some talk radio, but we couldn't find out what time it was. Right after we began climbing onto the Kaibab Plateau, we found what seemed like a promising station, but we drove out of its broadcast range and had to look for another. We found one just before what I thought would be noon, and waited eagerly for the announcer to confirm it.

High-tension electrical wires loomed ahead, and we kept driving toward them. The wires passed over the road ahead of us. We drew closer to them as it drew near to the hour. Then, just as the announcer began the station identification that would have included the time, we passed under the wires, and interference blotted out the broadcast.

I laughed, but Keith said, "Turn off the radio. God's reminding us we're on vacation, and we don't have to worry about what time it is."

Open my heart to praise You, Lord, whatever time it is.

—RHODA BLECKER

DAILY GIFTS

1 _____

2 _____

3 _____

4 _____

5 _____

6 _____

7 _____

8 _____

9 _____

10 _____

11 _____

12 _____

13 _____

14 _____

15 _____

16 _____

17 _____

18 _____

19 _____

20 _____

21 _____

22 _____

23 _____

24 _____

25 _____

26 _____

27 _____

28 _____

29 _____

30 _____

December

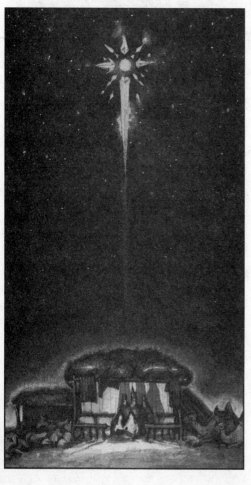

We love him,
because he first
loved us.

—I JOHN 4:19

S	M	T	W	T	F	S
						1
2	3	4	5	6	7	8
9	10	11	12	13	14	15
16	17	18	19	20	21	22
23	24	25	26	27	28	29
30	31					

IMAGE IN THE MIRROR

By now, it's obvious that Christmas is coming. Everywhere we look, the decorations are going up, the carols are playing in the stores, the crowds of shoppers are getting thicker at the malls and in the city streets. These days, most of us spend a lot of energy—and a lot of money—preparing to celebrate the birth of Jesus. But think back to the time before the first Christmas day, when a young Jewish girl carried an angel's message in her heart and the Word made flesh in her womb. This year, Carol Knapp invites you to look at the gospel stories of Mary and her baby with a new eye and to see, through Mary's eyes, the image of her Son. Carol is ready today to tell you how her Advent journey started. —THE EDITORS

1/_{SAT} *And blessed is she that believed: for there shall be a performance of those things which were told her from the Lord.* —LUKE 1:45

Christmas was approaching, and I had been invited to give an informal talk for a small group of friends from church. We met one evening in Kathy's home on Big Lake in Alaska—gathered around her dining table, snow piling up outside.

After dinner I brought out my scribbled notes and we began to think about Mary, the mother of Jesus. Who was she? What must it have been like for her to bring God's own Son into the world? Each of us had sons, and we knew that close mother-child bond. None of us felt so far removed in age or place or time that we did not long to see into Mary's heart and know her more. Most of all, we hoped to find mirrored in her heart images of Christ that would inspire and motivate and comfort us, that would help us to grasp that we, too, are among those to whom the promise of a Savior is given.

That night Mary's awestruck voice seemed to call to me from the

Scriptures: "Join with me in receiving the amazing benefits that Jesus, the Savior, gives. Don't be hesitant or unbelieving. You, too, are included." And so, during this Advent season, it is my hope that through a closer look at the events of Mary's life recounted in the first chapters of Luke, each one of us will be better able to recognize the images of Christ in Mary's life in our lives, also. Then, placing our praises alongside Mary's, we can truly say, "My spirit hath rejoiced in God my Savior" (Luke 1:47).

Jesus, You are come as the fulfillment of all God's promises—born into this world to fill our needy hearts. —CAROL KNAPP

IMAGE IN THE MIRROR

2 / SUN

FIRST SUNDAY IN ADVENT: IMAGE OF IDENTITY
And behold, you will conceive in your womb and bear a son, and you shall call his name Jesus.
—LUKE 1:31 (RSV)

I have often wondered if the angel Gabriel's visit to Mary seemed like a dream to her once he had departed. She must have pored endlessly over his every word, trying to make sense of them. Above all, the one thing she could cling to was a name: Jesus. Mary was the first to hear the name of God's incarnate Son.

I can imagine Mary repeating that name throughout her pregnancy, trying out the sound, saying it over and over until Jesus was a name more familiar than her own. Perhaps holding her baby's name in her heart comforted her when she felt overwhelmed by the magnitude of being His mother.

I learned how truly important a name can be when I discovered I was to become a grandmother for the first time. At first the news was shocking. I wasn't ready to step back a generation. My solution was not to think about it, which was easy to do because my daughter and her husband lived far away.

A few months later, however, my daughter called to tell me that they'd settled on names for their baby-to-be. If the baby was a boy, he would be named Zachary Peter. If it was a girl, Hannah Ruth. My ambivalence disappeared in an instant. The baby, boy or girl, had a name, and I had a connection. This unknown baby sprang to life for me. And when red-headed Zachary finally arrived, Grandma was ready to love him—fiercely and forever.

Mary believed God's promise, but that doesn't mean that she never felt confused or scared. How wonderful for her to have been given her child's name right from the beginning as a personal connection with the great miracle God was creating within her!

Heavenly Father, in Your tender mercy, You have sent us a Savior, and His name is Jesus. —CAROL KNAPP

WHEN GOD REACHES OUT . . . THROUGH OTHER PEOPLE

3/MON *O Lord, open thou my lips: and my mouth shall show forth thy praise.* —PSALM 51:15

The letter came on the stationery of a pottery barn in Vermont. "You probably won't remember me," the woman wrote, "but I want to thank you for your part in launching this business."

I read on in bewilderment. A pottery business in Vermont? We'd met, the letter continued, at the Mohonk Mountain House some years ago. I remembered the occasion very well—a Wildflower Weekend at a nature preserve in upstate New York. But there had been eighty or more flower enthusiasts taking part, and I didn't, in fact, recall this particular lady.

She, however, remembered a remark of mine on one of the guided walks. The leader had pointed out a cluster of bluets at the edge of the woods that, unlike their vigorous cousins carpeting the meadow, were stunted and colorless. "They just got started in the wrong place," he said. And I, apparently, had commented, "It's a good thing people can pick up and move."

"Your words were like a shaft of light in a dark place," the woman wrote. Miserable in a desk job in the city, she'd eventually sold her condo, moved to Vermont and turned her ceramics hobby into a full-time business.

All this, I wondered, *from a throwaway remark I can't remember making?* But, of course, mine was just a tiny piece in a design only God saw whole. The plan for her life was His, that shaft of light on her path, His words to her alone. The significance of my comment was beyond my knowing. What I do know, what this letter tells me, is that the role each of us is given to play in the lives around us is greater than we dream.

Remind me during the year ahead, Father, that You can reach out to Your children through anyone at all . . . even me.

—ELIZABETH SHERRILL

4/ *TUE* "He has sent me to proclaim release to the captives and . . . to set at liberty those who are oppressed. . . ."
—LUKE 4:18 (RSV)

The wall clock was ticking away my father's life.

I was a helpless twenty-one-year-old, sitting by the white mounded bed that was slowly swallowing his great body into that sea, or heaven, where independent oil operators go when all the wells are dry and the last field pump has ceased. I could picture his heart as a rusty, creaking field pump, awkwardly dipping like an arthritic black iron woodpecker, sucking out the black gold from long-forgotten strata in the rocks.

And then the pump seemed to come alive, in a frenzy to get the last drop out of life. He groaned, and a hooded Sister of Charity appeared from nowhere and took his hamlike hand. "Can you hear me?" she said gently.

"Umm." He nodded, his eyes still closed.

"Have you ever accepted Jesus as your Savior?"

He shook his head slightly.

"Would you like to?"

Silence.

As he decided, my mind flew back down the years to our childhood Depression dining table: Mother; my only brother, later killed in a wartime plane crash; and me, eyes wide as Father took us on imaginary flights to Paris, the Grand Canyon, Hollywood—places he'd take us really "when our ship comes in!" But the Depression had ground him down, and the ship of hope he'd seen so vividly had disappeared in a gray fog of unpayable bills and unspeakable fears.

"Do you accept Jesus as your Savior now?" the soft angel voice of the sister said.

"Oh, yes, I do!" he whispered, nodding, much to my surprise. Then he sat up in bed, wide-eyed with wonder.

"I see a ship!" he said.

And then he fell back and disappeared from my life and sailed into the "otherwhere" with Jesus.

Lord, thank You for reaching out, past doubt and failure, to take our hands and lead us across the sunset waters home. Amen.

—KEITH MILLER

5/ WED

And do not neglect doing good and sharing; for with such sacrifices God is pleased.

—HEBREWS 13:16 (NAS)

When our daughter Gae and son Glen were preschoolers, they were given an Advent calendar. Behind each little door marking off the days until Christmas was a tiny picture depicting some aspect of Christ's nativity. Every morning Gae and Glen jostled for the chance to open the day's door and tell me how the picture behind it fit into the Christmas story:

"That's the star that led the wise guys to Baby Jesus."

"That's the angel who singed to the shepherds."

"That's Jesus' mommy. She wears a scarf over her head because it's cold in the barn."

While their innocent explanations were delightful, their daily squabble about who should open the door often carried over into playtime.

"It's my turn!"

"No it's not!"

"Yes it is!"

I issued an ultimatum. "From now until Christmas, neither of you opens the Advent door if you bicker about it. Not only that, but if you misbehave during the day, you also lose your turn."

Interesting remarks soon started filtering out of the playroom.

"We've only got a few days left, Glen. I'll share my toys."

"Not many days left, Gae. You can have my cookie."

This year when I opened the door on December, I thought back to Gae and Glen's Advent calendar, only now I was the one who didn't want to share. "I know it'll soon be Christmas, Lord, but I just don't feel like baking for shut-ins this year, or sewing stocking stuffers for singles, or taking the elderly shopping. Can't You find somebody else to do it?"

That's not how my Son responded, God seemed to say.

A few minutes later my husband Leo came in from outside, where he had been clearing a neighbor's driveway with the snow blower. "Mmmm, what's that I smell?"

"Christmas cookies for Vera and Betty," I replied. "Not many days left."

Father God, remind me of the ways You've given me to share Your love with others.
                                                            —ALMA BARKMAN

6/ THU   *I pray that you . . . may . . . grasp how wide and long and high and deep is the love of Christ, and to know this love that surpasses knowledge. . . .*
                                                            —EPHESIANS 3:17–19 (NIV)

Seeking some Christmas cheer one day in early December, I drove to a plant nursery. All five of my children lived far away and would not be coming home this year, and my mother had been admitted to the hospital for cancer surgery. Mom had told me once, "When life is hard, plant some flowers. They'll speak of God's love to you." So taking her advice, I asked the clerk for an amaryllis bulb that would have bright red blossoms at Christmastime. She found one eager bulb already forming a bud at the end of a thick green stalk.

I put my potted plant into a bay window facing west, and eagerly watched the bud unfold. By Christmas it sported four radiant bell-shaped blossoms, each one eight inches in diameter. Two weeks later, just as the blossoms were drooping, a bud on a second stalk began to burst open. This time six brilliant red blooms crowned the plant. I used an old windshield wiper to support the drooping stalk.

But there was more: A third stalk appeared and grew to a height of thirty inches. Soon another cluster of four giant red trumpet-flowers appeared.

"Is it unusual for one bulb to grow fourteen blossoms?" I asked a clerk at a nursery.

"You definitely got a bonus," she said with a smile.

My mother, who'd recovered enough to visit me, agreed with the clerk. "I've never seen anything like it," she said.

I'd wanted a sign of God's love, and He had given me an extravagance. From Christmas Day until Valentine's Day, fourteen times over, God said in the most exquisite way, "I love you." But then, He never stops saying, "I love you." I just have to tune my heart to receive His tokens of love all year round.

Thank You, Father, for sending me Your love in a way I can grasp.
—HELEN GRACE LESCHEID

7/*FRI* *And this day shall be unto you for a memorial. . . .*
—EXODUS 12:14

I'd heard about Pearl Harbor all my life . . . in every U.S. history class I took, and from my father and father-in-law, both of whom served in the Navy. But when Gary and I visited Hawaii and took a day trip to see Pearl Harbor for ourselves, I was amazed at the emotion I felt.

A gleaming white structure rested out in the bay, a memorial built over the sunken *Arizona.* We boarded a boat with other tourists and listened as the guide talked about December 7, 1941. "The USS *Arizona* is the final resting place for many of the 1,177 crewmen who lost their lives. In the shrine room of the memorial, you will find the names of those killed."

As we walked onto the memorial, I looked over the side. I could see the sunken ship! Its outline was visible in the clear water below us. I imagined the sailors that morning, roused from their sleep. Young, confused, frightened, brave. Did they have mothers, sweethearts, wives? I sensed someone standing next to me at the rail. I looked up to see a Japanese woman. For a moment I stiffened. What right did she have to be here? Then I realized what she was doing:

dropping flower petals into the water. In that instant I knew that death—like bravery and love—knows no national boundaries, that we are all enlarged by the noble and diminished by the tragic.

The water lapped quietly against the sides of the memorial, and when the lady looked my way, I smiled.

Forgive us, Father, for the tragedies we inflict on each other. May we be inspired by brave men and noble causes. —MARY LOU CARNEY

8/SAT *For how great is his goodness, and how great is his beauty! . . .* —ZECHARIAH 9:17

I've always loved to travel, but I haven't been able to for the last few years. My friend Sue McCully, on the other hand, has always dreamed of traveling, but didn't have the chance until she recently retired from teaching school.

Sue's face was radiant as she described her adventures. "In England, I saw the beautiful white cliffs of Dover. Pilots returning from dangerous missions during World War II said they always knew they were safely home when they saw those gleaming cliffs."

She remembered the beauty of the tulips in Amsterdam, and the magnificence of Notre Dame in Paris. Then her voice softened and her face became very solemn. "On our trip to the Holy Land," she whispered, "I walked where Jesus had walked and I prayed where He had prayed. I saw the olive trees and the pomegranates that the Bible speaks about. Oh, it was all so wonderful, so beautiful!" She paused, closed her eyes briefly and then continued. "In Greece, I relived the second journey of Paul, and in Rome, I had an opportunity to see St. Peter's church."

Sue's most recent trip was to Colorado where she sat, warm and snug, before a floor-length hotel window and admired the crystalline brilliance of winter glistening in the snow. "Many people were sledding, and on a distant pond, I could see others ice skating. But I wasn't about to risk my old bones on any of that! So I sat and marveled at the loveliness of it all.

"And then we were almost home again. The automobile carrying us covered familiar ground, and soon we were crossing the Tennessee River. Then we turned into the driveway of my house, and there was the sweet sense of love awaiting me inside the front door."

She reached for my hand and we two sat very still, each in her own heart thanking our wonderful Lord for the beauty He's given His people.

Father, You have so generously blessed us, including those who go and then return to tell the stay-at-homes so that all may rejoice in Your lovingkindness. Amen. —DRUE DUKE

IMAGE IN THE MIRROR

9/SUN

SECOND SUNDAY IN ADVENT: IMAGE OF OBEDIENCE
And Mary said, "Behold, I am the handmaid of the Lord; let it be to me according to your word." . . .
—LUKE 1:38 (RSV)

When Gabriel told Mary that she—a virgin—would conceive a son by the power of God, she quickly said yes. How did she arrive at that moment of complete surrender? How did she become so perfectly the Lord's "handmaid," as she so humbly calls herself? Could it have been without pain and tears and self-denial? In the house in Nazareth, did she feel the cold shadow of the Cross?

One Sunday afternoon before Christmas several years ago, my husband Terry and I were sitting in our living room, watching a football game on television. As we sat there, one of our children quietly told us some devastating medical news—a checkup had revealed a serious, perhaps fatal illness. We were stunned.

That night I lay in bed in agony. Christmas was supposed to be a celebration of birth—of life—and I had just learned that my child was probably going to die. Not even tears could relieve the pain in my heart.

From out of the dark the Lord brought to my mind two Bible verses: Philippians 4:6–7 (RSV): "Have no anxiety about anything, but in everything by prayer and supplication with thanksgiving let your requests be made known to God. And the peace of God, which passes all understanding, will keep your hearts and your minds in Christ Jesus."

Deep in the night, I had a crucial decision to make: I could bow to God's Word and find peace as His obedient daughter, or I could surrender to my fear.

I chose to believe what He told me. I repeated that verse many times in the following months. And hardly understanding how it happened, I learned in my own small way to become a "handmaid"—to accept God's will for me, even if it led to a cross.

O God, Mary sets me an example of obedience. When my understanding fails me, let me repeat her yes to You. —CAROL KNAPP

10/_{MON} *The inward man is renewed day by day.*
—II CORINTHIANS 4:16

The morning before my birthday, I stand in line under the big renewal sign at the Department of Motor Vehicles. I've been whisked through the eye test, had a photo snapped so quickly it felt like an ambush, and now find myself in a bit of a bottleneck waiting for a clerk to certify the paperwork and take my check.

I keep thinking about that word *renewal*. It seems an unlikely description of the process a dozen of us are going through, moving sleepily from station to station (we're the ones who are convinced that the earlier we get here, the faster we'll be out), studying the newspaper and sipping coffee from Styrofoam cups ("Hold the cup down so it doesn't show up in the photo, please"). *Ordeal* would be more apt.

The older I get, the more I think of my birthday as an unwanted reminder of the inexorable aging process. *Another one down,* and all at once I realize I have more birthdays behind me than I am likely to have left. It's a strange thought.

I glance at my four-year-old license picture. *Not a bad shot,* I muse. As a rule I am very critical of myself in photos, a kind of reverse vanity. I was wearing my hair slightly longer four years ago—or maybe I had just needed a haircut; I can't recall. I don't look that different, otherwise. I remember feeling old on that day, too, yet looking at the picture now I seem young, younger than my age, even. Four years from now, will I look at the ambush photo taken today and think, *Not bad?*

The thought strikes me: When I look at my life *today,* when it counts most, can I help but think, *Not bad?* Things have changed in the past four years, certainly, and most of what has come to pass couldn't have been foreseen when I last stood here in the DMV renewal line. And life will change more in the four years to come. But today, standing in this line on a gray, sleepy morning, waiting for a free clerk, I can't help but feel grateful for God's careful guidance and for what I believe is my increasing awareness of it. In that respect, I know I am different. I am four years closer to God.

I look up again at the sign that says renewal, and smile. *Not bad.*

Lord, in Your presence my life is a process of rebirth in You.

—EDWARD GRINNAN

11/ TUE   *Oh, that men would give thanks to the Lord. . . .*
—PSALM 107:31 (NKJV)

Lord, I can't manage this meeting. I know we have to act fast to save this company, but this new manager is taking us out on the high seas in a rowboat. How will we ever reach all these goals?

"Those who go down to the sea in ships, Who do business on great waters, They see the works of the Lord, And His wonders in the deep" (Psalm 107:23–24, NKJV).

There's an ill wind blowing, Lord. This manager has been here three months, and already there is talk of mutiny. I think I'm getting seasick.

"For He commands and raises the stormy wind, Which lifts up the waves of the sea. They mount up to the heavens, They go down again to the depths; Their soul melts because of trouble. They reel to and fro, and stagger like a drunken man, And are at their wit's end" (Psalm 107:25–27, NKJV).

Lord, if this company breaks up, I don't have a lifeboat. I need this job, God. Please do something quick!

"Then they cry out to the Lord in their trouble, And he brings them out of their distresses. He calms the storm, So that its waves are still" (Psalm 107:28–29, NKJV).

Well, what do you know? This guy is beginning to make some progress. Look at these numbers! He just might turn this ship around. I can't believe how much he's accomplished in just one year. I actually look forward to coming to work each day, and he says we will all get raises next quarter.

"Then they are glad because they are quiet; So He guides them to their desired haven" (Psalm 107:30, NKJV).

Father, I'm sorry I doubted Your providence. For a moment I forgot that You are my true Captain. It's been a whale of a ride, but I wouldn't have missed it.

"Oh, that men would give thanks to the Lord for His goodness, And for His wonderful works to the children of men!" (Psalm 107:31, NKJV).
                                                            —DANIEL SCHANTZ

12/_{WED} *Good tidings of great joy, which shall be to all people.*
                                                            —LUKE 2:10

Last Christmas my wife Joy and I wanted to plan a family trip. Our boys were twenty-three, twenty-one and nineteen, and we figured we might not have many more Christmases when we were all together. I assumed the boys would want to go skiing, as we had often done before. But when we asked them, they said in unison, "Let's go to the beach!"

"The beach? How could you have Christmas at the beach?" I grumbled. But my objections were drowned out by a trio that soon became a quartet as Joy reverted to her Southern California up-bringing. So I asked some well-traveled friends where we should go for sun, sand and adventure.

We finally hit on Ambergris Cay, an island off the coast of Belize in Central America. Warm sun, beautiful reefs for snorkeling, trips to the mainland to see Mayan ruins, crocodiles and monkeys. . . it sounded like fun, but not like Christmas, so on the plane trip down, I read the Christmas story in all four gospels, trying to find a way to connect beaches with Bethlehem.

Ambergris Cay was a paradise. On our first night we walked to town to find dinner, and Nathan pointed to a big sign by a restaurant door: NO SHIRT, NO SHOES? NO PROBLEM! "See, Dad," he said, "they'll take anybody here, even wackos who wish they were skiing!"

Nathan's words brought to mind a phrase from Luke's Gospel: "Good tidings of great joy, which shall be to all people." Like the restaurant, Jesus takes anybody. A bunch of guys smelling like sheep at the door? Great, send them in. A grumpy Minnesotan pining for snow? That's okay, Jesus will give him six days of love and laughter with the most precious people in his world and hope he gets the message that Christmas is about people and not places.

Lord, thank You for coming into the world in a way all of us can take into our hearts and make our own. —ERIC FELLMAN

13/ THU *Christ Jesus . . . being in the form of God . . . made himself of no reputation, and took upon him the form of a servant, and was made in the likeness of men.*
—PHILIPPIANS 2:5-7

We are halfway through Week Three of the flu at our house. This week Mary has it, while John recovers and Elizabeth is getting her first coughs. I have had so little sleep lately that the few thoughts that make their way across my weary synapses are mostly about how sleep deprivation is a form of torture.

Last night my feverish baby was unable to sleep except in my arms. Even then, she awoke frequently, crying, "Mama! Mama!" with the high-pitched whine of a toy doll. I held her and rocked her and whispered to her. Sometime in the blur of the early morning hours, I asked God to give me something good to think about.

Nothing dramatic happened. I stroked my baby's hot, smooth skin and idly wondered if Baby Jesus ever had the flu. Surely, He must have been sick sometime. Surely, His mother nursed Him, held Him, comforted Him. Perhaps she stroked His back to ease the aches. My hand lingered on my own baby's back as I paused to think about Jesus with the delicious, smooth skin of a baby. It seemed amazing. God with baby skin. God you could touch. God you could hold tenderly in your arms. God Who is . . . human.

Mary moved restlessly in my arms. Jesus once weighed twenty-five pounds, too. Odd, isn't it, how in some ways it's harder to understand the smallness of God-made-man than the greatness of His heavenly Father?

Infant Jesus, help me hold You in my heart as surely as I hold my baby in my arms. —JULIA ATTAWAY

PRAYER FOR DECEMBER

You're never alone
  But
  if you find at times
that you're feeling lonely
Listen
  to the laughter of small children
welcoming the first flakes
of winter's white
  to the rain rattling the downspout
punctuating the thunder dance
of spring's morning storms
  to the beat of your heart
jogging the memories
of summer's deep heat
  to the stir of the brisk wind
strumming the dry leaves
of autumn's retreat.
  For when you hear
the silence in those songs
You'll know
I, too, am with you.

       —J. R. RINK

14/ *FRI* *"An evil and adulterous generation seeks for a sign. . . ."* —MATTHEW 12:39 (RSV)

"A plane slid off the runway." My sister Lori's voice was tense. "I'm watching it right now on TV." It wasn't our parents' plane, but the winter storm would only worsen by the time theirs left for Bermuda. My sister, still fixated on the jetliner perched precariously at the runway's end, said what we were both thinking. "It's a sign."

We were very big on signs in my family. We always searched for a sign when making important—or not-so-important—decisions, from which college to attend to whether the car would make it home without stopping for gas. Of course, we were convinced these signs came right from God.

Now, Lori and I feared the runway mishap was a sign that our parents shouldn't go. Six hours later, I was convinced of it as I hung up the phone after hearing from airport operations that my parents' plane was still on the runway, three hours behind schedule.

Didn't they see that plane go off the runway? I fumed frantically to myself. *Why don't they just come home?*

To pass the time before I called the airline again, I began thinking about signs. True, our family had always relied on them, but had we only sought those we expected? While panicking over the skidded plane, I'd not considered any number of other signs, like the professional, helpful airline staffers who'd been calm and informative every time I'd called. Or that my parents had driven to the airport without mishap. Or that no one on the "de-runwayed" plane had been injured. Or even God's presence with me now.

I dialed the airline number one last time, but before I could even say hello, the customer service representative said, "Marci, they're in the air!"

Lord, help me remember that You ask me to walk by faith, and not by sight—or signs.
                                        —MARCI ALBORGHETTI

A WHOLE AND HOLY LOVE

15/_{SAT} *How shall we sing the Lord's song in a strange land?*
                                        —PSALM 137:4

One morning, a few months after Robert and I were married, I woke up with an insistent longing I didn't understand. I knew it wasn't dissatisfaction with our marriage. I had never in my life felt so happy and fulfilled. What could possibly be missing?

Rather than try to figure it out, I gave the question to God and went back to sleep. A few days later Robert said something about "community," and it went straight into my heart where the ache was.

When we were first married, we were so busy setting up a household that all we wanted was to be with each other. We kept talking about finding a church and we visited a few, but we didn't feel a real need to belong. Since we prayed together daily, we felt we already were a community of two. But could it be that wholeness in a relationship calls for a third dimension—the dimension of *reaching out together*?

Suddenly I remembered a day when I was about seven years old, when the new music teacher asked each child to sing a line from the songbook so she'd know where to seat us for class. My heart was pounding because I'd been told that I couldn't carry a tune. My singing that day was way off-key, but Miss May was a wise teacher. She placed me in the center of a group of children with good pitch. And I found, to my utter surprise, that in that situation I really could carry a tune.

I think it's like that in a church family. A beautiful chorus is created by all the voices singing together. When one gets off pitch, the influence of the whole can bring that person back into harmony. Robert and I have now found our place as part of a spiritual community, and I've come to see that as we reach out together, our own song becomes more harmonious. It's a big part of what makes our holy love whole.

Be the Conductor of our chorus, O God, and let us always seek to blend our notes with others into Your perfect harmony.

—MARILYN MORGAN KING

IMAGE IN THE MIRROR

16/SUN

THIRD SUNDAY IN ADVENT: IMAGE OF HOPE
"He will be great, and will be called the Son of the Most High... and of his kingdom there will be no end." —LUKE 1:32-33 (RSV)

The journey that began the December night I received my child's frightening medical news continued into the next summer. One evening I was sitting at the end of a dock beside a clear mountain lake. A few last rays from the setting sun tinted the scattered clouds, which earlier had brought a light rain. I was praying yet again for my child. Suddenly, I flung my open arms to the sky and spoke to Jesus with complete conviction: "If You have allowed it, then I can trust it." It was my way of giving up my child to Him—of giving up my desire to say how this should end.

No sooner had I spoken than a magnificent rainbow formed right before my eyes, filling the sky with color. I wanted to leap into the air and run under that rainbow, treading the clouds. I still had no answer for our family's crisis, but I had hope.

Six months later, after another Christmas celebration of the miracle of the Christ Child, our own child received miraculous news of perfect health!

Even in the dark times, Mary had a hope anchored in that first angelic promise, "Of his kingdom there shall be no end." I believe this hope supported her from the flight into Egypt clear to the foot of the Cross. For all her joy in holding her Bethlehem baby, I picture her most keenly—even at Christmas—rushing into the outstretched arms of her risen Son.

Jesus, You give such hope and power and purpose to Your people! The tiny flailing fists of Bethlehem have become the strong arms of my salvation. —CAROL KNAPP

17 / MON

Seek that ye may excel to the edifying of the church.
—I CORINTHIANS 14:12

I had a mild case of the Christmas "blahs." Preparing for Christmas at home and at our ministry Mission Mississippi was getting me down. I wouldn't have minded sleeping right through till December 26.

Then, two days before Christmas, my telephone rang; on the other end was my friend Shelby. "Dolphus," he said, "do you know a place where my family and I could go to help on Christmas morning? We would love to serve at a homeless shelter or help someone working with the poor." Shelby and his wife have two sons and a daughter; perhaps they were looking forward to Christmas at home, so I asked him if he was sure this was what he wanted to do.

"Yes, Dolphus," he answered, "we all really want to do this."

I hung up the phone and thought a few minutes. Then I began to call people I knew, until I found a mission in Jackson that needed volunteers. I called back Shelby and gave him the news. "Praise the Lord!" he said. "We'll have the privilege of serving others this Christmas rather than concentrating on ourselves. And it will be a great opportunity for us to teach our children about the real meaning of Christmas."

Shelby and his family were reaching out with more than a dollar in the kettle or a check to a charity—as good as those gifts are—to share food and their own presence with the hungry. What a beautiful way of "doing Christmas"! And not only were they helping the people they'd be serving, they had helped me, too, by the example of their caring.

Lord, help me to take my eyes off of myself and to seek ways to remember Your special gift—Your Son.   —DOLPHUS WEARY

18 / TUE

Weeping may endure for a night, but joy cometh in the morning.   —PSALM 30:5

Each year as Christmas approaches, I take down a painting from our wall and replace it with a carefully framed strip of wrapping paper. Across the paper's surface my father's familiar scrawl declares, "Oh, I'm dreaming of a white Christmas, just like the ones I used to know."

It was December 1983. My father had died the previous spring, and now Christmas was coming. I couldn't imagine celebrating without him. Yet I had my family to consider, so one bleak night I began dragging out the decorations.

The long strip of paper was lining the bottom of the first box I opened. The year before, the paper had wrapped a large box filled with new boots for everyone in the family. Daddy had always believed we would have a white Christmas. He would buy boots, gloves, hats and insulated underwear to prepare us for the big snow. But it never came, and now he was gone. So I tucked away the paper scrap and carried on as best I could.

We made it through that Christmas and the year that followed. Then one day, I walked into a store and realized that the holidays were coming once again. Lights wound their way around the walls and up the escalator, and "White Christmas" played over the loudspeakers.

It was a funny place for an epiphany, the perfume aisle of a department store, but that's where I first realized that although Daddy always anticipated a white Christmas, the absence of snow never seemed to disappoint him. It was never about snow; it was about joy! My daddy had always had a white Christmas!

I hurried from the store. There was a tree to buy, cookies to bake, and there were mittens, warm socks and scarves to buy.

So, all these years later, I straighten the frame and smile at my daddy's happy scrawl. "I'm dreaming of a white Christmas, Daddy," I whisper, "just like the ones we used to know."

Father, as we anticipate the birth of Your Son, let us know joy as lovely as snow falling fresh and clean.
—PAM KIDD

19 / WED

Did the Lord God make coats of skins, and clothed them. —GENESIS 3:21

I have often wondered what Joseph thought about the coat his father gave him—did he take delight in its many colors? Did Aaron really appreciate the "broidered" coat he was given as a priest? They couldn't have been more thrilled than I have been with a coat that seems to last evermore. I think it will be here long after I have gone.

It happened on a steamy day in July more than thirty years ago. My friend Harold and I were in Saks when I noticed two elegant coats made of fake fur so reduced in price that they almost pleaded to be bought. I tried one on. It was three-quarter length, and it had a hood that when I pulled it up almost covered my face. The inside was something like silk, carefully crafted, and the outside was made of quantities of long, wooly hair, all chocolate brown, resembling some unrecognizable beast.

"Wow," said Harold as he slipped on the other coat, and we kept laughing all the way to the cashier. Back at the office, we produced an uproar when we swept in. Harolds coat was eventually stolen at a restaurant, but I continued to put mine on at every cold snap.

At Christmas my little nephew Eric fled in terror from me, while his older sister Katrin ogled me from a safe distance. My coat and I became a terrific squealy game, and Eric and Katrin waited for my return year after year.

"Hey! Come join us monkeys," cried a pal as he began scratching himself with both hands curled. "Don't wear it in the park," said another friend. "Somebody will shoot you for a bear." It doesn't matter where or when I wear my coat, the reaction to it is always glee. I bet Joseph and Aaron didn't have the fun with their coats that I and others have had with mine.

Father, there are so many serious matters to address in this life. Thank You for providing me with this little bit of fun.
—VAN VARNER

20 / THU   *Then the shepherds went back again to their fields . . . praising God for the visit of the angels, and because they had seen the child. . . .*   —LUKE 2:20 (TLB)

"Did you put up a tree?" my sister Amanda asked when we visited by telephone the week before Christmas.

"Don did. And, yes, it's a six-footer." My husband Don and I have argued over tree size for thirty-eight years, the length of our marriage. Our family can tell by the size who chose the tree. "My other decorations are up, too, such as they are. I envy those talented people who carry out a Christmas theme!"

"I have a theme," Amanda said. "It's called 'Early Attic.'"

"Since I don't have an attic, I guess my theme is 'Terribly Tacky,'" I responded.

Later, I walked around the house and studied the decorations. The Nativity on the piano was made from cornshucks, not porcelain, but it reminded me of the stable and the humble surroundings of Christ's birth. The cut-tin candleholder came from our church bazaar and shone as brightly as the star over Bethlehem. And the ornate stick-on window Nativity (number seven in a magazine list of "Ten Trashiest Decorations") had stunning colors that brought to mind the rich gifts of the wise men.

Then there was the tree, which even at six feet could barely contain all the ornaments. We bought the treetop star the Christmas after we married. We were in North Carolina, miles from friends and family. Michael and Rebecca's Sunday-school craft projects adorned the lower branches. Halfway up was the plaster-of-paris bell Patrick made in kindergarten; it hung right above paper decorations made by his three sons.

I didn't need talent or creativity or more money. I didn't even need a theme, because I already had one: Jesus. The ornaments and decorations are merely reminders of Him and His love. I looked over my beautiful Christmas house one more time, then went to the telephone to call Amanda.

Jesus, help me to remember it's You I'm celebrating this and every Christmas!
—PENNEY SCHWAB

21/*FRI* *When all the people saw it, they shouted for joy. . . .*
—LEVITICUS 9:24 (NIV)

I love books, and I like people. At least I thought I did, until I got caught in the holiday rush in the giant bookstore where I staffed the information desk during the holiday season. "Please, God, give me patience," I'd murmur when yet another customer would come up to the counter and say, "I don't remember the author, but someone was talking about it on the radio the other week."

I'd force a cheery smile. "Do you know the title?"

"Well . . . it had something about golf in it. At least I think it did."

That was when I'd think, *Well, why didn't you write down the name when the guy on the radio was talking about it?* But usually a silent prayer would keep me patient.

One night, however, near closing, a man came in with a long list of gifts to buy. He said, "Now, I don't know any of these titles, but my wife said there was a new biography that she wanted and it was on display near the front of the store."

I stared. We moved merchandise around daily. "Don't you have any more information than that? There are hundreds of biographies."

"Oh, sure," he said. "She said it had a blue cover."

That was it. "Oh, sure," I snapped. "We keep the books arranged by color in the warehouse." It was meant to be a joke, but it sure didn't sound funny when I said it.

He stared at me, and I wondered if he would report me to the manager for having a bad attitude. But he laughed. "I guess you've been pretty busy finding stuff for people who don't have a clue."

"And I guess you've been pretty busy, too, trying to get the right gift for the right person. Come on, I'll help you find something your wife will like." We headed off to the biography section, and all the while I was thinking:

Lord, thank You for kind people. Help me to be as forgiving and patient with other people as You are with me. —LINDA NEUKRUG

22 / SAT *"For to the snow he says, 'Fall on the earth' . . . that all men may know his work."* —JOB 37:6–7 (RSV)

On a Sunday afternoon in December our church holds its annual Bethlehem Day. With temperatures in the seventies in Arizona, we turn the courtyard outside the sanctuary into our idea of old Bethlehem. Families enjoy Christmas music and cookies while little costumed shepherds and angels tromp on the straw-covered ground from one craft booth to the next, making star-shaped candles or a clothespin Baby Jesus in a wooden manger.

The day is usually sunny and bright, but a few years ago an uncharacteristically blustery morning had turned cold by afternoon. And as my little daughter Maria and her Sunday-school choir rehearsed "Away in a Manger," I looked out the windows of the choir room in delighted shock. A soft, wet snow was falling, blanketing Bethlehem Day in dazzling white.

"It's snowing!" someone shouted, and folks ran to the windows and then outside, giddy at this incredible sight. It's hard to say who was more excited, the kids or the grownups, as we stood with our arms outstretched, heads tilted toward the sky and mouths open, literally drinking in God's wonderful surprise. The snow in Phoenix lasted only a short time, but it brought a joy that carried well beyond the day.

Christmas began with a wonderful surprise from God, too. The world awaited its Messiah but no one expected a tiny baby to be the

One. Christ's actual birth was a small moment, unnoticed by all but a few shepherds. But the joy He brought into the world is everlasting. And unlike our once-in-a-lifetime desert snowfall, Christ comes again and again—each year at Christmas, and every time we invite Him into our hearts.

Come, Lord Jesus, as I stand with my arms outstretched, ready to welcome You. —GINA BRIDGEMAN

IMAGE IN THE MIRROR

23 / SUN   *FOURTH SUNDAY IN ADVENT: IMAGE OF SHARING*
"He has helped his servant Israel . . . as he spoke to our fathers. . . ." —LUKE 1:54-55 (RSV)

It must have been difficult for Mary to share her newborn son so soon after He arrived. But the shepherds were right there on her doorstep within hours. From the beginning, Jesus belonged far beyond Mary's little family. He had come as Savior of the world!

On my dresser I used to have a small brown ceramic plaque with 1939 on the back. On the front precise block lettering read, JESUS NEVER FAILS. Squeezed beneath that was a portion of Hebrews 13:5, I WILL NEVER LEAVE THEE, NOR FORSAKE THEE. I learned about the plaque from my aunt, my father's sister, who mentioned it to me at his graveside. He had given it to her when she miscarried her first baby.

Several years later, after my aunt's death, I asked her daughter if I might have the plaque. I greatly treasured it as something that came from my father's heart. Sometimes I would trace the lettering with my fingers and pretend I was reaching back in time to touch my dad.

Then the cousin who had given me the plaque lost her son in an accident. It seemed only right that this gift, given by my father to her mother years ago, should pass from me to her and again offer its comfort.

I finally sent the plaque just before Christmas. I remember sitting in front of our Christmas tree holding that little package in the palm of my hand, and crying until the Christmas lights became a blur. I was crying because I knew I had to give it up—and for my cousin's pain. But mostly I was crying for all the generations of my family's tears.

Then I thought of the shared faith in Christ that I knew ran far back in our heritage. Deeper than our individual or collective sorrow was that River of Life flowing through the tears. And that faith—not the plaque that was merely one of its expressions—was what I needed to hang on to.

Oh, God, thank You for sharing Your very self with me in Jesus.

—CAROL KNAPP

IMAGE IN THE MIRROR

24 / MON   *CHRISTMAS EVE: IMAGE OF PRAISE*
"My soul magnifies the Lord."   —LUKE 1:46 (RSV)

I didn't know it was to be, after fourteen years, my last Christmas Eve in Alaska. Yet had I known, I wouldn't have changed a thing.

After a wonderful dinner with friends at their alpaca farm, I slipped outdoors in the chilly night air to spend time alone with God under the stars—and to enjoy the woolly animals quietly bedded down in their lean-to shelter near the house. The earthy aroma of hay filled my nose. More than a dozen alpacas followed me curiously with their intelligent big brown eyes. They weren't the traditional ox and donkey, but the scent and feel of the scene transported me to that first Bethlehem Christmas Eve.

All at once I began to softly sing "Away in a Manger" to the animals. This roused the inquisitive rooster, who fluttered out from his crumpled bed of straw beneath the deck. He strutted about, pecking at bits of hay in the snow. My song ended, but I couldn't stop praising God.

I looked up at the stars and called out, "Glory to God! Peace on earth! Christ is born!" Suddenly the rooster stopped his pecking and crowed three times, as if he were repeating my praise. We kept it up for several minutes, until I was bursting with such laughter and rejoicing that I ran inside to share it with everyone.

Was there, I wonder, a rooster in the hay the night Jesus was born? If there was, did he let out a zesty crow at the young Savior's first cry? It's something I'd like to ask Mary. Somehow, I don't think she would find my question strange at all.

Jesus, You are so glorious that all creation sings Your praise!

—CAROL KNAPP

IMAGE IN THE MIRROR

25 / **TUE** *CHRISTMAS DAY: IMAGE OF SATISFACTION*
"He has filled the hungry with good things. . . ."
—LUKE 1:53 (RSV)

For my husband Terry and me and our four children, Christmas was always a gift of joy—tramping through the snowy woods to cut our tree, twisting candy-cane cookies in the kitchen, filling the house with candlelight, wrapping presents (always leaving a few unlabeled), guessing who the "mystery" presents were for. But at last there came a Christmas that was very different.

My husband had accepted a job promotion that moved us far from our now-grown children. We were strangers to Minneapolis, our

new hometown, and it was almost December 25. Our tiny temporary apartment was so crammed with boxes that we couldn't put up
a tree. Out on the road we saw car after car loaded with college students heading home for the holidays. Our hearts filled with a deep
loneliness for our own children. We longed for Christmases past.

"Well, Lord," I prayed, "You are the meaning of Christmas, and
we still have You." Then my brother called with an invitation to his
home in Colorado. We accepted gratefully. The decorations were different, the tree was charmingly artificial, and the children weren't
ours, but oh, what a good gift that Christmas was for two empty-
nesters learning to live by themselves again.

On the first Christmas morning Mary held everything she—and
we—would need for her—and our—whole life in her arms. God's Son
had come to satisfy every hunger of the soul, as she had proclaimed
in her song. And in obedience and faith, she had given the world its
Savior, the one Good Gift from Whom all other good gifts would
come.

*Jesus, on this Christmas day, fill my soul with Your presence, the
Good and Perfect Gift.* —CAROL KNAPP

26/WED *Then Joseph being raised from sleep did as the angel
of the Lord had bidden him, and took unto him his
wife.* —MATTHEW 1:24

In my early twenties I wrote a Christmas play that was published in
a magazine. Shortly thereafter I received a phone call from a Sunday-
school superintendent. "We would like our junior high group to put
on your play, and we're wondering if you'd direct it for us."

I'd never directed anything in my life, and Christmas was only six
weeks away. But the superintendent said that they would get the costumes and assign the parts. All I had to do was show up.

I did. And what I found terrified me: fifteen seventh- and eighth-
graders jumping over benches, throwing paper airplanes, shouting,
laughing. The rehearsal was abysmal. The kids wouldn't settle down.
Joseph, a big guy with flaming red hair, was the ringleader. Clowning, making faces, he egged the others on. The only one who was serious about her part was Mary, a sweet, brown-eyed girl with long hair.

"If these kids don't settle down, we're not going to be able to do
the play," I said to the other teachers at the end of the evening.

"Let's pray," the superintendent said. So, forming a circle and holding hands, she led us in a prayer for a miracle.

Two more awful rehearsals passed. The teachers and I reasoned, threatened, pleaded. We now had only three weeks until the play, and I was ready to quit. But each time the superintendent said, "Let's pray. God can work a miracle."

And so He did. At the fourth rehearsal, Joseph was transformed. He'd fallen in love with Mary. Shuffling and awkward, he gazed adoringly at her and she at him. Paper airplanes ceased to fly. Everyone, from shepherds to angels to wise men, followed Joseph's lead and pulled their acts together.

We'd asked for a miracle; we got one. But, as so often happens, God made it out of what was already there: a boy, a girl and adolescent hormones.

Lord, thank You for answers to prayer that sneak up on us from right under our noses. Just like the first Christmas.   —SHARI SMYTH

27 / THU *And I saw the dead, small and great, stand before God; and the books were opened: and another book was opened, which is the book of life: and the dead were judged out of those things which were written in the books. . . .*   —REVELATION 20:12

"In the beginning was the Word," begins St. John's Gospel, and I know the answering refrain: In the end is the Word, too.

I sit here in my forty-second year, watching, with stereoscopic vision, both ends of my life. Even if I am to outlive the biblical allotment of three score years and ten, I have to acknowledge that my middle years have fully arrived, that my trajectory has mounted the summit and is beginning its descent.

I'm reading *Young Men and Fire* by the late Norman MacLean. Ordinarily, I would add MacLean to the list of people I can't stand—sheer professional jealousy at his enormous gift. But as I cross my midpoint, my capacity for such envy diminishes. I know I'll never be the next MacLean; I'm having enough trouble being the present Mark Collins.

I've been a writer for nearly twenty years. Writing is what I know, but maybe not all I know. In the next several months, I'm going to let go of it—perhaps for now, perhaps for a while, perhaps forever.

I can't say I'll miss it. It will be a pleasure to unplug my editorial buzz saw, to control those impulses that make me see metaphor in every blessed thing. My wife will have a dream about eating breakfast or something, and I'll glean some simile that explains her entire childhood.

Of course, now that I've finished writing this piece, now that I've survived another deadline, it doesn't seem so bad. I mean, MacLean was writing into his late eighties. It's almost as if his life were a metaphor for. . . .

Forget it.

Eternal Word, may my words always reflect the truth, goodness and beauty that the Father has written in You. —MARK COLLINS

28/<small>FRI</small> *The Lord had said unto Abram . . . And I will bless them that bless thee . . . and in thee shall all families of the earth be blessed.* —GENESIS 12:1, 3

When Keith and I arrived at the monastery for a Christmas visit one year, Mother Hildegard met us at the gate and said, "I have to warn you. My mother is visiting, and she's always been very prejudiced against Jews."

Keith and I looked at each other and shrugged, "Look, we can't be other than we are," I said to her. "We'll deal with it."

We are usually the only Jewish people at the monastery, and we're used to that. Sometimes we're the first Jews other visitors have ever met. But to my knowledge, this was the first time we'd ever shared the guesthouse with someone who started out not liking us.

During the week of our stay, we acted no differently than usual. We tease each other a lot, so we laugh a lot. We are always friendly toward the other guests, help them if they need our help, answer their questions openly, work alongside them if our work assignments happen to coincide. We ate two meals a day with other guests, and we were such a varied group of people that on Christmas Eve I wrote a carol just for all of us, to the tune of "Twelve Days of Christmas." It went (from "four calling birds" on downward): Four Romanians, two young girls, one Irish priest, two Jews, and a Presbyterian."

When we all sang it, around the table at a dinner of traditional Romanian Christmas foods, Mother Hildegard's mother piped up, "Say, *I'm* a Presbyterian," and we all laughed.

We left before she did, since we wanted to be home for New Year's. When I called Mother Hildegard after the Rose Parade was over, to find out how things were going, she said, "Well, you'll never guess what! Since you've been gone, my mother's been moping around, and when I asked her what was wrong, she said, 'I miss my little Jewish couple!'"

Lord, no matter what our differences, let us bless You by blessing each other. —RHODA BLECKER

29 / SAT *Ask where the good road is, the godly paths you used to walk in, in the days of long ago. Travel there, and you will find rest for your souls. . . .*
—JEREMIAH 6:16 (TLB)

I've always considered myself to be forward-moving, flexible, adaptable, living on the innovative edge of life, but lately I find myself clinging to the comfort of the old and familiar.

Perhaps that's why I'm looking at my new Bible with apprehension. I certainly need a new Bible, but months after having received it, it is still pristine, beautiful and virtually untouched. I know that all my favorite passages of Scripture are in there, exactly where they ought to be, but I can't seem to find them. So I continue to reach for the Bible that has been the most familiar of all my companions for more than forty years. Its pages are held together with sticky tape, its binding is falling apart, and snippets of inspiration clipped from here and there or given to me by those who know me best are stuffed between its pages. With scribbled notes in its margins and underlined passages, I can find anything I'm looking for in less than half a wink!

Sure, bring on an exciting, new, innovative year, but it is with a thankful heart that I find myself singing "For Auld Lang Syne" (For Days of Long Ago). I'm grateful for the comfort of familiar names on greeting cards, familiar faces that jump out at me from a crowd of strangers, familiar things (especially my Bible), and places, all of which chronicle my life with the sweetness of memories shared, disappointments prayed over, friendships kindled and love celebrated.

For the paths of yesteryear, thanks, dear Lord. For the road that lies ahead, strength. —FAY ANGUS

30/ SUN   *"For the Son of man also came not to be served but*
to serve. . . ."   —MARK 10:45 (RSV)

According to a friend of mine who is a member, a local church, St.
George's by the Gas Station, recently had a debate about their budget for the new year. Instead of giving the receipts from their annual
rummage sale to the town's soup kitchen, some people wanted to use
the proceeds to carpet the sanctuary. One of the old-timers said
those favoring new carpet needed to remember the church's mission.
Then he told them this story:

Because they lived on a dangerous coastline, the villagers of
Rockymoor constructed a hut on the shore and bought a boat to go
to sea whenever a ship went down and sailors needed rescuing. Over
the years many lives were saved, and the little outpost became famous.
They bought bigger boats and constructed a larger building, which
became a sort of clubhouse for members. But gradually the members tired of going to sea and risking their lives, so they hired trained
crews to do the rescuing. And that sufficed until one day a large shipwreck occurred and the crews brought many cold, dirty, half-
drowned survivors to the clubhouse. Afterward the place was a mess.

"I think we need to build a shower outside to clean up the victims
before we bring them in," one member suggested. "Otherwise, we're
going to ruin the place, and who will want to be part of our club?"
An argument about priorities ensued, and eventually the organization split in two. About half the members went down the way and
built another lifesaving station. It was a ramshackle place, and they
were short of equipment and expertise, but the rescuers were dedicated and they saved lots of lives. Their operation grew and became
famous, and they enlarged their building and formed a club, and. . . .

Today, there are many fancy clubhouses along that dangerous
stretch of shoreline. There still are many shipwrecks and many people cast into the sea, but most of the foundering drown.

What did St. George's do? They decided to forego new carpet this
year, at least, in favor of the soup kitchen. The vote was 47 to 42.

> *In the new year, Lord,*
> *Jerk my chain when I forget my mission,*
> *And ask to trade my serving job for a position.*
>
> —FRED BAUER

31 / MON

> *Behold the day, behold, it is come. . . .*
> —EZEKIEL 7:10

We never celebrated New Year's Eve when I was growing up in California. In fact, we went to bed early that night because we would be up early on January 1. Awake before dawn, we downed our cereal, grabbed our ladders and chairs, and drove to Colorado Boulevard in Pasadena, parking in the first place we could find. Walking several blocks, we passed the balloon sellers and program hawkers, part of the crowd surging toward the parade route. Inevitably there would be drowsy-eyed celebrants heading in the opposite direction to catch up on lost sleep. We scowled at them. How could they skip the bands, the floats, the horses and celebrities? In my family it was heresy to miss the Rose Parade. We didn't go to the Rose Bowl every year— you had to pay money to see that—but the parade was free. And it happened in our own backyard.

These days, if I'm not back home in Pasadena for January 1, I still feel the same sense of anticipation on New Year's Eve. In my childhood it was about which float would win the sweepstakes, which band would sound the best and which Big Ten or Pac Ten team would obliterate the other in the Rose Bowl. The main event was never at midnight; it began at 8:00 A.M. when the first float lumbered down the parade route. Similarly, my sense of anticipation on New Year's Eve now is about the year ahead, the goals I've set for myself and the blessings to come. I suppose that someday I'll stay awake late enough to croon a teary-eyed "Auld Lang Syne" for the year that has passed. Out of old habit, I prefer to keep my gaze on the wonders to come.

Thank You, God, for the year that has passed. I look with wonder on the one to come.
—RICK HAMLIN

DAILY GIFTS

1 _____

2 _____

3 _____

4 _____

5 _____

6 _____

7 _____

8 _____

9 _____

10 _____

11 _____

12 _____

13 _____

14 _____

15 _____

16 _____

17 _____

18 _____

19 _____

20 _____

21 _____

22 _____

23 _____

24 _____

25 _____

26 _____

27 _____

28 _____

29 _____

30 _____

31 _____

FELLOWSHIP CORNER

Welcome to Fellowship Corner, our annual family reunion, where our fifty-three writers are waiting to tell you what's been happening in their lives during the past year. Whether you're a first-time visitor or have been this way before, pull up a chair and be prepared to share some smiles—and a tear or two—as they let you know some of the ways God has been reaching out in their lives.

In her second year as a contributor to *Daily Guideposts*, MARCI ALBORGHETTI has experienced many new beginnings in her own life. After twenty years of living in Hartford, Connecticut's capital city, she moved to Stonington, in the southeastern part of the state, and now lives in a condominium directly on Stonington Harbor. "This is what people mean by the writing life," reports Marci, whose computer faces Long Island Sound. "It's just beautiful here, peaceful and very inspiring." Marci's children's and family book, *The Miracle of the Myrrh*, hit the bookstores in mid-2000, and is, she hopes, on its way to becoming a Christmas classic. Marci is also working on more children's stories and a book of essays about living with cancer. She summarizes her year, "Change is usually very hard for me, but God has given me more than my share of the grace I've needed."

"Thanks be to God we're back in a digital year! writes FAY ANGUS of Sierra Madre, California. At the turn of the century, all those 00s kept staring up at me like a pair of oogly, unblinking eyes that gave me the uncomfortable feeling of being watched, especially when it came to writing checks. 'That's just your conscience prodding you for spending t00 much money,' said my husband John. Now we have 01, a *numero uno* year! I've always liked number one. Since 1992, I've been alphabetically listed as number one here in the Fellowship Corner, and now I find it a bit disconcerting to be bumped into second place by Marci Alborghetti. Bother! I think I'll change the spelling of my name to Aangus, which will assure me first place, at least here on earth, if not in heaven (where Matthew 19:30 tells us the first shall be last, the last first).

Happy *numero uno* to all—a year reaching out to us with the promise of God's presence and never-failing love, moment by moment, day by day. Rejoice!"

"As our family has grown, each year has seemed richer than the last," says *Daily Guideposts* editor ANDREW ATTAWAY of New York City. "As each day goes by, the children seem to become more themselves, and Julia and I see more and more of what God made them to be from the very first instant of their lives. They are each so different. Elizabeth is an eager and joyful learner with a hunger to absorb new facts and master new skills. John will sit for hours listening to stories and enjoys spinning tales of his own. Mary's smile can melt the stoniest heart and light up the darkest room." The *Daily Guideposts* family is also an important part of Andrew's life. "In this twenty-fifth anniversary year, I've been moved by reports from readers and writers alike of the ways *Daily Guideposts* has ministered to them. And I thank God every day that He's made me a part of two such wonderful families."

"This has been a really fun year for us," reports JULIA ATTAWAY of New York City. "We began home schooling Elizabeth in the fall and have only good news to report." Younger brother John enjoys sitting in for Bible study, read-alouds and science experiments, switching his attention to building elaborate Duplo towers whenever the topic changes to math. "Mary the Wonder Baby" cheerfully interjects herself into all activities and has scaled every flat surface in the house except the refrigerator. "It's such a blessing to spend so much time with my children," Julia says. "As they discover more about the world God has given us, I discover more about how God wants me to share the gifts He has given."

KAREN BARBER and her husband Gordon, of Alpharetta, Georgia, have seen their sons take off on new adventures. Jeff recently graduated from Duke University and was commissioned as a second lieutenant in the U.S. Air Force in Colorado Springs. Chris is a sophomore at USC in Los Angeles. John is in fifth grade and is becoming quite well-traveled on visits to see his brothers. "Having my oldest sons so far away has changed how I reach out to them," Karen says. "I guess you could call me 'cyber-mom' because e-mail is now the main means of communication with the older boys. I have also depended on another means of reaching out to them over the distance that has been with us since ancient times—good old-fashioned prayer." Karen has been working on a book entitled *Surprised by Prayer*. "I have discovered that petition is not as easy as it may seem. I'm often reluctant to bother God with personal needs. I've concluded that it isn't what we ask for, but rather the simple act of asking that holds the power. When we ask, we reach out to God in the faith that He will reach down to us with His helping presence."

ALMA BARKMAN of Winnipeg, Manitoba, Canada, writes, "One of our callings this past year was to accompany my sister to the end of her life's journey, a sad time for both my husband Leo and me. And yet in that community of suffering, we experienced, as never before, people reaching out to share their unique gifts and talents with fellow pilgrims. They became the bright side to that valley of shadows, people whom God sent to teach us anew the value of 'just being there' for others in their time of trouble. Someone has called it 'the blessing of your presence,' as indeed it is. We continue to enjoy our quiet suburban neighborhood, although we are noticing, with some chagrin, that our yard is mysteriously expanding with each successive garden we plant. Surely we're not aging, are we?"

"Why don't we reach out to others more?" FRED BAUER of Englewood Beach, Florida, and State College, Pennsylvania, asks. "In the past, I think I may have been afraid of 'being a fool for Christ,' to borrow Paul's phrase. But in my dotage (Webster calls that our second childhood), I'm learning. Like hymn writer Isaac Watts, I've determined that God's love 'so amazing, so divine, demands my soul, my life, my all.'" In addition to church work, Fred and his wife Shirley have found satisfaction in volunteering for Meals on Wheels and pet therapy visits to nursing homes. They have also worked on behalf of Habitat for Humanity and Heifer Project International. "A new stone house in Pennsylvania has put us close to a golf course, the Penn State campus, the football stadium and, most importantly, our children and grandchildren. Ah, those wonderful hugs and kisses from grandchildren. They are, indeed, sweeter than wine."

"Well, last year I said I was hoping for future publication and I guess God heard me," says RHODA BLECKER of Los Angeles, California. "I sold a novella and short story (both science fiction), and four historical novels. The novels are a combination of adventure and love stories, and they are being published by Wildside Press of New Jersey. Every time I write a book, I am reaching out to hundreds of people I might never have a chance to meet. It pleases me so much to think that I could be making contact with—and perhaps a difference to—people all over the United States. Oh, and my husband Keith got his A+ certification as a computer service technician, and I'm so very proud of him!"

GINA BRIDGEMAN, of Scottsdale, Arizona, and her husband Paul celebrated their fifteenth wedding anniversary last June. "That passage of time seems incredible to me," Gina says, "as does the growth of our children. Ross is in sixth grade now, and following in his dad's footsteps as a Boy Scout. He's also turned into quite a left-handed pitcher, and added the trombone to his musical repertoire. Maria started kindergarten this fall, and loved playing piano in her first recital. They've changed so much and, of course, Paul and I haven't changed a bit!" Paul continues to teach technical theater at Grand Canyon University. Gina was happy to return to her first love, singing, by rejoining the church choir after several years away. "Singing is my favorite way to reach out and connect with people, to tell them of my love for God and the joy it brings into my life. No one can resist the power of a song."

This past year MARY BROWN and her husband Alex of East Lansing, Michigan, celebrated fifteen years of marriage. "We had a wonderful anniversary trip to Mackinac Island," writes Mary, "but I think the daily ways we've learned to reach out to each other bring the greatest joy—meeting for lunch, taking a walk together after dinner, leaving notes on pillows or in suitcases when one of us goes out of town." Daughter Elizabeth, 12, plays flute and piano, sings in the choir, and joined cross-country and volleyball teams this year. After watching his hometown favorite Michigan State University win the NCAA basketball championship, son Mark, 7, is determined to be a star basketball player. He and his buddies spend every spare minute shooting hoops in the driveway. "The children inspire me to stretch adventurously beyond my usual limits—from trying roller-blading with them (with lots of protective gear!) to substitute teaching and pursuing renewing my teaching certificate. Even at age 50, it feels good to be reaching for new goals."

Life continues to be wonderfully hectic for MARY LOU CARNEY and her family in Chesterton, Indiana. Daughter Amy Jo finished her first year of law school and spent the summer working for the Chicago Coalition for the Homeless. "She is sixth in her class at Valparaiso University, but I promised her I wouldn't tell anyone." Son Brett spent this year buying old houses—dilapidated, burned, abandoned—and renovating them with everything from new roofs to custom stained glass. Husband Gary's heart problems have been kept at bay by a mostly vegetarian diet and weekly jogging. Mary Lou has found new ways to reach out to her favorite slice of humanity: kids and teens. In addition to editing *Guideposts for Kids* and *Guideposts for Teens,* she helped launch a new children's Web site (www.gp4k.com) featuring the character Wally T. Turtle, and helped create "Phone Friends"—a free daily source of wholesome messages and songs for kids (1-800-233-0773). "Whenever I think of God's limitless love for me, it always gives me the energy and courage to reach out to others."

"This has been a wonderful year for us, as the wisdom of our move from Louisville, Kentucky, to Bellaire, Texas, has been constantly confirmed," says KENNETH CHAFIN. "My wife Barbara enjoys living in a house without stairs. Instead of visiting our children several times a year, we are now in daily contact. The church received us with such love and were so supportive when Barbara had major surgery in the fall. I'm teaching a new Bible study class for young couples with roots in the church but who are no longer involved. Helping them find a faith that speaks to the issues that are raised in their careers and marriages has been very fulfilling. I'm still writing poetry and beginning to do performances of my poems. Being closer to the farm and the porch swing is going to help my muse. Our grandson Daniel Kenneth lives just thirty minutes from us, and I enjoy reading *Green Eggs and Ham* and other children's classics to him. I feel very blessed."

MARY JANE CLARK of Durango, Colorado, learned something new about her husband Harry this year: He's a great nurse. A diagnosis of malignant melanoma for Mary Jane sent them on several trips to the M.D. Anderson Cancer Center in Houston, Texas, for surgery and radiation treatments. "Our little laptop computer enabled us to reach out to far-flung family and friends, and they reached back with encouraging e-mails, funny jokes, housecleaning, meals and lots of prayers. The skill and competence of the medical staff and the fact that the cancer was caught early, combined with the prayers of so many, make us hopeful that future checkups will find nothing amiss." All six kids are doing well, in spite of the inevitable ups and downs of their lives: joy in the birth of the first grandchild; the disappointment of a daughter's broken engagement; one son and his wife moved back to Africa; another published his first book; a daughter received her master's degree; another son and his wife are going through the pain and uncertainty of several lost pregnancies. "As we repeatedly experience God reaching out to us in our fear and hurt, so we want to reach out to others in our broken world."

"A friend of mine heard that my mom passed away," writes MARK COLLINS. "He wrote a very sweet note that said, 'These must be trying times for you and your family.' And in the midst of all that grief, my first thought was, *This is trying—I just can't figure what these times are trying to be. . . .*" Perhaps the answer came from 8-year-old Hope, Mark's middle daughter. During evening prayers, Hope whispered to her sister Faith, "We don't have to pray for Grandma anymore. She's off the list." Indeed, she's now on the list of the Choir Invisible. May Light Perpetual shine upon her. Faith, Hope and sister Grace are all doing well. Mark's wife

Sandee is in the Ph.D. program in Religion at the University of Pittsburgh. Mark also works at Pitt as a faculty member in Environmental Science—a radical departure from his days as a writer. "Very, very hard work," he says of his new position, but quickly adds, "No more writing means no more deadlines. This is good."

BRIAN DOYLE is the editor of *Portland* magazine at the University of Portland in Oregon. He and his wife have three small children and spend a great deal of time reaching out to keep the children from falling off the porch, trying to slice down local trees with overmuscled action figures, diving to catch crows and jays, slathering each other with mud, trying to bathe the horrified neighborhood cat, digging vast holes in the lawn in which to bury each other up to the eyeballs, etc. When not reaching out to save his children from their own exuberant headlong pursuit of hilarity, Brian is also an essayist. His collection of essays on faith, *Credo*, was published by St. Mary's Press, and he and his father Jim Doyle are the authors of *Two Voices*, a collection of their essays, which won a Christopher Award as a "work of art celebrating the human spirit."

DRUE DUKE of Sheffield, Alabama, writes, "I have moved into a new phase of my life. My beloved husband Bob died last February after almost fifty-seven years of totally happy marriage. I am lonely, of course, but the constant presence of God with me makes it bearable. Bob was progressively ill for several years, during which time our Lord taught us many lessons. One of them was reaching out to neighbors, friends and family for help. And now I rejoice in knowing where Bob is, Whom he is with and that he suffers no more pain."

KJERSTIN EASTON is a senior at the California Institute of Technology, where she studies electrical engineering. Trying her hand at research over the summer, Kjerstin made friends with a robot at the National Aeronautics and Space Administration's Jet Propulsion Laboratory. Now she's working on her senior thesis, using the robot to study moving object detection. "When I'm not in the lab," Kjerstin writes, "I sing and play trombone with the Caltech jazz bands—I've even found people in the audience who read *Daily Guideposts!*" She looks forward to recording two CDs with the jazz bands in the next few months. Somehow she still finds time to keep her journal and play with her cats Antimony and Nickel. "The cats don't care much about the future, as long as it involves tuna, but I'm looking ahead. With graduation drawing near, I'm still debating whether to go to graduate school or start that corporate ladder climb." We'll find out next year!

ERIC FELLMAN and his wife Joy live in Falls Church, Virginia, where he is a writer and part of a group that helps build relationships between the U.S. Congress and international visitors to the National Prayer Breakfast. Joy is a nurse, specializing in outpatient infusions and administration. Eric says, "We have really been blessed with opportunities to reach out this year as my role with international visitors has intersected with Joy's medical background. Many underdeveloped countries need help in securing medical training, supplies, and ongoing training from visiting doctors and nurses. With my contacts and Joy's administrative abilities, we are working on putting teams of doctors and others together with the leadership of a few countries in Africa and Asia. When asked why we come, we say because Jesus sent out His friends to teach and to heal. I've also had a lot of time to read this year, since all three of our sons, Jason, Nathan and Jonathan, are off to college. One title sticks out, *If Those Who Reach Could Touch*. It reminds me that reaching out is just the first step in making a connection that creates a relationship."

SHARON FOSTER of Glen Burnie, Maryland, writes, "A year ago I could never have imagined all the changes the year has brought. Since I joined the *Daily Guideposts* family, I have completed my first novel, *Passing by Samaria,* published by Multnomah Publishing, Inc. Now, I write full-time (keep me in your prayers), and I'm completing my second novel, *Meemaw's Rules,* which will be available early this year. My daughter Lanea is away attending graduate school and working full-time. My son Chase has passed the six-foot mark and is looking to get his learner's permit to drive any day now. As they grow older, I have found myself blessed to meet many people as I reach out through my writing and speaking engagements. I am grateful, pleased and surprised that I have been able to connect not only with adults, but also with some wonderful young people. What a blessing to be able to spread this joy to others!"

Reaching out is something DAVE FRANCO knows a lot about. "Not because I've reached out so much, but because I've been reached out to," he says. "In the letters of Paul you'll notice he often tells the recipients of his writings that he thanks God for the love they have showed each other. I can't help but feel that he would have been so pleased with what has gone on in our little enclave New York City. All the people here have reached out to us by watching our kids, caring for Nicole after she gave birth to Noelle, helping us move, praying with us in uncertain times." That's what Dave, his wife Nicole, and kids Julian and Noelle will try to do in their new neighborhood in Solana Beach, California. "We're going to try to reach out," Dave says. "I really believe that's how the Lord wants it."

ARTHUR GORDON of Savannah, Georgia, writes, "The other evening at a restaurant table next to ours there was a young mother and in a highchair a baby just about a year old. When their meal was over the mother stood up and held out her arms to the child, who in turn reached out to her in a gesture so simple, so trusting that I was reminded of the theme of this year's *Daily Guideposts*: 'Reaching Out.' I was reminded, too, of how profound this theme really is. It underlies almost every worthwhile activity, almost every rewarding relationship that I can think of. Take this book, for example, that you are holding in your hands. Year after year the writers in these pages are reaching out to you, the reader, offering fragments of their own lives, their own insights, their own thoughts, their own experiences. And you, the reader, are reaching back by accepting these offerings, honoring them with your attention, making this publishing venture ever more successful and worthwhile. In our local movie house one of the notices flashed on the screen before the feature begins says, 'Without advertising a terrible thing happens: nothing.' Might not the same also be said of 'Reaching Out'?"

OSCAR GREENE of West Medford, Massachusetts, has been retired for nineteen years, but he has never been as busy. He continues to contribute a monthly article to the Grace Episcopal Church newsletter. He completed his terms with the Medford Cultural Council and as usher-in-charge at Grace Church. In May he and Ruby attended grandson Jeremy's graduation from Champlain College in Burlington, Vermont. Oscar continues with the Monday evening Bible study, and in August he taught at the State of Maine Writer's Conference at Ocean Park. In September Ruby and Oscar motored to Williamstown, Massachusetts, to participate in Aunt Ruth's funeral. "She died on our 57th wedding anniversary at age 99. She was buried on Jeremy's 21st birthday. This great lady would have reached 100 on February 11, 2000."

In his second full year as editor-in-chief of Guideposts publications, EDWARD GRINNAN of New York City continues to reach out to a broader audience with the Guideposts message. "Mostly, though, I've learned about reaching the people I work with," says Edward. "Managing a staff is one of the most extraordinary challenges I've ever faced. It's not about being a boss but rather being a leader. That's fun and very tough, like climbing a mountain." Speaking of reaching out, Edward would like to thank his friends who help him when he yearly insists that he has run out of ideas for *Daily Guideposts* devotionals, especially Amy, Andrew, Brigitte, Celeste, Colleen, Elizabeth, Estelle, Rick, Van and, of course, his wife Julee and his dogs Sally and Marty. "I hope that doesn't sound too much like the Academy Awards."

"I've always been thankful for a neighbor boy who convinced me God was reaching out for my heart," says RICHARD HAGERMAN of Wendell, Idaho. "Since God took it sixty years ago, He has let me reach out in writing to tell others how exciting life is when your heart rests in His hands. One attempt is a devotional book based on the book of Ecclesiastes titled *Eat, Drink, and Be Especially Joyful*. Dot, my wife, and I have agonized through a burned-out dental office and the loss of a middle daughter. We have also thrilled at the witness of God's joy and peace through the lives of two other daughters. These trials and thrills and God's comfort convince me God is real and available. I pray the Lord will reach out for your heart as you read this book of inspirational experiences. But, more than that, I pray you will let Him take it."

"I seem to be doing a lot of performing lately," says RICK HAMLIN of New York City. "In January I did a benefit concert for our church, and that program endured another eight performances as a cabaret act in the theater district. And right now I'm in eighteenth-century Venice as the gondolier Marco in a production of Gilbert and Sullivan's *Gondoliers*. In it I share the stage with my son William, 13, and I suspect he will get the most accolades. It's good to have one family member comfortable in the limelight. His brother Timothy, 10, studies guitar and sings in the choir at church. At the Christmas caroling concert he sang a beautiful solo, but he prefers that we don't all stare at him when he performs. At *Guideposts* magazine, where I'm managing editor, we've had a wonderful year, keeping the magazine's ageless message current. When people ask me what I do here, I tell them I write, I edit, I read, I plan, and on Monday mornings I pray with the staff at Prayer Fellowship. Each letter and concern gives me a chance to reach out to people whose faith remains an inspiration to me. It's a great gift."

MADGE HARRAH of Albuquerque, New Mexico, writes, "As we move into the year 2001—what a portentous sound that has!—I think of the possibilities that lie ahead, such as sending a human being to Mars or finding a cure for Alzheimer's. I can't achieve those things myself, but someone can and will, probably sooner than we think. Meanwhile, I concentrate on possibilities closer to home: the completion of a biography I'm writing about Joseph Kesner, a Jewish refugee from Belgium, who became an agent of the British intelligence service in North Africa in World War II; my first trip to Mt. Rushmore; serving on the personnel committee in our church; continued visits from our children and grandchildren; the installation of a washer and dryer in our cabin in Colorado (no more wet blue jeans hanging around our old Ben Franklin stove!); and my husband Larry's third retirement. Life is good. God is good. Possibilities abound!"

"Ever since my dad went into a nursing home, I've been bringing my two dogs, Suzy and Tara, to visit him," says PHYLLIS HOBE of East Greenville, Pennsylvania. "They love it and so does he. And so do many of the other residents who hang around Dad's room when they know I'm coming. Finally, I took a friend's suggestion and enrolled in a pet therapy program. With a little more training, my dogs and I were ready to visit other nursing homes and hospitals, and it's been one of the most touching, rewarding experiences of my life. People's eyes light up when they see the dogs, and when they pet them they often talk to them about the pets they had. As for Suzy and Tara, well, they have a wonderful time, too. Of course, they're tired and they sleep all the way home, but all I have to do is say, 'Let's go visit!' and they're eager to get in the car. I think they like doing something that makes people feel good. Don't we all?"

"This past year has been one of significant changes," reports BROCK KIDD of Nashville, Tennessee. "Most importantly, my girlfriend Candy and I were married in beautiful Bermuda. After experiencing my sister Keri's wedding and all its fun but complicated intricacies, Candy and I opted for a low-key ceremony led by my father. It was especially meaningful to have both of our families there. The other big change in my life? Nashville's last great locally based bank and the parent company of the investment division that I work for were acquired by a company based in Birmingham, Alabama. I couldn't believe it. What would become of the investment division that I worked for? Would they have a need for my skills? I spent the next several days reaching out to God, asking Him for guidance, for faith. Then I got a phone call. It was my manager. 'Congratulations, you have been promoted to senior vice president.' It turned out that the new parent company was excited about our division, and it has turned out to be just one more fantastic change that God has brought to my life."

"All my life I've laughed about my 'monkey arms,' arms so long my sleeves always fall hopelessly short," says PAM KIDD of Nashville, Tennessee. "But this past year, long, long arms have become my chief asset, embracing a huge, hurting continent. Last summer my husband David and I traveled to

Africa in answer to a plea that I might write about the plight of the street children in that AIDS-ravaged continent. Ten months later my daughter Keri and I returned to follow up on the first booklet, *Pray for the Children of Zimbabwe,* to write about and photograph an AIDS crisis nursery in Zambia. We returned to clean running water, refrigerators filled with food, and closets spilling out with clothes and shoes. But a part of our hearts will always linger on the streets of Harare, Zimbabwe, where a lone woman rises at first dawn to bring tea and bread to the street children, and in a makeshift center in Lusaka, Zambia, where babies are being rocked and fed and loved in their last days on earth. And don't we all need long arms? Wide enough to hold all the goodness life offers, yet extended out toward God's hurting children, in whatever direction our Father points."

MARILYN MORGAN KING continues to find great joy in her marriage. "Robert and I celebrated our first anniversary and the millennium at the same time. Well, maybe *celebrated* isn't quite the right word. We were both sick with the flu!" But it's been an exciting year for the Kings, who moved into their new home in Green Mountain Falls, Colorado, in November. "We've tried to carry a sense of the spiritual into our home, with three stained glass windows in the living room and a special room for daily prayer and meditation." The Kings are reaching out together by becoming part of a spiritual community, making new friends, attending retreats and traveling. Karen's daughter Saralisa started school and is already typing e-mail letters to her grandmother; John finished his second year of graduate school; and Paul became a grandfather, making Marilyn a great-grandmother—not once, but twice! "I'm delighted that all members of the family are healthy," says Marilyn.

ROBERT KING of Green Mountain Falls, Colorado, recently retired from the academic world. "It was the only world I had really known for more than thirty-five years," he said. "Half of my career had been spent as a professor of philosophy and religion at a liberal arts college in the Midwest and the other half as vice president and dean of Millsaps College in Jackson, Mississippi. I wondered at the time what life would be like outside of this world, but I knew that I didn't want to simply withdraw from life.

I wanted to reach out in new ways. So in the past three years, I have traveled to Japan and France, made a new home for myself in the mountains of Colorado, nearly completed a book, become a grandfather for the first time, and entered into a beautiful marriage with a woman I had known and admired most of my life." Retirement, he has decided, feels like commencement, in the true sense of the word.

CAROL KNAPP writes, "I never thought that I would land in Minnesota, where I have Norwegian family roots on my mother's side. But my husband Terry and I love it here. The richness of the farm fields, the history in the old barns, the quaint churches and scrubbed Main Streets, the commanding presence of the sky—all seem to embrace us. And living near Minneapolis we are, of course, serious Vikings fans! We were thrilled recently to move into a home we built on two and a half acres. I call it my 'twirly' house, because I can spin around and see out the windows in all directions! Three of our young adult children—and two grandchildren—remain in Alaska. Our other child Kelly is soon to be married here. We eagerly await the rare opportunity to gather as a family for the occasion. I am often asked if it was hard to leave Alaska. My answer is we fulfilled our time there. God showed us something new and reached out to us with it, and it was up to us to reach toward Him in faith and do it. I won't deny that it was scary, but every time I breathe in a Minnesota sunset I am glad we did."

"Again this year, our Christmas card contained a wedding picture," writes CAROL KUYKENDALL of Boulder, Colorado. "Kendall, our 'baby,' married David Parkhurst in a Colorado mountain wedding in May. The year of wedding preparations coincided with the rewriting and recent re-release of my first book, *Loving and Letting Go,* which reminds me that learning to let go is a lifelong process. For my husband Lynn and me, one of the joys of this life season is visiting our children in their various places: Derek and his wife Alexandra in Portland, Oregon, where he is getting a master's degree in social work; Lindsay in San Diego, California, where she works at her church and takes classes at Fuller Seminary; Kendall and David, now living in the '.com' world of San

Francisco. This season also makes us more aware of the importance of reaching out and investing in relationships, which pull us into God's seamless circle of love. It works like this: We receive God's love so that we can reach out and give God's love to others. So in receiving, we give, and in giving, we receive. Praise God!"

HELEN GRACE LESCHEID of Abbotsford, British Columbia, writes, "I want to reach out to people who are hurting. One opportunity came to me recently. A woman walking her dog came toward me on the narrow path near my new townhouse. 'Hi,' I said. 'We met in the hot pool, remember?' Her face grimaced like she was about to burst into tears. 'He died,' she said. *What? Who? Oh, the man she was with did say he wasn't well.* 'I'm so sorry,' I stammered. A couple of days later, she invited me into her home. 'I'm so lonely since my friend died,' she choked. 'I'm afraid I'll go crazy.' A few minutes later, I brought over an audiocassette on loneliness and we huddled close to each other. Strangers no longer, but fellow pilgrims sharing a common road, we drank in words of hope and comfort to be found in Jesus Christ, our Lord. In reaching out to a neighbor, I'd found solace for my own heart and made a friend in the bargain."

PATRICIA LORENZ of Oak Creek, Wisconsin, writes, "Now that I'm in my third year of empty nesting, I'm reaching out across the country more all the time to make new friends and cherish the old ones. Some trips are for fun, others for giving speeches. The best trips of all, however, are to visit my four children: Jeanne, an artist in New York, and her significant other Canyon, who is in medical school; Julia and her husband Chris and their three little ones Hailey, Casey and Riley, who live in Lodi, Wisconsin; Michael and his wife Amy, who have two redheads, Hannah and Zachary, and live in Madison, Wisconsin; and Andrew, in his third year of college at Arizona State University. When my little 1987 station wagon was about to turn over 150,000 miles last year, I actually got off the interstate and drove around in a parking lot until the zeros all lined up, and I took a picture of the odometer! That car still gets me where I want to go . . . reaching across the miles to new friends and old. What a life, eh?"

"*Daily Guideposts* readers really know the secret of reaching out," says ROBERTA MESSNER of Huntington, West Virginia. "This past year has been a difficult one, with the death of my mother and my father's deteriorating health, along with changes in my personal and professional life. There have been many times I've wanted to give up when a letter of encouragement would arrive from one of our readers, extending a hand of comfort in the midst of—or as a result of—their own personal pain. They bring to mind II Corinthians 1:3-4 (NIV): 'Praise be to . . . the God of all comfort, who comforts us in all our troubles, so that we can comfort those in any trouble with the comfort we ourselves have received from God.' I'm learning from them to reach out to others when life threatens to overwhelm me."

KEITH MILLER and his wife Andrea, both writers, speakers and consultants, live in Austin, Texas. Keith's three married daughters and their husbands live in different cities in Texas. The seven grandchildren are "wonderful." About his work, Keith says, "I am writing song lyrics and hymns now, and *loving* doing that! And I'm writing a book about discovering what Jesus taught concerning the overcoming of blocks to loving and being loved. The working title is *Love at the End of the Tunnel*. I'm very grateful to have a part in 'reaching out' through such fascinating and fulfilling work."

"I have reached out in yet another new job," says LINDA NEUKRUG of Walnut Creek, California. "I work in a bookstore part-time now. It's quite different from the fantasy of standing around reading—after all, all those customers do come in and deserve to be helped! I have finally joined the twenty-first century, e-mailing my two nephews in New York. I have been reaching out for God through the year. When life gets hurried, a 'sixty-second prayer' can be calming and enriching in between the times I try to spend in deeper prayer. While reaching out has always been easy for me when it was to comfort someone else or to give a pat on the back to a friend, reaching out for myself when I needed comfort has been a whole different ball game. A girlfriend said to me in mock frustration, 'Linda, when you give a hug, you have to let yourself get the hug from the other person at the same time. Otherwise, a hug just won't work!' I tried it. I reached out to her, I let her reach out to me, and it felt good! May you all know the joys of reaching out and being reached out to in the coming year."

RUTH STAFFORD PEALE of Pawling, New York, says, "This year has been an important one for me as we celebrated in the attainment of our one thousandth volunteer at Peale Center's Prayer Ministry! To have so many people entrust their cares, worries and concerns to us means that we have a great responsibility, prayerfully lifting their needs up to God. Our volunteers are screened and then trained to be sensitive to the intricate way to reach out to each person reaching out to us with their requests. Also, this year I've been privileged to represent Guideposts and the Peale Center at community prayer breakfasts in Huntsville, Alabama; Cape May, New Jersey; and even at the National Prayer Breakfast in Washington, D.C.! Reaching out can actually be a cause for celebration!"

" 'Reaching out' took on a wonderful new aspect for me this year," says ROBERTA ROGERS of White Plains, Maryland. "My first book, *Is That You, Lord?*, was published by Chosen/Baker Books. Sharing what I and others have learned about hearing God's voice in everyday life has been a joyous experience. I love being able to reach out in this way! With the boys gone—David flying Army helicopters, Tom working in Atlanta (his MBA thesis won an international award!), John winning his first (teeny) PGA tournament and Peter moving to a larger airline on Cape Cod—Bill and I find ourselves reaching out for new ways to relate to each other. We reach out by long distance to our mothers, Marian and Kathryn, as they age gently into their nineties in Ohio and Connecticut. Most of all, we reach out from our new home in Virginia's Shenandoah Valley to rejoice in entertaining new—and old—friends."

DANIEL SCHANTZ of Moberly, Missouri, writes, "The year 1999 was one of magnificent monotony for the Schantzes, and the new millennium tiptoed in like a kitten." But the calmness stirred a bit when a little redheaded boy named Abram was born to Dan's elder daughter Teresa, of Kansas City, Missouri, making a total of four grandchildren for Dan and Sharon. Dan's other daughter Natalie lives nearby and often comes to town to visit him and Great-Grandma Dale, Sharon's mother. Dan's wife of thirty-six years continues her work as assistant teacher at West Park Elementary School, and she comes home each day with both funny and sobering tales to tell. In his thirty-three years of teaching at Central Christian College, Dan feels as if he is in the pause before the race, as the school begins to reach out to a global base for recruitment and service. Already many of Dan's students are involved in internships and ministries all over the world. "I feel like my final decade of teaching could be the most interesting of all. I have a worldwide family of former students, and we have the same Father watching over us all."

GAIL THORELL SCHILLING of Lander, Wyoming, reports, "Last summer Trina, 13, Tom, 15, and I visited family and toured my old haunts in New Hampshire and Boston, some of which I hadn't seen for twenty years. Our family reached out in a special way when we later traveled to Irvine, California, where Trina met her paternal grandmother, uncle, aunt and cousin for the first time. With our 'new' family, we enjoyed a regatta, art galleries and the Mission at San Juan Capistrano. Back home, I briefly considered installing a revolving door. In July Tom moved to California, where he attends school, studies jazz guitar, and lives with his dad and brother Greg, 16. Greg also plays electric guitar. (May they have tolerant neighbors!) In August Tess moved back to Lander, where Hannah Elizabeth, my first grand-blessing, was born in October. Baby met her amusing uncles and proud Grandpa when they visited for Christmas—the most special ever!"

"I'm grateful for the opportunity to reach out to readers of many faiths through the pages of *Daily Guideposts*," writes PENNEY SCHWAB of Copeland, Kansas. "My work as director of United Methodist Mexican-American Ministries allows me to reach out to people who experience barriers to obtaining health care and social services. A special joy is watching someone we've helped reach out to love and care for someone else. Grandchildren Ryan, David, Mark, Caleb and Olivia continue to bring joy and excitement to my husband Don and me. A special joy was a November reunion with family from Kansas, Oklahoma, Texas, California, Hawaii and Colorado."

A book project this year showed ELIZABETH (Tib) SHERRILL of Chappaqua, New York, how God continually reaches out to us. "I wanted to write about *heaven*," she says. "What it's like, where it is, how we get there. But as I began to recount actual experiences, my own and others', I discovered that heaven isn't 'out there' somewhere in the future, it's right here, right now. In our bad times especially, in the hardest things we have to bear, God is reaching out to take our hand." Now titled *All the Way to Heaven*, the book is about how we can take that outstretched hand any time, in any place. "When we do that, we live in heaven every day."

"All of us go through periods when God seems far away," says JOHN SHERRILL, who recently went through such a time. "My prayers seemed to wander off into space." On a fishing trip off the Florida Keys with his sons Donn and Scott, John mentioned his spiritual numbness. Donn pressed for details. The personal connection with God just wasn't there, John said. How could God be in charge of the whole universe and still care for one individual? And so on, with the usual litany of these spiritual dry spells. Shortly after John returned to Chappaqua, New York, he found a message from Donn on his answering machine. "Please call. I want to tell you about a dream I just had." When John called back, the dream, which Donn recounted, reached out across the miles and the generations, bringing a resounding end to John's depression. "I was sound asleep," Donn said. "Next instant I seemed to be totally awake, surrounded by a brilliant light, though it was still night." Then a voice came from the light. "I can hear it right now, in my head, Dad. *'Where's John?'* the voice said. *'Tell him I miss him. Tell him that I'm still here.'*"

SHARI SMYTH of Kingston Springs, Tennessee, says, "At my children's urging, I have finally succumbed to e-mail as a way of reaching out. My children tell me this new thing will grow on me as the telephone grew on my grandmother. I've made some new, dear friends this year, such as Sally Thomas. She's walked me through a hard time in my life and reminded me that reaching out involves both giving and receiving. The latter is often hard for me. Or, more precisely, humbling. Which brings me to God, Who *asks and waits* to receive His rightful place in my life. The Lord of the universe *asks and waits*. It boggles my mind. It brings me to my knees again and again. Another huge gift this year has been my daughter Sanna's move from Florida to Nashville. I love having her close by. She glows with health, beauty and faith. Thank You, Lord. And thank You for my other three children who keep close via e-mail, telephone and even the occasional antiquated letter."

"By modern statistics I am not 'that' old at seventy-seven," writes VAN VARNER of New York City, "but according to my way of thinking I am. My body informs me of it with a constant need for resting. My head feels it when I can't formulate a sentence (I struggle writing this piece—my stroke, I maintain), and memory is, shall I say, unreliable. I recognize age worse when friends, one after another, die, especially old schoolmates, and the fact that I have lived longer than anyone in my family, including grandparents, has become a conversation piece of sorrow and peculiar pride. But then there are the friends who are still here—some of them young, and even younger, former business associates, the families of godchildren and of two good nephews—and suddenly my age doesn't seem to matter. I enjoy watching while they wrestle with a world increasingly different from the one I knew. They reach out to me, thank

God, and I reach out to them, and I regularly say a prayer of gratitude for the honor of being alive."

The last year for SCOTT WALKER's family has been characterized by *rites of passage.* "On December 28, 1999, Beth and I celebrated our twenty-fifth wedding anniversary. These twenty-five years together have been wonderful, and my relationship with Beth is the most delightful gift God has ever given to me. In a few short weeks my oldest son Drew will graduate from high school. He will be traveling from Texas to attend Furman University in Greenville, South Carolina. While Beth and I are already grieving his departure, we are proud of him and support his move toward growth and independence. Our children sure grow up in a hurry. In July 2000 I will begin my eighth year of ministry at First Baptist Waco, Texas, and continue to teach at the George W. Truett Seminary at Baylor University. These are rich years filled with challenge and wonder. Finally, with each year that passes, my *Daily Guideposts* family means more and more to me. We all share a special relationship through our common devotion times that bring love and support into each of our lives. I am so grateful to God for *Daily Guideposts.*"

DOLPHUS WEARY lives in Richland, Mississippi, ten miles outside of Jackson and twenty-five miles north of his hometown Mendenhall. He is busy these days preaching a message of reconciliation and unity within the body of Christ across racial and denominational lines through Mission Mississippi, a nonprofit Christian organization. One of his responsibilities is to organize functions where people can come together across racial lines for fellowship and to get to know one another. The vision is to take this model throughout the state. His wife Rosie is working from their home, helping to build REAL Christian Foundation—a concept they developed by selling Dolphus's book, *I Ain't Comin' Back,* and using the proceeds to build the foundation that will one day support rural ministries in Mississippi. Danita graduated from medical school last June and is now doing her residency in Mobile, Alabama. Reggie, a college graduate, works in sales. Ryan is in the eighth grade. Dolphus is asking the question, "Is our faith and unity in

Christ stronger than racism and those things that will separate the body?"

BRIGITTE WEEKS has had a year somewhat like a roller coaster, with the wonderful news of her only daughter Charlotte's engagement to her longtime boyfriend Joshua and her eldest son Hilary doing some very tough and serious work at an international business school in France. Son Daniel, while working his day job, still managed to attend acting school at night, and the whole family showed up to wildly applaud his performance in Georges Feydeau's comedy *A Flea in Her Ear*. On the other side of the ledger, an unexpectedly prolonged illness put all of Brigitte's travel plans on hold, but as she says, "Being ill was no fun, but it truly reminded me of what a wonderful family and friends I have. My support group couldn't have been more powerful and loving. My colleagues at Guideposts also took on extra projects with generosity and good cheer. Reaching out to others sometimes seems impossible to fit into our busy lives, but somehow they all made the time to come, to call and to care."

MARION BOND WEST of Watkinsville, Georgia, writes, "Gene Acuff, my husband of thirteen years, is an incredible example of God reaching out to meet my needs. I believe God is giving us simple, but powerful ways to reach out to each other. I've stopped (well, almost) nagging him about all the clutter he stacks on the dining room table. He's about stopped ranting because I sometimes let English peas go down the drain in the kitchen sink. I remain convinced that the lovely assisted-living retirement home (almost across the street from us) was recently built so my 91-year-old mother could be cared for there. I can run over several times a day to take her pansies or ice cream or drive her to the beauty shop. God even reached out in compassion to allow our vet to discover the problem with my 16-year-old cat Minnie, who had used up her nine lives. I begged Him to let me have her a little longer. After the removal of eleven diseased teeth, Minnie is her marvelous, old, grouchy self again—affectionate only when she's hungry or wants the back door opened, so she can sit in the sun for a bit. Indeed, 'Thy faithfulness reaches to the skies' (Psalm 36.5, NAS)."

BRENDA WILBEE writes, "A second year of empty nest still finds me living in Bellingham, Washington, where I've been teaching part-time at Whatcom Community College. Ten years ago, I occasionally came across a student who lived a difficult or dangerous life. I've been disturbed, however, to learn that this is no longer the exception but almost the rule. Outside my office window is a commemorative garden for one of our students who was murdered three years ago. Inside my office I read student journals that reveal ongoing abuse, fear and seemingly impossible struggles. My most satisfying moments come in reaching out to the receptive students—being their friend, as well as their teacher, and finding tangible ways to express God's love for them. One of those ways has been through knitting socks. Dana wants socks with lace edges; Judy, socks with colored toes; Justin, socks that reflect. With each stitch of these special socks, I pray that God's protection and love will accompany the student who wears them. I pray a lot these days. And I knit a lot of socks!"

After her husband's death in 1998, ISABEL WOLSELEY determined not to marry again. That decision changed soon, however, after friends introduced her to Lawrence Torrey, proving that even though both were in their seventies, one should never say never about love. "Devotions and prayer have been important parts of Lawrence's and my times together prior to—and since—our marriage, so we're anticipating that God will soon show us He has a place for a pharmacist-writer team somewhere. We're hoping it will be with my son John Champ's mission or with Lawrence's Christian pharmacist group. Also praying for God's answer for us are my two sons—John, with Wycliffe Bible Translators in Portland, Oregon, and Kelly Champ, who recently started a new church in the Boise, Idaho, area. Meanwhile, Lawrence is becoming better acquainted with my sons, their wives, my six grandchildren and great-grandson as I learn about his family. We live in Syracuse, New York, where I'm a newspaper columnist for the *Post-Standard* and he is semiretired."

SCRIPTURE REFERENCE INDEX

An alphabetical index listing the Scripture references to verses appearing either at the top of devotionals or, on occasion, within the text. Chapter and verse numbers are in bold type on the left. Numbers in regular type, on the right, refer to the Daily Guideposts page(s) on which the complete verse or reference can be located.

Authors, Titles and Subjects Index

An alphabetical index to devotional authors; titles of special series; poems and songs; proper names of people, places and things; holidays and holy days; biblical persons and events appearing in the text; and subjects with subheading breakdowns that will help you find a devotional to meet that special need. Numbers refer to the Daily Guideposts page(s) on which these can be located.

A Note from the Editors

This original Guideposts book was created by the Book and Inspirational Media Division of the company that publishes *Guideposts,* a monthly magazine filled with true stories of people's adventures in faith.

If you have found enjoyment in *Daily Guideposts, 2001,* and would like to order additional copies for yourself or as gifts, the cost is $13.95 for either the regular print or the large print edition. Orders should be sent to Guideposts, 39 Seminary Hill Road, Carmel, New York 10512.

We also think you'll find monthly enjoyment—and inspiration—in the exciting and faith-filled stories that appear in our magazine. *Guideposts* is available by subscription. All you have to do is write to Guideposts, 39 Seminary Hill Road, Carmel, New York 10512. Each month you can count on receiving exciting new evidence of God's presence, His guidance and His limitless love for all of us.

Guideposts is also available on the Internet by accessing our home page on the World Wide Web at www.guideposts.org. Send prayer requests to our Monday morning Prayer Fellowship. Read stories from recent issues of our magazines, *Guideposts, Angels on Earth, Guideposts for Kids,* and *Guideposts for Teens,* and follow our popular book of devotionals, *Daily Guideposts.* Excerpts from some of our best-selling books are also available.